10659232

Bangladesh

Stuart Butler

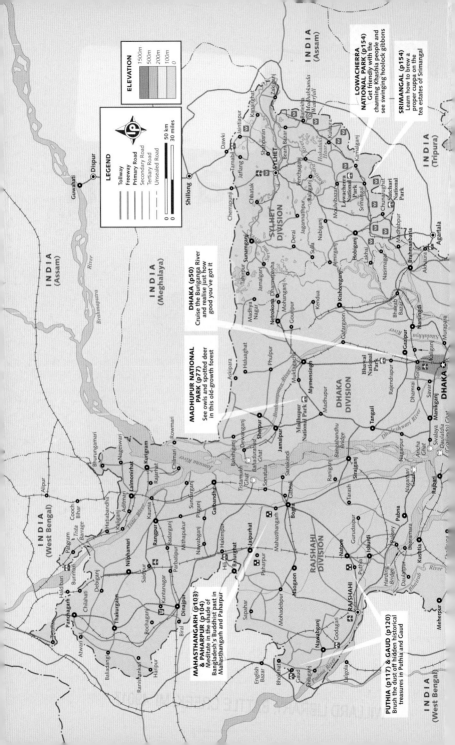

LEGEND

Tollway
Freeway
Primary Road
Secondary Road
Tertiary Road
Unsealed Road

ELEVATION

1500m
500m
200m
100m
0

0 — 50 km
0 — 30 miles

INDIA (Assam)

INDIA (Meghalaya)

INDIA (West Bengal)

INDIA (Assam)

INDIA (Tripura)

LOWACHERRA NATIONAL PARK (p154)
Get friendly with the charming Khasia people and see swinging hoolock gibbons

SRIMANGAL (p154)
Learn how to brew a proper cuppa on the tea estates of Srimangal

DHAKA (p50)
Cruise the Buriganga River and realise just how good you've got it

MADHUPUR NATIONAL PARK (p77)
See owls and spotted deer in this old-growth forest

MAHASTHANGARH (p103) & PAHARPUR (p104)
Meditate in the shade of Bangladesh's Buddhist past in Mahasthangarh and Paharpur

PUTHIA (p117) & GAUD (p120)
Brush the dust off hidden historical treasures in Puthia and Gaud

SYLHET DIVISION

DHAKA DIVISION

RAJSHAHI DIVISION

DHAKA

Guwahati
Dispur
Shillong
Agartala

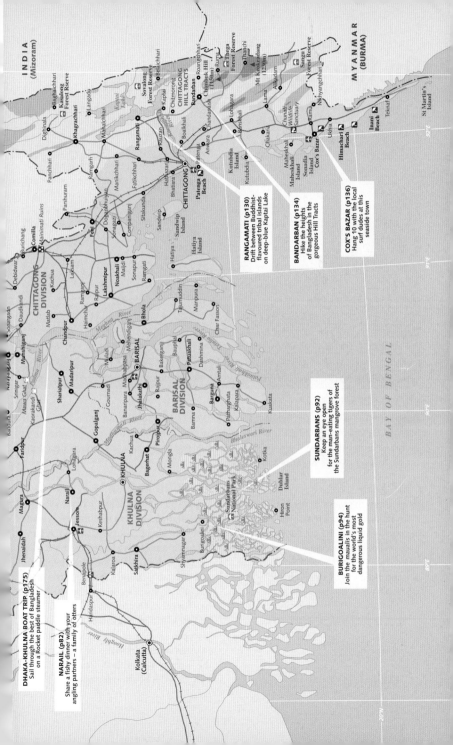

INDIA
(Mizoram)

MYANMAR
(BURMA)

CHITTAGONG
HILL TRACTS

CHITTAGONG
DIVISION

BARISAL
DIVISION

KHULNA
DIVISION

BAY OF BENGAL

DHAKA-KHULNA BOAT TRIP (p175)
Sail through the best of Bangladesh
on a Rocket paddle steamer

NARAIL (p82)
Share a fishy dinner with your
angling partners – a family of otters

BURIGOALINI (p94)
Join the maualis in the hunt
for the world's most
dangerous liquid gold

SUNDARBANS (p92)
Keep an eye open
for the man-eating tigers of
the Sundarbans mangrove forest

RANGAMATI (p130)
Drift between Buddhist-
flavoured tribal islands
on deep-blue Kaptai Lake

BANDARBAN (p134)
Hike the heights
of Bangladesh in the
gorgeous Hill Tracts

COX'S BAZAR (p136)
Hang 10 with the local
surf dudes at this
seaside town

On the Road

STUART BUTLER Author

This photo was taken on the Buriganga River in Old Dhaka (p50). I'm looking a little uneasy because my boatman thought it was hilarious playing chicken with the 200-tonne cargo ships and ferries that steam up and down the river ploughing over anything in their path. Let's just hope that he never becomes a bus driver…

DON'T MISS

I'd seen the chimneys of the brick factories many times, but didn't realise just what making bricks entailed. The guys doing it have to have one of the most dangerous jobs in the world; they're literally working on top of a volcano. Go and visit one. A bad day at the office will never be the same again!

ABOUT THE AUTHOR

English-born Stuart Butler has travelled extensively in South Asia over the past decade in search of empty surf, unlikely stories and fodder for his camera lenses, but he considers Bangladesh to be the most refreshing and enjoyable country in the region. When not getting stuck in Dhaka's rickshaw jams he writes about his travels, which have taken him beyond the borders of Bangladesh to places as diverse as the coastal deserts of Pakistan and the jungles of Colombia, for the world's surfing and travel media. He now calls the beaches of southwest France home.

Bangladesh Highlights

Bangladesh's flat terrain cradles mangrove swamps, Buddhist kingdoms, lush tea plantations and stunning beaches, and its people are some of the most generous and open-hearted you'll meet. Here, travellers and Lonely Planet staff share their top experiences in Bangladesh. Do you agree with their choices, or have we missed your favourites? Go to www.lonelyplanet .com/worldguide/bangladesh and tell us your highlights.

RICHARD I'ANSON

① RICKSHAWS

Pure exhilaration or pure terror, it's hard to decide: take a rickshaw (p179) in rush hour and admire how the world's tiniest man navigates you through a seemingly unmoving mass of vehicles, people and animals.

Emma Kate Stroud, traveller

TEA ESTATES, SRIMANGAL

Srimangal (p152) is tea territory – high and cool and green and mellow. Just show up at an estate and ask to crash. Pick tea. Lounge. Drink fresh tea. Lounge some more.

'savvyjake' (online name), traveller

PADDLE-WHEEL STEAMER

There are boat rides to be had anywhere, anytime – but the 19th-century Rocket (p175) is king.

Stuart Butler, author

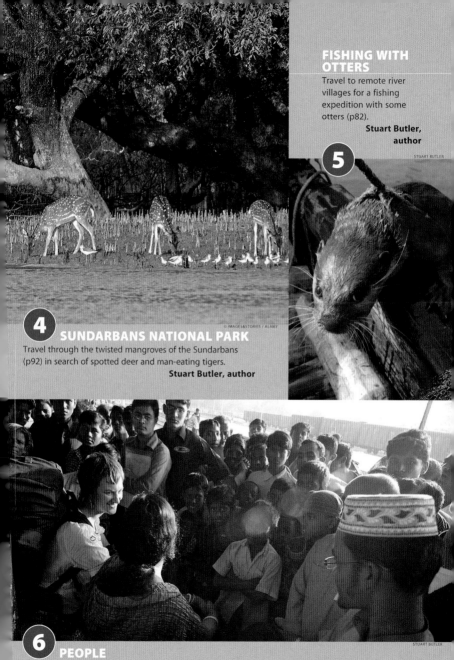

FISHING WITH OTTERS

Travel to remote river villages for a fishing expedition with some otters (p82).

Stuart Butler, author

5

STUART BUTLER

© IMAGES&STORIES / ALAMY

4

SUNDARBANS NATIONAL PARK

Travel through the twisted mangroves of the Sundarbans (p92) in search of spotted deer and man-eating tigers.

Stuart Butler, author

6

PEOPLE

No matter where you go or who you're with, give it half a minute and you'll be surrounded by a crowd of 30 or so nonplussed locals. They will then escort you to your destination whether you want them to or not. And giving away pens doesn't work.

Emma Kate Stroud, traveller

STUART BUTLER

SHANKHARIA BAZAR

My first trip to Shankharia Bazar (p52) felt more like an adrenaline shot than a shopping expedition. I passed stalls piled high with clothing, jewellery and handicrafts, all thrown together in a labyrinthine mess that defied both gravity and common sense. 'One size fits all' was a lesson learned – it seems one size often fits no-one.

Karl Smith, Lonely Planet staff

7

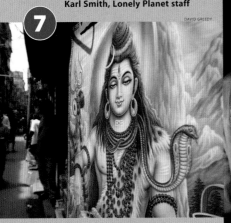

DAVID GREEDY

WATERWAYS

Take a small boat out onto the river in Dhaka (p50) and watch the extraordinary scenes of daily life unfold on the water and river banks.

Stuart Butler, author

8

RICHARD I'ANSON

STUART BU

9

CHITTAGONG HILL TRACTS

The Hill Tracts (p129) are set among rolling hills covered with banana plants, bamboo huts and Buddhist temples. Here I encountered some of the most distinctive people I'd seen anywhere in the world. I'll never forget the experience of being invited to eat with members of the Marma royal family. Feasting on frog legs and rice wine, it felt like I'd arrived in another country altogether.

Trent Holden, Lonely Planet staff

Contents

Destination Bangladesh

In late 2007 a rumbling occurred deep in the tropical waters of the Bay of Bengal. Within hours of Cyclone Sidr smashing into southwest Bangladesh, the world's media and aid organisations were on the move and Bangladesh was about to find herself wrenched back out of obscurity and once again presented to the global community as a classic 'basket case' (as Henry Kissinger once described the country) of disaster. The pictures and stories that emerged from Bangladesh at that time portrayed an entire nation on its knees, but this was only a half-truth for within hours of the storm hitting, the majority of the country was back on its feet and operational.

This wasn't the first time that Bangladesh had been dismissed as a no-hope nation, and it probably won't be the last. But no matter what the opinion of the wider world is, this dynamic country proudly considers itself to be an active participant in an increasingly global community. In defiance of its stuttering development and the weight of historical tragedy that it bears, it is a nation charged with perseverance and promise, and one from which we could all learn a thing or two. For the great irony is that while images of devastation were beamed nightly into Western living rooms and the talk was of an unfolding humanitarian disaster, nobody bothered to say that Bangladesh could make good news. In the years preceding Cyclone Sidr, the country had been quietly doing something considered nearly impossible in richer Western countries – banning all petrol and diesel vehicles from the major conurbations (and, if things go to plan, the entire nation) and replacing them with cleaner alternatives. If striving for cleaner air isn't enough, they've also banned plastic bags and created a flurry of national parks and protected areas.

The same holds true for the country's tourism profile. The majority of the world considers Bangladesh to be a frying pan–flat country. Yet within this flat framework are primeval swamps full of man-eating tigers, the unseen relics of long-forgotten Buddhist kingdoms, lush and lurid tea plantations, tribal groups with Burmese faces, glorious beaches that stretch for eternity, freshwater dolphins and deep-water whales, and some of the most open-hearted people you will ever have the honour to meet. This is a country where genuine adventure is not just a possibility but a certainty. You can chug down mile-wide, slug-brown rivers on a 19th-century riverboat, fish with otters, and hunt for the world's deadliest honey. All this in a country whose loftiest peak is as tall as the highest mountain in Scotland.

It just goes to show how much the world has to learn about the trendsetting, breathtaking and hard-working country that is Bangladesh.

FAST FACTS

Population: 150 million

Percentage of the population living below the poverty line: 45%

Percentage of the population living on less than US$1 per day: 30%

GDP per capita: US$1400

Life expectancy at birth: 63.21 years

Female adult literacy rate (over 15 years old): 31.8%

Male adult literacy rate (over 15 years old): 53.9%

Year women received the right to vote: 1972

Getting Started

Bangladesh is designed for the traveller who revels in genuine adventure. There is little here that can be described as organised, comfortable or reliable, and the backpacker scene of next-door India is completely unheard of. The fact that there are so few tourists in Bangladesh means that you won't have to contend with crowds at hotspots or with booked-out accommodation, but it also means that the going can be rough.

WHEN TO GO

Bangladesh has three main seasons: the monsoonal season (wet season) from late May to early October; the cool season from mid-October to the end of February; and the hot season from March to mid-May.

See Climate Charts (p159) for more information.

Between October and February is the best time to go: skies are blue, days are sunny and the weather is dry, with daytime temperatures averaging 24°C. By April the temperature rises to around 40°C, the humidity can be intolerable and hailstorms aren't uncommon. On average, Bangladesh is hit by one major cyclone every three years. The worst times for these are May and June, and October and November.

The only festival that may really inconvenience you is Ramadan. During this month-long period of fasting, getting food (especially in small towns) can be difficult. Some budget hotels stop operating altogether.

COSTS & MONEY

Whatever budget you're travelling on, you can be certain that you'll get more for your money in Bangladesh than just about anywhere else on earth. If you're the type of traveller who sees a cockroach-infested room as just a place to sleep, then you'll enjoy Bangladesh. For as little as Tk 60 you can have a room all to yourself, for Tk 30 you can get an enormous meal and for around Tk 5 you can buy a street snack. A backpacker looking to stretch the pennies can easily get by on US$6 a day or less. At the 'you only live once' end of the spectrum, you can pay a couple of hundred US dollars for a lavish room, and buy a meal of the same quality and for the same price that you would expect at home (though travel at this end of the scale is only really feasible in Dhaka and Chittagong).

DON'T LEAVE HOME WITHOUT...

Given that the safety situation in parts of Bangladesh is particularly subject to change, don't leave home without checking some reputable travel advisories. Although you can buy almost anything if you know where to find it, there are a couple of things you might want to bring:

- Loose-fitting, modest clothes
- Earplugs for inconceivably loud bus rides and neighbouring passengers
- Sunglasses for sun and stare protection
- Glasses in case contact lenses become irritated by the pollution
- Torch (flashlight) for power failures
- Appropriate visa (p167) and a passport valid for six months after you intend to leave Bangladesh
- A good book or two
- An open mind

Most people, even those who are confirmed budget travellers elsewhere, travel on a midrange budget in Bangladesh. For between Tk 400 and Tk 1000 a night you will be able to find a nice place to stay with all the necessary amenities. A Tk 120 meal is large and tasty. In the way of transportation, there is a range of classes on trains and boats, and different types of buses, which offers enormous flexibility when weighing up value and comfort. A couple staying together in good quality hotels, travelling on 1st-class train carriages and eating in decent restaurants should budget about US$15 each a day.

TRAVEL LITERATURE
Budding writers will be happy to hear that there is very little travel literature on Bangladesh published in the West. However, there is a growing range of books that will give the traveller an insight into the people and culture.

Monica Ali's best-selling *Brick Lane* (2003) has brought Bangladesh to the world. In this beautifully written novel, set in London and Bangladesh, the trials and tribulations of its multi-dimensional characters reveal the complexity of both Bangladeshi culture and human nature. It's recently been given the full Hollywood makeover and turned into a major film.

The Bangladeshi government should make it illegal to come here and not have *Songs at the Rivers Edge* (1991) by Katy Gardner in your luggage. The story of a year spent living in a small village in the Sylhet region, it's more than a memoir, and answers some of the many questions regarding village life throughout South Asia.

A Golden Age (2007) by Tahmima Anam is a superb debut novel of love, betrayal and family loyalties, set against the backdrop of the War of Independence.

If you're caught reading *Lajja* (Shame; 1993) by Taslima Nasrin in Bangladesh (where the book is banned) you're unlikely to make many friends. When first published this half novel/half political treaty earned its outspoken feminist author a *fatwa*. It's essential predeparture reading, but is unfortunately a little hard to find. See also boxed text, p30.

Shame (2007) by Jasvinder Sanghera is the true story of one woman's struggle to break away from Asian tradition and live her life in the UK. The issues raised by this book may make you think about your opinion on both Asian culture and immigration to the West. It is a gripping read.

TRAVELLING RESPONSIBLY
Tourism in Bangladesh is so little established that there are currently very few 'eco' options in the classic sense of environmentally sustainable hotels and restaurants. Instead, responsible travel in Bangladesh is more about the way you behave and think, and your interactions with local people. You might be the only foreign tourist that many Bangladeshis will see all year and therefore your every movement will be judged. In Bangladesh it's essential to interact with the local people: drink cha with them, share meals with them and answer their questions, however tiring they become, and in return ask your own. Be aware that the tribal groups living in the Chittagong Hill Tracts (p129) and elsewhere are suffering heavily from government policies of marginalisation. By buying their handicrafts, visiting their villages and expressing an interest in them there is some slim hope of change.

The government has put a lot of effort recently into environmental policies and by visiting the newly created national parks and voicing your approvals of the banning of plastic bags and phasing out of diesel and petrol, you can help to further encourage this development.

Avoid purchasing shell, coral or animal products and historical artefacts.

HOW MUCH?

Bottle of Coke Tk 10-20

Cup of cha (tea) Tk 2

Newspaper Tk 7

Sundarbans National Park tour US$150

Toilet paper Tk 10

TOP 10
BANGLADESH
India   Dhaka

TOP READS

Reading is an ideal way to get into the mindset of the nation. There are some great books that touch on various issues that have shaped Bangladesh. See also p13.

1 *Brick Lane* (2003) Monica Ali
2 *Songs at the Rivers Edge* (1991) Katy Gardner
3 *A Golden Age* (2007) Tahmima Anam
4 *Lajja* (Shame; 1993) Taslima Nasrin
5 *Interpreter of Maladies* (1999) Jhumpa Lahiri
6 *The Departed Melody* (2003) Raja Tridiv Roy

7 *Rabindranath Tagore: An Anthology* (1998) Krishna Detta and Andrew Robinson (eds)
8 *Seasonal Adjustments* (1995) Adib Khan
9 *A Quiet Violence: View from a Bangladeshi Village* (1983) Betsy Hartmann and James Boyce
10 *Midnight's Children* (1981) Salman Rushdie

WHO'S WHO OF BANGLADESH

On your travels through Bangladesh, you'll see portraits prominently displayed in family homes and shops throughout the country. Here is a list of people you should have heard of.

1 Begum Khaleda Zia – former prime minister and General Zia's widow; on trial for corruption at the time of writing
2 General Ershad – former president, jailed in 1991 for corruption and illegal possession of weapons
3 General Zia Rahman – sector commander of Z force, former president; assassinated 1981
4 Iajuddin Ahmed – president of caretaker government
5 Kazi Nazrul Islam – national poet; died 1976

6 Mohammad Ashraful – captain of the Bangladesh cricket team
7 Rabindranath Tagore – Nobel Prize-winning poet; died 1941
8 Sheikh Hasina Wajed – Awami League president, former prime minister and daughter of Sheikh Mujibur; on trail for corruption at the time of writing
9 Sheikh Mujibur Rahman – founder of Bangladesh; died 1975
10 Taslima Nasrin – exiled author

BEST OF GREEN BANGLADESH

1 Banning of petrol and diesel vehicles (p38)
2 Banning of plastic bags (p38)
3 Creation of new national parks (p39)
4 Sundarbans National Park (p92)
5 Bandarban (p134)

6 Lowacherra National Park (p154)
7 Otter fishing (p82)
8 Tea estates (p154)
9 Rocket ride (p175)
10 Rice paddies (countrywide)

INTERNET RESOURCES

Bangladesh continues to become ever more tech-savvy and the following are the current hot sites to help with background reading and predeparture research.

Bangladesh Development Gateway (www.bangladeshgateway.org) A guide to the numerous development projects, organisations and activities in Bangladesh.

Bangladesh Parjatan Corporation (www.bangladeshtourism.gov.bd) The national tourism organisation website is user-friendly and has a wealth of information.

Daily Star (www.thedailystar.net) Online edition of one of the country's best regarded newspapers.
Discovery Bangladesh (www.discoverybangladesh.com) A great place to start getting an idea about the country and its people.
Independent (www.independent-bangladesh.com) Online edition of this highly regarded newspaper.
Lonely Planet (www.lonelyplanet.com) Succinct information, useful links and the popular Thorn Tree Travel Forum, which, though we say so ourselves, is easily the best place to get up-to-the-minute Bangladeshi travel advice.
Virtual Bangladesh (www.virtualbangladesh.com) Regularly updated, this is an extremely extensive resource for both cultural and historical facts, and travel information.

Itineraries
CLASSIC ROUTES

TIGERS & TREKKING – THE BEST OF BANGLADESH

Two weeks/
Dhaka to Rangamati

A fortnight in Bangladesh is the perfect amount of time to give you an overview of the country's scenery and culture.

Spend the first couple of days being swallowed up by **Dhaka** (p46). After following the city itinerary outlined on p49, head out on the **Rocket** (p175). This memorable boat ride to **Khulna** (p79) is a return to the age of romantic travel. After exploring Khulna's hectic markets and bazaars, head north for some **angling with otters** (p82) or south on a day trip to the landmark-filled historical town of **Bagerhat** (p88) where you will experience serene scenery and one of the most famous buildings in Bangladesh, the **Shait Gumbad Mosque** (p58).

Next, don your sea legs and join a cruise boat for a few days drifting through the tiger-haunted swamps of the **Sundarbans** (p92) before hopping on a flight back to Dhaka.

From here head east to the Buddhist tribes and forest peaks of **Bandarban** (p134) and then, if time allows, finish up with some island-hopping in plain-sailing **Rangamati** (p130).

An action-packed fortnight that takes in epic adventure on a Rocket ride, a hunt for the legendry otter fishermen, history in the shape of the mosques and temples, wildlife and wild spaces in the Sundarbans National Park and hiking in the Buddhist-flavoured hills of the east.

MONTH IN MOTION
Four weeks/Dhaka to Cox's Bazar

A month in Bangladesh will allow ample time to soak up many of the country's unexpected surprises.

Take your time in **Dhaka** (p46), following our two-day itinerary (p49). Ease yourself into the rhythm of rural life with a day trip out of the city to stately **Sonargaon** (p71) before heading further afield to the fascinating, but little visited, town of **Mymensingh** (p74) where gold dust, and lazy parks and gardens grace the town centre. Further out of town, search for the Mandi and monkeys in the **Madhupur National Park** (p77). Return to Dhaka and then zoom on a Rocket to **Barisal** (p97), from where any number of adventures await on the backwater tributaries to the south of the city. Head across to **Khulna** (p85) and incorporate the suggestions of the Tigers & Trekking itinerary (opposite). Be sure to take your time in the **Sundarbans** (p92).

Make your way back to Dhaka overland by bus, with a break in **Kushtia** (p83) to pay homage to saints, gurus and poets. After soaking up city life again, retreat to the peace of **Srimangal** (p152) for a nice cup of five-flavoured tea, tribal villages and a glorious jungle.

From Srimangal catch the train to **Chittagong** (p123). If you're an archaeology buff, get off en route at Comilla to visit the **Mainimati ruins** (p144). Spend a couple of days exploring sweaty Chittagong before venturing into the stunning Chittagong Hill Tracts for boating and Buddhas around **Rangamati** (p130), and mountain walks around the mist-swirling peaks of **Bandarban** (p134).

If you still have time, finish off by doing the beach Bangladeshi-style at **Cox's Bazar** (p136), four hours by bus from Chittagong.

This month of steady travel will show you the breadth and beauty of Bangladesh, from its tea plantations and beaches to its tribal hill tracts and cities. After this mammoth journey on buses, boats and trains, you will be able to say with utter confidence that you have experienced Bangladesh.

ROADS LESS TRAVELLED

FOR THE INDIANA JONES IN YOU

Three weeks/
Rajshahi to Chittagong Hill Tracts

Bangladesh isn't known for its past glories but, for the discerning histori-cal buff, there's plenty of treasure to be found if you know where to look. This itinerary will take you on an amble through time, and through some Bangladeshi backwoods.

In Rajshahi division, spend a couple of weeks exploring some hard-to-get-to archaeological sites. From **Rajshahi** (p113) visit picturesque **Puthia** (p117) with its plethora of temples and palaces, and **Natore** (p118) with its sadhus (holy men) and ponds. You could also head out to **Gaud** (p120) on the Indian border; it's a messy journey but the scenery and a flurry of glorious mosques make it worthwhile.

Bogra (p101) is a happy base from which to travel to the majesty of king-doms gone at **Mahasthangarh** (p103) and **Paharpur** (p104). From here you can also make the trip to **Sariakandi** (p103) and hire a boat to explore life on the Jamuna River.

Head back to Dhaka then take a train to **Chittagong** (p123), stopping on the way to check out the **Mainimati ruins** (p144) at Comilla. From Chittagong, don't miss out on the chance to vary the scenery with a sortie to the **Chittagong Hill Tracts** (p129) for some trekking, tribal encounters and gold-plated Buddhist stupas.

Juggle buses, boats and boats and borders on a quest to reach the remote ruins and historical artefacts of Bangladesh. This three-week dream run is a real rural experience, and your visit might be a major event for the population of a far-flung village.

History

For much of history, the state that we today call Bangladesh has been a part of a greater India and was known only as Bengal; what happened elsewhere on the subcontinent affected Bengal. The history of the modern state of Bangladesh has been short and, rarely, sweet. Born in a war that some call genocide, the nation's history has been filled with an almost unnaturally large guest list of villains, tyrants, soldiers and politicians, as well as one or two ever so rare heroes.

Prior to the creation of Bangladesh, the history of Bengal was one that seemed to involve the constant meddling of foreign powers – sometimes this resulted in the glow of cultural splendour, but more often than not it descended into the tears of war.

Virtual Bangladesh (www.virtualbangladesh .com/history/overview .html) gives a simple overview of a compli- cated history.

BUDDHISM IN BANGLADESH

Strange though it may now seem in such an overwhelmingly Muslim country, Buddhism in Bangladesh is no small player in the nation's history and culture. Countrywide it's the third major religion but in certain areas, such as Chittagong division, Buddhists make up an impressive 12% of the population.

It's not mere numbers though that makes Bangladesh important in the Buddhist world, but history. It's not far from Bodhgaya (in present-day India, where the Buddha reached enlightenment) to Bengal, and the region has played a huge part in the development of Buddhism, including the creation of the mystical Tantric Buddhism.

By the reign of the great Indian Buddhist emperor Ashoka (304–232 BC), Buddhism was firmly entrenched as the number one religion of Bengal and, aside from a few minor blemishes, it continued to thrive in the region until the 12th century AD, making Bengal the last stronghold of Buddhism in an increasingly Hindu and Muslim dominated subcontinent.

In the 6th century, Sasanka, a powerful Buddhist king, founded the Gauda Empire in Bengal, which was eventually overthrown by the warrior king Sri Harsa, who ruled the Bengal area until the 8th century.

Gopala, a Kshatriya tribal chief from Varendra, became the founding figure of the Buddhist Pala dynasty (8th to 11th centuries). He was succeeded by his son Dharmapala, who established the gigantic Somapura Vihara in Varendra, known today as Paharpur (p104).

In the 12th century, Hindu *senas* (armies) came to rule Bengal, and crushed Buddhism. Surviving Buddhists retreated to the Chittagong area. In less than a century the senas were swamped by the tide of Islam.

The army (known to the Greeks as Gangaridai) that chased Alexander the Great from India in 325 BC was supported by 4000 trained elephants and horses.

TIMELINE

Back in time	326 BC	262 BC
The earliest mention of the region is in the 9th century BC Hindu epic *Mahabharata*, which tells of Prince Bhima's conquest of eastern India, including Varendra, an ancient kingdom in what is now Bangladesh.	Storming out of ancient Greece, Alexander the Great subdues most of western Asia but flees India when word reaches him that the Gangaridai people of Bengal have amassed an army on the banks of the Ganges.	Chandragupta Maurya creates an empire, then known as Pundravardhana Bhukti, now as Mahasthangarh. It spreads across northern India under his grandson, the emperor Ashoka, whose conversion to Buddhism in 262 BC has a lasting effect.

Though somewhat beaten, Buddhism never totally died out in Bangladesh and in the Chittagong Hill Tracts there are several monasteries which lean to Myanmar (Burma) for religious inspiration and a number of schools in which children learn to read Burmese and Pali (an ancient Buddhist language). As in neighbouring Myanmar, many Buddhist men in this region spend a part of their lives as monks. The large number of Burmese refugees who have fled the terror of their country have brought their religion with them and this has had a profound effect on Bangladeshi Buddhism. The Ministry of Religious Affairs helps to maintain Buddhist religious sites.

THE MUSLIM PERIOD

They took some time to arrive, but when they did they left a legacy that continues to define the country to this very day. The arrival of the Muslims began with the trickle of a few Sufi (Muslim mystic) missionaries in the 12th century and the construction of the odd mosque on the fringes of Bengal. Then came Mohammed bin Bakhtiar (a Khilji from Turkistan) who, with only 20 men under his command, made short work of capturing Bengal and bringing the area under the rule of the sultanate of Delhi, the centre of Muslim power in India.

In his book *Heroes* (1987) the ever-emotive John Pilger discusses ordinary people in extraordinary situations. The words he dedicates to Bangladesh luridly evoke the fervour of its formation and the passion of the people involved.

Under the Muslims, Bengal entered a new era. Cities developed; palaces, forts, mosques, mausoleums and gardens sprang up; roads and bridges were constructed; and new trade routes brought prosperity and a new cultural life. In 1576 Bengal became a province of the mighty Mughal Empire, which ushered in another golden age in India. Mughal power extended over most of Bengal except the far southeast around Chittagong, and it was during this period that a small town named Dhaka emerged from obscurity to become the Mughal capital of Bengal.

BRITS ABROAD

For decades the Portuguese, Dutch, British and French tussled for influence over the subcontinent, but it was the British East India Company that prevailed.

Originally a mere clerk for the British East India Company, Robert Clive rose to become local head of the company and, eventually, the effective ruler of Bengal.

It was during the reign of Mughal emperor Aurangzeb (1618–1707) that a Bengali nawab (Muslim prince) sold three local villages to the British East India Company. Today one of those villages is a mega-city that goes by the name of Kolkata (Calcutta). From here the British gradually extended their influence to take in all of Bengal and finally all of the subcontinent, but the going was far from easy.

It has been said that the British Raj ushered Bengal into a period of growth and development, but historians hotly dispute this. To quote Monty Python, 'What have the Romans actually done for us?' The answer is that the British brought a great many positive changes to India, particularly in regard to infrastructure, law and government. Conversely, they also brought a great many

4th century AD	1202	1342–1487
In the 4th century AD, northern India comes under the imperial rule of the Guptas; during their reign Buddhism reaches its zenith. The Guptas succumb to a wave of White Hun invasions.	The Muslims storm into Bengal and quickly convert the region. The Mameluk sultanate is established, until the Tughlaq dynasty overthrows it in 1320. The Tughlaqs are defeated by another wave of Muslim invaders in 1398.	Under the Ilyas Shahi dynasty, a distinct Bengali identity begins to form. The city of Gaud emerges as a cosmopolitan metropolis, remaining the centre of power until the capital is moved to Dhaka in 1608.

bad things, including dictatorial agricultural policies and the establishment of the zamindar (feudal landowner) system, which many people consider responsible for draining Bengal of its wealth, damaging its social fabric and directly contributing to today's desperate conditions in Bangladesh.

Most Hindus cooperated with the British, entering British educational institutions and studying the English language. The majority of Muslims, on the other hand, refused to cooperate, preferring to remain landlords and farmers. This religious dichotomy formed a significant basis for future conflict.

Though the British Raj has long since been relegated to the history books, the truth remains that the British adventure in South Asia remains one of the most significant events in the history of both Bangladesh and Britain. Today trade ties are strong between both nations and a large proportion of Britain's Asian community hails from Bangladesh. Whereas once upon a time it was Britain exporting its culture and industry to India, recent years have seen something of a reversal, especially in regards to culture with Indian art, food, film and philosophy being exported to Britain.

PARTITION & PAKISTAN

At the close of WWII it was clear that European colonialism had run its course. The Indian National Congress continued to press for Indian self-rule and the British began to map out a path to independence.

With the Muslim population of India worried about living in an overwhelmingly Hindu-governed nation, the Muslim League was formed. It pushed for two separate Muslim states in South Asia. Lord Mountbatten, Viceroy of British India, realising the impossibility of the situation and, quite possibly looking for a quick British escape, decided to act on these desires and partition the subcontinent.

The Partition of East Pakistan did not lead to the extraordinary levels of bloodshed that marked the creation of West Pakistan, which led to the deaths of an estimated half a million people.

Though support for the creation of Pakistan was based on Islamic solidarity, the two halves of the new state had little else in common. Furthermore, the country was administered from West Pakistan, which tended to favour itself in the distribution of revenues.

The Awami League, led by Sheikh Mujibur Rahman, emerged as the national political party in East Pakistan, with the Language Movement as its ideological underpinning. The 1971 national elections saw the Awami League win with a clear majority; in East Pakistan it won all seats but one. Constitutionally, the Awami League should have formed the government of all Pakistan but faced with this unacceptable result, President Khan postponed the opening of the National Assembly.

In July 2002, Pakistani president Musharraf visited Bangladesh and expressed his regret at excesses carried out by Pakistan during the Liberation War.

1575	1707	1756–57
Under the command of Akbar, the Mughals show the Bengali sultan Daud Karrani who the boss is at the Battle of Tukaroi. His defeat announces the beginning of the Mughal adventure in Bengal.	The last great Mughal ruler Aurangzeb dies and the Mughal empire is thrown into disarray. Bengal has long had autonomy, and now breaks away completely from the rest of the empire.	Suraj-ud-Daula, the nawab of Bengal, attacks Calcutta. British inhabitants are packed into an underground cellar, where most of them suffocate. To avenge them Robert Clive kills Suraj-ud-Daula and becomes the de facto ruler of Bengal.

WAR & PEACE

At the racecourse rally of 7 March 1971 in Dhaka (at what is now Ramna Park), Sheikh Mujibur (Mujib) stopped short of declaring East Pakistan independent. In reality, however, Bangladesh (land of the Bangla speakers) was born that day. Sheikh Mujib was jailed in West Pakistan, igniting smouldering rebellion in East Pakistan.

Visit Dhaka University (www.univdhaka.edu) – the setting of significant moments in history and now a repository of historical records.

When the Mukti Bahini (Bangladesh Freedom Fighters) captured the Chittagong radio station on 26 March 1971, Ziaur Rahman, the leader of the Mukti Bahini, announced the birth of the new country and called upon its people to resist the Pakistani army. President Khan sent more troops to quell the rebellion.

General Tikka Khan, known to Bangladeshis as the 'Butcher of Balochistan', began the systematic slaughter of Sheikh Mujib's supporters. Tanks began firing into the halls of Dhaka University. Hindu neighbourhoods were shelled and intellectuals, business people and other 'subversives' were hauled outside the city and shot.

By June the struggle had become a guerrilla war. More and more civilians joined the Mukti Bahini as the Pakistani army's tactics became more brutal. As documented in media reports at the time, and in several book-length studies since, napalm was used against villages, and rape was both widespread and systematic, although the actual number of women affected remains disputed.

By November 1971 the whole country was suffering the burden of the occupying army. During the nine months from the end of March 1971, 10 million people fled to refugee camps in India.

With border clashes between Pakistan and India becoming more frequent, the Pakistani air force made a pre-emptive attack on Indian forces on 3 December 1971, precipitating a quick end. Indian troops crossed the border, liberated Jessore on 7 December and prepared to take Dhaka. The Pakistani army was attacked from the west by the Indian army, from the north and east by the Mukti Bahini and from all quarters by the civilian population.

By 14 December the Indian victory was complete and West Pakistan had been defeated, but at what cost? According to Bangladeshi sources around three million people were killed in the nine month war, 200,000 women raped and 10 million people forced from their homes. Pakistani sources claim that

POLITICS & STUDENTS

Probably nowhere in the world do students play such a pivotal role in politics as in Bangladesh. Students today are empowered by recent tradition, stemming largely from the key role they played in the Liberation War. When the war started it was no mistake that the Pakistanis aimed their tanks first at Dhaka University. Many students were among the intellectuals targeted for death.

1758–1857	1885–1905	1947
The British East India Company controls Bengal but their policies hardly endear them to the Bengalis. The Sepoy Mutiny further inflames local passions. Westminster intervenes and in 1857 the British government takes over control of India.	Supported by Hindus and Muslims, the Indian National Congress is founded in 1885. But the division of Bengal in 1905 by Lord Curzon, seen as a religious partition, prompts the formation of the All India Muslim League.	Pakistan and India come to life. Pakistan is divided into two regions, in the Punjab and Bengal. Bengal is known as East Pakistan. A bloody exodus occurs as Hindus move to India and Muslims to East or West Pakistan.

THE SLAUGHTER OF THE INTELLECTUALS

Immediately following Sheikh Mujib's arrest on 26 March 1971, all hell broke out. Blaming the Hindu intellectuals for fomenting the rebellion, the generals immediately sent their tanks to Dhaka University and began firing into the halls, killing students. This was followed by the shelling of Hindu neighbourhoods and a selective search for intellectuals, business people and other alleged subversive elements. One by one they were captured, hauled outside the city and shot in cold blood. Over the ensuing months, the Pakistani soldiers took their search for subversives to every village. By then, if there had ever been a distinction made between intellectuals and Hindus, it was gone. When captured, men were forced to lift their lungis (sarongs) to reveal if they were circumcised; if not, they were slaughtered.

The perpetrators were never punished; indeed today they are heroes. General Tikka Khan, for example, retired in comfort and years later, in 1989, this 'grand old man' of the Pakistani army, as he was affectionately called, became the Governor-General of Punjab Province.

26,000 deaths occurred, whilst the international community quote anything from 200,000 to three million deaths.

BIRTHING PAINS

The People's Republic of Bangladesh was born into chaos – it was shattered by war, had a ruined economy and a totally disrupted communications system. Henry Kissinger once described the newly independent Bangladesh as an 'international basket case'. As if to reinforce this point, famine struck between 1973 and 1974 and set the war-ravaged country back even further.

After a couple of years of tumultuous power struggles, General Ziaur Rahman, now the head of the army, took over as martial-law administrator and assumed the presidency in late 1976.

The overwhelming victory of President Zia (as Ziaur Rahman was popularly known) in the 1978 presidential poll was consolidated when his party, the newly formed Bangladesh Nationalist Party (BNP), won two-thirds of the seats in the parliamentary elections of 1979. Martial law was lifted and democracy returned to Bangladesh. Zia proved to be a competent politician and statesman. Assistance began pouring in and over the next five years the economy went from strength to strength.

Though the country progressed economically during the late 1980s, in early 1990 the economy began to unravel and massive rallies and hartals (strikes) were held. During this period Zia's wife, Begum Khaleda Zia, who had no political experience, became head of the BNP and, in the ensuing election, the Awami League won about 33% of the vote compared to the BNP's 31% – but the BNP won about 35 more seats in parliament. Begum Khaleda Zia became prime minister in 1991.

In *Bangladesh: From a Nation to a State* (1997), Craig Baxter discusses the development of national identity throughout history. A comprehensive and ambitious work that contextualises the nationalistic pride evident in Bangladesh today.

1952	1970	1971
The Pakistani government declares that Urdu will be the national language. Riots break out in Dhaka and on 21 February, 12 students are killed by the Pakistani army. Pakistan's waning democracy gives way to military government.	A catastrophic cyclone kills around 500,000 people in East Pakistan. The Pakistani government appears to do little. War between East and West Pakistan looms large on the horizon.	War breaks out between East and West Pakistan. After nine months, the Indian army intervenes in December. Within two weeks, Pakistan's General Niazi surrenders and Sheikh Mujib takes over the reins of an independent government.

Never fully accepting the election result, the Awami League, headed by Sheikh Hasina, began to agitate against the BNP. A long and economically ruinous period of hartals (strikes) eventually brought down the BNP government in June 1996, and the Awami League took power.

THE FUTURE IS BRIGHT(ER)

The past eight or nine years have seen no respite in the political twisting and turning. Khaleda Zia's Nationalist Party and its three coalition partners won the 2001 elections. Arguing that the elections were rigged, the now-opposition Awami League began parliamentary boycotts. In August 2003, two opposition Awami League politicians were murdered, triggering a spate of hartals. In February 2004, the opposition called a series of general strikes in a failed attempt to force the government from power.

The Bangladeshi constitution states that at the end of its tenure the government must hand power over to an unelected, neutral caretaker government who must organise elections within 90 days. In January 2007, with elections due and neither side able to agree on a suitable caretaker government, and street protests over the stalemate becoming increasingly large and violent, a military-backed caretaker government under the leadership of Fakhruddin Ahmed took over. One of its first acts was to declare emergency rule, postpone the elections to late 2008 and ban all political activity. In the meantime they promised to stamp out the corruption that in recent years had seen Bangladesh rated the world's second most corrupt nation after Nigeria. For much of 2007 the caretaker government was genuinely popular with many Bangladeshis, but by August of that year a curfew was imposed on many Bangladeshi cities after students took to the streets demanding an end to the emergency.

The country has suffered from a series of low-key bomb attacks by local Islamic militant groups, but in general Islamic militancy hasn't taken root here in the way many feared it might. Other good news can be found in the economy, which, in recent years, has been steadily growing at around 5% to 6% per annum, fuelled primarily by the country's burgeoning textile industry. Though still one of the world's poorest and least developed nations, Bangladesh normally manages to feed itself and, so long as the 2008 elections pass without hitch, the future of the country looks brighter than it has done for years and the 'basket case' metaphor can be safely laid to rest.

The exact origin of the word Bangla is unclear, but is thought to derive from the Dravidian-speaking Bang tribe that lived in the region around 1000 BC.

See Amnesty International (www.amnesty .org) for reports on human rights in Bangladesh.

1974–6	1981	2007
A state of emergency is declared in 1974 and Sheikh Mujib proclaims himself president. He and most of his household are killed in a military coup on 15 August 1975. His surviving daughter Sheikh Hasina becomes prime minister in 1996.	During an attempted military coup in May, President Zia is assassinated in Chittagong. Justice Abdul Sattar is appointed as acting president and, as candidate for the BNP, wins 66% of the vote in the ensuing general election.	Fakhruddin Ahmed's caretaker government declares emergency rule and arrests former prime ministers Begum Khaleda Zia and Sheikh Hasina Wajed. Elections are rescheduled for late 2008. Cyclone Sidr leaves 3500 dead.

The Culture

THE NATIONAL PSYCHE

It is Bangladeshi curiosity that you will encounter first, in the form of awe-struck stares and a line of questioning that begins with your country, ends with your marital status and takes in your academic qualifications, opinion about Bangladesh and your observations about the state of the world. Yes, Bangladeshis are curious and worldly wise. It's almost as if Bangladesh keeps its finger on the pulse of the world to spite the world's apathy towards it. From American politics to Australian cricket, there are opinions aplenty.

Bd Chat (www.bdchat .com) is the Bangladeshi Facebook – the forum contains some interesting topics.

The streets are the economic, social and political veins of human activity. Markets burst into life on back streets at night, students and businessmen stand on street corners to exchange ideas over cha (tea), and politicians are held accountable by protestors on the main roads.

This eagerness to squeeze the juice out of all endeavours goes hand in hand with Bangladeshi pride. Bangladesh's bloody history is a proud one. The legacy of ordinary people turned heroes resonates today to spur Bangladeshis on to shape their country's identity. You will be frequently asked, 'what do you think of Bangladesh?'. Regardless of your answer, you will be run through a check list of national assets and regaled again with the history of the country's birth.

For serious news, take a look at either Online News Bank (http://on linenewsbank.com) or the online version of national newspaper the *Daily Star* (www.the dailystar.net).

Fortunately, this national pride is not of the ilk that gives license to rest on the laurels of previous triumphs. Rather, it is a pride that is driven by a sense that while Bangladesh is economically poor it is intellectually rich. The right to an education is valued, along with a duty to be educated. It isn't uncommon to be asked, 'What is your country?', followed immediately by, 'What is your academic qualification?'.

Your 'all men are equal' sensibilities will be thrown into turmoil when a self-righteous businessman commands an employee to move an ashtray slightly left of its current location. You will wonder just how much everyone really loves Bangladesh after the 100th request to help a stranger on the street obtain a visa for your country.

But above all, the prevailing impression you will have about Bangladeshis is their overwhelming and sincere hospitality. In a country where it is a privilege and honour to welcome travellers, it is indeed a privilege and an honour to be welcomed.

LIFESTYLE
Poverty & Economy

Circumstance always seems to be stacked against Bangladesh in its bid for economic security. Every time the country takes a step forward some event,

---

STARING

For most of us, visiting Bangladesh is the closest we'll come to achieving celebrity status. Anything unusual is a crowd magnet. After a few minutes, you get the feeling that you wouldn't be met with more dumbstruck looks if you were dressed in drag, and moon-walking down the street (though we wouldn't test this).

Keep it in perspective. You may be the most interesting thing that's happened for a long time. Believe it or not, the best way to gain control of the situation can be to engage with the audience. Start to interact and you may discover that what was once a crowd has become company. But if you don't have the energy for conversation and can feel your rage-o-meter creeping into red, seek refuge in a shop.

CHILD LABOUR

As if cyclones, floods and civil strife aren't enough, Bangladesh has another dark blotch to its name – child labour. It's estimated that there are 4.9 million working children in Bangladesh (Unicef 2005 report). More than half of these children are working in the agricultural sector, but there are also domestic workers, garage assistants, porters and brick makers. However, it's the use of underage children (under 14) in the textile factories supplying clothing to the West that has caught the most attention. Under pressure from the UN, child labour in the textile factories was banned in 1994, but it is thought to continue regardless. In 2006 British supermarket chain Tesco was accused of selling clothes manufactured in factories using child labour. In some of these factories the working conditions are indeed horrendous and the hours very long – at least from the perspective of a Westerner, but this is where the problems arise. Nobody doubts that the use of child labour is a terrible thing but, thanks to dreadful levels of poverty, many of these children simply have no choice but to work. If the children are barred from the legal textile factories, they may end up in the unregulated, illegal factories, or involved in brick-breaking, begging or prostitution.

An interesting short film on this subject can be viewed on www.insightnewstv.com.

Tiziana Baldizzoni's *Tales from the River: Brahmaputra* (1998) is a lavish coffee-table travelogue. Sumptuous photos and text capture the Indian, Tibetan and Bangladeshi lives that shape and are shaped by the Brahmaputra.

crop failure, population growth, corruption, cyclone or flood seems to push it back again. Back in the mid-70s the number of people living below the poverty line was around 83%, but things are slowly improving and today, that figure has been reduced to 40%. Even so, problems of inequality and unemployment are rife for Bangladesh's rural poor, who comprise the majority of the population. At least 28% of the population are without regular work and of those who are working a great many are involved in highly unpredictable, seasonal agriculture for pitiful wages and security. This goes some way to explaining the fact that 30% of the population live on less than US$1 per day and that, on average, four people live on one person's earnings.

In avenues of health, Bangladesh is also making some progress though a lot still remains to be done. Bangladesh is one of the few developing countries on target to meet the Millennium Development Goals of reducing its under-five mortality rate to 51 per 1000 live births and reduce its maternal mortality ratio to 143 deaths per 100,000 live births by 2015. Since 1990, Bangladesh has halved its under-five mortality rate from 151 deaths per 1000 live births to 77. Diarrhoea is the leading killer of children in Bangladesh, while drowning accounts for 26% of deaths.

Child labour remains a problem in Bangladesh, despite official denials (see above).

The subcontinental head waggle is a ubiquitous form of nonverbal communication. Waggling the head from side to side in response to a question may mean 'no', or 'not sure', while a single tilt to one side is a sign of assent or agreement.

Family

The extended family forms the basis of social and economic life in Bangladesh and remains a cornerstone, despite the recent shift towards nuclear families. The head of the household assumes much of the responsibility and provides for parents, children and other relatives. All may occupy one house or compound area, establishing separate kitchens as the family grows and more independence is sought. Almost all marriages are arranged and when a son marries, his wife is brought to the family home and assumes the duties outlined by her mother-in-law. The family is a tightly knit group, not only for economic and protective reasons, but as a major centre for both recreational and social activities.

Though rural lifestyles have remained largely unchanged for millennia, the small urban middle class live much like their Western counterparts. Young people from richer families are under great pressure to get a good education at a prestigious university.

POPULATION

In July 2007 the population of Bangladesh stood at around 150 million. Since then, it has grown by 1.34% per year, making it the seventh most populated country in the world. Though technically Bangladesh is *only* the fourth most densely populated country in the world, the three countries ahead of it (Monaco, Singapore and Malta) are all tiny city states and therefore Bangladesh, with 1090 people per sq km, is considered by many to be the most densely populated country in the world. By 2015 it's estimated that Bangladesh's population will be 181.5 million.

Despite these frightening figures, Bangladesh has done a reasonable job of reducing its birth rate. Where women in the 1970s were having around seven babies, today the average birth rate is 2.9.

Urbanisation is a big problem as job seekers flock to the cities. At the time of writing, around 25% of the population live in cities and this is expected to grow to 50% by 2025. Massive shanty towns exist on the fringes of the largest Bangladeshi cities and with the urban drift continuing, these will become an ever bigger problem for the government. The least populated area in the country is the Chittagong Hill Tracts, though the government is trying to change this with policies designed to promote an influx of Muslim Bangladeshis to the area. The population of this 13,180-sq-km area is estimated at between one and 1.5 million people.

There is much emigration to the Arab Gulf States and Western nations and this expatriate community, who often go for years without seeing their

They Ask if we Eat Frogs: Garo Ethnicity in Bangladesh, by Ellen Bal, is a scholarly examination of the life and society of the Garo tribe from the Mymensingh area.

A NOBEL BANK

Founded in 1976 by Nobel Laurete Muhammad Yunus, the Grameen Bank now operates services in virtually every village in Bangladesh (some 79,000 at the last count) and has provided micro credit to over seven million Bangladeshis.

Yunus opposes the traditional concept that a borrower must be educated to be risk-worthy and that micro-loans can't be profitable. He feels that if financial resources are available to poor, landless people at existing commercial terms, millions of small families with millions of small pursuits can create a development wonder.

Grameen Bank targets destitute women as Yunus believes that women are more reliable and tend to plough money into the needs of the family while men more often spend it on themselves. By the bank's statistics, the default rate is around 2% and it claims that about a third of the borrowers have crossed the poverty line.

Under the bank's lending formula, prospective borrowers form small groups who vet each others loan requests and ensure weekly paybacks. If one member fails to pay, the group receives no further loans; peer pressure tends to keep things straight.

The programme is not without its sceptics. The bank's claims are difficult to verify because of slow reporting. Its default rate calculation may be suspect; some say that by normal banking standards the rate would be much higher.

Repayment of loans begins after the first week; many borrowers complain that this is too limiting. Some don't know how they'll use the loan, but because the money is there and they're eligible, they accept it. Reportedly, some borrowers lie about the purpose of the loan and use it for personal reasons such as dowry demands.

In the past decade the bank has expanded its activities enormously and alongside various trusts and funds it also runs separate communications, energy, education and even knitwear businesses, all with the goal of helping the poor of Bangladesh.

There is little doubt that the Grameen Bank has become the most recognised Bangladeshi business on the world stage and there is equally little doubt that it has made a positive impact on millions of lives. It was thanks to this that in 2006 the Nobel Peace Prize was awarded to the bank's founder, Muhammad Yunus and to the Grameen Bank itself.

family, send a significant proportion of their income back to Bangladesh. These remittances are an important part of the nation's economy.

RELIGION

Only Indonesia, Pakistan and India have a larger Muslim population than Bangladesh. Around 83% of Bangladeshis are Muslim, 16% are Hindu, leaving Christians and Buddhists to make up the remaining 1%.

The Departed Melody by former Chakma chief and member of the legislative assembly Raja Tridiv Roy is an all-encompassing account of the history, culture and political dispossession of the people of the Chittagong Hill Tracts.

Islam

Bangladesh's Muslim majority is almost entirely Sunni. Although there is a very small (but vocal) fundamentalist minority, the Liberation War – during which some fanatics collaborated with the Pakistanis because they believed that rebelling against Pakistan, the 'land of the pure', was a crime against Islam – affected the general attitude towards fundamentalist Islam.

On the Indian subcontinent, Islam was mostly spread by Sufis, followers of a branch of Islam from Central Asia. Sufism is a philosophy that holds that abstinence, self-denial and tolerance – even of other religions – are the route to union with God. Sufi missionaries were able to convert Hindus in Bangladesh with beliefs that have similarities to some branches of Hinduism. Major Sufi sects in Bangladesh include the Naqshbandhis, originally from Central Asia, and the Chishtis, which was founded in Ajmer, India.

Islamic fundamentalism, though present in Bangladesh, has not become the problem that it has in Pakistan, Indonesia or even India.

TRIBAL PEOPLE

The tribal population of Bangladesh numbers almost one million. They generally live in the hilly regions north of Mymensingh, the Sylhet area, and more than 500,000 are concentrated in the wooded Chittagong Hill Tracts.

The major tribal groups living in the Chittagong Hill Tracts are the Bengali-looking Chakma and the Burmese-looking Marma (or Maghs), who are also found in Cox's Bazar and the Khepupara region near Kuakata. Both these tribal groups are primarily Buddhist. These, and the other smaller tribes inhabiting this region, are sometimes collectively known as Jhumias, from *jhum*, their method of slash-and-burn agriculture. Despite their population size, the Chakma are not the original inhabitants of the area – that honour goes to the Mros, who traditionally live in fortified hilltop villages. The Mros have no written language of their own and though many claim to be Buddhist, a lot of their religious practises are in fact largely animistic.

The Garos (or Mandi, as they call themselves) are the largest group living in the hilly regions north of Mymensingh and the Garo Hills. Interestingly they have a higher literacy rate than Bengalis, yet few make it into higher education. They are said to number close to 100,000.

The tribes in the Mymensingh area were originally nomads from the eastern states of India and China, and those in the Chittagong Hill Tracts originate from Myanmar (Burma). They have distinct cultures, art, religious beliefs, superstitions, farming methods and attire.

Many of the tribes still have very little contact with the outside world, but as modern civilisation encroaches on their territories, more and more of the younger villagers are moving to urban areas for employment. The Chakmas, for instance, now make saris and tribal jewellery and have established, or joined, weaving industries. They have begun to accept Western education and clothing, and even use Western medicine in lieu of herbs and mantras.

Found within the broad racial group of the plains people, who make up the vast majority of Bangladeshis, are subgroups who, although apparently integrated into the culture, continue to pursue strikingly different lives. The Bauls, for example, are wandering beggar-minstrels, whose sexual freedom and fondness for bhang (marijuana) are abhorred by the mainstream, but they are good musicians and are welcomed at weddings and parties.

BEHAVIOUR IN MOSQUES

One person's tourist attraction is another person's place of worship, so it is important to respect religious etiquette.

You may not be permitted to enter a mosque either because you are a non-Muslim or female (or perhaps both). Sometimes you may simply have to forgo close inspection during prayer times. If in doubt, ask, and be respectful of the answer.

If you *are* granted admittance, behave with appropriate solemnity and decorum. Displays of affection are highly inappropriate, as is smoking. Never step over or walk in front of someone praying. Ask permission before taking photographs.

A way of showing respect and increasing your chance of gaining entry is by dressing appropriately. Women, if not wearing a *salwar kameez* (a long, dress-like tunic over baggy trousers), should at least wear long pants, long sleeves and a headscarf. Shorts and singlets are inappropriate for men. Both sexes should take care not to rock up in dirty and/or tatty clothing.

Hinduism

The Hindu minority was persecuted during the Pakistani era, but since 1971, relations between Hindus and Muslims have by and large been peaceful. One notable exception was in 1992, when the destruction of India's Babri mosque by Hindu fanatics unleashed a wave of violence against Bangladeshi Hindus. Since Partition in 1947, many Hindus have fled to India.

Buddhism

Buddhists today are mostly tribal people in the Chittagong Hill Tracts. A small ethnic Bangladeshi community also exists. The once-flourishing Buddhist culture faded under pressure from Hinduism before the arrival of Islam (see p19), but its influence lingered in the styles of sculpture and the generally relaxed way of life.

Christianity

Although there is a small Christian population, mostly descendants of Portuguese traders, there is quite a strong Christian presence courtesy of foreign aid organisations and missionary groups. Since overt proselytising is forbidden by the government, these groups focus on providing aid and serving Christians in the community, rather than attempting to make converts.

WOMEN IN BANGLADESH

One thing you may notice quite quickly is the absence of women on the streets and in the marketplaces. All the shopkeepers, produce sellers and hawkers are men, and the outright majority of those doing the buying, the tea sipping, and the standing around are men.

Strict purdah (the practice of keeping women in seclusion in keeping with the Quranic injunction to guard women's modesty and purity) is not widely observed in Bangladesh. It is sometimes found in middle- to lower-class families, who tend to be the most conservative element of society, but most of the poorer segment cannot afford the luxury of idle females. The generally progressive upper class, with the benefit of an urban education, consider themselves too sophisticated to put up with it. Even in the absence of purdah, however, cultural tradition and religious custom serve to keep women 'under wraps', and relationships between men and women outside of the family are very formal.

The birth of a daughter is met with less fanfare than that of a son. Though there has been a massive increase in the amount of girls attending school in the past few years (now 85% of male and female children attend primary

On the Brink in Bengal, by Francis Rolt, is an out-of-print travelogue focusing on the author's encounters with the minority tribal populations in and around the Chittagong Hill Tracts.

The annual Biswa Ijtema, an international Muslim gathering second in size only to the haj (pilgrimage) to Mecca in Saudi Arabia, is held on the outskirts of Dhaka, usually in January.

Bangla2000 (www .bangla2000.com) is a popular portal to news, entertainment, sport, business and lifestyle links.

TASLIMA NASRIN & THE POLITICS OF SHAME

Dubbed the 'Salman Rushdie of Bangladesh', Taslima Nasrin became Bangladesh's most internationally famous writer with the publication of her book *Lajja* (Shame) in 1993.

Lajja is the fictional story of the Dutta family, Bangladeshi Hindus victimised by Islamic extremists. It's based on the real-life destruction of the Babri mosque in India in 1992 by Hindu extremists, which unleashed a wave of religious violence in India and Bangladesh that left hundreds dead. *Lajja* details the atrocities committed against an innocent minority, and the Dutta's indignation at being branded second-class citizens in their own country.

Born in 1962, Nasrin started writing at the age of 15. Over the years she has written seven novels and numerous short stories, essays, poems and newspaper articles. She first drew the ire of Islamic extremists in 1990 in a series of newspaper features where she criticised some Islamic statutes, described herself as an atheist and called the Quran obsolete. Nasrin has since said, 'I don't believe in the Quran…I've called for the abolition of Quranic law on the grounds that it is a discriminatory law which oppresses women in Bangladesh'.

When *Lajja* was first published it caused a storm – huge street protests by Islamic militants calling for her death took place, hartals (strikes) were held in support of her arrest, and some Islamic clerics declared a fatwa (death sentence for blasphemy) against her. Rather than acting to protect her, Begum Khaleda Zia's government banned the book in Bangladesh, confiscated her passport and put out an arrest warrant for her. With the help of various humanitarian organisations in the West, Nasrin eventually managed to flee to Europe in 1994, where she was awarded the prestigious Sakharov prize for freedom of thought.

Nasrin returned to Bangladesh in September 1998 to be with her cancer-stricken mother and her arrival relit the protests. Further fatwas were issued, as were further arrest warrants on the basis of 'hurting people's religious feelings'. She was eventually forced out of Bangladesh again and fled to India, but life hardly improved for her there. In March 2007, the All India Ittehad Millat Council offered 500,000 rupees for her beheading, while in August 2007 she was attacked during a book launch in the Indian city of Hyderabad. In March 2008 she was forced out of India and went into hiding in an undisclosed location in western Europe.

For more about Nasrin see her website http://taslimanasrin.com/.

school compared to 46% in 1991). Despite this, only around 31% of women are literate (compared to 54% of men). Most marriages are arranged by parents, and in rural villages the general marriageable age for girls is well below the legal minimum of 18 years.

Poorer Bangladeshi women bear the brunt of many of the country's problems. Numerous pregnancies, hard work and a poor diet mean that many women suffer ill health. Among the wealthier classes, a high number of women go to university and there are many professional women.

There are a number of development projects that are directed at women's concerns. These focus on training programmes about health care and legal representation and are intended to foster independence and self-sufficiency. There are also signs that the government is taking women's rights increasingly seriously. In response to increased public anger over violence against women, the government introduced a law in 2002 making acid attacks (usually committed by family members over marital disputes) punishable by death. There is still a long way to go though, as was demonstrated in early 2008 when male protestors took to the streets to air their grievances over a new law entitling women to the same inheritance rights as men.

Scout around the superb website of the Sustainable Development Networking Programme (www.sdnpbd.org) for detailed information on poverty, environmental, women's and tribal issues in Bangladesh.

MEDIA

The press in Bangladesh is relatively free. Newspaper ownership and content are not subject to government restriction and there are hundreds of daily and weekly publications, mostly in Bengali. However, the government does seek to influence newspapers through the placement of its advertising, and media-rights organisation, Reporters Without Borders, reports that journalists are targeted by Islamists and Maoist groups as well as government politicians.

There are eight English-language daily newspapers. The ones with the most international news and, reputedly, the most unbiased reporting are the *Daily Star* and the *Independent*. The *Bangladesh Observer* is also fairly good, as is *New Age*. Satellite TV has revolutionised local TV viewing habits and there are now nearly more channels than you can handle (though still rarely anything to watch!). These are mostly entertainment channels from India such as the various Star channels (films, music) and Zee TV, but you'll also find CNN, Discovery, BBC and other European channels.

The national government TV broadcaster is BTV. You may prefer an early night than an evening spent with this channel, though it does have nightly news in English, as does Radio Bangladesh. Satellite channel ATN Bangla is the biggest private TV channel in Bangladesh. Check local newspapers for broadcast times.

Sirajul Islam's multi-volume *Banglapedia* covers history, politics, culture and government. This complete library will adorn the bookshelf but encumber the backpack. Fortunately it's available in a no-frills online form at http://banglapedia .search.com.bd/.

SPORT

Cricket is enormously popular in Bangladesh, and Indian satellite TV broadcasts it practically nonstop. In 2000 Bangladesh earned Test and one-day international status, but maybe an even more momentous event in Bangladeshi cricket occurred in 1999 when the national team qualified for the World Cup and became national heroes by beating Pakistan. This rare victory was the cause of national rejoicing, and the prime minister described it as the greatest day in the country's history.

Though not as popular as in other parts of the world, Bangladeshis enjoy their football (soccer) more than most people on the subcontinent. It goes without saying that Manchester United are far and away the most popular team (yawn, yawn). Most big premiership and international matches are shown on TV.

The national sport of Bangladesh is kabaddi, in which two teams battle each other by capturing members of the opposing team. The 'raider' enters the opposition's half and has to 'tag' as many opponents as he can, while continuously chanting 'kabaddi-kabaddi' to prove he is not taking any breaths. If the opposing team manages to detain the raider in its half until he takes another breath, the raider is declared out.

Women don't play much sport, except for badminton, which is one of the country's most popular sports.

Expatriate Games – 662 days in Bangladesh, by Mark Trenowden, takes this popular genre away from the wine-filled clichés in the south of France to the noise-filled days in Dhaka.

ARTS

The people of the Bengal region share a similarity of language, dress, music and literature across the national boundaries. Weaving, pottery and terracotta sculpture are some of the earliest forms of artistic expression and the necessities of clothing and cooking utensils also provided a medium for aesthetic creation.

Literature, too, had an early place. Hindu and Buddhist translations and local mythology were preceded by theatre groups, whose rural wanderings date back 2000 years.

Architecture

The oldest and most basic Bangladeshi building style is *bangla*. A classic example of this 2500-year-old style is the bamboo-thatched hut with a distinctively curved roof, still seen in villages today.

Of remaining ancient architectural styles, most are religious. The oldest of these are the Buddhist structures built between the 4th and 7th centuries.

These generally consisted of a square plinth surmounted by a circular plinth and topped by a dome, which tapered off sharply near the top – this was known as the Gupta style. The great brick temples and monasteries at Mahasthangarh (p103), Comilla (p142) and Paharpur (p104) all date from this period.

The earliest surviving Hindu buildings are the tall, god-lined towers (that are still built in southern India today). A perfect 18th-century example of this can be seen in Puthia (p117), while the Kantanagar temple (p111) near Dinajpur is a good example of home-grown Hindu temple architecture.

Get down with the kids at www.banglamusic.com and learn all about the happenings in the world of Bangla pop.

When the Muslims first arrived in the area that is now Bangladesh they set about creating mosques so stunning that modern Bangladeshi architecture has been hard pushed to catch up. Of particular note are the mosques of the Turkistan Khiljis period (13th to 15th centuries), including the famous Shait Gumbad Mosque (p89) near Bagerhat and the Goaldi Mosque (p72) at Sonargaon. From 1576 to 1757 the Mughals ruled Bengal and altered the simple design of preceding Muslim architecture, without following the traditional designs employed in India. The best examples are Dhaka's Lalbagh Fort (p53) and Sat Gumbad Mosque (p58).

Once the British arrived on the scene, the art of religious architecture was largely thrown out the window and energy was focused instead on grandiose public buildings and palaces. The Hindu rajbaris – the generic name for palaces built by the zamindar (feudal landowners) – are a uniquely Bengali construction from this period. Although rajbaris are essentially very large Georgian or Victorian country houses, the cosmopolitan ideas of their owners were often expressed in a barrage of neo-Renaissance features, creating a mixture of styles. Many rajbaris are in ruins after being vacated at Partition in 1947.

Most public structures built during the British era combined Renaissance and Mughal styles. Examples of this include Curzon Hall (p55) at Dhaka University, and Carmichael College (p106) in Rangpur.

Many government circuit houses resemble the British bungalow style, with high-pitched corrugated-iron roofs and low verandas.

Modern architecture has been less kind to Bangladesh with the most notable modern building being the very '70s style National Assembly building (p58), designed by American architect Louis Kahn to incorporate bold geometrical patterns. The orthodox Islamic architecture of Baitul Mukarram Mosque (p55) is interpreted with very sharp and spare lines.

Literature

Best known in the literature of Bangladesh are the works of the great Bengali poets Rabindranath Tagore (1861–1941) and Kazi Nazrul Islam (1899–1976), whose photos are displayed in restaurants and shops countrywide. Tagore received international acclaim in 1913 when he was awarded the Nobel Prize for Literature for his book *Gitanjali* (Song Offerings). Despite his Hindu upbringing, Tagore wrote from a strong cultural perspective that transcended any particular religion. He celebrated 'humble lives and their miseries' and supported the concept of Hindu-Muslim unity. His love for the land of Bengal is reflected in many of his works, and a portion of the lyrics in one of his poems was adopted as the national anthem.

Jhumpa Lahiri's Pulitzer Prize-winning *Interpreter of Maladies* covers the theme of emigration and displacement amongst Bangladeshis.

The 'rebel poet' and composer Kazi Nazrul Islam is considered the national poet. When the country was suffering under colonial rule, Islam employed poetry to challenge intellectual complacency and spark feelings of nationalism.

Of modern writers, the most famous by far is the exiled feminist writer Taslima Nasrin (see p30).

NAKSHI KANTHA

Once only found among a woman's private possessions, *nakshi kanthas* (embroidered quilts) can be seen in Bangladesh hanging on the walls of upmarket hotels, offices and in museums. The humble but indigenous *nakshi kantha* has become an artistic symbol, not just of Bangladeshi women but the nation as well.

Traditionally, *nakshi kantha*-making was mostly done in the central and western divisions of Bangladesh. They are made from worn-out clothing, particularly saris, and six or so layers of material are stitched together in a way that leaves a rippled surface. They are often given as wedding gifts to a daughter leaving home, or to a grown son as a reminder of his mother. Besides the usefulness of recycling old material, there is also a folk belief that a *nakshi kantha* made from old material brings good luck. The jealous gods won't harm someone dressed in rags – infants are often dressed in *nakshi kantha* nappies for this reason.

Nakshi kanthas share many motifs with another female art form, the ground drawings made with powder called 'alpanas'. Alpanas have a long connection to religious rites held to bring rain, protect families, celebrate the harvest and secure a successful new rice sowing. The lotus symbol, often the central symbol, evokes both sun and water. The plant opens as the sun rises and, seemingly dead in the dry season, revives as soon as the water rises. The tree-of-life motif is an ancient fertility symbol. In one ritual, a newlywed couple plant a banana sapling to mark their new life together. Patterns made of twined leaves relate back to the tree-of-life. Images of fish and rolling waves reflect the dominance of the rivers on the Bangladeshi landscape.

There are women's cooperatives that produce *nakshi kantha* commercially. One good place to look is Aarong in Dhaka (p66).

Folk Art

Weaving has always held a special place in the artistic expression of the country. In the 7th century, the textiles of Dhaka weavers found their way to Europe, where they were regarded as *textiles ventalis* (fabrics woven of air).

The most artistic and expensive ornamental fabric is the *jamdani* (loom-embroidered muslin or silk), which was exclusively woven for the imperial household centuries ago and evolved as an art form under the influence of Persian design.

Needlework has become a cottage industry. Most well known are *nakshi kantha* (see above), embroidered and quilted patchwork cloths that hold an important place in village life, with the embroidery recording local history and myth. There are women's cooperatives that produce *nakshi kantha* commercially.

The Art of Kantha Embroidery, by Naiz Zaman, uses drawings and photographs to explain the technique of nakshi kantha and give a face to the women involved in its production.

Modern Art

The paintings on rickshaws and trucks, the most pervasive form of popular culture, are purveyors of history and myth (see boxed text, p34).

The turbulence of life in Bangladesh has given artists much to express, which they do with wondrous artistry and diversity. The Shilpakala Academy (p65), just next to the National Museum in Dhaka, showcases some of the finest contemporary work. The Osmani Auditorium (p65) also has good examples, such as Zianul Abedin's powerful depictions of famine, while the National Museum (p55) has a section devoted to modern Bangladeshi art.

Cinema

Dhaka, or Dhallywood as the local movie fanzines call it, has a thriving film industry that produces 150 to 200 films annually. Every commercial movie follows the immortal formula of romance, comedy, violence and song-and-dance, often spliced together in ways gloriously free of Western

Get with the stars at www.dallywood.com profiling all the big names in Bangladeshi cinema and offering a brief historical analysis.

RICKSHAW ART

Your first and last impression of Bangladesh is likely to be the rainbow colours of a cycle rickshaw. More than just a cheap and environmentally sound form of transport, the humble rickshaw is a work of art and a fleet of rickshaws the finest art galley Bangladesh can conjure up. Art passing by on wheels needs to be bold and eye-catching, and able to be taken in quickly. Rickshaw artists aim to decorate the vehicles with as much drama and colour as possible, and paint images that are both simple and memorable. This is street art for the ordinary man, and it is unashamedly commercial.

Maliks, the owners of rickshaw fleets, commission *mistris* (rickshaw makers) to build and decorate the machines to their specification. The artists working in the *mistri's* workshop learn on the job, sometimes starting out as young as 10, when they work decorating the upholstery and smaller sections of the vehicle.

The main 'canvas' is recycled tin, from a drum of cooking oil for example. This forms the backboard of the rickshaw. Enamel paints are used. The artist may also decorate the seat, handlebars, the curved back of the seat, the chassis, the hood, and just about every other surface. The handlebar decorations in particular can be wildly elaborate, with intricate coloured plastic tassels 20cm long.

All the dreams of the working man appear on rickshaws. Common themes include idealised rural scenes; wealthy cities crammed with cars, aeroplanes and high-rise buildings; unsullied natural environments; and dream homes with sports cars parked outside. Images of Bangladeshi and Indian film and pop stars are by far the most popular designs. The portraits often make the actors plumper than in real life – a slim figure isn't a fantasy when so many go hungry. The images of women with heart-stopping stares are a great contrast to the real women on the street, who by custom avoid eye contact with unfamiliar men.

Another theme is animals behaving as humans. Many are just playful: birds playing music, or lions, tigers and deer dancing and singing in a wedding procession. Others have coded messages, such as a fat lion sitting in the back of the rickshaw roaring at a skinny pedal-pushing deer, or a tiger (Bangladesh?) feasting on a cow (India?).

In the more pious Muslim towns such as Sylhet and Maijdi, rickshaw paintings have fewer human or animal figures, due to the Islamic injunction against depicting living creatures. In their place appear landscapes and religious imagery such as crescent moons and stars, Arabic calligraphy, Mecca and the Taj Mahal. Islamic green is the main colour used on these rickshaws. For a short time Osama Bin Laden and Saddam Hussein were seen grinning off the back of some rickshaws, though their popularity seems to have rapidly diminished.

Mass-produced photographic images of film stars applied to the backboard are increasingly challenging the hand-painted art, especially in Dhaka. The rise of motorised traffic in the big cities is another threat to the non-polluting rickshaw industry. Some people say that nowadays the smaller towns of Mymensingh and Tangail have the freshest and most original rickshaws tinkling by on the streets.

notions of plot continuity. Given the ban on anything sexually explicit, movie makers are pushing the boundaries of what sexually implicit entails. They may not be high art but they are certainly entertaining, both for the audience participation and the fact that an understanding of Bengali probably wouldn't make them any less obscure.

Environment

THE LAND

First, let's state the obvious – Bangladesh is flat and wet; very flat and very wet. The two exceptions to this are the hills around Sylhet, which mark the beginnings of the hills of Assam, and the steep mountains of the Chittagong Hill Tracts, which run along the Myanmar (Burma) border. In fact, in a country as famous for being flat as Bangladesh is, it might come as something of a surprise to learn that the highest peak in the country (1230m-high Mt Keokradang in the Chittagong Hill Tracts) is only 100m lower than the highest peak in Scotland.

Bangladesh has a total area of 143,998 sq km, roughly the same size as England and Wales combined. It is surrounded to the west, northwest and east by India, and shares a southeastern border with Myanmar for 283km. To the south is the Bay of Bengal.

The great Himalayan rivers, the Ganges and Brahmaputra, divide the land into six major regions which correspond to the six governmental divisions: northwest (Rajshahi), southwest (Khulna), south-central (Barisal), central (Dhaka), northeast (Sylhet) and southeast (Chittagong).

Almost all the Bangladesh coastline forms the Mouths of the Ganges, the final destination of the Ganges River, and the largest estuarine delta in the world. The coastal strip from the western border to Chittagong is one great patchwork of shifting river courses and little islands. Over the whole delta area, which extends into India, the rivers make up 6.5% of the total area.

In all of Bangladesh, the only place that has any stone is a quarry in the far northwestern corner of Sylhet division, bordering India. That is one reason you will see bricks being hammered into pieces all over the country: the brick fragments are substituted for stones when making concrete.

Ganges, the 2007 BBC TV series and DVD, is a sumptuously filmed exploration of the Ganges River, its people and its wildlife. The last programme in the series focuses largely on the Sundarbans.

WATER WORLD

Floods are almost the first thing that people think of when talk turns to Bangladesh, but even so, if you arrive by air during the monsoon season, you'll be astounded at how much of the country appears to be under water – around 70%. And this will probably be just the normal flooding that occurs. When there is a *real* flood, even the fish start to feel a little out of their depth! Many first-time visitors to Bangladesh assume that the flooding is due to heavy rainfall during that time of year. In fact, local rainfall is only partly responsible – most of the water comes pouring down the Padma (known as the Ganges upstream in India), the Meghna and the Jamuna (Brahmaputra) Rivers.

For Bangladeshis, annual flooding is a fact of life and one that, with an ever-increasing population, bad land management and global climate change, is only likely to get to worse. However, much of the flooding (which affects about a third of the country) is regarded by farmers as beneficial, as worn soils are replenished with nutrients. It's when the rivers rise above their normal limits that problems arise.

Major flooding struck northwest Bangladesh and Chittagong in 2007, but in 2004 really heavy flooding over much of the country resulted in the deaths of around 800 people, while in 1998 all three of the country's major rivers reached flood levels at the same time and 16 million people were left homeless. In Dhaka, even houses on fairly high ground were inundated, and Zia airport was covered with water and had to be shut down.

WILDLIFE
Animals
Bangladesh is home to the Royal Bengal tiger and other members of the cat family including leopards and the smaller jungle cat. Tigers are almost exclusively confined to the Sundarbans, but their smaller relations prey on domestic animals all over the country. There are three varieties of civet, including the large Indian civet, which is now listed as an endangered species. Other large animals include Asiatic elephants (mostly migratory herds from Bihar), a few black bears in Chittagong division, wild pigs and deer. Monkeys, langurs, gibbons (the only ape on the subcontinent), otters and mongooses are some of the smaller animals.

Reptiles include various ocean turtles, mud turtles, river tortoise, pythons, crocodiles and a variety of venomous snakes. The voluble gecko, named for the sound it makes, is known here as *tik-tiki*.

> The Sundarbans Tiger Project (www.sundarbanstigerproject.info) tells you all you ever wanted to know about tigers, the Sundarbans and the on-going conservation projects taking place there.

ENDANGERED SPECIES
The Royal Bengal tiger is endangered and although the government has set aside three areas within the Sundarbans as tiger reserves (see p93), numbers are low.

Other rare or threatened species include the Indian elephant, the hoolock gibbon, the black bear and the Ganges River dolphin. Reptiles under threat include the Indian python, the crocodile and various turtles.

Many of the diverse bird species are prolific, but some are vulnerable, including Pallas' fishing eagle and Baer's pochard.

BIRD-WATCHING
Sitting like a cushion between the plains of India, the hills of Myanmar (Burma) and just a mere Yeti's footstep from the Himalaya, the waterways of Bangladesh are a bird-watchers dream. The country contains more than 650 species of birds – almost half of those found on the entire subcontinent.

The country's positioning means that Bangladesh attracts both Indian species in the west and north of the country, and Malayan species in the east and southeast. It is also conveniently located for migrants heading south towards Malaysia and Indonesia, and those moving southwest to India and Sri Lanka. In addition, there are a number of Himalayan and Burmese hill species that move into the lowlands during the winter.

The plundered Madhupur National Park (p77) is an important habitat for a variety of owls, including the rare brown wood owl, wintering thrushes and a number of raptors. The Jamuna River floods regularly, and from December to February provides winter habitats for waterfowl, waders and the occasional black stork.

The low-lying basin of Sylhet division has extensive natural *haors* (wetlands), and during winter it is home to huge flocks of wild fowl, including Baer's pochard and Pallas' fishing eagle, along with a great number of ducks and skulkers. The remaining fragments of evergreen and teak forests are also important habitats, especially along the Indian border near the Srimangal area, where the blue-bearded bee-eater, red-breasted trogon and a variety of forest birds are regularly seen.

One of two important coastal zones is the Noakhali region, particularly the islands near Hatiya, where migratory species and a variety of wintering waders (including large numbers of the rare spoon-billed sandpiper, Nordman's greenshank and flocks of Indian skimmers) find suitable refuge.

The Sundarbans (p92), with its miles of marshy shorelines and brackish creeks, supports a number of wetland and forest species, along with large populations of gulls and terns along the south coast. Eight varieties of kingfisher have been recorded here, including the brown-winged, the white-collared, the black-capped and the rare ruddy kingfisher.

The most exciting time of year for bird-watching is during winter, from November to March.

Plants

About 10% of Bangladesh is still forested. Half of the forest is in the Chittagong Hill Tracts and a quarter in the Sundarbans, with the rest scattered in small pockets throughout the country.

The forests fall into three distinct regional varieties: the tidal zones along the coast, often mangrove but sometimes hardwood, in much of the Sundarbans; the sal trees around Dhaka, Tangail and Mymensingh; and the upland forests of tropical and subtropical evergreens in the Chittagong Hill Tracts and parts of Sylhet.

Away from the forests, Bangladesh is still a land of trees. Lining the old trunk road in the west are huge rain trees, and every village is an arboreal oasis, often with spectacular *oshot* (banyan) trees. The red silk-cotton (kapok) tree is easily spotted throughout the countryside in February and March, when it loses its leaves and sprouts myriad red blossoms. Teak was introduced into the Hill Tracts in the 19th century and the quality approaches that of Myanmar.

Flowering plants are an integral part of the beauty of Bangladesh. Each season produces its special variety of flowers. Among them is the prolific water hyacinth, its carpet of thick green leaves and blue flowers giving the impression that solid ground lies underneath. Other decorative plants that grow easily are jasmine, water lily, rose, hibiscus, bougainvillea, magnolia and an incredible diversity of wild orchids in the forested areas.

The world's single surviving wild Corypha taliera Roxab palm tree grows in the grounds of Dhaka University.

Wild buffaloes and rhinoceroses once inhabited the Sundarbans, but became extinct last century.

NATIONAL PARKS & FOREST RESERVES

For many years, conservation has been on the back burner in government circles, but at last the government has woken up to its immense natural wealth and in recent years several new parks have opened, and old ones have had security, facilities and care beefed up.

Bhawal National Park (p74) Comprising regrowth sal forest and open picnic spots. There are a few walking trails, and its proximity to Dhaka makes it a popular escape from the city.

Chunati Wildlife Sanctuary (p139) An easy-to-visit region of semi-open coastal forest and grassland that is home to wild Asian elephants. There are walking trails and viewing platforms.

Lowacherra National Park (p154) A beautiful tropical forest containing diverse insect and bird life and a number of primates. The park has walking trails, tribal villages and eco guides, and is one of the most rewarding and easiest national parks to visit.

Madhupur National Park (p77) A degraded sal and mixed forest with some remaining old growth. A fascinating place, with plenty of wildlife and increasingly easy to visit .

Rema Kalenga Wildlife Sanctuary (p156) The least visited of the three protected forests around Srimangal, but its walking trails reveal a wealth of wildlife.

Satchari National Park (p156) A virtual continuation of the Lowacherra National Park, but the tropical evergreen forest here is less frequently visited. Has several walking trails, and is an excellent park for bird-watching and primates.

Sundarbans National Park (p92) The finest natural area in the country, mostly due to its impenetrable jungle and maze of rivers. Located in the southern half of the Khulna division, it's part of the world's largest mangrove forest and home to the world's largest population of Bengal tigers.

Bird-watchers will enjoy A Photographic Guide to the Birds of India & the Indian Subcontinent by Bikram Grewal and Bill Harvey. It has useful maps and pictures, and is compact enough to take with you.

ENVIRONMENTAL ISSUES

Bangladesh faces huge environmental problems, but having turned a blind eye for years the government is finally starting to implement plans and ideas that we could all learn from.

Starting with the bad news (which usually boils down to over-population): farmland soils are being damaged by overuse, rivers are being polluted by chemical pesticides and forests are being chopped down at an alarming rate. The water table is under threat as deep tube-wells extract clean water for drinking.

Annual flooding during the monsoonal season is part of life in Bangladesh. Some experts are questioning whether the flooding is getting worse, and, if so, whether deforestation in India and especially Nepal (which causes increased runoff), is the reason. Another theory holds that the river beds have become choked with silt from once-forested land, making flooding more severe. Regardless, there has been increased pressure to 'do something' and find a 'permanent solution'. Part of the problem of doing anything, however, is that the country depends on regular flooding for its soil fertility, and simply building massive dykes along river banks could be disastrous for agricultural output.

With the continuance of global warming, Bangladesh, as one of the 10 countries most vulnerable to a rise in sea level, will be drastically affected. And, if predications are correct, a 1m rise in the Bay of Bengal would result in a loss of 12% to 18% of the country's land.

Loss of land is just one consequence – severe flooding and reduced agricultural potential are almost inevitable. This is indeed a cruel twist of fate, since Bangladesh, as a poor, agricultural society, has contributed very little to global warming. Even with assistance from the Dutch, who are helping to devise a strategy to cope with rising water levels, the question remains whether Bangladesh will have the capacity to develop and apply the appropriate technology.

However, there is some good news. Bangladesh is now taking environmental issues very seriously and has implemented policies that should make richer Western nations cringe in embarrassment that they haven't adopted them. Responding to the high levels of litter, much of which was plastic, Bangladesh has become one of the first countries to almost completely ban plastic bags. The only places you will see plastic bags are where there are no viable alternatives for carrying certain goods. Everywhere else, goods are now packaged in paper or jute bags (so also supporting the local jute industry).

The government has also taken steps to reduce the horrendous pollution levels in Dhaka – caused largely by vehicle emissions – by banning all petrol and diesel vehicles from the capital and replacing them with cleaner, greener (and cheaper to run) CNG (compressed natural gas) vehicles. This has worked so well that the project has been extended to Chittagong and, with the amount of CNG fuel stations multiplying rapidly across the

The Sustainable Development Networking Programme (www.sdnbd .org) is one of the most valuable sources for environmental, agricultural, social and developmental information.

ARSENIC POISONING

As if war, floods and famine weren't tumultuous enough for Bangladesh, the 1970s also marked the beginning of its exposure to arsenic poisoning.

In the early 1970s people were relying on ponds and rivers for drinking water. The lack of sanitation at these sources was killing around 250,000 children annually. To address this, NGOs instigated massive tube-well projects to tap into underground water sources but, in doing so, neglected to test arsenic levels in the water. The presence of arsenic is a natural phenomenon, likely originating from the Himalayan headwaters of the Ganges and Brahmaputra Rivers. Bangladesh's special receptivity to dangerously high levels of arsenic has been attributed to its high quantity of arsenic-absorbing mud.

The battle over who is to blame for this crisis rages on. Meanwhile, more people than anyone seems to be able to count are dying every year. The social impact of this manifests itself in ostracism of affected people – children are turned away from school, and women are divorced and deserted. Physical symptoms (which often only show after a decade or so of drinking poisoned water) often begin with blisters on palms and soles, which may later become cancerous.

Needless to say, when you buy bottled water, always check that it reads 'arsenic free' and that the seal is unbroken.

THE CYCLONE ZONE

Every few years it seems Bangladesh is hit by another disaster. While there are periodic floods and droughts, the most catastrophic disaster in terms of human life are cyclones.

Bangladesh is in the world's worst area for cyclones, averaging one major storm every three years. The worst months are May and June, and October and November, and the area where damage tends to most frequently occur is in the east around Chittagong and Cox's Bazar.

People still talk about the 1970 cyclone when between 300,000 and 500,000 people died. The 1991 cyclone, which occurred during big spring tides, was stronger, affected over twice as many people and destroyed four times as many houses. However, the death toll of between 140,000 and 200,000 was less than half that of the1970 disaster.

Halfway through the research period for this book, Cyclone Sidr, the strongest storm in 15 years, struck the southwest coast and left 3500 people dead. It's generally acknowledged that the death toll would have been far higher were it not for the early warning system that was installed after the 1991 storm.

Another major reason for the reduction of fatalities was the presence of storm shelters, a number of which were constructed since 1970. Some are multi-functional, serving as schools as well as shelters, though in the investigation following Sidr it was discovered that many of shelters had fallen into such a state of disrepair as to have been unusable. Others were occupied by 'criminal elements'.

country, it will hopefully come into effect across the nation within the lifetime of this book.

Finally, the government has created a number of new national parks in the past couple of years and have stepped up environmental education for the public. All this makes Bangladesh a country that should be lauded for its environmental awareness, and shows that there is hope for the rest of the world!

Food & Drink

The fiery curries and delicately flavoured biryanis that make up so much of Bangladeshi cuisine will keep your taste buds drooling throughout your adventures in this country. Bengalis (both in Bangladesh and India's West Bengal) consider their food to be the most refined in the subcontinent and though this causes debate, everyone is in agreement that Bengali sweets truly are the finest you can dip your sticky fingers into. Chinese food has made its presence strongly felt, with decent Chinese restaurants popping up in all but the most obscure places.

STAPLES & SPECIALITIES

Thanks to its small size, it's no real surprise to learn that Bangladeshi food is not nearly as varied as that of its neighbours and, out in the rural sticks, many dishes begin to look and taste the same after a while. If you are arriving from India you will quickly notice that meat forms a much more important part of the daily diet than in Hindu India – you will also find that in most places the level of hygiene is higher! A typical Bangladeshi meal includes a curry made with vegetables and either beef, mutton, chicken, fish or egg, cooked in a hot spicy sauce with mustard oil and served with *dahl* (cooked yellow lentils) and plain rice. Rice is considered a higher-status food than bread – therefore, at people's homes you will generally be served rice.

Many menus refer to *bhuna* (or *bhoona*), which is the delicious process of cooking spices in hot oil and is the basis for many Bangladeshi dishes. It also refers to a specific type of dry curry cooked in coconut milk (more common in India than Bangladesh). Another common dish is *dopiaza* (literally 'double onions'), which, as the name suggests, contains large amounts of onion added to the curry in two separate stages. Finding purely vegetarian dishes can be quite difficult because in Bangladesh meat is highly prized. Ask for *bhaji* which, as well as being a ball of fried vegetables (such as the onion *bhaji*) is also a general term for a simple vegetable curry. A mixed vegetable dish would be *shobji bhaji*. At fancy dinners an all-vegetarian meal would not be well received.

The three main forms of rice dishes that you're likely to encounter are biryani, *pula* (also known as *polao*), which is similar to biryani but without the meat, and *bhat* (plain rice). Rice and lentils mixed together and cooked is called *khichuri* and is perfect for upset tummies. In restaurants, chicken tikka is also common and usually served with Indian-style naan (slightly puffed wholewheat bread cooked in a tandoori oven).

Fish is every Bangladeshi's favourite meal. Traditionally it's all been about freshwater fish and most Bangladeshis have long considered saltwater fish a poor cousin, but with the rivers and lakes becoming overfished, the Bengalis are reassessing their relationship with marine life.

The fish you are most likely to eat – boiled, smoked or fried – are *hilsa* and *bhetki*. These are virtually the national dishes of Bangladesh and it's said they can be prepared in around 50 different ways. Smoked *hilsa* is very good, but be prepared to pay five-star prices for it. *Bhetki* is a variety of sea bass with lots of flesh and few bones. It's one of the best fish you'll eat and is served in midrange restaurants along with prawn and crab dishes.

Beef is widely available, although the quality is low. Kebabs come in a wide variety including *shami kebab*, made with fried minced meat, and shish kebab, which is prepared with less spice and usually with mutton or beef.

Bengali Cooking: Seasons & Festivals, by Chitrita Banerji and Deborah Madison, has the approval of Bengali food aficionados. It contains a smorgasbord of recipes and authoritative insights into the historical and cultural role of Bengali food.

The Book of Indian Sweets, by Satarupa Banerjee, is a godsend for those who develop a craving for *roshogullas* (a syrupy dessert) and other teeth-rotting Bengali treats.

Tea: Addiction, Exploitation and Empire, by Roy Moxham, is a sweeping and disturbing behind-the-scenes look at the tea industry. It reveals the blood that was spilt in Sylhet to make your cuppa.

A Bengali breakfast is usually *bhaji* or *dahl* on *rooti* (chapati). It's not always vegetarian, though – sometimes there's a lump of bone served on top.

The Bangladeshis have a sweet tooth, and there are many sugar-loaded desserts. One popular dessert is *misti doi* (sweetened yoghurt) and everyone loves jaggery, a fudge-like sweet made from sugarcane or date palm.

DRINKS

There are very few sources of drinking water in the country that are guaranteed to be safe. People in Dhaka are advised to boil and filter tap water. In a restaurant, even if the water comes from a tube well, it can easily be contaminated by the glass.

It's possible to buy bottled water nearly everywhere, but local newspapers have revealed that quite a few brands are made by companies that don't actually filter the water all the time. If the filter breaks, for example, they might choose not to jeopardise their business by stopping production. When buying bottled water from outdoor stalls, make sure that the plastic cap has not been tampered with in any way. Recycling takes many forms, including 'rebottling' water. See also boxed text on arsenic poisoning, p38.

Bengalis use the pith of the banana tree as a vegetable.

Nonalcoholic Drinks

Maybe one of the best reasons for going to Bangladesh is for the milky sweet tea known as cha! Costing just Tk 2 or Tk 3 a cup and available everywhere, each cup is made individually (rather than stewing all day), meaning that it leaves the undeniably excellent Indian version for dead. It also means that it's no problem getting tea without sugar (say *chini na* or *chini sera*), but as sweetened condensed milk will be used it doesn't make much difference.

The magic words to get a pot of tea, usually with just one weak tea bag, are 'milk separate'. Miming a tea bag produces hilarity but not much else. Coffee is difficult to find and those who can't do without should consider buying a jar of the instant stuff in Dhaka.

There is no such thing as 'curry' – the word is a purely British invention taken from the Tamil word *kari* (black pepper) and used to describe any spicy dish.

International soft drinks, such as Pepsi, Coke and Sprite, are readily available throughout the country and cost between Tk 10 and Tk 20.

Fresh lime sodas are generally available at the better restaurants in Dhaka and at some of the top-end hotels outside Dhaka. Sometimes it's no more than antacid – highly recommended for an upset stomach.

Green coconut water is a safe and refreshing drink, and is helpful in treating diarrhoea. A whole young coconut costs about Tk 5.

Lassi, the refreshing yogurt drink found throughout India, is not as common in Bangladesh.

Alcoholic Drinks

Every major town has at least one government-owned shop selling alcohol, but they're invariably hidden in very discreet locations (to avoid upsetting Islamic sensibilities). The 'selection' is usually only hard liquor such as whisky. In Dhaka, Chittagong, Cox's Bazar and Teknaf you can sometimes find Asian whisky and cans of Heineken or Tiger beer sold on the sly; the price is at least Tk 160 per can.

WHERE TO EAT & DRINK

Budget restaurants are all very similar; plain rooms where men shovel down rice, *dahl* and maybe a meat curry, as quickly as possible. In the cheapest places, notions of hygiene are pretty basic; extra rice might be served by hand, for instance. In low-end restaurants, it's rare to see women eating, but they are welcomed. Some restaurants have family rooms, often just a curtained

Bengali Spice (www .bengalispice.com) is a well-maintained, colourful site with recipes and information for Bengali food lovers.

POTTY FOR PAAN

The red patches that coat walls and roads throughout Bangladesh aren't blood but the delicately disposed of remnants of *paan*. Ubiquitous throughout the subcontinent (though most people will be glad to hear that it's not quite as common in Bangladesh as India) *paan*, a melange of betel nut, lime paste and spices wrapped in an edible *paan* leaf, is the perfect finish to any meal. Sold by *paan-wallahs*, whose little stalls dot the streets of every town and city, *paan* is eaten as a digestive and breath-freshener (though as the teeth of heavy users are horribly rotten, we remain sceptical over breath-freshener claims!). The betel nut is mildly narcotic and many people get heavily addicted to it. In addition to its digestive properties, certain *paan* mixtures are said to enhance a man's performance where it counts – though we're yet to meet a woman who'll back this claim!

There are two basic types of *paan*: *mitha* (sweet) and *saadha* (mixed with tobacco). For an unaccustomed Westerner either form tastes very bitter, but if you want to partake just pop the parcel in your mouth and chew slowly. When you've had enough find a nice, freshly painted white wall and spit the blood-red mess onto it.

---

booth, where women and families are supposed to eat. These offer a welcome opportunity for both men and women to go 'off stage'.

In Dhaka you can also find excellent Indian, Thai, Chinese and Korean restaurants. Outside Dhaka, the only cuisine that you'll find besides Bangladeshi food is Chinese, or rather a Bangladeshi interpretation of Chinese, which you'll find everywhere, even in small towns. The prevalence of Chinese restaurants is something of a mystery, given that there are estimated to be only around 700 Chinese people in Bangladesh! Prices at these establishments typically start at Tk 100 a dish, but the cost can almost triple in Dhaka. For a foreign tourist, Chinese restaurants are something of a godsend – aside from the fact that you can finally get your jaws around something other than curry and rice, they also provide a handy escape from the hordes.

> Bengali Food on the Web (www.angelfire.com /country/bengalifood/) offers easy-to-find and easy-to-make recipes.

Quick Eats

Breads and biscuits are available everywhere, and in some small towns they might be all that you feel like eating. 'Salt' biscuits are usually not salty, just not the usual extremely sweet variety.

VEGETARIANS & VEGANS

The Bengali culinary tradition evolved on the basis of what was available and, given the scarcity of meat, vegetarianism was often necessary. This means that if you can make yourself understood, you should be able to find some delicious meatless meals. You may have to explain that by 'no meat' you mean any kind of animal, including fish, and that just a little bit isn't OK.

> In a Bengali meal, flavours are usually fused by introducing the more delicate-tasting dishes first, followed by the stronger ones.

If in doubt you can always resort to fresh fruit, which isn't so poor a consolation, given the range. Major fruit-growing areas include the hilly fringes of Sylhet division, the Chittagong Hill Tracts and Rajshahi division.

Oranges and bananas are the most common fruits on sale in winter. Mango orchards along the banks of the Padma in Rajshahi division are said to grow the best mangoes.

HABITS & CUSTOMS

Traditionally, Bengali meals are served on the floor. Each person sits on a *pati* (a small piece of straw carpet). In front of the *pati* is a large platter or banana leaf, around which bowls are placed.

DOS & DON'TS

■ It is courteous to use only the right hand to receive or give things. This is especially important when it comes to food. The left hand is considered unclean, given its use in the bathroom.

■ You may break bread with both hands, but *never* put food into your mouth with the left.

■ Water may be drunk from a glass with the left hand because it is not being directly touched.

■ Always wash your hands before you eat – for the sake of courtesy as well as of hygiene.

For the uninitiated, eating in the proper Bengali fashion involves disregarding everything you've ever been taught about table manners. *Do* slurp, *do* burp and, above all, *do* play with your food. Eating with your hands is not only functional, but is also said to allow for an appreciation of textures before they are enjoyed by the tongue.

EAT YOUR WORDS

It's hard to get what you want if you can't explain what it is. For more on the Bengali language, including pronunciation tips, see the Language chapter (p190). See also the Menu Decoder (p44) for more Bengali terms.

Useful Phrases

Can you recommend a ... ?	একটা ভাল ... কোথায়	*qk*·ta *b'a*·lo ... *koh*·ṭ'a·e
	হবে বলেন তো?	*ho*·be *boh*·len ṭoh?
café	ক্যাফেটেরিয়া	*kq*·fe·te·ri·a
restaurant	রেস্তোরা	*res*·ṭoh·ra

Where would you go	...জন্য কোথায়	*john*·no *koh*·ṭ'a·e
for (a) ... ?	যাবো?	*ja*·boh?
cheap meal	সস্তা খাবারের	*shos*·ṭa·e *k'a*·ba·rer
local specialities	এখানকার বিশেষ	*e*·k'an·kar *bi*·shesh
	খাবারের	*k'a*·ba·rer

I'd like to reserve a	রিজার্ভ করতে চাই।	*aa*·mi ... *qk*·ta *te*·bil
table for ...	...আমি একটা টেবিল	*ri*·zarv *kohr*·ṭe chai
(two) people	(দুই) জনের জন্য	(dui) *jo*·ner *john*·no
(eight) o'clock	(আটার) সময়	(*aat*·tar) *sho*·moy

What would you	আপনি কি খেতে	*aap*·ni ki *k'e*·ṭe
recommend?	বলেন?	*boh*·len?
What's in that dish?	এই খাবারে কি কি	ei *k'a*·ba·re ki ki
	আছে?	*aa*·ch'e?
I'll have that.	আমি ওটা নিব।	*aa*·mi *oh*·ta *ni*·boh
I'm vegan.	আমি মাছ মাংস ডিম	*aa*·mi maach *mang*·shoh
	দুধ খাই না।	dim dud' k'ai na
I'm vegetarian.	আমি ভেজিটেরিয়ান।	*aa*·mi *ve*·ji·te·ri·an

I don't eat (meat/chicken/fish/eggs).
আমি (মাংস/মুরগী/মাছ/ডিম) খাই না।   *aa*·mi (*mang*·shoh/*mur*·gi/mach/dim) k'ai na

Is this bottled water?
এটা কি বাতলর পানি?   *e*·ta ki *boh*·ṭoh·ler *pa*·ni?

Not too spicy, please.
মশলা কম, প্লিজ।   *mosh*·la kom pleez

No more, thank you.
আর না, ধন্যবাদ।   aar naa *d'oh*·noh·baad

I'm allergic to ...	আমার ... -এ এ্যালার্জি আছে।	*aa·mar ... -e q·lar·ji aa·ch'e*
nuts	বাদাম	*baa·dam*
shellfish	চিংড়ি মাছ	*ching·ṛi maach'*
Please bring ...	... আনেন প্লিজ।	*... aa·nen pleez*
an ashtray	একটা এ্যাসট্রে	*qk·ta qsh·tre*
the bill	বিলটা	*bil·ta*
a fork	একটা কাঁটা	*qk·ta ka·ta*
a glass	একটা গ্লাস	*qk·ta glash*
a knife	একটা ছুরি	*qk·ta ch'u·ri*
a menu	মেন্যু	*me·nu*
a spoon	একটা চামুচ	*qk·ta cha·much*
That was delicious.	খুব মজা ছিল।	*k'ub mo·ja ch'i·loh*

Menu Decoder

MAINS

bhaji	ভাজি	a ball of fried vegetables; also general term for vegetable curry
bhat	ভাত	rice
bhuna/bhoona	ভুনা	food fried in spices over high heat for a long period
biryani	বিরিয়ানি	rice casserole, often cooked with chicken, beef, mutton and/ or vegetables
dahl	ডাল	cooked yellow lentils
dopiaza	দোপিয়াজা	curry cooked with lots of onions
gorur mangsho	গরুর মাংস	beef
hilsa/ilish	ইলিশ	species of fish
kalia	কালিয়া	rich, spicy meat curry, often with potatoes
kebab	কাবাব	small pieces of meat, skewered and usually cooked over charcoal
khasir mangsho	খাসির মাংস	mutton
kofta/bora	কোফতা/বড়া	ground meat or vegetables bound by spices and egg
korma	কোরমা	meat cooked in a mild yogurt sauce and butter
mach	মাছ	fish
mangsho	মাংস	meat
murgi	মুরগী	chicken

SNACKS

alur chop	আলুর চপ	fried potato cutlet
chotpoti	চটপটি	hot chickpeas with potato, egg, spices and tamarind sauce
luchi	লুচি	deep-fried flatbread
moghlai paratha	মগলাই পারাটা	*paratha* stuffed with egg, vegetables and spices; delicious for breakfast
paratha	পারাটা	thick flatbread, lightly fried in oil or ghee
puri	পুরি	deep-fried bread stuffed with *dahl* or mashed potato
samosa	সামুসা	wheat-flour pastry triangle stuffed with spiced vegetables or minced meat
shingara	সিঙ্গারা	similar to a samosa but round and with a slightly heavier filling, typically spiced potatoes or liver

DESSERTS

firni/paish	ফিরনি/পায়স	rice pudding cooked with milk, sugar, flavouring and nuts, popular at Eid celebrations
halua	হালুয়া	common dessert made with carrot or pumpkin, butter, milk and sugar

jorda	জরদা	yellow sweet-rice with saffron, almonds and cinnamon
kalojam	কাল জাম	fried milk-and-flour balls, soaked in syrup
kheer	ক্ষীর	rice pudding with thick milk
molidhana	মলিধানা	milk-based dessert similar to *halua*
pitha	পিঠা	blanket term for all kinds of cakes or pastries, including specific varieties such as *chitoi, dhupi, tokti, andosha, puli, barfi* and *pua*
rosh malai	রস-মালাই	*roshogulla* floating in a thick milk
roshogulla	রসগোল্লা	soured-milk balls boiled in syrup
shemai	সমাই	vermicelli cooked in milk and sugar
shirni	সিরনি	rice flour with molasses or sugar
shondesh	সন্দেশ	milk-based dessert, one of the best available
shooji	সুজি	semolina, almond and pistachio nuts

OTHER

cha	লেব	milky, sweet tea
chamoch	চামুচ	spoon
churi	ছুরি	knife
dim	ডিম	egg
glas	গ্লাস	glass
kata	কাটা	fork
lebu	লেবু	lemon, lime
morich	মরিচ	chilli
pani	পানি	water
rooti	রুটি	*chapati* (bread)
shobji	সবজি	vegetable

Dhaka

Dhaka is more than just a city, it is a giant whirlpool that sucks in anything and anyone foolish enough to come within its furious grasp. Around and around it sends them, like some wildly spinning fairground ride bursting with energy. Millions of individual pursuits constantly churn together into a frenzy of collective activity – it is an urban melting pot bubbling over. Nothing seems to stand still. Even the art moves, paraded on the back of the city's sea of 600,000-plus rickshaws, which throb with colour and restlessness even when gridlocked.

It doesn't matter how many times you experience this city, the sensation of being utterly overwhelmed is always the same. Sights and experiences come at you so thick and fast that it would take a lifetime to know this mega-city's every mood. A day spent alternating between the filthy riverbanks of Old Dhaka and the swish restaurants of Gulshan is a day spent seeing the haves and have-nots of the world in crystal clarity. We can't guarantee you'll fall for Dhaka's many charms, but sooner or later you will start to move to its beat and when that happens Dhaka stops being a terrifying ride and starts becoming a cauldron of art and intellect, passion and poverty, love and hate. Whatever happens, this is one fairground ride you'll never forget.

HIGHLIGHTS

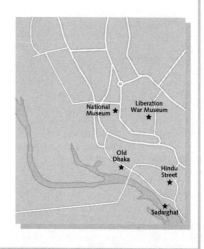

- Staring dumbstruck at the panorama of life and death unfolding in front of you on a boat ride from **Sadarghat (p50)**
- Shielding your eyes from the horrors of war at the heart-stirring **Liberation War Museum** (p55)
- Getting noisy and colourful on Old Dhaka's **Hindu Street** (p52)
- Exploring the echoing halls of the treasure-filled **National Museum** (p55), a multi-storey insight into the cultural heritage of Bangladesh
- Being completely engulfed by the chaos that is **Old Dhaka** (p50) – and loving every minute of it!
- Being trapped in an hour-long traffic jam consisting entirely of **rickshaws** (p54)

- TELEPHONE CODE: 02
- POPULATION: 12.5 MILLION

HISTORY

Founded in the 4th century, Dhaka first received principal status in 1610, when the Mughals transferred the capital from Rajmahal to Dhaka, and renamed it Jahangirnagar. During the Mughal period, Dhaka became the chief commercial emporium. This encouraged a much greater concentration of commerce: maritime trade brought industry, Islamic education and increasing sophistication in the arts. Dhaka's prosperity was also considerably enhanced – the Mughals built mosques, palaces, caravanserais (accommodation for camel caravans), bazaars and gardens. This development began to attract European traders from southern India.

In 1666 the British East India Company established a trading post in Dhaka; however, Dhaka's decline as a maritime trade centre had already begun. Dhaka remained the capital under the Mughals until 1704, when they moved it to Murshidabad.

The British East India Company extended its power to such an extent that by 1757 it controlled all of Bengal except Dhaka, which it took eight years later. It was under the British, during the late 18th and early 19th centuries, that the dominant forms of current economic development were established: indigo, sugar, tobacco, tea and, of course, jute.

In 1887 Dhaka became a district capital of Bangladesh, and in 1905 Bengal was divided into east and west, the eastern section incorporating Assam (with Dhaka as its winter capital). From this point on Dhaka again began to assume some measure of importance as an administrative centre. Government buildings, churches, residential enclaves and educational institutions transformed it into a city of great prosperity. During the existence of East Pakistan, Dhaka was classed as a subsidiary capital, and it was not until Independence in 1971 that Dhaka once again achieved its former capital-city status.

ORIENTATION

Dhaka is not too difficult to figure out, though you'll probably have a different opinion when you're standing in the street.

The city can be divided into three areas. Old Dhaka is a maze of crowded bazaars and equally crowded narrow streets lying between the northern bank of the Buriganga River and Fulbaria Rd. It's brimming with points of interest for tourists, but not many facilities. The much larger 'modern' city begins about 2km to the north. The heart of Central Dhaka is Motijheel (moh-tee-jeel), which is also an important commercial district. Major landmarks here include the National Stadium, the Shapla (Lotus Flower Fountain) Circle on Inner Circular Rd and the Raj-era Supreme Court, just north of Dhaka University. Beyond are the suburbs, including the cantonment and the upmarket quarters of Banani, Gulshan and Baridhara. These three quarters have the best restaurants, guesthouses, almost all of the embassies and many of the swishest shops.

Most major arteries run north–south. Starting in the east these include DIT Rd/ Shaheed Suhrawardi Ave, Airport Rd, Kazi Nazrul Islam Ave, the shorter Begum Rokeya Sarani, and Mirpur Rd. The airport is on Airport Rd between Uttara to its north and the rest of the city to its south.

An important road connecting Old Dhaka and the central area is North-South Rd, heading south from Kakrail Rd past the main post office and the Gulistan (Fulbaria) bus station into Old Dhaka, and leading almost all the way to the Buriganga River. The intersection of North-South and Fulbaria Rds is known as Gulistan Crossing.

Travelling around Dhaka is complicated by the fact that the main roads are known by the names of the areas through which they pass, and rarely by their official name. Adding to the confusion is that side streets and lanes often take the same name as the nearby main road. If the driver of your rickshaw, bus or baby taxi (auto-rickshaw) doesn't speak English, you'll be better off giving sections of the city or landmarks, and addresses only after you get there.

Between 5pm and 8pm the traffic jams are phenomenal and walking is almost always quicker. Around Dhanmondi, which sees about the worst of the jams, the traffic is a mixed bag of buses, cars and rickshaws whereas in Old Dhaka, where motorised vehicles are banned, the traffic jams consist entirely of hundreds upon hundreds of rickshaws. Friday morning is the best time for wandering around – although few commercial businesses are open, a number of public markets and tourist sites can be visited. Some shops reopen in the afternoon, when traffic on the streets picks up.

DHAKA

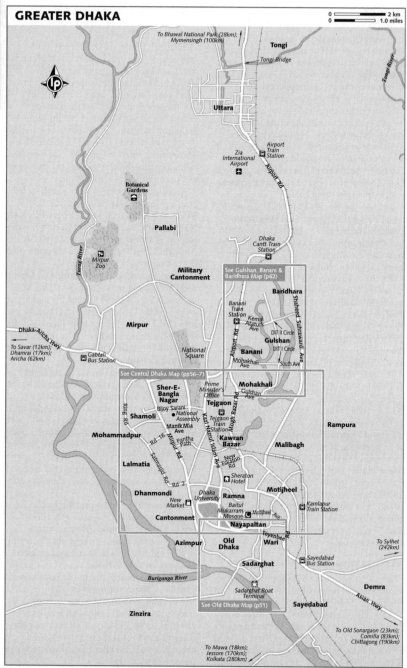

GREATER DHAKA

0 ——————— 2 km
0 ——————— 1.0 miles

To Bhawal National Park (28km);
Mymensingh (100km)

Tongi

Tongi Bridge

Uttara

Airport
Train
Station

Zia
International
Airport

Airport Rd

Botanical
Gardens

Pallabi

Dhaka
Cantt Train
Station

Mirpur
Zoo

See Gulshan, Banani &
Baridhara Map (p62)

Baridhara

Military
Cantonment

Banani
Train
Station

Kemal
Ataturk
Ave

Shaheed Suhrawardi Ave

DIT II Circle

Gulshan

Turag River

Mirpur

National
Square

DIT I Circle

Banani

Mohakhali
Ave

South Ave

Dhaka-Aricha Hwy

To Savar (12km);
Dhamrai (17km);
Aricha (62km)

Gabtali
Bus Station

See Central Dhaka Map (pp56-7)

Mohakhali

Gulshan
Ave

Sher-E-
Bangla
Nagar

Prime
Minister's
Office

Tejgaon

Mogh Bazar Rd

Shamoli

Bijoy Sarani

National
Assembly

Tejgaon
Train
Station

Ring Rd

Manik Mia
Ave

Kawran
Bazar

Rampura

Mohammadpur

Rd 16

Mirpur Rd

Pantha
Path

Kazi Nazrul Islam Ave

Malibagh

Lalmatia

New
Eskaton
Rd

Satmasjid Rd

Rd 2

Sheraton
Hotel

Dhanmondi

Dhaka
University

Ramna

Motijheel

Kamlapur
Train Station

New
Market

Baitul
Mukarram
Mosque

Motijheel Ave

Cantonment

Nayapaltan

Azimpur

Old
Dhaka

Wari

Toyenbee Rd

To Sylhet
(242km)

Sadarghat

Sayedabad
Bus Station

Buriganga River

Demra

Sadarghat Boat
Terminal

Sayedabad

Asian Hwy

See Old Dhaka Map (p51)

Zinzira

To Old Sonargaon (23km);
Comilla (83km);
Chittagong (190km)

To Mawa (18km);
Jessore (170km);
Kolkata (280km)

DHAKA IN TWO DAYS

After a long journey, you'll probably want to take the first day in Dhaka a bit easy so start off by heading to the **National Museum** (p55). Afterwards travel serenely in a rickshaw to Dhanmondi's **Mirpur Rd** (p64) for lunch. In the afternoon, spend some time wandering around nearby **Suhrawardi Park** (p55), and **Dhaka University** (p55). Next, mooch on over to the **Liberation War Museum** (p55) for a lesson on the painful birth of a nation. At night head to DIT II Circle in Gulshan and choose one of the many fine **restaurants** (p64) as the setting for the post-mortem of your day.

An exploration of **Old Dhaka** (p50) is the only way to spend your second day in the city. Start with a leisurely wander through history at **Lalbagh Fort** (p53) and the next door **Khan Mohammed Mirdha's Mosque** (p54). From here walk in any direction and you will find fantastic sights and unexpected adventures at every turn. Pace yourself with a few cha (tea) breaks and delicious street snacks. Don't miss out on **Shankharia Bazar (Hindu St)** (p52) and Nazira Bazar, the birthplace of **rickshaw art** (p66). After lunch in one of the old town's atmospheric eateries, blast on over to the fabulous **Ahsan Manzil** (Pink Palace; p52) and then, shortly before sunset, board a small boat at the chaotic **Sadarghat boat terminal** (p50) and drift out on the Buriganga River for a view of life at its grittiest – it is undoubtedly the highlight of a visit to Dhaka.

Wind down with an indulgent dinner in **Gulshan** (p64).

Maps

The best map of Dhaka is produced annually by **Mappa** (Map pp56-7; 112 Green Rd, Farmgate); you will be able to find it at most bookshops and occasionally at markets. The **Parjatan Corporation** (Map pp56-7; 233 Airport Rd) also has a map of Dhaka, available from its office and other tourist offices, as well as many bigger hotels. It has enough detail to enhance your sightseeing experience.

INFORMATION
Bookshops

There is a great literary culture in this city. The five-star hotels have bookshops that carry international newspapers, maps and a few interesting books on Bangladesh. There is a host of small but well-stocked bookshops on Mirpur Rd in Dhanmondi.

Other recommended bookshops:

Books Express (Map p62; Gulshan Ave, Gulshan) Specialises in English-language titles. Also sells CDs and has a good selection of Lonely Planet guides. The cakes in the upstairs coffee shop are epic.

Narigrantha Prabartana (☎ 811 465; 5/3 Ring Rd, Shaymoli) A feminist bookshop and restaurant. For a nice change, men must be accompanied by women.

New Market complex (Map pp56-7; Azimpur Rd, Azimpur) The bibliophile's fantasy. When entering through the main entrance, turn left and walk as far as you can: you will be surrounded by great bookshops.

Words 'n' Pages (Map p62; ☎ 989 0832; Gulshan Ave, Gulshan; ☯ 10am-9.30pm) This new bookshop is open every day and stocks a large range of Lonely Planet books and numerous English language novels as well as a large section devoted to South Asian studies. There's a small upstairs café.

Emergency

Fire (☎ 199)
Gulshan police station (☎ 988 0234)
Holy Family hospital (Map pp56-7; ☎ 831 1721/5)
International Centre for Diarrhoeal Disease Research in Bangladesh Hospital (ICDDRB; Map p62; ☎ 881 1751; 68 Shahid Tajuddein Ahmed Sharani, Mohakhali)
Police (☎ 999)

Internet Access

There are numerous small business centres (Map p51) offering fax, telephone, photocopying and internet access. The connections are normally good though most only have one or two computers.

Adda (Map p62; 3rd fl, Banani Super Market, Kemal Ataturk Ave, Banani; per hr Tk 40) Serves coffee.

Big-B (Map p62; 2nd fl, Banani Super Market, Kemal Ataturk Ave, Banani; per hr Tk 50)

Dynasty IT Cyber Café (Map pp56-7; Dewan Complex, cnr Elephant & New Elephant Rds; per hr Tk 50)

D-Zone Cyber Café (Map p62; Gulshan DIT II; per hr Tk 50) One of several small cyber cafés on Gulshan II circle.

Golden Cyber Café (Map p62; Gulshan DIT II; per hr Tk 50) Also on Gulshan II circle.

Speednet (Map p62; 1st fl, Banani Super Market, Kemal Ataturk Ave, Banani; per hr Tk 40)

Medical Services

International Centre for Diarrhoeal Disease Research in Bangladesh Hospital (ICDDRB; Map p62; ☎ 881 1751; 68 Shahid Tajuddein Ahmed Sharani, Mohakhali) Has a traveller's clinic.

Japanese-Bangladesh Friendship Hospital (Map p62; ☎ 818 7575; House 27, Rd 114, Gulshan)

Money

Citibank (Map pp56-7; ☎ 955 0060; 122-4 Motijheel) North of Dilkusha II Circle.

Eastern Bank (Map pp56-7; ☎ 955 6360; Dilkusha II Circle, Motijheel)

HSBC (☎ 01199 884722) Gulshan (Map p62; cnr Gulshan Ave & Rd 5); Motijheel (Map pp56-7; 1/C DIT Ave) Both have ATM.

Janata Bank (Map pp56-7; ☎ 956 0000; Dilkusha I Circle, Motijheel)

Pubali Bank (Map pp56-7; ☎ 955 1071; 26 Dilkusha Rd, Motijheel)

Sonali Bank (Map pp56-7; ☎ 955 0426/34; Shapla Circle, Motijheel)

Standard Chartered Bank Banani (Map p62; ☎ 882 1718; 14 Kemal Ataturk Ave); Motijheel (Map pp56-7; ☎ 956 1465; Inner Circular Rd) Both branches have ATM.

Post

Main Post Office (Map pp56-7; ☎ 955 5533; cnr Abdul Ghani & North-South Rds; ☾ Sun-Thu) Near Baitul Mukarram Mosque. Parcel-wallahs (who sew up large parcels) can be found in a small shelter on the left of the building.

Tourist Information

Parjatan (Map pp56-7; ☎ 811 7855/9; 233 Airport Rd) National tourism organisation. Tourist brochures, car rentals and a couple of local tour options.

Travel Agencies

Hac Enterprise (Map pp56-7; ☎ 955 6211; 5 Inner Circular Rd, Motijheel)

Regency Travels (Map p62; ☎ 882 4760; 18 Kemal Ataturk Ave, Banani)

Unique Tours & Travel (Map p62; ☎ 988 5116/23; 51/B Kemal Ataturk Ave, Banani)

Vantage Tours & Travel (Map pp56-7; ☎ 811 7134/9; Pan Pacific Sonargaon Hotel, Kazi Nazrul Islam Ave, Mogh Bazar)

DANGERS & ANNOYANCES

Considering its massive size and high levels of poverty, Dhaka is a remarkably safe city and few travellers experience any problems. The biggest annoyance in Dhaka is air pollution, which though vastly improved since the banning of petrol and diesel vehicles a couple of years ago (see p38) is still able to conjure up sore throats and headaches.

Bag-snatchings and muggings are rare but not unheard of. One trick is for a baby-taxi driver to snatch the belongings of an unsuspecting rickshaw passenger, often through prior arrangement with the rickshaw-wallah. As in the rest of the world, pickpockets operate in crowds, of which there are plenty in Dhaka. Be a little cautious, especially in markets.

Take particular care when withdrawing money from an ATM; it's a good idea to use ATMs with private booths so you can hide your money before you hit the streets.

Train and bus stations can be dodgy after dark, so try to avoid leaving or arriving at night.

Hartals (strikes) and accompanying violent demonstrations are common. During hartals it is safe enough to drive around the Gulshan area, and it is usually possible to move around the central city area by rickshaw; rickshaw-wallahs usually know which areas to avoid. Don't let your photojournalistic fantasies get the better of you – be curious from a safe distance.

See also p160 for more about scams.

SIGHTS
Old Dhaka

No matter where in the world you've just come from, Old Dhaka, the chalk next to rural Bangladesh's quiet cheese, will side-swipe you with its overwhelming intensity, and leave impressions that will never fade. Time spent getting lost in its streets is time spent falling in love with this city.

SADARGHAT

Running calmly through the centre of Old Dhaka, the Buriganga River is the muddy artery of Dhaka and the very life blood of both this city and nation. To explore it from the deck of a small boat is to see Bangladesh at its most raw and grittiest. The panorama of river life is fascinating. Triple-towered ferries leer over thousands of bustling ant-like canoes. Country boats bump off the dirty hulks of domineering cargo and fishing boats. On the grease-and-mud stained foreshores, you'll find children fishing with homemade nets in the lee of rusting tankers. Further out, repair men busy themselves crashing, bashing and scrubbing ship hulls while floating on planks of wood. Barges overloaded with sand

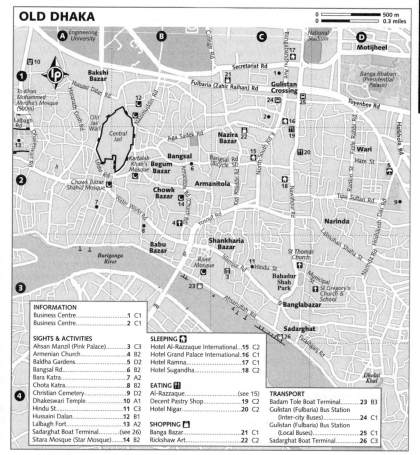

OLD DHAKA

0 ____ 500 m
0 ____ 0.3 miles

and other building materials float down river with barely an inch of clearance above water. Extended families step fresh-faced and nervous off creaky craft that have brought them to a new life full of hollow promises.

Among all the large ships are the tiny wooden ones that you can hire. These are available almost everywhere along the waterfront, though most people hire them from around **Sadarghat boat terminal** (Map p51; Ahsanullah Rd; admission Tk 4). An increasing number of foreigners in Dhaka are starting to hire boats out, so things are becoming more organised and most boatmen will know what you want to do (a lack of a common language isn't much of a hindrance). It does however mean that prices are starting to rise and touts are beginning

to come to life. The standard rate is Tk 100 per hour but many boatmen will push for a higher price.

When out on the river, ask your boatman to take you to the far bank where you can disembark for few minutes and mingle with those whose lives revolve around the dirty riverbank. Keep an eye out for some of the *baras* (ancient houseboats) moored along the river bank. These worn-out boats, some half-a-century old, are popular floating restaurants catering to the poorest of the poor, where meals are served from 8am until midnight.

Do bear in mind that these river trips are not entirely safe – the multi-hulled ferries won't think twice about ploughing over the top of your puny little craft and the foreshore

NAWAB ABDUL GHANI

Nawab Abdul Ghani, born in 1830 of Kashmiri descent, was the most influential person in East Bengal in the last half of the 19th century. Unlike most zamindars, Ghani was Muslim. He, his son, Nawab Ahsanullah, and his grandson, Salimullah Bahadur, contributed greatly to Dhaka's development. Along with elephants, horses, boats and other materials donated to the British government, they also contributed large sums to local colleges. As Ghani's land-holdings grew to include most of Dhaka, he ruled like a king.

Politically astute, Ghani participated in both Hindu and Muslim festivals, and both groups admired him. He also introduced professional horse racing to Dhaka. When he returned from a voyage to Calcutta by steamer, flags were flown along the river, a band played lively tunes and guns were fired.

The demise of the family occurred when Ahsanullah, for whom Ahsan Manzil (Pink Palace) was named, died suddenly in 1901 without a will. Under Islamic law the monolithic estate was broken into nine parts and Ahsanullah's son, Salimullah, received only one part. Although residing at the Pink Palace, Salimullah was reduced to being a relatively poor man. Nevertheless, he contributed more to Muslim schools than anyone in the city's history, and founded Dhaka Medical School. Because of this he is revered today perhaps even more than his illustrious grandfather.

is little more than a filthy building site without the slightest nod to health and safety concerns. Don't let this put you off though because this river, with its powerful theatre of life and death, is probably the very reason you came to Bangladesh.

AHSAN MANZIL

About 600m west of Sadarghat is the must-see **Ahsan Manzil** (Pink Palace; Map p51; Ahsanullah Rd; admission Tk 2; ⏰ 10.30am-5.30pm Sat-Wed, 3-7.30pm Fri Apr-Sep, 9.30am-4.30pm Sat-Wed, 3-7.30pm Fri Oct-Mar), one of the most interesting buildings in Dhaka.

Dating from 1872, Ahsan Manzil was built on the site of an old French factory by Nawab Abdul Ghani (see above), the city's wealthiest zamindar (landowner). Some 16 years after the palace's construction, it was damaged by a tornado. It was altered during restoration, becoming even grander than before. Lord Curzon stayed here whenever he came to visit. After the death of the nawab and his son, the family fortune was dispersed and the palace eventually fell into disrepair. It was saved from oblivion by massive restoration in the late 1980s, aided by photos of each of the 23 rooms, taken during the high point of the palace's history. The photos are still on display as are various family portraits and the skull of Nawab Abdul Ghanis's favourite elephant, Feroz Jung.

SHANKHARIA BAZAR (HINDU ST)

A crash of drums, a cloud of incense and a bursting paintbox of colours signal a welcome to **Shankharia Bazar** (Map p51), also known as **Hindu St**. Lined on either side with ancient houses, garlands of lurid orange marigolds, and dark doorways leading to matchbox-sized shops and workshops, this is by far the most photogenic street in Old Dhaka. While exploring the bazaar keep one eye on the upper levels, where many of the houses have beautiful carvings. The *shankharis* (Hindu artisans) busy themselves creating kites, gravestones, wedding-hats, jewellery, and bangles carved out of conch shells.

Shankharis first came here over 300 years ago, but these days their art is slowly dying out. If you pass a shop and hear some faint grinding sounds out the back, ask to see the tiny quarters where they make the jewellery; most owners will be delighted to show you around. At the western end of the street you'll find a standpipe around which sari-clad women can normally be found collecting water for the household. If your stay in Dhaka coincides with a Hindu festival then you're in for a treat. At any excuse, the inhabitants of this road build oversized clay-and-papier-mâché figures depicting Hindu gods and goddesses (Kali is a favourite) and parade up and down the old city, as noisy and boisterous as they can be. However, even if a festival isn't taking place there is always plenty going on.

To find Hindu St, head north along Nawabpur Rd from Sadarghat. After two long blocks you'll pass a small square on your right called Bahadur Shah Park, which has a cenotaph to commemorate the Indian Uprising of 1857. From the northwestern corner, cross the street and head west, parallel to the river. After 100m you'll come to some small shops selling tombstones – that's the beginning. It continues for about 400m until it merges with Islampur Rd.

ARMENIAN CHURCH

About 1km northwest of Sadarghat, and north of Badam Tole, is an area called Armanitola, named after the Armenian colony that settled here in the late 17th century.

The peach-pink **Armenian Church of the Holy Resurrection** (Map p51; Armanitola Rd), is the soul of this now almost extinct community. The church, which dates from 1781, is an oasis of tranquillity in the heart of the crowded city. During the course of the Liberation War, the silver setting and organ were stolen and many of the graves were desecrated. **Mr Martin** (☎ 731 6953), the caretaker, has done much to restore the church, and delights in giving personal tours. Note that you can't get in without him unlocking the door for you.

The Armenian archbishop from Australia comes here about twice a year to hold services.

The church is open so long as Mr Martin is around – and even if he isn't someone in the neighbourhood will almost certainly go and summon him. From Badam Tole head north for two blocks to Islampur Rd, then left for one block and right for another.

SITARA MOSQUE

About 350m north of the Armenian church, you'll come to **Sitara Mosque** (Star Mosque; Map p51; Armanitola Rd), one of the city's most popular tourist attractions. Its striking mosaic decoration makes it look like your granny's best teacups. The mosque dates from the early 18th century, but has been radically altered. It was originally built in the typical Mughal style, with four corner towers. Around 50 years ago a local businessman financed its redecoration with Japanese and English china-tiles, and the addition of a new veranda. If you look hard you can see tiles illustrated with pictures of Mt Fuji. Non-Muslims are normally welcome outside of prayer time, but you should dress appropriately and women should bring something with which to cover their hair. Sitara Mosque is pictured on the Tk 100 note.

BARA KATRA & CHOTA KATRA

These dilapidated Mughal-era structures are about the oldest buildings in Dhaka. **Bara Katra** (Map p51), once a palace of monumental dimensions, was built in 1644 and now has a street running through its arched entrance. While only a small portion of the original structure remains standing, the building is still occupied and has a small prayer room on top.

Chota Katra (Map p51), which dates from 1663, was a caravanserai for visiting merchants. It was similar in design to Bara Katra, but there's not much left.

To find Bara Katra head west along Water Works Rd (the continuation of Islampur Rd) to the landmark Chowk Bazar Shahid Mosque, which has a very tall red-brick tower – you can't miss it. Bara Katra is located 100m south of the mosque, towards the river. Finding Chota Katra is a little more difficult. From Bara Katra head south and take the first left. Follow this road for a few hundred metres and Chota Katra is along a street to your left.

LALBAGH FORT

Along with Sadarghat, **Lalbagh Fort** (Map p51; admission Tk 10; ☻ 10am-5pm Mon-Sat, 2.30-5.30pm Fri Nov-Mar, 10.30am-5.30pm Mon-Sat, 3-6pm Fri Apr-Oct, closed holidays) is one of the big hitters of Old Dhaka. Unlike the waterfront, which is full of raw energy, the fort is a slightly melancholy step back in the misty Mughal past of emperors and princesses. It's particularly atmospheric in the early morning light.

Construction of the fort began in 1677 under the auspices of Prince Mohammed Azam, third son of Aurangzeb, who handed it to Shaista Khan for completion. The death of Khan's daughter, Pari Bibi (Fair Lady), was considered such a bad omen that the fort was never completed. However, three architectural monuments within the complex – Diwan (Hall of Audience), Mausoleum of Pari Bibi and Quilla Mosque – were finished in 1684.

On the eastern side of the fort, to your far left as you enter, is the residence of the governor containing the Hall of Audience. It's an elegant two-storey structure. Inside there's a small museum of Mughal paintings and calligraphy, along with swords and firearms. Beyond the Hall of Audience, on the western side, a massive arched doorway leads to the central square *hammam* (bath house).

The middle building, the Mausoleum of Pari Bibi, is the only Bangladeshi building in which black basalt and white marble (from Bangladesh), and encaustic tiles of various colours have been used to decorate an interior. The inside central chamber, where Pari Bibi is buried, is entirely veneered in white marble.

You'll find Lalbagh Fort near the intersection of Dhakeswari and Azimpur Rds.

KHAN MOHAMMED MIRDHA'S MOSQUE
Some 500m west of Lalbagh Fort is **Khan Mohammed Mirdha's Mosque** (off Map p51; Lalbagh Rd). Erected in 1706, this Mughal structure is stylistically similar to Lalbagh Fort. It is built on a raised platform, up a flight of 25 steps. Three squat domes, with pointed minarets at each corner, dominate the rectangular roof. To get a good view of this walled mosque, enter the main gate off the main road. Unfortunately, unless you're here during prayer times (around 1pm), you'll probably find the gate locked.

DHAKESWARI TEMPLE
About 1km north of Lalbagh Fort, up a short alley off Dhakeswari Rd, is the city's main Hindu temple, **Dhakeswari Temple** (Map p51), dating from the 12th century. There are two sets of buildings. The one often seen in tourist photos consists of four adjoining *rekha* temples (buildings with a square sanctum on a raised platform with mouldings on the walls) covered by tall pyramidal roofs of the typical curvilinear *bangla* (bamboo-thatched hut with curved roof) style. It's nothing special, but it is colourful and you are likely to find some long-haired sadhus (itinerant holy men) hanging around smoking ganja.

HUSSAINI DALAN
A block north of the central jail is **Hussaini Dalan** (historic building; Map p51; Hussaini Dalan Rd, Bakshi Bazar) that looks more like a Hindu rajbari (landowner's palace) than an Islamic building. It was built in the 18th century, near the end of the Mughal period, as the house of the imam of the Shi'ia community. The Ashura festival (see p162), on the 10th day of the Islamic month of Muharram, is celebrated here .

Though the architecture seems baroque in inspiration, the original building was purely Mughal. It changed somewhat with restorations after the 1897 earthquake, when the roof collapsed. You can see a silver fili-

---

COUNTING RICKSHAWS

The Dhaka police estimate there are about 600,000 rickshaws in the city. However, the revenue department of Dhaka City Corporation, the body responsible for collecting licence fees from rickshaw-wallahs, has a different figure. When a newspaper reporter asked a top official from the department about the number of rickshaws in Dhaka, the official replied, 'There are 88,700-and-something rickshaws in the city'. When the reporter pointed out that other estimates were somewhat higher, the official replied, 'As far as we are concerned there are only 88,700-and-something rickshaws in the city. If you disbelieve me, why don't you start counting?'

---

gree model of the original building in the National Museum (opposite).

BALDHA GARDENS & CHRISTIAN CEMETERY
At the eastern end of Tipu Sultan Rd, and a block south of Hatkhola Rd, the **Baldha Gardens** (Map p51 ; admission Tk 5; 🕑 9am-5pm Sat-Thu, closed at lunch) in Wari provide a nice break from the rest of the sightseeing you'll be doing in the area. The two walled enclosures, Cybele and Psyche, were once the private gardens of Narendra Narayan Roy, a wealthy zamindar, whose grandson gave them to the government in 1962 as a tribute to his family.

Just opposite is the **Christian Cemetery** (Map p51), which, as well as all the expected British names, contains a large number of Portuguese graves.

BANGSAL RD (BICYCLE ST)
For a souvenir of Bangladesh, you can't beat a piece of rickshaw art. The place to find this art is in Nazira Bazar on **Bangsal Rd**, popularly known as **Bicycle St**.

The street begins 700m south of Gulistan bus station, heading west from North-South Rd, a block south of the well-marked Hotel Al-Razzaque International.

See p66 for more on rickshaw art.

Central Dhaka
North of Old Dhaka is the old European zone, now the modern part of town.

BAITUL MUKARRAM MOSQUE

West of Motijheel on Topkhana Rd, the modern **Baitul Mukarram Mosque** (Map pp56–7) is designed in the style of the holy Ka'aba of Mecca. Non-Muslims can normally enter outside of prayer time. The boisterous market in the surrounding streets is interesting.

DHARMARAJIKHA BUDDHIST MONASTERY

The largest Buddhist cultural centre in the country is the **Dharmarajikha Buddhist Monastery** (Map pp56–7), located east of Sayedabad Rd. It has an enormous bronze statue and a marble statue of Buddha. There's a peaceful pond here too – bring a book and get some reading done. The monastery is open during daylight hours (vague, but true). Take off your shoes before entering the temple and don't take photos of any shrines without permission.

OLD HIGH COURT & AROUND

The imposing **Old High Court** (Map pp56–7), once the governor's residence, is just north of Dhaka University's main campus. It is the finest example in Dhaka of the European Renaissance style. Nearby is the newer **Mausoleum for Three Martyrs** (Map pp56–7) and the **Mosque of Hazrat Haji Khawja Shahbaz** (Map pp56–7), a popular shrine dedicated to a rich merchant who devoted much of his energy and money to helping the poor of Dhaka. A little to the east of this is the **Supreme Court** (Map pp56–7).

SUHRAWARDI & RAMNA PARKS

Beginning near the Old High Court and stretching all the way to the National Museum, **Suhrawardi Park** (Map pp56–7; ⏰ 6am-10pm) covers an enormous area. This was once a racecourse, where both the Bangladeshi Declaration of Independence and the surrender of Pakistani occupation forces took place in 1971. At night the park turns into an open-air market and also attracts hundreds of homeless who, living by the 'safety in numbers' motto, set up camp each evening on the pavements outside. A few unsavoury characters mean you should keep your wits about you at night around here.

Northeast of Suhrawardi Park is **Ramna Park**, which is well tended and has a boating lake.

DHAKA UNIVERSITY & CURZON HALL

Dating from 1921, **Dhaka University** (DU; Map pp56–7) has some fine old buildings. North of the Engineering University campus is the **British Council Library** (Map pp56–7) and further north, on Kazi Nazrul Islam Ave, is the **Institute of Arts & Crafts** (Map pp56–7), which has an art gallery.

On the main campus, south of the Old High Court, **Curzon Hall** (Map pp56–7) is the university's architectural masterpiece and science faculty. It's a fine example of the European-Mughal style of building erected after the first partition of Bengal in 1905. The red-brick building has eye-catching detail, and an elegant façade.

Two blocks west, on Secretariat Rd and just north of the College of Medicine, is the **Central Shaheed Minar** (Map pp56–7), built to commemorate the historic Language Movement of 1952.

NATIONAL MUSEUM

A visit to the **National Museum** (Map pp56-7; Kazi Nazrul Islam Ave; admission Tk 5; ⏰ 9.30am-4pm Sat-Wed, 3-7pm Fri) is a good way of downloading information about Bangladesh. Sprawling over several floors it begins at the beginning with the geological formation of Bangladesh, whisks you through a rundown of the nation's flora and fauna, saunters through a Buddhist and Hindu past, and brings you bang up to date with the War of Liberation and the creation of the modern state. Some of the exhibits are a little stale – the stuffed birds are looking more stuffed and less bird with every passing year, and it's amazing how badly lit, displayed and labelled everything is.

It's a good idea to avoid visiting on Friday when most of Dhaka will be here and you'll be as much of an attraction as the ancient relics.

LIBERATION WAR MUSEUM

This **museum** (Map pp56-7; ☎ 955 9091; 5 Segun Bagicha Rd; admission Tk 3; ⏰ 10am-5pm Mon-Sat), chronicling one of the 20th century's more deadly wars, is spread out over two floors and has been put together with enormous pride and respect. The display on the 1971 War of Independence is arranged chronologically, with English and Bengali newspaper reports, photographs and various memorabilia. The displays start off tame enough but gradually become more graphic before culminating in a room full of personal items (each of which comes with a short story on the owner's life); a large pile of human skulls and bones; and some very disturbing photos of rotting corpses with bound hands being eaten by dogs and

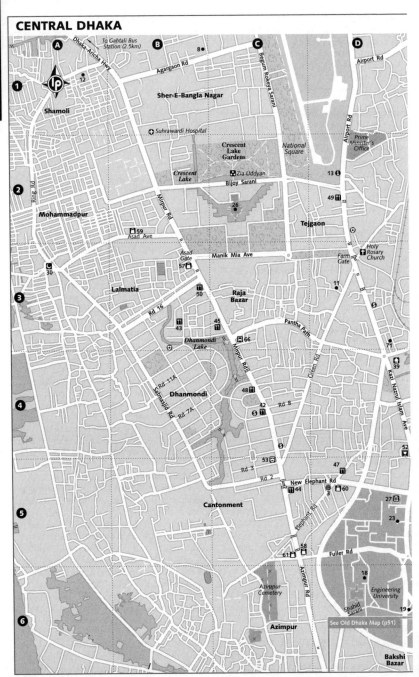

CENTRAL DHAKA

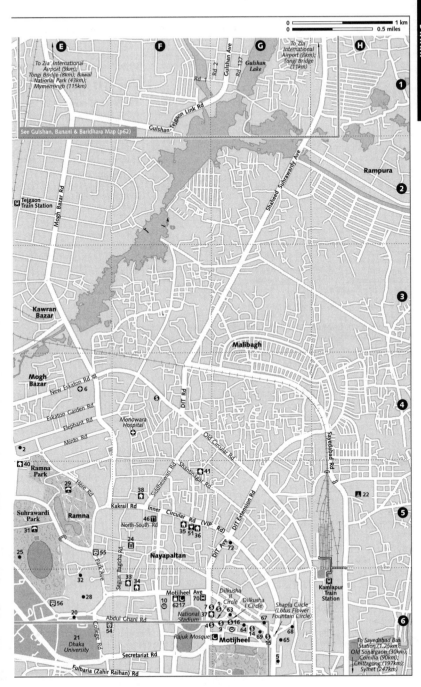

DHAKA

vultures. Though the displays might not make for happy holidays, this museum should be a compulsory stop for everyone.

From Topkhana Rd head north up Segun Bagicha Rd; it's on the second street on the right. Contact the museum to find out about its cultural events.

NATIONAL ASSEMBLY
In 1963 the Pakistanis commissioned Louis Kahn, a world-renowned American architect, to design a regional capital for East Pakistan. Due to the liberation movement and ensuing war, the **National Assembly building** (Map pp56–7) wasn't completed until 1982. The building often features in books on modern architecture, and is regarded as among Kahn's finest works.

It's a huge assembly of concrete cylinders and rectangular boxes, sliced open with bold, multi-storey circular and triangular apertures instead of windows, and is probably only considered attractive by fans of grim '70s architecture.

It is not usually possible to approach the building too closely. On the opposite side of the road is a large and enjoyable park full of loving couples.

SAT GUMBAD MOSQUE
Dating from 1680, **Sat Gumbad Mosque** (Map pp56–7) is a white-washed onion dome mosque, and the finest example of the pure Mughal-style mosque in Dhaka.

Unfortunately, few travellers see Sat Gumbad because of its somewhat remote location. Head north from Dhanmondi on Mirpur Rd, turn left through Asad Gate and go to the end of the road (1.5km). Then begin asking; it's nearby, towards the river. Women are admitted if appropriately dressed.

Suburban Dhaka
BOTANICAL GARDENS
The shady, tranquil **botanical gardens** (Map p48; admission Tk 5; ⏰ 9am-5pm), stretch over 40 hectares and contain over 1000 species of local and foreign plants. It's a nice respite from the

city's mass of humanity. In the distance you'll see the Turag River.

These gardens are probably the best place in the city for bird-watching. The quiet early mornings are especially good. Next door to the gardens is a zoo, but it isn't a pleasant place.

The gardens are on the northwestern outskirts of Dhaka. To get there take a bus from Gulistan bus station to Mirpur via Begum Rokeya Sarani, then take a rickshaw (Tk 15 to Tk 20).

ACTIVITIES
Language Courses
See Courses in the Directory chapter (p159) for information about learning Bengali.

Rickshaw Rides
One of the best ways to see the sights of Dhaka is by rickshaw. The going rate is about Tk 80 per hour. Rickshaw-wallahs who speak English can generally be found outside five-star hotels, but charge more and expect a tip. You can also approach a tour company to organise a sightseeing tour on a rickshaw.

River Trips
There are several companies offering trips on the rivers encircling Dhaka.

Contic (☎ 881 4851; mail@contic.com; House 183, Rd 69, Gulshan II), a river-cruise specialist with an elegant boat, the *Fleche D'Or*, cruises along the Turag River (west of the city) down to the Buriganga River. Contic cruises get excellent reviews.

Guide Tours (Map p62; ☎ 988 6983; www.guidetours .com; 1st fl, Darpan Complex, DIT II Circle, Gulshan; ☺ cruises Mon, Fri & Sat) offers a 4½ hour cruise along the Sitalakhya River on its yacht, the *SB Ruposhi*, departing from Demra (a river town about 15km east of Dhaka). You'll get to stop at a village of *jamdani* (muslin-cloth) weavers en route.

Swimming
Non-guests can use the pool at the Sheraton Hotel (Map pp56–7) for Tk 1200 per day.

TOURS
Guide Tours (Map p62; ☎ 988 6983; www.guidetours .com; 1st fl, Darpan Complex, DIT II Circle, Gulshan), the company with the best reputation, offers half- and full-day tours in and around Dhaka. Half-day tours cover Sadarghat, Lalbagh Fort, the Liberation War Museum and other sights,

and cost Tk 1500 per person. Full-day tours include Savar or Sonargaon and cost Tk 2300 per person (minimum four people). Guide Tours also runs day trips to a pottery village near Savar and overnight stays in a village.

Bengal Tours (Map p62; ☎ 883 4716; www.bengal tours.com; Block A, Banani) offers half- and full-day city tours. The half-day tours focus on Old Dhaka while the full-day tour spins you around both the commercial city and Old Dhaka. Prices are virtually identical to those of Guide Tours.

There are several other companies offering city tours and, at this stage in Bangladesh's foray into tourism, it's a good idea to give some of the smaller up-and-coming operators a go.

FESTIVALS & EVENTS
One of the most exciting events to be part of in Dhaka is the colourful Hindu festival of **Durga Puja**, commemorating the victory of the mighty warrior goddess, Durga.

On the last evening of the five-day festival, devotees parade their clay-and-bamboo effigies through the streets toward Sadarghat. At nightfall the statues of Durga are immersed in the Buriganga River, ending the festivities. The festival is held at the Dhakeswari Temple (p54) around the second week of October.

Around the same time as Durga Puja, there's a colourful boat race on the Buriganga near Postagola. It's quite a spectacle and is inaugurated each year by the president of Bangladesh. Each longboat is crammed with about 60 oarsmen and the competition ensues amidst continuous clapping by the spectators. Advance publicity is poor. Contact **Parjatan** (Map pp56–7; ☎ 811 7855/9; 233 Airport Rd) for details.

An interesting experience in Dhaka is the **International Mother Language Day** (held on 21 February), commemorating the martyrs who fought in the 1952 Language Movement. Blood was shed (where the Central Shaheed Minar now stands) to establish Bengali as the national language. Mourners gather at the monument at midnight each year to pay their respects with songs, prayers and the laying of wreaths.

Bangladeshi New Year's Day falls in mid-April.

SLEEPING
Accommodation is more expensive in Dhaka than elsewhere in Bangladesh, but it's still cheap by international standards. Almost all

midrange and top-end hotels offer large, year-round discounts on stated rates (up to 50% off) and most of the time this will be volunteered before you've had a chance to ask. However if you're booking online or by phone, you're less likely to be offered a discount. Fortunately, it's rare that Dhaka hotels are full, so you can safely just turn up and find something to suit. The highest concentration of budget and midrange hotels is in the area extending from Inner Circular Rd down to Old Dhaka. There aren't any top-end hotels in Old Dhaka.

Old Dhaka
BUDGET
There are numerous hotels on Nawabpur Rd costing no more than a handful of Taka, but they almost universally refuse to accept foreign tourists.

Hotel Sugandha (Map p51; ☎ 955 6720; 243-4 Nawabpur Rd; s/d Tk 120/350) It's cheap and it's one of the very few that will let you stay, but hygiene isn't a strong point, and female guests aren't welcome. The double rooms are quite large and have balconies overlooking a grey wall.

Hotel Al-Razzaque International (Map p51; ☎ 956 6408; 29/1 North-South Rd; s/d with bathroom Tk 210/270) The al-Razzaque offers great value budget beds in rooms that are kept lovingly clean. For once the sheets aren't disturbingly stained and it has sit-down toilets. The signs asking guests and staff to not drop rubbish work; the signs saying 'no spitting' don't. Women will almost certainly not be allowed to stay.

MIDRANGE
Hotel Ramna (Map p51; ☎ 956 2279; 45 Bangabandhu Ave; s/d from Tk 350-630) Don't get too excited by the glass-fronted reception area; the rooms are much more down-to-earth. However, they are kept clean and what you get for the price is excellent. It can be a little difficult to find in the maze of tailor shops.

Hotel Grand Palace International (Map p51; ☎ 956 1623; 11-12 North-South Rd; s with/without air-con TK 500/250, d with/without air-con 700-800;) The small and tidy rooms would be a good bet but for the bedlam of noise echoing up from the road below, which is certain to make sleep an impossible dream.

Central Dhaka
BUDGET
Asia Hotel (Map pp56-7; ☎ 956 0709; 34/1 Topkhana Rd; s with shared bathroom Tk 180, d with/without TV Tk 450/350) One of the few hotels on Topkhana Rd that accepts foreigners, the Asia Hotel is on a quiet side street and has spacious rooms that offer good value for your Taka. Bring a torch (flashlight) though, as the electricity supply isn't too hot.

Hotel Cairo International (Map pp56-7; ☎ 956 2594; 19 Topkhana Rd; s/d Tk 250/300) Small and shabby rooms, but this is one of the rare cheapies happy to have you to stay and, quite frankly, at this price you can't knock it. It has a more reliable electricity supply than the nearby Asia Hotel.

MIDRANGE
Hotel Midway International (Map pp56-7; ☎ 831 9315; hotelmid@aitlbd.net; 30 VIP Rd, Nayapaltan; s/d Tk 610-980, d with air-con Tk 1220;) The rooms, which have big wooden wardrobes, dressing tables and tiled bathrooms, must once have been the star of the show, but today the first signs of tropical rot are setting in. The lacklustre staff doesn't exactly help either, but if everywhere else is full then this is good for a night or two.

Hotel Pacific (Map pp56-7; ☎ 955 8148; www.hotelpacific dhaka.com; 120/B Motijheel; d with/without air-con Tk 1200/800, deluxe d Tk 1600;) The Hotel Pacific continues to rule the roost as the best value cheapie in Central Dhaka. There is a wide range of room types, and all are spacious and homely with hot water in the bathrooms. The staff are unfailingly polite and welcoming without being overpowering. They are quite used to foreigners and their strange ways.

Hotel Royal Palace (Map pp56-7; ☎ 716 8972; www .hrpalaceltd.com; 31/D Topkhana Rd; s/d with air-con Tk 1300/1700;) A palace fit for royalty it ain't, but for the rest of us the clean and tidy rooms ferreted away in this hotel offer everything likely to be required. There are numerous different classes of rooms – the prices given are for the standard air-con joints.

Hotel Razmoni Isha Kha (Map pp56-7; ☎ 832 2426; razmoni@bdcom.com; VIP Rd; s/d Tk 2000/2800) A vast auditorium-like reception leads onward to some of the better midrange rooms in this part of town. The highlights are the big puffy, bubble chairs and the massive views over the city. There is free breakfast and plenty of parking, but the staff could be more welcoming.

White House Hotel (Map pp56-7; ☎ 832 2973/6; fax 831 7726; 155 Shantinagar Rd; s/d with fan US$14/17, deluxe s/d with air-con US$25/30;) This place has small but lovingly maintained rooms that are cleaner than most places of a similar price. Be warned though that the management aren't keen on unmarried couples.

our pick Hotel Victory (Map pp56-7; ☎ 935 3088; www .hotelvictorybd.com; VIP Rd; s/d US$40/60; ❄ ▯). Stated rates are little more than make-believe and as soon as you enter you'll be offered a 50% discount. Even if you were paying top dollar these rooms would be good value, but with the price you'll end up paying it's a certified bargain. The newly built Victory has small, comfortable, spick-and-span rooms that are as quiet as a library, and the staff have a professional attitude. The restaurant is guaranteed to keep you coming back for more. It's easily the best in the class and gives the top-end hotels a good run for their money.

TOP END

Hotel Orchard Plaza (Map pp56-7; ☎ 933 0829; fax 989 4573; www.hotelorchardplaza.com; 71 VIP Rd; r US$70-80; ❄ ▯) The cheapest of the big boys, the Orchard Plaza is all neon lights and equally flashy rooms – this business class hotel has large rooms kept very clean and staff who keep smiling. Rates include a free breakfast, internet access and an upstairs gym. The stated rates are a bit high, but like many Dhaka hotel there seems to be a no-questions-asked 30% discount.

At the time of writing we received reports that a major gas explosion had severely damaged this hotel. It is uncertain when, or if, it will reopen (and even if it does you may not want to commit to their wiring!).

Sheraton Hotel (Map pp56-7; ☎ 833 0001; www .sheraton.com/dhaka; 1 Minto Rd; r excl 27% tax from US$130; ❄ ▯) The facilities might be similar to the Pan Pacific and prices much the same (after the near-standard 50% discount at the Pan Pacific) but, with its '70s architecture and musty smelling rooms, the Sheraton is definitely the poorer cousin. The nice pool is open to non-guests for a whopping Tk 1200 per day.

Pan Pacific Sonargaon Hotel (Map pp56-7; ☎ 811 1005; www.panpacific.com; 107 Kazi Nazrul Islam Ave; d excl 30% tax from US$250; ❄ ▯) Leave the chaos of the outside world behind and step into the tranquillity of the Pan Pacific. It has everything you'd expect of a top-dog hotel – large and tasty rooms, numerous restaurants and relaxation facilities (though the pool was under refurbishment at the time of research), and a couple of nice little touches that add class (for example, sofas in the elevators and, from

some rooms, wonderful views of the slums below…). The price stated here is the standard rack rate, but discounts of 50% are normal.

Gulshan Area

The greater Gulshan area, including Banani and Baridhara, is the heart of the diplomatic zone and hence something of a foreigners ghetto. This can be a pro or a con, depending on what you're looking for, but it is hard to see the peace, quiet and cleanliness of this area as a negative. Prices are higher here than elsewhere in Dhaka.

MIDRANGE

The Royal Inn (Map p62; ☎ 882 5139; fax 882 3007; House 38, Rd 18, Banani; s/d Tk 1000/1200) The cheapest rooms in Dhaka's poshest corner have a nice white-washed and wicker feel to them. However, bring your own sheets as the ones it provides are coated in very suspect stains.

The Jame Prestige Abode (Map p62; ☎ 882 9474; jame@bijoy.net; House 97, Rd 4, Block B, Banani; economy/ standard/deluxe r Tk 1300/1700/2300, ste Tk 3300 plus 15% tax) In a former incarnation, this charming guesthouse was known as the French Inn and was about as close as Dhaka got to a travellers centre. Today, the name might have changed but not the game. The welcome remains as warm as ever and the staff as knowledgeable. The single rooms can be a little stuffy but the pastel-blue doubles are perfect for the discerning traveller couple.

Sky Park Guesthouse (Map p62; ☎ 989 9894; sky park_net@hotmail.com; House 65, Rd 15, Banani; r Tk 1500) Backpackers – when you want one you can't find one for love or money. That's the problem Sky Park is facing. It's as cheap and cheerful as this part of Dhaka gets and its rooms are all jazzed up for the party, but alas, there's not a backpacker in sight.

The Chalet (Map p62; ☎ 881 5689; fax 881 2709; House 5/A, Rd 32, Gulshan I; s/d US$30-40; ❄ ▯) Offering some of Gulshan's cheapest and best value rooms, the Chalet may lack some of the gloss of the more expensive hotels, but its immaculate rooms really do have everything you actually need. An almost instant 20% discount is offered on the above rates. There's free breakfast and internet, and the downstairs restaurant gets votes of approval.

Eastern House (Map p62; ☎ 988 2216; www.eghouse dhaka.com; House 4, Rd 24, Gulshan I; s/d US$50-55; ❄) It might look like a private residence but it is in fact a hotel, and a pretty good one at that. The

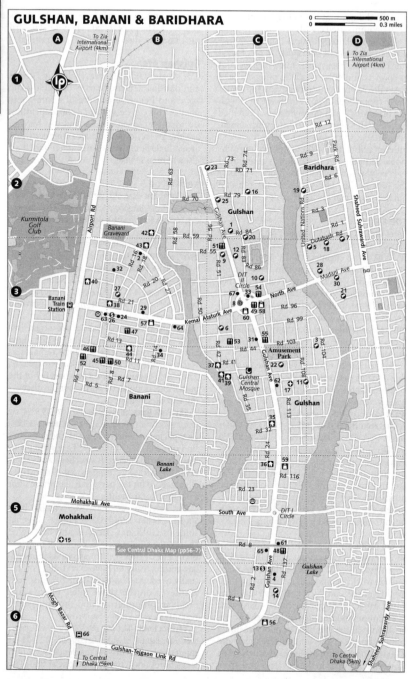

GULSHAN, BANANI & BARIDHARA

comfortable front rooms have balconies and road noise, while in the back rooms you say goodbye to the balcony, but gain the peace. The horror-house dolls inhabiting some of the alcoves are certain to give you nightmares.

Green Goose Guesthouse (Map p62; ☎ 882 1928; ggoose@citech-bd.com; Rd 38, Gulshan; r US$60; 🕸) Super-sized rooms with bizarre, but kind of cool, wood panelling over the walls. The little kitchenettes make this a good one for long-stay guests. Rates are, as normal, highly flexible. On a quiet side street and, just in case you're interested, the bird on their logo is a male mallard duck not a green goose…

Hotel De Castle (Map p62; ☎ 881 2888; www.hotel decastle.com; House B/72, Rd 21, Banani; s/d US$70/80; 🕸 🖳) Reliably clean and inviting rooms with a quiet and cool atmosphere. The location is good, just a stone's throw from all the action but far enough away to avoid all that commotion. There's a standard 40% discount.

TOP END
Laurel Hotels (Map p62; ☎ 883 4009; www.laurelhotelbd .com; House 54, Rd 18, Block J, Banani; s/d US$66/90; 🕸 🖳) With 50% discount virtually compulsory, this hotel packs a real punch in the bargain department. It has the look of a business-class hotel, but without the formality. It's large, airy, and

sunshine-bright rooms are kept spotless, and prices include internet and breakfast. The only downside is that if you are of Bangladeshi/ Indian descent (even if it's two generations removed and it's your first time on the sub-continent), you will not be allowed to stay for security reasons!

Hotel Golden Deer (Map p62; ☎ 882 6259; Rd 35/A, House 31/B, Gulshan II; s/d with breakfast US$70/90) Not only is dirty old Dhaka home to the ever so rare Golden Goose but, hiding down a leafy lane, is the equally scarce Golden Deer. This creature offers large, shiny, white-tiled rooms – just make sure you get a front room in order to enjoy massive views over the cityscape and the lake out front. Discounts are standard and breakfast is included.

ourpick Lake Shore Hotel & Apartments (Map p62; ☎ 885 9991; www.lakeshorehotel.com.bd; House 46, Rd 41; r/ste from US$160/240; 🕸 🖳) Everything about this hotel, from the modern glass bathroom fittings to the rooftop pool fit for a New York millionaire, is simply magnificent. If you fit in this price category then you fit in this hotel.

EATING
Old Dhaka
Decent Pastry Shop (Map p51; Nawabpur Rd) A slightly incongruous sight in the den of the old town

the Decent Pastry Shop is a towering pillar of calm, sanity, and Western cleanliness and tastes.

Al-Razzaque (Map p51; ☎ 956 6408; 29/1 North-South Rd; meals Tk 80) When locals tell you that this restaurant (belonging to the Hotel Al-Razzaque International) is the king of old-town eateries, you'd better believe it. There are separate booths for women, and the attached cake shop and juice bar are equally good.

Hotel Nigar (Map p51; Nawabpur Rd; meals Tk 80) Step down that dimly lit alley/tunnel and cheap and reliable tastes await.

Central Dhaka

New Café Jheel (Map pp56-7; ☎ 955 2255; 18/1 Topkhana Rd; ☺ 6am-midnight; mains Tk 80) If you want to know what Bengali food is supposed to taste like then check out the thick, fiery curries at this bright and clean favourite. Tk 120 will get you a curry, rice and naan bread.

Café Mango (Map pp56-7; ☎ 913 6686; ☺ 10am-10pm; mains Tk 100) It's hard to find but persist, because this little chestnut is well worth the hunt. Without even trying, the super-chilled atmosphere encourages you to linger far longer than you intended and, just as you've finished your delicious sandwiches and salad and plucked up the courage to face the outside world again, you spy the rich, creamy chocolate cake and kiss goodbye to the afternoon. Everything is freshly and hygienically made, and the walls are often adorned with the works of local artists. The breakfast is great too. To find it, turn onto Rd 13 (formerly Rd 32) from Mirpur Rd and take the first right. It's a block up on the left.

Malancha Restaurant (Map pp56-7; 50 New Elephant Rd; mains Tk 120) The many students in this neighbourhood fill their tummies on the cheap and memorable fried chicken and delectable kebabs up for grabs here.

Santoor (Map pp56-7; ☎ 812 3336; Mirpur Rd; mains Tk 150) Simply superb Bengali cooking! The higher than normal prices are justified by both the food and the prim-and-proper atmosphere.

Sung Garden Restaurant (Map pp56-7; ☎ 831 251; 65 North-South Rd; mains Tk 200-250) It might be discreet but that hasn't prevented the well-to-do of Dhaka finding this little Chinese restaurant. The service is attentive and the dishes delectable. Everything about the place is immaculately clean.

Xian (Map pp56-7; ☎ 861 9805; 126 Elephant Rd; mains Tk 250) A popular and refined Chinese restaurant where you're expected to dress sharp and enjoy the equally smart food.

Bigger and bolder than Xian, and certainly not the place for an intimate meal, is **Xinxian** (Map pp56-7; ☎ 815 3745; Mirpur Rd; mains Tk 250).

The two branches of **Yummy Yummy** (Map pp56-7), on Mirpur Rd and Airport Rd, and **Bronx Café** (Map pp56-7; Mirpur Rd) will offer you similar homely reminders.

Gulshan Area

Gulshan area has the widest range of restaurants in the country and is the best place in which to indulge.

Gulshan Plaza Restaurant (Map p62; Gulshan DIT II; ☺ 7am-midnight; mains Tk 90) Cheap and basic workman's restaurant that has all your Bangladeshi favourites, as well as kebabs and roast chickens – all of which are near enough perfect. The boss is English-speaking.

King's Confectionary (Map p62; ☎ 989 4321; House 25, Rd 11, Block F, Banani; ☺ 7am-10.30pm; lunch Tk 100) Not only does it have a good range of light lunches and a mouth-watering selection of cakes (including Portugal's finest, the *pastéis de Belém* for Tk 70), but it gets one of Dhaka's only green-and-social awards for running a bring-and-buy scheme for old clothes. All proceeds go to charity.

Dhaba (Map p62; Rd 11, Banani; mains from Tk 120) Come and pretend you're on a tropical beach in this foliage-covered, beach shack–style restaurant selling what it describes as 'street food', but this is civilised street food and very tasty it is too.

El Toro (Map p62; ☎ 885 2863; House 1A, Rd 138, Gulshan I; ☺ 11.30am-10.30pm; mains Tk 160) The dark and cool el Toro is the only Mexican restaurant in Bangladesh, and surely one of the best on the Indian subcontinent. The chunky chicken quesadilla is a Trojan Horse of flavour – it looks benign on the plate but stages a coup in your mouth. They even have cocktails...sort of.

Cofi II (Map p62; Gulshan DIT II; mains Tk 180) One of the current hot spots with younger expats and locals for after-work drinks (non-alcoholic of course), stingy but enjoyable meals, and internet use. Try the chicken cooked in honey. It's on the second floor of the shopping centre.

Kebab-E-Q (Map p62; ☎ 989 1301; House 48, Rd 11, Banani; mains Tk 200) Downstairs is like eating in someone's front room and upstairs is like chowing down in the jungle, but what exactly will you be chowing down? Some memorable Bangladeshi treats.

Samdado Restaurant (Map p62; ☎ 882 8499; House 27, Rd 35, Gulshan II; ◷ 12-3pm & 5-11pm; mains Tk 200) Sleek design and sleek food characterise this lonely Japanese restaurant.

ourpick Spaghetti Jazz (Map p62; ☎ 882 2062; 43 North Gulshan II; ◷ 12.30-3pm & 6.30-10pm; mains 400) An excellent Italian restaurant, just off DIT II Circle, that produces pastas and pizzas stuffed with cheese in just the right places, and covered in tomatoes just where they're needed. Very popular with expats.

Topkapi (Map p62; ☎ 881 2646; 134 Gulshan Ave; lunch buffet Tk 450) This is one of several large and similar ventures on Gulshan Ave whose all-you-can-eat lunch buffets are much less tacky than the venues themselves. Also open for dinner.

Spitfire's Barbeque & Grill (Map p62; ☎ 885 1930; cnr Rd 55 & Gulshan Ave; ◷ 11.30am-3pm & 6-11pm; mains Tk 400-1000) Located in the heart of the diplomatic quarter, the bevy of shiny 4WDs with ambassadorial standards and multi-national logos should tell you something about both the quality and price of the food here. Steaks are the staple, but you can also opt for quail and duck breast (but it would be cheaper to wait until you get back home). The atmosphere is far more relaxed than you'd expect.

Khazana (Map p62; ☎ 882 6127; Gulshan Ave; mains Tk 400-1000) Khazana, next door to Spitfire, is its Indian-cuisine equivalent, though it's much more of a shirt-and-tie kind of place.

For some 'what-you-see-is-what-you-get relief', head to **Dominous Pizza** (Map p62; Rd 10) or **Helvetia** (Map p62; Tower Hamlet, 16 Kemal Ataturk Ave, Banani). There's also **Club Gelato** (Map p62; Rd 11, Banani), a perfect replica of an Italian café, serving posh coffee and every rainbow-coloured flavour of ice cream.

DRINKING

There are licensed bars at the **Pan Pacific Sonargaon Hotel** (Map pp56–7) and the **Sheraton Hotel** (Map pp56–7).

For a cheaper beer (Tk 160 for a cold Heineken) try the **Peacock Restaurant** (Map pp56–7) or the **Sukura Restaurant** (Map pp56–7), both located opposite the Sheraton. A discreet mutter at other similar establishments might also prove fruitful.

Not quite as racy but certainly very tasty is the cha (tea) brewed up by the **Mohamad**

Isobali Teashop (Map pp56-7). This tea stand, which rickshaw-wallahs insist is the best in the city, is about halfway between the Hotel Orchard Plaza and the Hotel Victory in Central Dhaka.

ENTERTAINMENT
Cinemas
With the plethora of Bengali movies available (p33), cinemas only very occasionally play mainstream Western films. Check newspapers. Expats find the range of pirated DVDs is adequate compensation for the lack of variety on the big screen.

Sport
There are often cricket, soccer or hockey matches at the National Stadium; check English-language newspapers for details. Women usually don't go to sporting events – it's considered unseemly.

Traditional Music & Dance
The best place for cultural performances is **Shilpakala Academy** (Map pp56-7; ☎ 956 2801), the national academy of fine art and the performing arts. The major cultural event of the year is the month-long **Asian Art Biennial** in November (held on odd-numbered years). The exhibition, which spills over into the National Museum, attracts top artists and the quality is high. Contact the Shilpakala Academy for details of other upcoming events. The academy is in a side street off Segun Bagicha Rd, next to the National Art Gallery.

Cultural events are also held at **Shishu Academy** (Map pp56-7; Old High Court Rd), southwest of the Supreme Court; the **National Museum** (Map pp56-7; Kazi Nazrul Islam Ave), 1km northwest of the Supreme Court; **Osmani Auditorium** (Map pp56-7; Abdul Ghani Rd), 1km southeast of the Supreme Court; and **Dhaka University** (Map pp56–7). Finding out about events is a challenge – they seem to be advertised only among the cultural elite. Your best option is to ask at the Shilpakala Academy or the **Alliance Francaise** (Map pp56-7; Mirpur Rd).

SHOPPING
Clothing
Dhaka is a fantastic place for purchasing cheap ready-made garments, all of which are produced locally for export. If you're ready to haggle, then head for **Banga Bazar** (Map p51; Fulbaria Rd), a block west of Gulistan

bus station. Although some of the clothes are seconds, with small flaws, most are over-runs. Banga Bazar is usually closed on Friday, but always check.

For easier but pricier purchasing, try the upmarket clothing shops around the Gulshan area.

Handicrafts

Many handicraft shops accept credit cards. Most open at 9am and close between 7pm and 9pm, and are closed on Friday.

For painless shopping, the Pan Pacific Sonargaon and Sheraton Hotels have handicraft shops in their malls, but you can pay less elsewhere, including at the row of shops on New Elephant Rd.

If you're looking for jewellery, avoid buying items made from white conch shells in Shankharia Bazar; other seashells and corals; anything made of ivory; and jade products that may have come from Burma – all these items come with bad karma.

Leading handicraft shops and jewellery shops:

Aarong Handicrafts (www.brac-aarong.com) Gulshan (Map p62; Gulshan-Tejgaon Link Rd, Gulshan I); Lalmatia (Map pp56-7; 1/1, Block A, Mirpur Rd) The biggest name in quality handicrafts. Aarong is the retail branch of the Bangladesh Rural Advancement Committee (BRAC), which aims to create employment for economically and socially marginalised people through the promotion of traditional Bangladeshi handicrafts.

Halima Handicrafts (11/20 Iqbal Rd, Block A, Mohammadpur) A project to help abandoned and widowed women support themselves and their children by producing goods such as wall hangings, bedspreads, cushions and tablecloths.

Kumudini Gulshan (Map p62; 74 Gulshan Ave); Mogh Bazar (Map pp56-7; Pan Pacific Sonargaon Hotel, Kazi Nazrul Islam Ave) Specialises in jute products.

Mona Jewellers (Map pp56-7; 13 Baitul Mukarram Market, Nayapaltan)

Monno Ceramics (Map pp56-7; 334 New Elephant Rd, Mogh Bazar) For modern ceramics.

Monno Fabrics (Map p62; DIT II Circle, Gulshan)

Markets

The city's largest market is **New Market** (Map pp56-7; Mirpur Rd; ☽ closed Mon afternoon & Tue all day). You can find almost anything here including maps, material, saris and household items. It's a great place to get kitted up in local gear. You can find pre-made *salwar kameez* (a long dress-like tunic worn by women over baggy trousers) for as low as Tk 200.

Chandni Chowk Bazar (Map pp56-7), east across the street from New Market, is best place for local fabrics. It's also closed on Monday afternoon and all day Tuesday.

Stadium Arcade (Map pp56-7), north of the National Stadium, has an array of electrical goods, CDs and DVDs.

DIT II Market (Map p62), with its intense but friendly atmosphere, is particularly fascinating for its ground-floor fish and livestock market. The cockroaches look healthier than the chickens, and are even more free-range. Tucked away on the first floor of the market are a couple of framing stores that sell Bengali art.

Rickshaw Art

Bangsal Rd (Bicycle St; Map p51), in Old Dhaka's Bangsal, is the place to buy rickshaw parts. For rickshaw art try further along Bangsal Rd in Nazira Bazar, or Bangla Duair Lane. The art is painted on strips of tin and vinyl, and will fit in most suitcases. Prices are around Tk 50, sometimes more if it's special. Bargaining is required, of course.

GETTING THERE & AWAY
Air

There are several airlines in Bangladesh:

Best Air (☎ 988 2404) Office at the domestic airport.

Biman (Map pp56-7; ☎ 955 9610; Dilkusha II Circle, Motijheel)

GMG Airlines (Map pp56-7; ☎ 711 4155/7; Sena Kayan Bhaban, 13th fl, Motijheel)

United Airways (☎ 895 7640; www.uabdl.com) At the domestic airport.

GMG and United are the most reliable, both in schedules and safety. Routes and prices vary little between the competitors.

At the time of writing, there were services to Barisal (35 minutes), Chittagong (50 minutes), Jessore (40 minutes), Cox's Bazar (40 minutes), and Sylhet (45 minutes). Prices and times change constantly, and don't expect any of them to stick to their schedule.

See also regional chapters and p169.

Boat

Book 1st- and 2nd-class Rocket (paddle-wheel) tickets at the **Bangladesh Inland Waterway Transport Corporation office** (BIWTC; Map pp56-7; ☎ 955 9779, 891 4771; ☽ Sun-Wed to 5pm, Thu to 2pm, closed Fri & Sat) in Motijheel, a block east of Dilkusha Circle I. You may be told that only 1st-class tickets can be booked from this office. A smile and some persistence should change this policy.

The Rocket departs from Sadarghat (Map p51) and, on rare occasions, from Badam Tole boat terminal (Map p51), 1km north of Sadarghat. Get there in plenty of time. The trip to Khulna takes from 27 to 30 hours. Fares to Khulna are roughly Tk 1010/610/150 for 1st/2nd/deck class, depending on which Rocket you catch. Prices are sequentially less, depending on where you want to jump off along the way. For an explanation of classes see p175.

Boats depart for Khulna every day (except Friday) at 6pm sharp.

Those travelling deck class (good luck convincing someone to sell you a deck-class ticket) may want to stake a place before the hordes arrive. You could pay a local to occupy a place for you, sitting all day for a fee of around Tk 50.

Private launches operate up and down the major rivers but most head south. Short-distance destinations reached by services from Dhaka include Bandura (30km west), Munshiganj (25km southeast) and Srinigar (20km southwest). Long-distance destinations include Barisal (110km south), Bhola (110km south), Chandpur (60km southeast), Madaripur (60km southwest) and Patuakali (40km south).

Short-distance launches travel during the day. The large long-distance launches travel at night, arriving at Sadarghat in the morning and remaining there all day, until departing at around 6pm or 7pm. Tickets are usually sold on board on the day of departure and require some bargaining.

Bus

The bus 'system' in Bangladesh teeters between mind-bogglingly chaotic and surprisingly organised. When you arrive at a bus station, you will be swamped by panic-stricken men shouting like auctioneers. When you so much as mutter your intended destination, you will be frantically shunted onto a bus as if it's going to leave at any second, only to have to then wait for it to leave in its own sweet time. For your own safety and sanity, take the train if it's possible.

The government **Bangladesh Road Transport Corporation** (BRTC; DIT Ave) buses leave from Kamlapur station (Map pp56–7). It's best forgotten as the service is far inferior to that of the private lines.

GABTALI BUS STATION

The largest bus station in Dhaka, **Gabtali** (Map p48) is on the northwestern side of town on Dhaka-Aricha Hwy (an extension of Mirpur Rd), 8km from the heart of the city. (It will cost Tk 5 by bus to get to the city from Gulistan bus station.) It's a madhouse; be on guard for pickpockets (particularly after dark), but in general, people are very friendly and helpful. Most of the buses leaving from here are the cheaper 'local' buses. Luxury buses leave from in front of the relevant offices in the city centre.

Buses for most destinations leave every 20 to 30 minutes. Travel times vary considerably depending on traffic in Dhaka.

Gabtali serves destinations in the northwest and southwest such as Savar (Tk 30), Jessore (express/chair coach Tk 230/325, 6½ hours) and Khulna (Tk 280, eight hours). Buses leave between 7am and 4.30pm.

Between around 7.30am and 11pm buses leave for Barisal (Tk 250, five to seven hours), Bogra (Tk 120, five hours), Rangpur (Tk 250, eight hours), Dinajpur (Tk 200, 9½ hours) and Rajshahi (Tk 250, six hours).

SAYEDABAD BUS STATION

Sayedabad bus station (Map p48; Hatkhola Rd) is 1km before Jatrabari Circle, on the southeastern side of town. Buses leave every half an hour or so to destinations in the south and west, such as Comilla (Tk 60, three hours, between 5.30am and 10.30pm), Chittagong (Tk 200, six hours, between 5am and midnight) and Sylhet (Tk 200, five hours, between 5am and 11.30pm).

Fares to Barisal, Jessore, Khulna and Kushtia are the same as those from Gabtali.

For travel to Chittagong, the best bus companies are along a one-block stretch on Inner Circular Rd in the Nayapaltan area near the New Hotel Yeameni International. They charge between Tk 450 and Tk 600 depending on the class, and take six hours.

There are also buses from here to Cox's Bazar (Tk 400, 10 hours). Comparable companies serving Chittagong Division are **Soudia** (☎ 801 8445), **Hanif** (☎ 831 3869) and **Green Line** (☎ 710 0301). Private chair coaches usually leave from around 7am onwards.

MOHAKHALI BUS STATION

The **Mohakhali bus station** (Map p62; Mogh Bazar Rd) is 2km south of Banani. From here buses head north for Mymensingh (Tk 180, 4½ hours) and Tangail (Tk 80, 2½ hours) every 20 or 30 minutes, between around 6am and 8.30pm.

GULISTAN (FULBARIA) BUS STATION

Finally, there's **Gulistan (Fulbaria) bus station** (Map p51; North-South Rd), in the heart of town at Gulistan Crossing. Most buses depart from a block east at the chaotic intersection of Bangabandhu Ave and Toyenbee Rd. It's extremely crowded and traffic jams in the area are constant. Most buses are local and people are stuffed into them like sardines. Destinations include greater Dhaka as well as many towns within 30km or so of Dhaka, such as Mograpara (Old Sonargaon).

Train

Dhaka's main train station is **Kamlapur station** (Map pp56–7) in Motijheel. Many trains also stop at the smaller Banani and Airport train stations, both of which are more convenient if you're staying in Gulshan area. Buying tickets is easy and there's a large timetable in English. Double-check it for accuracy because the schedules change slightly in the summer and the board may not reflect this. The inquiry counter, which is open until 11pm, and the chief inspector are both helpful. The table below shows some examples of express trains from Dhaka. If you've just arrived from India, you will be in for a shock when you see how comparatively organised everything is here.

Destination	Departure	Approximate Duration (hr)
Sylhet	6.40am & 10pm	7
Sylhet	2pm	8
Chittagong	7.40am	7
Chittagong	3pm & 11pm	8
Chittagong	4.20pm	6
Khulna	6.20am	10
Mymensingh	10.10pm	4
Rajshahi	2.25pm	7
Rajshahi	11.20pm	6

GETTING AROUND
To/From Zia International Airport

The cheapest way to get to the city centre from the airport is by bus. They're extremely crowded, so it's possibly not a viable option if you have a lot of luggage. You'll find buses out on the main highway (Airport Rd), a five-minute walk from the airport. The fare is less than Tk 10 to most places. After 8pm you may have difficulty finding one.

There's a fixed-rate taxi booth just outside the airport exit. Taxis arranged through this booth will cost around Tk 750 for the journey into central Dhaka. If you go straight to the taxi drivers you should be able to negotiate a cheaper fare, but after a long international flight most people can't be bothered with the additional hassle this entails.

To get to the airport, buses and tempos (shared auto-rickshaw) leave Gulistan bus station throughout the day and cost around Tk 8. A baby taxi (auto-rickshaw) will probably cost a little over Tk 100 and a taxi around Tk 150. Rickshaws aren't allowed at the airport or on the major highway (Airport Rd) passing the airport.

Baby Taxi

Travel by baby taxi (known as auto-rickshaws or tuk-tuks in neighbouring countries) is as efficient as it gets in Dhaka, and can be great (hair-raising) fun. Though pricier than rickshaws over short distances, they have the advantage of speed. Despite the presence of meters it will be a rare day that a driver will agree to use one. Bargain before setting off. A baby-taxi fare from, say, Motijheel to Gulshan will cost around Tk 80 to Tk 100.

Bus

Cheaper than cheap, local buses have no English signs, and their numbering is in Bengali. They are always overcrowded, so boarding between major bus stops is virtually impossible. Fares vary, but around Dhaka you won't pay much more than Tk 8. Foreigners almost never use the local buses.

Car

Unless you have an International Driver's Licence, self-driving isn't an option (ironic when you consider how bad some of the locals are at driving!). Even if you do have a licence, hiring a self-drive car for cruising Dhaka (or anywhere else in Bangladesh for that matter) has got to be the silliest idea in the world. However, hiring a car or van with a driver can make a lot of sense (see p177).

There are numerous car/driver-hire places scattered around Dhaka. One is **Dhaka Tours Rent-A-Car Association** (Map pp56–7; ☎ 861 1313), with an office opposite the Sheraton, just off

THE MUSTANS

If you get a baby taxi from one of the larger taxi stands, you may see the driver give a young man a Tk 2 note before departing. This money ultimately goes to one of the *mustans* who wield Mafia-like power over their territories. Baby-taxi drivers have to pay for the privilege of using a public space to park. A man carting cargo through an area controlled by a *mustan* may be stopped by one of his lieutenants and forced to pay a small fee for the right to pass on a public street. Roadside food vendors also have to pay regular tolls to *mustans*. These thugs levy similar tolls on slum-dwellers occupying public lands. Refusal often draws a beating.

Mustans operate all over the country. Popular belief is that the most powerful *mustans* are connected with the major political parties.

Kazi Nazrul Islam Ave. If you venture out of Dhaka you will have to pay extra each day for the driver's food and accommodation. When you are negotiating with any company, make sure you are clear on what is included in the price.

The more upmarket option is to approach one of the big tour companies such as **Bengal Tours** (Map p62; ☎ 883 4716; www.bengaltours.com; Block A, Banani) or **Guide Tours** (Map p62; ☎ 988 6983; www .guidetours.com; 1st fl, Darpan Complex, DIT II Circle, Gulshan), who both charge around Tk 4500 (including fuel and driver's expenses) depending on what you want to do.

Rickshaw

You will find rickshaws (which in Bangladesh means cycle-rickshaws) everywhere, and when the streets are crowded (as they usually are) they're not much slower than anything else that moves. Aim for a basic fare of about Tk 6 for the first kilometre and Tk 5 per kilometre after that, and make your own judgment with regard to *baksheesh* (tip). The fantastically decked-out cycle-rickshaws of Dhaka are a tourist attraction in their own right (see p34) and you should go for a spin at least once.

Taxi

There are two types of taxis on the roads of Dhaka. The yellow taxis are more spacious, have air-con and are usually cleaner than their black counterparts, but you pay for the difference. Meters in yellow taxis clock more quickly and at a higher rate than the black taxis, but this is often irrelevant because, as with baby taxis, most drivers are reluctant to use the meters.

Tempo

Fast and cheap to use, tempos are a convenient way to travel if you aren't carrying much luggage and don't mind rib-cage compression. The close quarters might make women (and those around them) uncomfortable.

A trip from Gabtali bus station to Farm Gate costs around Tk 10.

Dhaka Division

Rub your eyes and blink. You are finally free of the last of the crazy Dhaka traffic jams and in front of you stretches a rural wonderland. This large district, comprising of some 25,000 villages and hardly any towns, is the most densely populated area of Bangladesh and epitomises the diversity of this surprising country.

While there are dappled forests, great rivers and hilly panoramas, much of the region is given over to radiant rice paddies, filling your vision with more hues of green than you ever knew existed. It's this farming soul, where life revolves around the gentle clip-clop of an ox and cart and the slow rotation of the seasons, that is, for the adventurous tourist, the appeal of this little visited region. It's the sort of place where brief encounters turn into solid friendships and a person can fall in love with a much maligned nation. This is the reason you came to Bangladesh, so dive right in.

HIGHLIGHTS

- Pace the streets of a city of gold in regal **Sonargaon** (opposite)
- Dance with cobras, get lovey-dovey with pythons and be spellbound by the magical residents of **Ghuradia** (p73)
- Munch on Monad, search for 99 elephants disguised as policemen and slither your hips like a pole dancer in **Muktagacha** (p77)
- Monkey around spotting the spotted deer in the patchy forests of **Madhupur National Park** (p77)

SONARGAON

A great day trip from Dhaka (about 23km) is an excursion to Sonargaon (sometimes known as Old Sonargaon), the country's first capital. Combining countryside, culture, archaeology, adventure and friendship in one tidy bundle, the village is an ideal way to experience all the best of Bangladesh in one easy step.

Except for some mosques, a bridge, a few tombs and stupas (Buddhist monuments), and some indistinguishable mounds (most of which are found around the small modern village of Mograpara), nothing much remains of the original city of Sonargaon. For most people, enchanting Painam Nagar (p72) is the real jewel.

Unfortunately the government's archaeological department has done precious little to preserve the buildings of Sonargaon and, on the rare days that work is undertaken, the results are normally totally out of keeping with the surrounding buildings. Some of the poorer residents reportedly sell the bricks from ramshackle buildings to be broken into gravel for construction work. Since

Independence, only Goaldi Mosque, a pre-Mughal bridge and a single rajbari (landowner's palace) called Sadarbari (now housing a folk-art museum) have been restored.

Sights & Activities

MOGRAPARA

A thriving village located on the Dhaka–Chittagong Hwy, Mograpara claims most of the remains of the old capital, including the **Tomb of Sultan Ghiyasuddin Azam Shah** (the oldest surviving Muslim monument in Bangladesh) and the **Panch Pir Dargah**. Most of these are 1km or 2km west of Mograpara. These monuments aren't very impressive and most visitors, believing only Painam Nagar to be Old Sonargaon, don't even know they exist.

SADARBARI (FOLK-ART MUSUEM)

Built in 1901, this stunning rajbari is an appropriate building for a **folk-art museum** (admission Tk 10; ☉ 9am-5pm, Fri-Wed). The building has two façades. The one facing the street, with steps leading down to the water and life-size English horsemen in stucco on either side, is one of

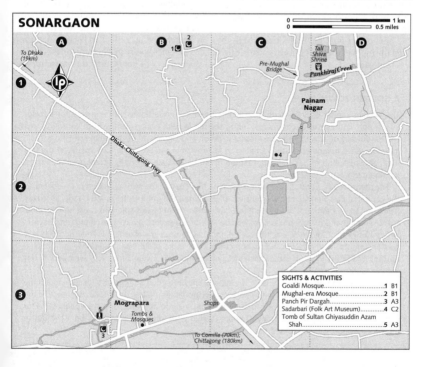

SONARGAON

To Dhaka (19km)

Dhaka-Chittagong Hwy

Pre-Mughal Bridge

Tall Shiva Shrine

Pankhiraj Creek

Painam Nagar

Mograpara

Tombs & Mosques

Shops

To Comilla (70km); Chittagong (180km)

0 — 1 km
0 — 0.5 miles

SIGHTS & ACTIVITIES	
Goaldi Mosque	1 B1
Mughal-era Mosque	2 B1
Panch Pir Dargah	3 A3
Sadarbari (Folk Art Museum)	4 C2
Tomb of Sultan Ghiyasuddin Azam Shah	5 A3

DHAKA DIVISION

the most picturesque in Bangladesh. The other, at the museum's entrance, is profusely embellished with a mosaic of blue and white tiles, and has something of an Andalucian look to it.

Inside, the unadorned rooms are stuffed full of folk art and handicrafts, but everything is very poorly labelled and badly displayed. Around the back of the rajbari, and on the opposite side of the lake, is a new building containing another museum of folk-art objects. This one is much better organised and laid out.

For most people though, the highlight of a visit are the beautiful water-soaked gardens where trees, lawns and ponds have come together in a close impression of heaven. Bird-watchers should bring some binoculars because the trees and bushes are full of different kingfisher species. Relaxed Bangladeshis from the city come here for some fresh air on Friday.

GOALDI MOSQUE

Built in 1519, the graceful, single-domed **Goaldi Mosque** is the most impressive of the few extant monuments of the old capital city, and a good example of pre-Mughal architecture.

The mosque 50m beyond Goaldi, built in 1704 during the Mughal period, is historically less important.

PAINAM NAGAR

The once elegant town of **Painam Nagar** is busy fighting a loosing battle with nature, and with every passing year the trees and vines drape themselves a little further over the decaying houses. The result is a delightful ghost-town quality where the buildings appear to hang like exotic fruits from the branches of the trees.

Constructed almost entirely between 1895 and 1905 on a small segment of the ancient capital city, this tiny settlement consists of a single narrow street, lined with around 50 (now dilapidated) mansions built by wealthy Hindu merchants. At the time of Partition, many owners fled to India, leaving their elegant homes in the care of poor tenants, who did nothing to maintain them. Most of the remaining owners pulled out during the anti-Hindu riots of 1964, which led up to the 1965 Indo–Pakistan War. Despite the rot, a few people do continue to live in some of the houses and their bright shades add a technicolour tint to the village.

Getting There & Away

Sonargaon is only 23km from central Dhaka and makes an easy day trip. From Dhaka's Sayedabad bus station, say the buzz word 'Mograpara' (Tk 30, 40 minutes – if the traffic is on your side!). If you ask for Sonargaon, you will likely end up at the Pan Pacific Sonargaon Hotel. Once you're in Mograpara, a short rickshaw ride will get you to the museum and

---

A GOLDEN TOWN

The ancient capital of Sonargaon (or 'Golden Town' in Hindi) flourished as the region's major inland port and centre of commerce during the pre-Muslim period. By the 13th century it was the Hindu seat of power. With the Muslim invasion and the arrival of the sultan of Elhi in 1280, its importance magnified as the region's de facto Islamic capital. Some 42 years later, the first independent sultan of East Bengal, Fakhruddin Mubarak Shah, officially established his capital in Sonargaon.

For the next 270 years, Sonargaon, known as the 'Seat of the Mighty Majesty', prospered as the capital of East Bengal, and the Muslim rulers minted their money here. Mu Huany, an envoy from the Chinese emperor, visited Sultan Ghiyasuddin Azam Shah's splendid court here in 1406. He observed that Sonargaon was a walled city with broad streets, great mausoleums and bazaars where business of all kinds was transacted. In 1558, famous traveller Ralph Fitch noted that it was an important centre for the manufacture and export of *kantha* (traditional indigo-dyed muslin), the finest in all of India. Ancient Egyptian mummies were reportedly wrapped in this *kantha* exported from Bengal.

When the invading Mughals ousted the sultans, they regarded Sonargaon's location along the region's major river as too exposed to Portuguese and Mogh pirates. So in 1608, they moved the capital to Dhaka, thus initiating Sonargaon's long decline into oblivion. Yet its legendary fame for incredibly fine muslin fabric continued undiminished until foreign competition from the British (and their import quotas) ruined the trade.

CENTRE FOR THE REHABILITATION OF THE PARALYSED (CRP)

An inspiring organisation that has been operating since 1979, the **Centre for the Rehabilitation of the Paralysed** (CRP; ☎ 771 0464/5; www.crp-bangladesh.com) helps paralysed people develop skills that enable them to become self-sufficient and productive.

In addition to selling fish, fruit, poultry, handicrafts and wheelchairs, CRP's funding is also derived from the guesthouses it runs in the tea gardens of Moulvibazar.

The centre has branches in Gonokbari, Gobindapur, Manikganj and Mirpur, but its headquarters is on the northeastern outskirts of Savar Bazar on the Dhaka–Aricha Hwy, from where you can buy postcards, stationery and other trinkets produced by CRP patients.

Visitors are most welcome at this sprawling complex; various training sessions and workshops are held daily from 8am to 1pm, and from 3pm to 6pm. The centre is closed Thursday afternoon and Friday. Volunteers, both skilled and unskilled, are always required – see the website for details.

---

other sights. Rickshaw-wallahs will guess what you're there to see.

SAVAR
☎ 06626

A popular day excursion for Dhaka locals is a trip to Savar (*shar*-var). The town, Savar Bazar, is on the Dhaka–Aricha Hwy, 15km north of Gabtali bus station in Dhaka. Tuesday is market day in Savar Bazar, which becomes very animated, especially along the banks of the Bangsi River just west of town.

The main attraction is the historic **National Martyrs' Memorial** (Jatiya Sriti Saudha), which is 8km further along the Dhaka–Aricha Hwy, just off the road. The tapering 50m-high structure is a memorial to the millions who died in the struggle for independence. The beautifully kept grounds contain a number of grassy platforms that cover the mass graves of some of those slaughtered in the Liberation War. This is an important place for Bangladeshis, who wander the grounds with an air of reverence.

If you need to eat, there's a large Parjatan restaurant across the road from the National Martyrs' Memorial. Downstairs the food is fast and cheap; upstairs it's more expensive and tasty. There is a well-marked Chinese restaurant on the main drag in the centre of Savar Bazar.

Buses for Savar (Tk 30, one hour) leave from Gabtali bus station throughout the day. Tell the driver that you want to get off at the memorial.

DHAMRAI
☎ 011

Dhamrai, an excellent side trip from Savar, is little more than a village, but its single main street packs quite a punch. Rotting slowly, and

in the most pleasant of manners, are a dozen or so extravagant century-old houses built by the wealthy Hindu families who once lived here. Today the town continues to be home to a substantial Hindu population and the inhabitants are renowned for their skill in brass work and for their *jamdani* (embroidered muslin or silk) weaving. Most of the finest Raj-era buildings are occupied by brass or weaving workshops, and are slowly being restored to their former glory. These workshops are well worth a peek, as the process of making brass objects (often Hindu religious statues) using the lost-wax technique is a fascinating one. The quality of the goods they turn out is generally excellent and, with no pressure or sales pitch whatsoever, it's a good opportunity to browse. One workshop that has received high praise is **Dhamrai Metal Craft** (☎ 832 620).

Saturday, which is market day, is a good time to come for some local colour. The multi-storey Jagannath (chariot), adorned with painted images from Hindu mythology, sits in the centre of town and is paraded down the street during **Rath Jatra**, the festival held here during the full-moon in late June/early July (see p162).

Dhamrai is 5km west of the Savar and 1km north off the Dhaka–Aricha Hwy. Buses between Savar and Dhamrai cost about Tk 5.

Buses to Dhamrai (Tk 35, one hour) leave from Dhaka's Gabtali bus station. A baby taxi will be quicker but costs around Tk 250.

GHURADIA

Are you scared of snakes? If so give Ghuradia a wide birth because it's in this little village on the banks of the Dhaleshwari River (a few kilometres from Savar) that your worst nightmares will come true. There are slippery serpents everywhere, but don't worry because the human inhabitants of the village are rumoured to have magical powers that allow them to handle deadly cobras without fear. The Badhi river gypsies are famous throughout the region for their skill as snake charmers, but are also employed to remove snakes from houses, and to milk cobras and other venomous snakes (the venom they milk is used in antivenin). The villagers will know what you have come for and there are always a few boxes of snakes lying around. Bidding for a snake-charming show will probably commence at around Tk 1000 but quickly drop to a more sensible Tk 100 to Tk 150. The snakes they use include cobras and much more harmless pythons, as well as various equally harmless water and tree snakes. In actual fact the cobras are also harmless – they've either been defanged or milked of all their venom (though it's probably best not to test this).

Getting to Ghuradia is complicated in your own car and almost impossible on public transport. The best advice is to hire a taxi or rickshaw in Savar as they should know the way. If not, the staff in the Parjatan restaurant opposite the National Martyrs' Memorial (p73) will be able to give you directions. Remember that by visiting you are encouraging the villagers to catch more snakes.

BHAWAL NATIONAL PARK

Located at Rajendrapur, and only one hour north of Dhaka, **Bhawal National Park** (admission per person Tk 6, per car Tk 30, per minibus Tk 50) is where the citizens of the city come to remember what a lungful of fresh countryside air feels like. While it certainly cannot be described as an untouched wilderness, its forest walks, angling and lake boating make it a favourite weekend haunt with the inhabitants of Dhaka. In recent years, the forest department have created a 'silent zone' where music is banned, and have reintroduced peacocks, spotted deer, fishing cats and pythons.

The park is on the Dhaka–Mymensingh Hwy, 38km north of Dhaka. From Mohakhali bus station in Dhaka, buses heading for Mymensingh run right past the well-marked park entrance, on your right. The trip takes at least an hour.

TANGAIL
☎ 0921

Crawling along the traffic- and pollution-clogged road out of Dhaka, it's hard to believe that Tangail has anything of interest except the possibility of a cold drink. Yet in the green fields just behind this scruffy town is a magnificent piece of Bangladeshi artistic heritage – **Atia Mosque**. Built in 1609 by Said Khan Panee, this pretty-in-pink mosque, depicted on the Tk 10 note, blends pre-Mughal elements with imperial Mughal architectural features. It has been diligently restored several times in its long life. Its location, among a rash of trees and fields and beside a deep pond, is sheer visual poetry after the nightmare of the road from Dhaka.

The mosque is located 9km south of Tangail on the tarred road to Nagarpur, and a rickshaw from the town will cost around Tk 100 with waiting time.

Tangail has little in the way of a tourist infrastructure and its proximity to the capital means there is no real reason to stay here. There are some friendly local restaurants on the main street, and more serving similar chicken, fish and mutton dishes at the intersection of Dhaka and Mymensingh Rds.

You will find the **District Forestry Office** (☎ 53524) for Madhupur National Park (p77) on the third floor of the well-marked Water Development Board building, a block north of the post office on Victoria Rd.

Getting There & Away

Ordinary buses leave Tangail every 20 minutes or so between 5am and 7pm to Dhaka (Tk 80, 2½ hours) and Mymensingh (Tk 90, 2½ hours). All leave from the main bus station on Mymensingh Rd, 2km north of the intersection with Dhaka Rd.

Buses for Tangail depart from Mohakhali bus station in Dhaka.

MYMENSINGH
☎ 091

Mymensingh presents maybe the most gentle of introductions you can have to the wonderful world of rural Bangladesh, yet the poor old girl is largely ignored by most visitors. In some ways this makes sense. The town is out on a limb and getting from there to almost anywhere else involves backtracking to Dhaka and, secondly, there are no drop-dead tourist attractions that just have to be seen.

DHAKA DIVISION

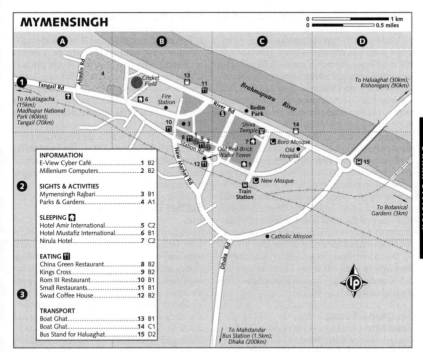

MYMENSINGH

0 —————— 1 km
0 —————— 0.5 miles

INFORMATION
E-View Cyber Café..........................1 B2
Millenium Computers.....................2 B2

SIGHTS & ACTIVITIES
Mymensingh Rajbari........................3 B1
Parks & Gardens.............................4 A1

SLEEPING
Hotel Amir International...................5 C2
Hotel Mustafiz International.............6 B1
Nirula Hotel....................................7 C2

EATING
China Green Restaurant...................8 B2
Kings Cross....................................9 B2
Rom III Restaurant........................10 B1
Small Restaurants..........................11 B1
Swad Coffee House........................12 B2

TRANSPORT
Boat Ghat.....................................13 B1
Boat Ghat.....................................14 C1
Bus Stand for Haluaghat................15 D2

Tangail Rd
To Muktagacha (15km); Madhupur National Park (40km); Tangail (70km)
Abadin Rd
Cricket Field
Fire Station
Brahmaputra River
River Rd
Bedin Park
Shiva Temple
Old Red-Brick Water Tower
Boro Mosque
Old Hospital
New Mosque
Train Station
New Market Rd
Station Rd
Dhaka Rd
Catholic Mission
To Haluaghat (30km); Kishoreganj (90km)
To Botanical Gardens (3km)
To Mahstandar Bus Station (1.5km); Dhaka (200km)

DHAKA DIVISION

Even so, this leafy town, built on the banks of the mighty River Brahmaputra, has a lovely riverside setting that the authorities have been quick to capitalise on. You'll also find one of the most interesting old quarters in the country, whimsical botanical gardens, lots of happy students and a wealth of nearby natural-world attractions. If you're hooked on rickshaws then you'll like Mymensingh – the zillions of rickshaw-wallahs here seem to be in fierce competition to see who can create the most colourfully decorated fleet.

There are some internet cafés on Station Rd. A good one with reliable connections is **Millenium Computers** (Mymensingh Online; 1st fl, Alimun Plaza; per hr Tk 20). **E-View Cyber Café** is further west on the same side of the road.

Sights & Activities

Built between 1905 and 1911, the **Mymensingh Rajbari** is a well-kept building in the middle of the city. It is now occupied by an organisation that trains female teachers, but much of the original structure remains. An ornamental marble fountain with a classical statue of a semi-nude nymph lies just beyond the arched

gateway entrance. Behind the main building is the Jal-Tungi, a small two-storey bathhouse once used as the women's bathing pavilion. You can politely ask the security guard for admittance to the grounds, but it is doubtful whether he will grant you a glimpse of the interior.

Several kilometres east of town, next to the Agriculture and Fisheries College, are the large and peaceful **botanical gardens** (entrance Tk 2; 9am-5pm). Well laid out, and with clear labels pinpointing some of the more interesting plants and trees, it makes an excellent place to relax on a bench with a book. A rickshaw from the town centre will cost in the region of Tk 30.

The original ancient core of the town, located between the train station and the waterfront, is, with its many absorbing **souks**, a fascinating place in which to get lost. Keep an eye open for the gold workshops, muddled away in the mess of streets, where people hammer down minuscule gold pieces found in the riverbed in order to make jewellery. The town has a large Hindu minority and there are several noticeable Hindu shrines in the old town area. The most obvious is the rotting stone Shiva temple just by the water.

Wind your day up in the **parks** on the waterfront at the western edge of town. This is one of the most enjoyable public spaces in Bangladesh and every evening half the Mymensingh population takes advantage by decamping down here to lull about in the shade of trees and watch multi-coloured boats criss-cross the river. There are several small tea stalls as well as an outdoor café. In the playing fields just behind the parkland, numerous cricket matches add their thunk and whack to proceedings and if you're an architecture buff you'll probably get some joy wandering around the back lanes admiring the glorious old colonial houses. Should you want a closer look at the other side of the river, one of the small wooden boats will happily take you over (Tk 2). From the far bank, set off across this rural oil painting towards one of the many little villages whose inhabitants are likely to be overjoyed to have you around. It's a perfect setting in which to create your own adventure!

Sleeping & Eating

Nirula Hotel (☎ 54285; r Tk 150/250/350) The best budget choice with windowless, but clean, rooms. The Tk 350 rooms differ only from the Tk 250 ones in that they have a TV. They won't be over the moon to let you stay in the Tk 150 room, but that's OK because you probably won't be either. It's in the Chowk Bazar and a little difficult to find.

Hotel Amir International (☎ 54030; 46 Station Rd; s/d Tk 600/800, with air-con Tk 1000/1260; ✷) Set around a central courtyard, the clean rooms here have desks, satellite TV, hot water and even sickly sweet pictures of the English countryside on the walls. The staff are friendly and the English-speaking room boy loves chatting to foreigners about their travels and where he dreams of one day going. The air-con rooms have sit down toilets; those without air-con have squat toilets. It's easily the best value hotel in town.

Hotel Mustafiz International (☎ /fax 63870; 6/B Gangadas Guha Rd; s/d Tk 800/1500) On a quiet side street, this new hotel has rooms so big they manage to fit in a sofa or two. The beds and bathrooms are equally large and everything has that newly constructed, immaculate feel, but it's a little overpriced.

There are some nice low-key Bangladeshi restaurants in the numerous side streets off Station Rd, but for something a little more upmarket try the superb curries at the **Rom III Restaurant**, (Station Rd; mains Tk 100) an eternally popular spot with local students, workers and holidaying Bangladeshis. There are also a couple of Chinese options for lunch and dinner, such as **Kings Cross** (☎ 01715 815399; Station Rd; mains Tk 150) or the slightly more authentically Chinese tasting **China Green Restaurant** (☎ 53331; Station Rd; mains Tk 150).

On the upstairs level of the Press Club complex, just off Station Rd, is the **Swad Coffee House** (☎ 53932; 10am-10pm; mains Tk 25) where teenagers strut and flirt over cheeseburgers and sandwiches.

Getting There & Away

BUS

The main bus terminal is Mahstandar bus station, 3km from the Station Rd Circle. Between 6am and 6pm you can get a bus to a zillion places including Tangail (Tk 80, 2½ hours), Madhupur (Tk 40, 45 minutes), Dhaka (Tk 80, 4½ hours) and Bogra (Tk 140, 4½ hours).

The bus stand for Haluaghat and other destinations on the other side of the Brahmaputra River is, logically, at the bridge. Buses to Haluaghat (Tk 45, 1½ hours) leave regularly between 8am and 7pm.

TRAIN

Mymensingh is no longer really on the way to anywhere since the new railway line over the Bangabandhu Bridge started providing a much faster Dhaka–Rajshahi link. Despite this, travelling by train to Dhaka is certainly a much more relaxing way to go than by the often scary buses. There is one train a day to Dhaka (1st/2nd class Tk 110/80, five hours, departs 4pm).

AROUND MYMENSINGH

To the north, the hill country of the Indian state of Meghalaya beckons in an enticing but unfortunately forbidden way. The area may be divided politically, but culturally it shares a common heritage among the tribal hill people – Mandi (known as Garos across the border in India), Hanjongis and Kochis – all of whom are ethnically distinct from the others around them.

Haluaghat

This is the end of the line, so to speak – the sealed road ends here, but a number of potholed dirt roads take off in various directions for smaller villages along the Indian border. Haluaghat, one of the Mandi tribal centres for the area, is a typical low-slung town less than two hours north of Mymensingh. It is one big market, with vendors selling a variety of rice, dried peppers, and melons in season. Blacksmiths work in small shops next to silversmiths and cloth dealers. You've got to feel for the people of Haluaghat: many must spend their entire lives staring at the hills just over the border, yet never personally get to experience the sensation of climbing a hill! Due to the fact that permits are required to explore anywhere north of Haluaghat, and that the nearby Indian border is closed to foreigners anyway, there is almost no reason to visit this small town.

Buses for Haluaghat (Tk 45, 1½ hours) leave from the bus stand near the Brahmaputra Bridge in Mymensingh.

Muktagacha

The little village of Muktagacha, situated 12km west of Mymensingh on the old Tangail–Dhaka Hwy, has two tourist draws – one cultural and the other dentist-inviting.

The cultural draw is a decaying 300-year-old **rajbari**. Spread over 10 acres, this is a special estate, even in disrepair, bedecked with Corinthian columns, high parapets and floral scrolls in plaster. Inside you'll find a former treasury with the last of 50 safes – a room that the caretaker quaintly describes as the 'finishing room', but is actually a less-quaint execution chamber. The main audience chamber has the remnants of a rotating dance floor, which might well be the precursor of the pole-dancing stage. The Rajeswari temple and the stone temple, believed to be dedicated to Shiva, are two of the finer temples within the complex. Just outside the rajbari are the former stables for the rajbari's 99 elephants. The stables are now occupied by the police, though we don't know if there are 99 of them.

Few locals visit the rajbari, but they do all visit the famous **Gopal Pali Prosida Monda Sweet Shop** (☎ 0902 875383), which makes the best *monda* (grainy, sweetened yogurt cake) in the country. Two hundred years ago the Pal family cooked these delicious sweetmeats for the zamindar (landowner), who liked them so much that he employed the family. When the landowner's family left during Partition, the Pal family opened up shop and have been in business ever since. This isn't just a shop though, oh no! Start thinking of a strait-laced Bordeaux wine chateau and you're on the right track. The tasting room is a delightful faded-yellow room with hard wooden roof beams and a handful of polished tables and chairs. Once safely installed on said chair, a silver plate with a few tasters of *monda* (Tk 10) will be presented to you for your sensual pleasure. It's open all day, everyday.

Coming from Mymensingh on the Tangail road, take the second road leading northeast into Muktagacha. Go down about three blocks and the shop will be on your right. Look for the lion motif over the door.

Madhupur National Park

Home of the beautiful capped langur monkey, wild boar, barking deer and a galaxy of bird species the Madhupur (*mode*-uh-poor) National Park, covering around 8500 hectares, is one of the last remaining patches of old-growth Sal forest left in the country. In addition to it's abundant wildlife, the park also provides a home to the Mandi tribal peoples (see p78) whom you are almost certain to encounter.

This area was once famous for tigers, unfortunately this was during the days when it was thought that tigers looked much better hung on the wall than in the forest, and they have long since been wiped out. Now, explorations of the forest will likely turn up some rhesus macaque, golden-coloured capped langurs and small herds of gorgeous spotted deer. There are also three species of civets here. Madhupur will turn twitchers twitchy as it's one of the country's finest birding locales. There are numerous species, but serious birdwatchers will be most interested in spotting the dusky owl, the brown fish owl, the spotted eagle owl and the famous brown wood owl, which is a speciality of the forest.

For many years the forest was used and abused by all and sundry, and though this continues, things are starting to improve thanks to government investment. For the moment, despite the presence of marked trails on the forest-office brochures, many locals (and forestry workers), citing bandits, will insist that is far too dangerous for you to explore the forest on your own. While there might be some truth to this, it's more likely that they don't want you stumbling into any of the illegal logging operations taking place here.

MANDI ON THE MOVE

Far into the Madhupur National Park, where there are fewer trees, are some small Mandi settlements. The atmosphere of these enclaves is quite distinct from that of Muslim villages. A matrilineal group, the Mandi (or Garo as they are commonly called by outsiders), may have originally migrated from China. The Mandi language is called Achichik Katha and has no written alphabet. Thanks to the efforts of Christian missionaries, most Mandi are now Christians (though they often maintain aspects of their tribal belief, Sangshareq).

Unfortunately for the Mandi, neighbouring Bengalis are slowly encroaching on their lands and cutting down their forests. Accustomed to having their own space, the Mandi are selling off their lands and heading to more remote areas further north. The rate of deforestation is high and poorly paid forestry officials have few resources to stem it.

However, take solace in the fact that though the official walking trials are still effectively off-limits, there is still a decent amount of wildlife to be found just by walking around the main routes (little more than empty mud trails linking up villages). One excellent day walk is the roundtrip from the forest resthouse to the 'zoo' halfway along the Raslpur-Chandar road in the hamlet of Laharina. Don't be put off by the word zoo, as it's more a feeding station for wild animals. The most frequent visitors are the spotted deer and rhesus macaque (who are near enough guaranteed to be hanging around). All up it's a 10km roundtrip walk for which you'll need a guide – ask at the Forest Resthouse.

The **District Forestry Office** (☎ 53524) for Madhupur National Park is in Tangail (p74).

SLEEPING & EATING

Pirgacha Mission (☎ 0171 3003523; Pirgacha village; dm Tk 100) This Christian mission in the small Mandi settlement of Pirgacha has good value dorm beds in traditionally styled mud-walled buildings. Meals are available at very specific times (don't be late!) with advance notice. The complex is run by an elderly American missionary, Father Homerich, who has been here forever and is quite a character.

Forest Resthouse (book through Tangail District Forestry Office ☎ 53524; house Tk 3300) This is a real countryside bolt-hole and a gem of a place to stay. The colonial era bungalow is well-maintained and has large verandas overlooking the forest, a couple of bedrooms (room for four people) and a pleasant sitting room. There are no organised eating options but someone in the nearby village will conjure meals up for you. If you arrive without pre-booking then you'll need to find the caretaker (rarely a problem) who'll sort everything out for you.

GETTING THERE & AWAY

There are frequent buses between Mymensingh and Tangail; take a bus to Pocheesh Mile (Tk 40) which is a little way before Madhupur, and from there hop on the back of a wooden goods rickshaw (Tk 50) to Pirgacha village. The Forest Resthouse is on the same road but a couple of kilometres before the village.

Dhanbari Nawab Palace

Some 15km north of the town of Madhupur is the old **Dhanbari Nawab Palace**. It was originally owned by a Hindu, Dhanwar Khan, but it fell into the hands of Muslims, which explains the presence of a mosque.

The interior of the elegant three-domed mosque, renovated in 1901, is marvellous – the inner walls are covered from floor to ceiling with mural decorations made from broken china pieces.

To get here from the town of Madhupur, take the tarred road north towards Jamalpur and after about 15km you'll see the palace on your right, just off the highway.

Khulna Division

If your idea of adventure is one of unexplored jungle swamps teeming with wildlife as deadly as it is beautiful, then you'll love Khulna division. Comprising in large parts of nothing but marshlands, waterlogged jungles and rivers, this archetypical explorer country is not easy to navigate, but it promises unlikely stories you'll be recounting for years to come. Imagine telling your friends of how you travelled by paddle-wheel steamer to secret villages where men fish with tame otters, and where steel masks are worn to provide protection from tiger attacks. Imagine their faces when you talk of crocodiles being hand-fed chickens in the grounds of a moody mosque, or of helping to steal honey from the hives of giant killer bees. Think of their surprise when you tell them you spoke with a guru who could cure illnesses through nothing but faith and a magic touch, and of a saint who sang his way to the throne of God.

Magical Khulna division is unquestionably the highlight of Bangladesh, so get out and explore!

KHULNA DIVISION

HIGHLIGHTS

- Keeping a nervous eye out for tigers while drifting through the surreal **Sundarbans** (p92), the world's largest mangrove forest

- Casting a line with the **fishing otters** (p82) of the Narail and Gopalganj areas

- Singing and dancing your way to religious ecstasy in the backwater town of **Kushtia** (p83)

- Wishing you had a suit of armour in the race to find the world's most dangerous **honey** (p94)

- Searching for crocodiles among the treasure-trove mosques of **Bagerhat** (p88)

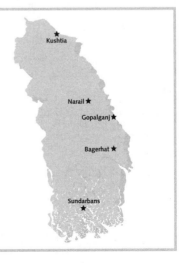

★ Kushtia

★ Narail
Gopalganj ★

Bagerhat ★

Sundarbans ★

JESSORE
☎ 0421

Standing close to the bold and brash gates of India, many travellers arriving from Kolkata bring with them a haughty notion that Bangladesh will be little more than India's vaguely entertaining side-kick. But give them two hours and such silly notions are utterly shattered – and the amazing thing about this transformation is that Jessore, like many Bangladeshi towns, has no real tourist sights. Rather, its attractions are all in the exotic and chaotic atmosphere and in the web of narrow winding backstreets overcrowded with possible adventures.

There's a **Cybercafé** (High Court Rd) at the western end of town, but no ATM.

Sleeping

BUDGET

Hotel Mid-Town (☎ 01711 940160; MK Rd; s/d from Tk 135/200) A strict hotel with a list of rules a mile long including a no-woman policy, which is a shame because it could do with a bit of a female touch. If you're a bloke on a tight budget then it'll do for a night or so. The hotel is visible from MK Rd but accessed just off it.

Grand Hotel (☎ 73038; grand@khulna.bangla.net; MK Rd; s/d Tk 150/400) This budget hotel is managed like a midrange one and is the best budget base in Jessore. You enter the rooms through red theatre curtains and discover carefully looked after rooms and the sort of boisterous welcome worthy of the theatre. Both men and women are welcome.

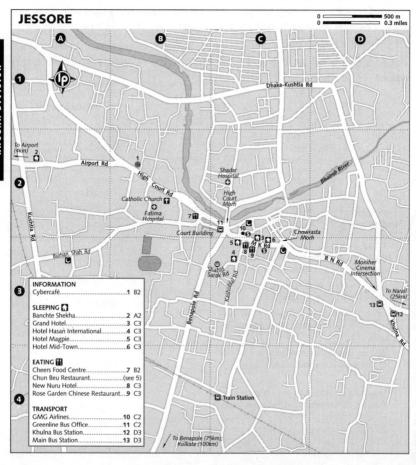

INFORMATION
Cybercafé.....................................1 B2

SLEEPING
Banchte Shekha............................2 A2
Grand Hotel..................................3 C3
Hotel Hasan International..............4 C3
Hotel Magpie................................5 C3
Hotel Mid-Town...........................6 C3

EATING
Cheers Food Centre.......................7 B2
Chun Beu Restaurant...............(see 5)
New Nuru Hotel.............................8 C3
Rose Garden Chinese Restaurant...9 C3

TRANSPORT
GMG Airlines................................10 C2
Greenline Bus Office......................11 C2
Khulna Bus Station........................12 D3
Main Bus Station...........................13 D3

LEARNING HOW TO SURVIVE Heather Butler

The Banchte Shekha Foundation (Learn How to Survive) was founded in 1975 by Angela Gomez, a non-Muslim teacher who, touched by the mistreatment of women in Bangladesh, endured death threats while trying to set up education and health centres for women and children (see bleow). She works directly with the villagers, encouraging them to empower women. Her efforts have earned her the Asia Nobel Prize.

Hotel Magpie (☎ 72162; MK Rd; s/d Tk 250/500) If it weren't for the crazy road noise then this would be a real find. It's bright, well lit, clean and friendly. For budget hotel prices you get midrange standards.

There are some more budget options near the bus station at the east end of town, on Khulna Rd.

MIDRANGE

our pick **Banchte Shekha** (☎ 66436/68885; Shaheed Mashiur Rahman Rd just off Airport Rd; r Tk 300-800) Just east of the bypass road to Benapole, Banchte Shekha (*bach*-tah *shay*-kah) is surrounded only by the noise of leaves blowing in the breeze and chirping birds. You could be forgiven for thinking this is just a cheap hotel, but make no mistake, this place is something special. It is in fact a small, local NGO-run women's training centre/hotel and your money goes directly towards funding its aid projects (see boxed text, above). The rooms are basic but more than adequate and come with hot showers, satellite TV and clean sheets smelling of mothballs. For single women travellers, this almost completely female-run establishment is a dream. If you let staff know in advance, you can share the family-style meals for a small fee. It's true that there are more luxurious hotels in Bangladesh, but Banchte Shekha is deserving of the 'Our Pick' selection, and your custom.

Hotel Hasan International (☎ 67478; cnr Kashoblal & Shahid Sarak Rds; s/d Tk 700/1200, ste Tk 2000-2500) On the surface, it's the best city centre hotel with large rooms, hot water and satellite TV, but thanks to some serious road noise and staff who haven't learnt how to smile, it won't be winning awards any time soon.

Eating

The K'Purti Rd area is a great place for street food, fresh produce and a carnival-like atmosphere.

Cheers Food Centre (High Court Rd; mains Tk 30) A new, shiny-orange snack bar modelled along Western lines with a variety of fried and unhealthy, but undeniably tasty, snacks of the burger ilk.

New Nuru Hotel (MK Rd; mains Tk 80) The unchallenged curry king of Jessore, but the fiery kebabs are also worthy of mention. Be prepared for some relentless staring.

Rose Garden Chinese Restaurant (Jess Tower, MK Rd; dishes around Tk 180) All your favourite (or by this stage in the game, possibly not) Bengali Chinese dishes. It's tucked away on the upper floors of a small shopping centre.

Chun Beu Restaurant (4th fl, Hotel Magpie, MK Rd; soup Tk 100, mains Tk 250) A rare, authentic Chinese restaurant with a casual atmosphere helped along nicely by the equally casual blue-and-white checked tablecloths. It's ideal for a go-slow meal with friends.

Getting There & Away

AIR

The airport is around 6km and a Tk 100 rickshaw ride west of the city centre.

GMG Airlines (☎ 73280; RS Tower) flies from Jessore to Dhaka (Tk 2770, 40 minutes) daily at 8.50am and 5.25pm (Saturday 3.55pm). **United Airways** (☎ 171 3398783; at the airport) has flights to Dhaka (Tk 2645) every day except Friday.

BUS

From Dhaka, buses for Jessore leave from Gabtali bus station (p67).

Buses leave for Dhaka (ordinary/air-con coach Tk 230/325, seven to 10 hours, 6am to 10.30pm). There are also super deluxe coaches (whatever that might be) for Tk 475 from the main bus station. Several companies have offices around the main bus station.

There are buses for Benapole (Tk 30, 1½ hours, periodically from 6am), also from the main bus station, and if you're headed to Kolkata count on about six hours for the entire trip.

There are also buses to Khulna (Tk 50, 1½ hours), Bogra (Tk 220, eight hours), Kushtia (Tk 100, three hours) and a hundred other places.

TRAIN

The **train station** (☎ 5019; Rail Rd) is 2km south of the central area. There's an express to Rajshahi (1st/*sulob* class Tk 215/75, daily at 7.59am).

It's simpler to travel by bus on the short journey to Khulna, although there is an inter-city (IC) train (1st/*sulob* class Tk 85/35, 1½ hours, daily at 12.30pm).

There is also a daily train to Benapole (Tk 20, 8.50am).

AROUND JESSORE

Baro Bazar Mosque

This pre-Mughal mosque, dating from the 15th or early-16th century, is a good example of a single-domed mosque with thick walls, arched doorways, a square shape, sparse exterior embellishment and a low semicircular dome. Not well-known by the locals, it's about 18km northeast of Jessore on the Jessore–Magura Hwy at Baro Bazar.

Sonabaria Temple

The Sonabaria Shyam Sundar Temple, built in 1767, is similar in style to Kantanagar Temple (p111). Like Kantanagar, it's a simple square structure, rising in three diminishing storeys, and extensively decorated with terracotta art. It's only about half the size though, and not as beautiful or well preserved.

As the crow flies, it's about 30km south-west of Jessore, near the Indian border. To get there from Jessore, take the road west towards Benapole for 25km to the tiny village of Navaron (about two-thirds the distance

to Benapole), where you'll find a country road heading south. It's about 15km along that road.

BENAPOLE

Benapole (also spelt Benapol) is the border town situated on the overland route from Kolkata. The town is essentially a 2km-long road lined with trucks waiting to cross the border. It's a friendly enough place, but not one you'd visit unless you were crossing the border.

If you've arrived at a reasonable time, it's probably best to spend your first night in Jessore. Failing that, there is some accommodation in Benapole – the **Parjatan Hotel** (r with/without air-con Tk 1000/600, ste Tk 1500) has large, clean suites that for some reason have two bathrooms and two bedrooms. Bickering couples will find it perfect!

There are a number of cheap **restaurants** with meals from around Tk 40.

Minibuses ply the route between Benapole and Jessore (Tk 30, 1½ hours). Ask for both 'Benapole' and 'border' to avoid confusion. The word 'India' may also come in handy.

OTTER FISHING VILLAGES

Human beings are a resourceful and enterprising lot, and over the centuries we've come up with all manner of weird and wonderful machines to help make life that little bit easier. Often though you just can't beat good old Mother Nature for pure design brilliance. In riverside villages in the **Narail** and **Gopalganj**

CROSSING THE BORDER

Border officials see quite a few travellers crossing at Benapole and things are relatively efficient. The border is open every day between 6am and 6.30pm.

Some travellers who've arrived in Bangladesh by air have been asked for a 'change of route' permit when trying to leave by land. These can be obtained for free at the Immigration and Passport Office (p167).

Changing Money

If you're coming into Bangladesh, be sure to have cash on you, as you'll be hard-pressed changing travellers cheques and the nearest ATM is in Khulna.

Entering & Exiting

Travelling from the railway station at Bangaon in India to the border costs Rs 50 by baby taxi (mini auto-rickshaw). Take a rickshaw or three-wheeler cart to the bus stand in Benapole (between Tk 10 and Tk 20). From here you can get a local bus to Jessore (Tk 30, 1½ hours).

If you're going into India, from Bangaon you can take the cheap and cheerful local train to Kolkata.

OF OTTERS AND MEN

Fishing with otters has been taking place for at least 1000 years and was once fairly widespread across the world; in the UK it didn't die out until 1880. There are two techniques employed by the fishermen; one involves the otters individually catching fish and returning them to the fishermen while the other (and the technique employed in Bangladesh) involves a net being lowered into the water and 'shuffled' along the river bed or against clumps of water plants to disturb the fish which the otters then chase into the net. On good nights the otters can help catch up to 50kg of fish, which can net the fishermen a not insignificant US$50 to US$60 a day. This makes skilled otters valuable possessions, and a pair of fishing otters can exchange hands for over US$100.

Whatever you do, don't try and cuddle them. Otters are powerful and aggressive and in 1992 a group of otters killed a fisherman in India!

---

areas (a couple of hours east of Jessore), the local fishermen know this and instead of using sea-bed devastating drag nets and other such fishing 'marvels', they've stuck with a technique that died out elsewhere in the world eons ago. Each night small groups of fishermen pile into little wooden boats and set out to catch fish using the ultimate fishing machine – the otter (see also boxed text, p84).

With a little patience, it's possible to visit the villages the fishermen live in and even go out fishing with them and their furry friends, but be warned it's not an easy task for independent travellers. However if you manage it this might well turn out to be one of your most memorable experiences in Bangladesh.

To get there, first take a bus from Khulna or Jessore to Noapra (Tk 15), a small riverside town. From here hop into a little passenger ferry (Tk 2) over the river and then take a tempo (auto-rickshaw) to the village of Gobra (Tk 20). Once in Gobra village, you must take a rickshaw or baby taxi to Singasolhur village and finally another little ferry to the tiny village of Hariar.

This is where the otter fishermen live, but don't worry if you get hopelessly lost and end up elsewhere as many of the riverside villages in these parts engage in otter fishing and most people will quickly grasp what you want to do. Even so, only about three or four tourists a year visit these villages and nobody speaks anything other than Bengali so trying to discuss anything of significance will be difficult. Note also that there is nowhere to stay or eat around here and the journey from Jessore or Khulna on public transport is likely to take all day. The hospitality of the villagers is such that you probably wouldn't be left to sleep on the street, but don't rely on them.

The real business of fishing takes place at night so you will probably have to rouse the fishermen and otters from their sleep and arrange an hour or two out on the river (for most people this is sufficient). There is no set fee for this but be generous in what you give – Tk 800 to Tk 1000 between two of you should be fine.

An easier, though undeniably less adventurous, alternative is to arrange a car and driver through one of the tour companies in Khulna. **Guide Tours** (☎ /fax 731 384; www.guidetours.com; KDA Bldg, KDA Ave, Khulna) can supply a car and the excellent, English-speaking Mr Shaheentoor, who knows the fishermen well. It can also arrange an overnight boat ride from Khulna, which is a superb way to get there. All these tours are customised and the price varies, but expect to pay around Tk 45,000 for a day-long road trip.

KUSHTIA
☎ 071

Kushtia is a bustling town just south of Rajshahi division, but largely in the middle of nowhere. At first sight it may appear an unlikely spot in which to find a living guru, and the shrine of a saintly man with a sweet voice and a sensible view on life, but then this is one of the poorest areas in the country, so maybe they did choose appropriately.

Sights
SHRINE OF LALON SHAH
The burning white shrine of Lalon Shah is, for most Bangladeshis, the first and only reason for visiting Kushtia and come they do, in their hundreds. Lalon Shah is one of the most famous holy men in Bangladesh (see p85) and his shrine is a fascinating peak into

a mystical side of Bangladeshi life, and proof that Islam here isn't as straight-laced as it may at first appear. The shrine centres on the holy man's tomb and that of his adopted parents, while around the perimeter of the shrine are the tombs of various local dignitaries. Behind the tomb complex is a covered area where musicians continually play and sing Lalon Shah's songs, and pilgrims sometimes burst into dance.

Outside the shrine complex are numerous stalls selling a variety of holiday tack and pan-religious knick-knacks, including small talismans, Christian crucifixes and Hindu tridents. Next to the shrine is a private house, used as a sometimes-home to an important guru who is reputed to be able to cure illnesses through faith and touch. If he is around you have a good chance of being invited in to meet him and his disciples.

In February/March and October, huge melas (festivals) take place here, attracting thousands of pilgrims, itinerant vendors and holy men from across the subcontinent.

The shrine is a Tk 15 rickshaw ride from the town.

TAGORE LODGE

It's a worthwhile trip to **Tagore Lodge**, as much for the journey there as for the lodge itself. A ride to the lodge on a three-wheeler affords the privilege of witnessing village life candidly unfold in front of you.

This picturesque home was built in the mid-19th century and the famous Bengali poet Rabindranath Tagore lived here for over 10 years from 1880, composing some of his immortal poems, songs and short stories. He returned in 1912 for several years, translating his works into English and earning the Nobel Prize for Literature (1913) in the process.

The estate is on the south bank of the Padma River, outside Shelaidaha, east of Kushtia. To get here, cross the Gorai River then hire a three-wheeler to take you the remaining 8km to the lodge. The cart should cost about Tk 150 return if you bargain successfully.

Opening hours depend on what the groundskeeper feels like doing, but if you rock up at a sensible time you'll generally be able to have a look.

Sleeping & Eating

Hotel Al-Amin (☎ 54193; Nawab Sirajuddula Rd; s from Tk 200, d with air-con Tk 550; ❄) It's not certain whether foreigners can stay here or not, but persistence normally pays off. The rooms, though not palatial, are clean and that's what counts. It's on the main drag.

Azmiree Hotel (☎ 53012; 107/1 RCRC Rd, Court Para; s with/without air-con Tk 230/180, d with/without air-con Tk 750/280; ❄) The old Azmiree (aj-mee-ree) has some impressively clean rooms and shutters that look as though they could withstand a siege. It's given some gentle touches with the addition of desks and chairs, and is the hotel most likely to accept foreigners. It's poorly marked so you'll have to ask directions near the train station.

There are the usual local eateries, the best of which is the **Jangail Hotel**. A renowned sweet shop, **Dodhi Bhander**, can be found on the way to the shrine. Its milk-based desserts and sweets are as superb as local opinion holds.

Getting There & Away

Coming into Kushtia, you'll likely be dropped off on a main road away from the main

---

MR RATAN – OTTER FISHERMAN

I have been fishing with otters for over 30 years now. There are around 200 otter fishermen in this area and this is the only part of Bangladesh where people fish with them. Winter nights at low tide are the best time to go as this is when the most fish are around, but the fish levels have been dropping over the last 20 years and now it's not easy to make a living from otter fishing. We take our fish to the village depot and from there they are sold to markets all over Bangladesh.

I learnt to fish like this from my father but I am not teaching it to my children as there isn't enough money in it and I want them to go to school instead.

Sometimes the otters are caught in the wild and trained, but other times they breed and the baby otters learn from their parents. It takes about a year for a baby otter to learn how to fish with us. I have three otters at the moment – a couple and their baby who is still learning to fish. We never handle our otters as they can bite.

Mr Ratan is an otter fisherman from the village of Hariar

THE SINGING SAINT

No one is quite certain when or where Lalon Shah was born. He claimed to have merely 'arrived' and certainly his discovery (aged 16, and suffering from smallpox, he was found by a local farmer floating in the river near Kushtia) lends credence to his claim that he 'came from water'. As the boy recovered, it became clear that he was posessed of great wisdom and he quickly attracted many followers.

Lalon was a humanist and vehemently opposed to all distinctions of religion and caste (throughout his long life he said nothing of the time before his discovery and nobody has ever been able to prove whether he came from an Islamic or Hindu background), though he often spoke positively on aspects of all religions. Instead he encouraged people to look 'into themselves' for answers and, being a talented poet and musician, he used music to get his messages across.

Lalon died in 1890 around the ripe old age of 116.

---

drag. It might be worth getting a rickshaw to Nawab Sirajuddula Rd so you can get your bearings.

The bus ride to Jessore (Tk 75, three hours) can be punctuated with stops, but the roads are reasonably well maintained.

There are a few luxury coach companies on Babar Rd, at College Gate, that service Dhaka (Tk 200 to Tk 300, 6½ hours).

KHULNA
☎ 041

Khulna, capital of the province, is a town on the frontier. Beyond its scraggly streets awaits a Boys Own range of extraordinary adventures that, for many travellers, are the sole reason for coming to Bangladesh. Though the town itself offers few tangible sights, this frontier sensation hangs heavy in the air and only the most jaded of travellers won't feel a flutter of excitement as they disembark from the bus or the boat that carries them here.

Orientation & Information

Most of the cheap hotels and restaurants are located in the city's heart. Khan A Sabar Rd, also known as Jessore Rd, is the main drag through the city, and KDA Ave is the major thoroughfare on the western side.

Bengal Tours (☎ 724 355; 236 Khan Jahan Ali Rd)
Cafe.net (2/2 Babu Khan Rd; per hr Tk 30) A cyber café that actually has a café.
Guide Tours (☎ /fax 731 384; www.guidetours.com; KDA Bldg, KDA Ave)
Hotel Royal International (☎ 721 638/9; royal@bttb .net.bd; 33 KDA Ave) General tourist information and car rentals. Also does package tours to the Sundarbans.
New Market (Upper Jessore Rd; per hr Tk 20) The best place for internet access, with a few different establish-

ments on the 1st floor. New Market is also a great place to shop; the environment is pressure-free and prices are fixed.
Standard Chartered Bank (KDA Ave) Changes money and has an ATM; near Shiv Bari Circle.

Sights & Activities

There are few physical sights in Khulna, but the **old town** streets, centred on the riverfront and Helatala Rd, are an energetic mish-mash designed to confuse and inspire the senses. From the ghats (steps or landings) down by the waterfront, you won't have to struggle to find someone to take you out in a small boat for a half-hour people-watching session along the river (Tk 100 to Tk 150 should be ample).

If you've got some time to kill before a boat or bus departure, the small collection of objects garnered from around Bagerhat and on display at the **Divisional Museum** (admission Tk 50; ☯ 2.30-6pm Mon, 10am-1pm & 1.30-6pm Tue-Thu & Sat, 12.30-6pm Fri Apr-Sep, 1.30-5pm Mon, 9am-1pm & 1.30-5pm Tue-Thu & Sat, 9am-12.30pm & 2-5pm Fri Oct-Mar) should help pass half an hour or so. Opposite the Hotel Jalico is a large **Hindu temple** (Sir Iqbal Rd) dedicated to Shiva, in which colour and incense are virtually compulsory.

For information about Sundarbans tours, see p94.

Sleeping
BUDGET

Khulna's cheap hotels are concentrated in the heart of the city in an area 1km south of the train station. Most are well marked in English.

Society Hotel (☎ 720 995; Helatala Rd; s/d 50/80 deluxe s/d Tk 80/130) The brightly painted and well-tended rooms make this one of the city's best value cheapies. Unusually for a bottom-end

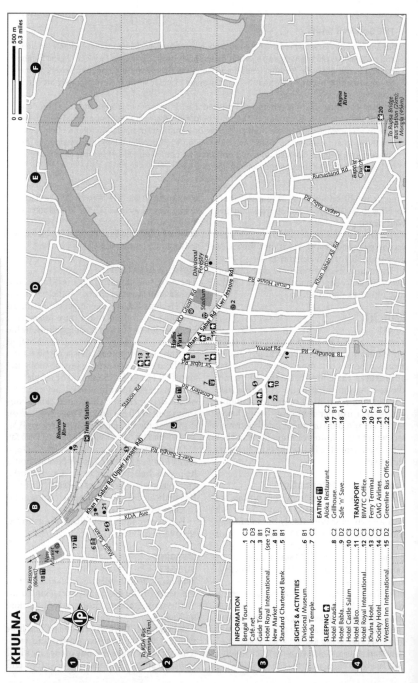

KHULNA

0 _____ 500 m
0 _____ 0.3 miles

INFORMATION
Bengal Tours.............................1 C3
Café.net...................................2 D3
Guide Tours..............................3 B1
Hotel Royal International...........(see 12)
New Market..............................4 B1
Standard Chartered Bank...........5 B1

SIGHTS & ACTIVITIES
Divisional Museum.....................6 B1
Hindu Temple............................7 C2

SLEEPING
Hotel Arcadia............................8 C2
Hotel Babia...............................9 D2
Hotel Castle Salam...................10 C3
Hotel Jalico..............................11 C2
Hotel Royal International...........12 C3
Khulna Hotel.............................13 C2
Society Hotel............................14 C2
Western Inn International...........15 D2

EATING
Aloka Restaurant......................16 C2
Grillhouse................................17 B1
Safe 'n' Save...........................18 A1

TRANSPORT
BIWTC Office............................19 C1
Ferry Terminal..........................20 F4
GMG Airlines.............................21 B1
Greenline Bus Office.................22 C3

hotel, the English-speaking staff are happy to see you. It's in a colourful neighbourhood.

Khulna Hotel (☎ 724 359; s/d Tk 120/150, ste Tk 500) Larger rooms than at the Society Hotel but because it's dirtier, it's the inferior option.

Hotel Arcadia (☎ 732 552; Khan A Sabar Rd; s/d Tk 250/350) Excellent value budget rooms with – are you ready for this – brand new, unsullied bedding! The rooms are small but well kept and the bathrooms have sit-down toilets, which is rare for this price range.

MIDRANGE
Hotel Babla (☎ 813 641; 65 Khan A Sabar Rd; s/d Tk 200/450, d with air-con Tk 600; ✷) The clean Hotel Babla has character, both in its uneven architecture and in its English- and German-speaking manager. It's something of a backpacker hang-out, but is a little difficult to find as its sign is in Bengali.

Hotel Jalico (☎ 811 883; Sir Iqbal Rd; s/d Tk 500/700, ste Tk 1600) This central hotel is large enough to ensure that there are always rooms available and when you get inside said rooms, you will find them equally large, with shiny, tiled floors and soft furniture. Some also have good views over the city. The management is charming and speaks some English. Add 15% tax for suite rates.

TOP END
Western Inn International (☎ 733 191; western@bttb.net.bd; 51 Khan A Sabur Rd; r from Tk 800, ste from Tk 1600) The garish, flashing Christmas-tree lights covering the outside of the building may not inspire much confidence, but once inside you will find one of the ritziest places in town, and the best value for its type. The Western Inn is extremely professional in its service and outlook. The very good attached restaurant is also a big plus. Add 5% tax for suite rates.

Hotel Royal International (☎ 721 638/9; royal@bttb.net.bd; 33 KDA Ave; s/d from Tk 800-950) If '70s disco is your favourite music then the décor at the Royal will please. The all-in-one desk/table/window combo in the rooms are especially funky and you can't fault the price. The service is pretty lacklustre though. There's a travel agency in the lobby where you can make arrangements for car rental and guided trips to the Sundarbans.

Hotel Castle Salam (☎ 730 725; castle@khulnanet.net; cnr Khan Jahan Ali Rd & KDA Ave; r Tk 960-1200) The boudoir red rooms of the Castle Salam vie with those of the Western Inn for king-of-the-castle status and offer good value for money. The service is warm and friendly and the staff keen for a chat. The lobby contains a display of cricket bats signed by the members of the respective national cricket teams who stayed here during the World Cup.

Eating
Aloka Restaurant (☎ 733 342; 1 Khan A Sabar Rd; mains Tk 60) We think this place is simply lovely and we're not the only ones. Locals flock here to gorge on a feast of quality Bangladeshi fare.

Grillhouse (☎ 730 245; New Market; mains Tk 150) Widely considered the best restaurant in Khulna, the locals rave about the kebabs and Chinese dishes (which form the bulk of the menu) at the Grillhouse, near New Market. There are also a few Indian and European dishes thrown in to leaven the mix. Be warned that the orange juice has salt mixed with it – apparently to improve the flavour of bad oranges! Fortunately the food doesn't need much improvement.

Safe 'n' Save (New Market; ☷ 9am-6pm) This supermarket is a good place to stock up on snacks and more before a Sundarbans adventure.

For really cheap food, head for the food stalls around the train station.

Getting There & Away
AIR
The nearest airport is at Jessore. **GMG Airlines** (☎ 732 273) provides a direct bus service (about one hour) between Jessore airport and their Khulna office.

BOAT
The **Bangladesh Inland Waterway Transport Corporation** (BIWTC; ☎ 721 532) office looks like a small house. It's just behind the train station and opens every day at around 9am.

Between Khulna and Dhaka there are six Rockets (1st/2nd/deck class Tk 1010/610/150) per week in each direction. They stop at Mongla (1st/2nd/deck class Tk 140/80/15), Barisal (1st/2nd/deck class Tk 530/310/70) and several smaller ports. Reserve several days in advance to ensure a 1st-class cabin.

Departures from Khulna are scheduled at 3am, though there can be delays.

BUS
The main bus station is **KDA bus terminal** (also known as Sonadanga bus terminal), 2km

KHULNA DIVISION

northwest of the city centre. A rickshaw costs about Tk 10 from the city centre and Tk 20 from the Rupsa ghat. Inside KDA terminal, bus companies servicing common destinations are grouped in the same area. The station serves all points except Mongla and Bagerhat; for these two towns you have a choice of either catching a bus from the new bus station on the southern edge of town (near the new bridge) or taking a little ferry over the Rupsa river (Tk 2) and catching one from there.

Buses headed to Mongla (Tk 35, one hour) and Bagerhat (Tk 30, 45 minutes) depart throughout the day.

Country buses to Dhaka (Tk 280, 7½ hours) depart throughout the day. **Greenline Buses**, just along the road from Hotel Castle Salam, charges between Tk 525 and Tk 775 depending on the class.

Buses for Barisal (Tk 250) mostly leave in the early morning and early evening, while buses for Jessore (Tk 50 to Tk 60, one hour) leave frequently until the early evening.

CAR
You can rent a car and driver through **Guide Tours** (☎ /fax 731 384; www.guidetours.com; KDA Bldg, KDA Ave) or **Bengal Tours** (☎ 724 355; 236 Khan Jahan Ali Rd) but at an average of Tk 4000 to Tk 4500 per day it isn't cheap. On the plus side, the drivers are excellent.

TRAIN
The main **train station** (☎ 723 222) is near the city centre. There are four IC trains a day to Jessore (1st/*sulob* class Tk 85/30, 1½ hours) and three mail trains, which also take passengers but are slower. The 6.30am IC express continues on to Rajshahi (1st/*sulob* class Tk 255/125, 6½ hours), and the 7.50am express goes to Saidpur (1st/*sulob* class Tk 355/170, nine hours).

There's a night train to Dhaka (1st/*sulob* class Tk 625/235, 11 hours, departs 10pm), though buses are preferable given the disruptive need to switch trains en route.

BAGERHAT
☎ 401

Unesco-protected Bagerhat, with its treasure-trove of historical monuments, will send a shiver of excitement down the spines of archaeology buffs. Hidden among the green folds of the surrounding countryside are more ancient mosques and mausoleums than anywhere else in Bangladesh (except Dhaka), but the crowning jewel of this fabulously little-known collection is the Shait Gumbad Mosque – a multi-domed medieval masterpiece.

The creators of such buildings also understood the value of good scenery and the tranquil countryside, full of tropical trees, ponds and birds, is a joy to walk through.

Bagerhat was also home to one of the most revered men in Bangladeshi history, Khan Jahan Ali (see opposite), and is a significant cradle of Islam in Bangladesh.

The town lacks decent hotels and restaurants, so it's sensible to visit Bagerhat as a day trip from Khulna or Mongla.

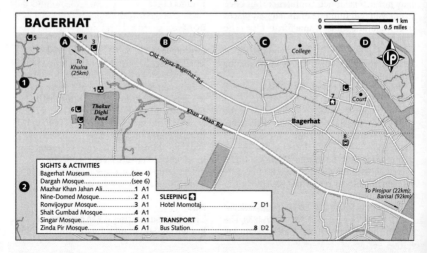

BAGERHAT

To Khulna (25km)

College

Court

Bagerhat

To Pirojpur (22km); Barisal (92km)

0 ——— 1 km
0 ——— 0.5 miles

SIGHTS & ACTIVITIES
Bagerhat Museum.............................(see 4)
Dargah Mosque.................................(see 6)
Mazhar Khan Jahan Ali.......................1 A1
Nine-Domed Mosque.........................2 A1
Ronvijoypur Mosque..........................3 A1
Shait Gumbad Mosque.......................4 A1
Singar Mosque...................................5 A1
Zinda Pir Mosque...............................6 A1

SLEEPING
Hotel Momotaj..................................7 D1

TRANSPORT
Bus Station..8 D2

KHAN JAHAN ALI

Khan Jahan Ali was a Sufi (a Muslim mystic, the counterpart of the Hindu sadhus or Indian yogis) from Turkey who settled in Bagerhat in the middle of the 15th century after decades of wandering and learning.

Upon arriving in Bagerhat with thousands of horsemen, clearing the jungle and founding Khalifatabad (as the town was originally named), this warrior-saint quickly initiated a huge construction programme. He adorned his capital city with an incredible number of mosques, bridges, brick-paved highways, palaces and other public buildings. Large ponds of water with staircase landings were built in various parts of the township to provide salt-free drinking water in this predominantly saline belt.

When he died, a mausoleum was raised to his memory, which you can still see standing, along with some of the major mosques. Today Khan Jahan Ali is the patron saint of the area and his name equates with a major pre-Mughal architectural style in Bangladesh.

Sights

The principal 15th-century mosques are in one large area 5km west of Bagerhat.

BAGERHAT MUSEUM

This small and neatly arranged **museum** (joint admission to museum & Shait Gumbad Mosque Tk 50; ⊙ 2.30-6pm Mon, 10am-1pm & 1.30-6pm Tue-Thu & Sat, 10am-12.30pm & 2.30-6pm Fri Apr-Sep, 1.30-5pm Mon, 9am-1pm & 1.30-5pm Tue-Thu & Sat, 9am-12.30pm & 2-5pm Fri Oct-Mar) is located opposite the Shait Gumbad Mosque. It contains relics from the surrounding area and is a good place to get your bearings before setting out to explore Bagerhat.

MOSQUES

Built in 1459, the same year Khan Jahan Ali died, the famous **Shait Gumbad Mosque** is the largest and most magnificent traditional mosque in the country. Shait Gumbad means 'the Temple with 60 Domes' – a misnomer given that there are actually 77. This fortress-like structure has unusually thick walls, built in the tapering brick fashion known as Tughlaq, and is an impressive sight.

Around Shait Gumbad are three other smaller, but equally worthy, mosques, all single-domed and in reasonably good condition. These are **Bibi Begni's Mosque**, which has some interesting floral motifs and is located about 500m behind Shait Gumbad and across a large pond; the bulbous **Chunakhola Mosque**, in a paddy field about 500m behind Bibi Begni's; and **Singar Mosque**, across the highway from Shait Gumbad.

On the western bank of the Thakur Dighi Pond, the recently repaired **Nine-Domed Mosque** is an impressive structure. The mihrabs (niches) are embellished with terracotta floral scrolls and foliage motifs, with a prominent chain-and-bell terracotta motif in the centre.

You might also want to check out the tumbledown **Zinda Pir Mosque** just north of the Nine-Domed Mosque.

About 2km east of Shait Gumbad is the splendid **Ronvijoypur Mosque**. It is singularly impressive, with the largest dome in Bangladesh, spanning 11m and supported by 3m-thick walls.

MAZHAR KHAN JAHAN ALI

Khan Jahan's Tomb is the only monument in Bagerhat that retains its original cupolas (domed ceilings). The cenotaph at the entrance is covered with tiles of various colours and inscribed with Quranic verses, but it is usually covered with a red cloth embroidered with gold threads. The mausoleum and the single-domed **Dargah Mosque** are enclosed by a massive wall with short towers at each corner and archways on the front and back. It's a popular pilgrimage site and therefore has a little more colour and flair than some of the other monuments around here. The pond out front has a couple of crocodiles lurking in its depths which get regular chicken dinners from the site caretaker.

KHODLA MATH TEMPLE

The 20m-high spire on this extraordinary beehive-like **Hindu building** makes it one of the tallest Hindu structures ever built in Bangladesh and a must see. It was built by a Brahman in the early-17th century. The entrance façade is thought to have originally been decorated with moulded terracotta art, but it's now badly weathered.

Khodla Math is just outside the village of Ayodhya, about 11km from Bagerhat. Take a rickshaw or baby taxi to the market town of Jatrapur. From there ask directions to Ayodhya, 3km east along winding, paved paths.

Sleeping & Eating

Pickings are slim on the sleeping front.

Hotel Momotaj (Rail Rd; r Tk 200) A very basic lodging – not only are the rooms only for the most hard core, but they're also highly overpriced. There are a couple of other similar places nearby.

There are some equally basic local **restaurants** and street stalls along the main road.

Getting There & Away

BUS

The bus from Khulna (Tk 30, 45 minutes) takes you through some enchanting countryside. The bus passes Shait Gumbad (5km before town) on the left, where you can disembark and start sightseeing.

If you're headed to Mongla, it may be faster to take a bus to the Khulna–Mongla Rd intersection and hail another bus there. You may have to stand, but the 33km trip from the intersection takes less than an hour. Buses from Khulna headed east to Pirojpur and Barisal also pass through Bagerhat, but finding a seat might be difficult.

CAR

You can organise a hire car from Khulna to take you to and around Bagerhat (see p88). The bus ride is an easy one though, and it's the sort of scenery in which you don't mind being delayed.

Getting Around

From the bus station, hire a rickshaw for a few hours to take you to the various sights and back to the bus terminal. You could start the bidding (and may be successful) at around Tk 70, but when you see the narrow bumpy roads that inflict wear and tear on the rickshaw, you may feel like upping the price.

MONGLA
☎ 04658

At its core Mongla, 42km south of Khulna, is nothing more than a single, sandy street and it can be hard to believe that the town is actually a major port. For many years Mongla has been plagued with that curse of ports the world over – a reputation for danger and seediness. This is a largely unfounded reputation and most people you meet here will go out of their way to help you have a good time.

The Sundarbans begins only 5km south from here.

Sights & Activities

BOAT TRIPS

At the outset, it's worth saying that despite Mongla's proximity to the Sundarbans National Park, if you really want to explore and appreciate the forest in any depth then Khulna is the better place from which to organise a **boat trip**. If, however, you just want a cheap and cheerful day trip then Mongla is the place to start.

In recent years, the forestry department has banned any independent boats from Mongla (and other towns) from taking tourists on overnight trips into the Sundarbans. This rule was brought in after a couple of nasty incidents involving lost boats. Nowadays, no matter what boatmen in Mongla may tell you, the only way to travel independently into the Sundarbans from Mongla is on a day trip to the **Karamjal Forest Station**. With raised walkways, viewing platforms and a small 'zoo' it's hardly the back of beyond, but surprisingly in recent years it's been one of the best places to see a tiger thanks to a lone cat that has developed a taste for chilling out in the vicinity.

In the past, many travellers reported bad experiences in the form of hostile negotiations, overcharging and/or failure to deliver on what was promised when organising a trip from Mongla, but the introduction of new regulations seem to have gone someway to reducing these. Even so, when you're shopping around for quotes, be clear on what is included in the price, where the boat will go and how long it will go for. Don't pay everything up front.

A day trip can costs between Tk 2000 and Tk 4000, depending on what's included, the length of time and your bargaining skills. Note that you do not need permits to visit Karamjal.

There are some good operators in Mongla – **Jahangir Enterprises** (☎ 880 04658 566/513), **Mr Emdad** (☎ 0171 6079829) and **Mr Sobhan** (no phone – ask for him at the Hotel Bangkok) have been recommended.

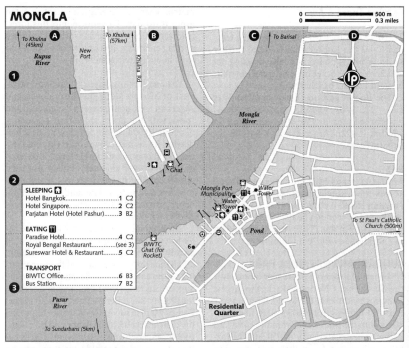

MONGLA

```
                                                    0          500 m
                                                    0          0.3 miles
```

To Khulna (45km) A | To Khulna (57km) B | C To Barisal | D

Rupsa River
New Port
Khulna Rd
Mongla River

SLEEPING
Hotel Bangkok.............................1 C2
Hotel Singapore..........................2 C2
Parjatan Hotel (Hotel Pashur)........3 B2

EATING
Paradise Hotel.............................4 C2
Royal Bengal Restaurant...............(see 3)
Sureswar Hotel & Restaurant........5 C2

TRANSPORT
BIWTC Office................................6 B3
Bus Station.................................7 B2

Mongla Port Municipality
Water Tower
Water Tower
Pond

To St Paul's Catholic Church (500m)

BIWTC Ghat (for Rocket)

Pusur River

Residential Quarter

To Sundarbans (5km)

KHULNA DIVISION

ST PAUL'S CATHOLIC CHURCH

Built in 1992, **St Paul's Catholic Church** is a fascinating Catholic church disguised as a mosque! Skilfully embroidered wall hangings depict a Bangladeshi Christ and there are some bold stained-glass windows. You can purchase stunning embroideries from the attached sewing centre (open 9am to noon and 2pm to 4pm, closed Sunday).

Sleeping

Hotel Bangkok (☎ 0171 3975311; Main Rd; s/d Tk 150/300, with shared bathroom Tk 80/150) The deep-green rooms are small, but well kept. Some rooms have nice river views – some have road noise. It is the friendliest hotel in Mongla.

Hotel Singapore (s/d Tk 100/200) There isn't much to pick between this and the Hotel Bangkok. Singapore might get a little more light but to counter this the rooms are a little tattier.

Parjatan Hotel (Hotel Pashur; ☎ 75100; Khulner Rd; r with/without air-con Tk 1200/600; ✷) The nicest place to stay is the Parjatan, across the river (an easy Tk 2 ferry ride) from town. It only rarely receives foreign tourists which is a shame as it's one of the chain's better bets. It looks a little like an old colonial palace (though it is in fact a modern creation) and is set in peaceful gardens. Rooms are bright and clean, with a small balcony overlooking Mongla River and the busy port beyond.

Staff can help you track down a boatman for a trip to the Sundarbans.

Eating

Mongla isn't overflowing with eating options. The local favourite is the **Sureswar Hotel and Restaurant** (Main Rd; mains Tk 30), located on the main drag, next to the Hotel Bangkok. It stocks the standards and has a handy 'food catalogue' painted onto the wall in English.

Also on the main drag, and identical in almost everyway, is the **Paradise Hotel** (Main Rd). If you need an escape, head across the river to the Parjatan Hotel (Hotel Pashur, Khulna Rd), where you'll find the **Royal Bengal Restaurant** (mains Tk 120), with a decent selection of Bangladeshi and European options in a quiet environment.

At the north end of town, before the bridge, there are a couple of bakeries with some basic snack foods.

Getting There & Away

BOAT

The BIWTC office is 150m south of the ferry ghat, and the Rocket ghat is 100m further south. You may have difficulty booking 1st and 2nd-class Rocket tickets here; if possible, book in Khulna or Dhaka.

The Rocket goes to Dhaka (1st/2nd/inter class Tk 870/530/135, departs 6.20am) via Barisal and in the other direction to Khulna (1st/2nd/inter class Tk 140/80/15, departs 5am).

BUS

Almost all buses leave from the bus station across the Mongla River, just outside the Parjatan Hotel. It costs Tk 2 to cross the river on the public wooden boats.

Buses for Khulna (Tk 35, one hour, 6.40am to 7pm) leave every 20 minutes or so.

SUNDARBANS NATIONAL PARK

A shroud of mystery and danger looms over the Sundarbans National Park, the largest mangrove swamp in the world. This gloomy forest of baffling waterways stretches some 80km into the hinterland from the coast and its name translates into the 'beautiful forest', a misnomer if ever there were one. For most people, the Sundarbans is a horrifying matrix where, on average, a person is eaten every third day. To venture into this forest is to return to a primeval world of big trees and big creatures. It is one of the wildest and least known environments in all of southern Asia.

The Sundarbans begins about 5km southwest of Mongla along the Pusur River, and covers an area (split between Bangladesh and India, with the tiger's share in Bangladesh), of about 10,000 sq km, which is around half of what it was just 200 years ago. About one-third of the total area of this forest is covered in water – river channels, canals and tidal creeks varying in width from a few metres to a few kilometres. The land is constantly being reshaped by tidal action, and cyclones also wreak their havoc.

The ecological balance of these impenetrable forests is extremely delicate and influenced greatly by tidal shifts that affect the salinity, and hence the growth rates, of the surrounding vegetation. The eclectic inhabitants of the Sundarbans range from deer, pigs and crabs to the mighty Royal Bengal tiger. The Divisional Forestry Office supervises activities to protect the delicate ecological balance and botanists, zoologists, environmentalists and conservationists around the world keep eager eyes on this ecological repository.

LIFE IN THE SUNDARBANS

There are no permanent settlements within the forest, apart from a few government camps housing the labour force for the extraction of timber. These camps are either built on stilts or 'hang' from the trees because of the soft muddy ground and the 2m-high tides that course through the coastal areas.

From November to mid-February thousands of fishermen from Chittagong converge on Dublar Island, at the mouth of the Kunga River, a Sundarbans estuary, to harvest schooling shrimp that come here to breed, and to catch fish and sharks.

During the same period, thousands of low-caste Hindus from Khulna, Barisal and Patuakhali come to the island for a three-day mela (festival). They set up statues of deities in makeshift temples, bathe in the holy waters and release or sacrifice goats. During the mela, sweetmeats, dried fruit, toys, hookahs, wooden clogs and religious paraphernalia are sold in the market (though in 2007 the authorities forbade the mela to take place – it remains to be seen if it will be allowed in the future). A few weeks after the festival-goers departure, the fishermen also return to Chittagong. For the next nine months the island is deserted.

You might also see fishing families who live like sea gypsies in the Sundarbans. They have large boats with thatched roofs and cabins. Some woodcutters working in the Sundarbans also live in boats or temporary dwellings on the edge of the forest, usually at a height of 3m or so, for protection from tigers.

Besides yielding fish in great quantities, the region produces the sundari tree (see boxed text, opposite). Other forest products include gol leaves (from a local shade tree of that name), reeds and snails.

> **THE SUNDARI TREE**
>
> The Sundarbans derives its name from the *sundari* trees that grow here. These 25m-high trees are very straight, have tiny branches and keep well in water – they become rock hard when submerged for a long time and are thus suitable for shipbuilding, electric poles, railway sleepers and house construction. *Gema* wood, also felled in the Sundarbans, is mainly pulped for the Khulna newsprint factory. Timber workers here are called *bawalis*.

The dry season, November to April, is the most popular season for visiting the Sundarbans.

History

The first record of settlement in the region is from the 13th century. Hindus fleeing the Muslim advance sought refuge in the forests, eventually settling and building a number of temples. They were later joined by the Khiljis, who were fleeing the Afghans. In the 17th century, Portuguese-Mogh pirates probably caused the population to leave the area, although lack of fresh water and an unhealthy climate must have been contributing factors.

The Sundarbans was added to the Unesco World Heritage list in 1997.

Wildlife

The Sundarbans is home to some unique subcontinental wildlife, though spotting them in the thick mangrove forests is difficult. Most visitors report seeing little, but many argue that it is the pristine environment and not the wildlife that is the real attraction. Elevated viewing towers have been constructed to help visitors spot wildlife.

ROYAL BENGAL TIGERS

The creature everybody wants to see (and the one that you really have very little chance of sighting) is the magnificent Royal Bengal tiger. Tigers, which have been known to grow to a body length of more than 2m, have a life span of around 16 years and prey on deer, boars and fish stranded on river beds at low tide. It is only in old age, when they have lost their physical agility and canine fangs, that they prey on workers in the area.

There are estimated to be around 5000 wild tigers left in the world, with the Sundarbans providing a home to 200 to 450 cats – the highest tiger density in the world. Above all else, the tigers of the Sundarbans are famous for their supposed taste for human flesh. Recent scientific surveys reveal that the number of people eaten by tigers in the Sundarbans may be as high as 120 a year – much higher than had previously been thought. Spread over the course of a year this is one death every three days, something to keep in mind on a four-day Sundarbans tour… Why Sundarbans tigers are so partial to human flesh remains a mystery, but for a long time people thought that drinking salty water may have turned the tigers a little crazy. However scientists are beginning to reject this idea.

The **Sundarbans Tiger Project** (www.sundarbans tigerproject.info) is a superb website put together by one of the world's leading authorities on Sundarbans tigers, Adam Barlow. His team are currently involved in a slightly controversial project to collar wild tigers, and though some people have expressed dismay at this, the information they have been gathering is of vital importance for tiger conservation. It's also slowly helping to change the way villagers, who live on the fringes of the forests and have long regarded the tiger as a fearful creature to be persecuted, view these wonderful animals.

BIRDS

Over 300 different bird species have been recorded in this region, including about 95 species of water birds and 35 species of birds of prey. Birds found here include snipes, white and gold herons, woodcocks, coots, yellowlegs, sandpipers, common cranes, golden eagles and the *madan-tak* (adjutant bird), which always looks worried and dejected.

OTHER WILDLIFE

Other wildlife in the Sundarbans includes deer, wild boars, clawless otters, monkeys, crocodiles, 35 species of reptiles (including large cobras and pythons, and eight species of amphibians) and numerous river dolphins.

There are an estimated 30,000 spotted deer in the Sundarbans. They're relatively easy to find given that they use clearings and riverbanks to drink. Monkeys have curiously been observed to drop *keora* leaves whenever deer appear on the scene.

KHULNA DIVISION

DEADLY HONEY

One of the most important natural resources to emerge out of the Sundarbans is honey. Indeed, this is one of the country's richest sources of honey (madhu or mau), producing over 250,000kg annually. About 90% comes from the far western area called Satkhira, where certain flowering trees thrive on the higher salinity.

The people who gather honey, known as maualis, occasionally constitute a part of the diet of the Royal Bengal tiger. Indeed, they are far more vulnerable to tiger attack than anybody else. The maualis carry no protection and in the frenzy of following the bees to their hives, can't keep an eye out for tigers as well. Tigers attack from the rear and in a matter of seconds can crush a victim's head or break his neck. On the Indian side of the Sundarbans, the forest department has developed iron head-masks for the maualis, which have proven quite effective. But in Bangladesh, honey collectors continue to work unprotected.

And if you thought the tigers were bad news, just wait till you meet the bees! The giant honey bee, which forms colonies sometimes tens of thousands strong, is renowned for its ferocious nature and for chasing attackers long distances in large swarms. In order to get close to their nests, the maualis must use smoke to subdue the bees, but it takes years of painful practise to get it right.

The honey-gathering season is tightly controlled and greeted with much festivity when it kicks off at **Burigoalini** on 1 April with a volley of gunshots. The boats of the maualis then race off downstream and into the forest in search of the best honey-hunting areas. The season lasts for around two months.

Guide Tours (Map p86; ☎ /fax 041-731 384; KDA Bldg, KDA Ave, Khulna) organises occasional tours to follow the maualis and hunt honey with them. It would be hard to think of a more fascinating, and gruelling, way of seeing the Sundarbans.

As if man-eating tigers weren't bad enough, the Sundarbans provide a home to another bad tempered animal – the giant honey bee (see boxed text, above).

Information

Unless you are just engaged on a day trip from Mongla to the **Karamjal Forest Station** (see p90), the only way to enter the forest is as part of an organised tour with a recognised travel agency. They will take care of all logistics for you. A small, local tourist industry has recently sprung up around Munshigonj in the northwest section of the park. Boatmen here will take you on day trips into a truly wild part of the forest (and the place where the most tigers are to be found). At the time of research it wasn't possible to stay overnight in this area, but getting to Munshigonj and organising the trip promises to be quite an adventure.

Organised Tours

The easiest (and indeed the only) way to penetrate the forest in any depth is on an organised boat tour. Most companies offer fairly similar packages and all concentrate on the far southeast of the swamp. Boat quality and environmental awareness varies between operators, and the less you pay the less you get.

The only complaint we have against any of the following tour operators is that a lot of time is spent just getting to this south eastern sector, during which time opportunities to see anything of the Sundarbans wildlife is limited.

Guide Tours Dhaka (Map p62; ☎ 02-988 6983; 1st fl, Darpan Complex, DIT II Circle, Gulshan); Khulna (Map p86; ☎ /fax 041-731 384; KDA Bldg, KDA Ave, Khulna) knows these forests like nobody else and is heavily involved in conservation and research projects here. It gets fantastic reports for its tours, and its guides are a wealth of information. The more people in a group, the less you'll pay, but to have any chance of seeing anything it's best

---

BEWARE THE WHITE FIGURE

Many people have reported an encounter with an unusual hitchhiker in the Sundarbans. It's said that a person wrapped in white cloth hails passing boats in order to help them cross the river. They say or do nothing while they are in the boat, but on reaching the opposite bank they simply vanish into thin air.

WHALE-WATCHING

The Swatch of No Ground, a deep-water canyon a short way offshore of the Sundarbans, acts as something of a magnet to Brydes whales and bottlenosed dolphins. Between December and February, **Guide Tours** (Map p86; ☎ /fax 731 384; www.guidetours.com; KDA Bldg, KDA Ave, Khulna) organises boat trips out to this canyon where schools of up to 750 dolphins have been seen, and whale sightings are virtually guaranteed. It's a one-day excursion that is added onto the Sundarbans tour at a cost of US$50. You will travel on a scientific boat and in addition to watching whales, you get to watch the scientists at work.

---

to go on a small group tour. The cheapest four-day trip will cost around Tk 9500 on the largest boats, while the small group tours on the most luxurious boat is Tk 15,000 per person. Fees include all food, accommodation and transport, but you will need to pay an additional Tk 2500 for permits.

Bengal Tours Dhaka (☎ 882 0716; www.bengaltours .com; house 66, Rd 10, block D, Banani); Khulna (☎ 724 355; 236 Khan Jahan Ali Rd) offers an almost identically priced package as Guide Tours to the same areas and is equally knowledgeable of the forest and as environmentally aware. We have received nothing but positive reports about its trips.

Unique Tours & Travels (Map p62; ☎ 988 5116-23; 51/B Kemal Ataturk Ave, Dhaka) has also been recommended.

Barisal Division

Barisal division is marked by the branches of the Padma that braid through it to the Bay of Bengal, creating a maze of waterways. This wide, flat region has little to offer in the way of historical monuments but, in many ways, Barisal division is the quintessential Bangladesh. There is hardly any industrial development in this luxuriously green region fringed by rivers and the sea. The land is intermingled with ponds, marshes and streams, which keep the soft, fertile ground moist.

Though first impressions might show that there is little here, Barisal division in general (and the southern half in particular) should get the hearts of explorers racing in excitement. The possibilities for adventure in this remote corner are almost limitless. The best way to tackle the area is just to pick a spot on the map and ask at chaotic Barisal port about boats heading there. It might take time, it might get uncomfortable and sweaty, it might involve numerous changes of boat and days spent stuck in muddy villages marked on no map and then, when you finally reach your goal there might be nothing of note to see, but rest assured that nothing will beat the experience of lying on the deck of a ship on a steamy night, listening to the sounds of the swamps and rivers, destined for a place you don't know.

HIGHLIGHTS

- Get lost in the grimy backstreets of atmospheric **Barisal** (opposite)
- Board a **boat** (opposite) from Barisal for an adventure through the chocolate-coloured rivers of southern Barisal division

Barisal ★

BARISAL
☎ 0431

Barisal (*bore*-ee-shal) is a major port city and one of the gateways to the world for Bangladesh, yet it's also utterly isolated from the rest of the country. Appropriately, perhaps, it's much easier to reach by boat than road. It's one of the more pleasant cities in the country, with several ponds in the city centre and handsome buildings from the Raj era in quiet backstreets – but it's the busy river port, constantly humming with life, that is the real star. To arrive here by boat in the early-morning mist is a quintessential exotic Bangladeshi experience.

Information

There are a couple of ATMs scattered around the city.

Dutch-Bangla Bank (Sadar Rd) Changes money and has an ATM.

Genius Café (Sadar Rd; per hr Tk 20) Most of your money will be spent waiting for the computer to do something.

Sleeping

Quite a few of the cheaper hotels near BIWTC Ghat Rd are loath to accept foreigners.

Hotel Ababil (East Bogura Rd; ☎ 0119 8038781; s/d Tk 100/200) Just above the Yan Thai Restaurant, this is a spot-on place for those on a tight budget. Rooms are startlingly clean and the price as low as Bangladesh can get. Single women may well be viewed with the utmost suspicion.

Paradise Hotel (☎ 64643; Hospital Rd; s/d from Tk 250/350) The exterior looks a bit shabby but there's private parking, a small garden and, besides some musty carpets, it's clean and well furnished. All rooms have attached bathroom.

Hotel Ali International (☎ 64732; Sadar Rd; s with/without air-con Tk 700/250, d with/without air-con Tk 1100/700; ⚡) One of the more salubrious places to stay; it's orderly, well-managed and has knowledgeable reception staff. Some rooms share a common bathroom, while the pricier rooms are large and spotless with comfortable armchairs and beds, fans, coffee tables and sit-down toilets.

Hotel Athena International (☎ 65233; Katpotty Rd; s with/without air-con Tk 900/400, d with/without air-con Tk 1100/700; ⚡) The most popular hotel in town with that rare breed, passing foreigners, the Athena has a clean design with equally clean and slick rooms for a decent price.

BARISAL GUNS

Since the 1870s, booming noises resembling cannon fire have been heard coming from the Bay of Bengal. Termed 'Barisal guns' by the British officials who first reported this strange phenomenon, their source remains a mystery. It is possible that the sound still occurs today…but who could hear a cannon above the traffic?

Eating

There are numerous small, cheap, seemingly makeshift restaurants in the area around the intersection of BIWTC Ghat Rd and Faisal Huq Ave. Some cha (tea) stalls specialise in 'red tea' – cardamom tea without milk.

Rose Garden Restaurant (Sadar Rd; mains Tk 50-60) One of the locals' favourite places is the Rose Garden. It's unidentifiable curries all the way, but unidentifiable certainly tastes good. Occasional female patrons soothe the atmosphere.

Kirtonkhola Garden Restaurant (Chnmari; mains Tk 80-100) Perfectly sited on the lazy banks of the Kirtonkhol River, this Thai- and Chinese-influenced restaurant is considered one of the more enjoyable places to get stuck in.

Yan Thai Restaurant (East Bogura Rd; mains Tk 100; ⚡) Bringing the spicy tastes of Thailand to the water world, this cosy and clean little restaurant serves Thai delights, and has plenty of Bangladeshi favourites to enjoy.

Getting There & Away
AIR

United Airways (☎ 893 2338) is about to launch twice weekly flights from Barisal to Dhaka (Tk 2595, 30 minutes). A baby taxi (auto-rickshaw) to the airport will cost around Tk 90.

BOAT

The Rocket (see p175) from Barisal to Dhaka (1st/2nd/deck class Tk 480/300/80, departs 6pm daily except Saturday) is supposed to arrive in Dhaka at 6am the following morning, but during the high-water season (monsoonal, July and August) it can take up to 16 hours.

The Rocket to Khulna (1st/2nd/deck class Tk 530/320/75, departs 5am daily except Saturday) also stops at Mongla (1st/2nd/deck class Tk 390/240/50).

On Tuesday there is a Rocket to Chittagong (1st/2nd/deck class Tk 850/560/120, departs

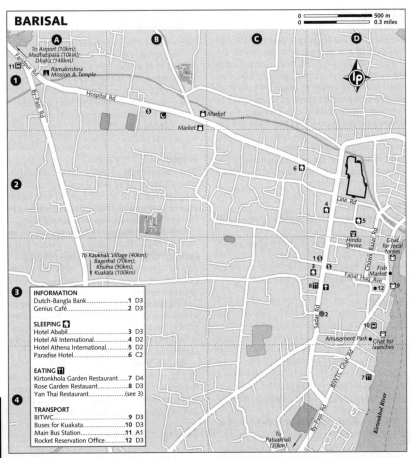

BARISAL

To Airport (10km);
Madhabpasa (10km);
Dhaka (148km)

Ramakrishna
Mission & Temple

Hospital Rd

Market

Market

Line Rd

Hindu
Shrine

Chowk Bazar Rd

Ghat
for local
ferries

Faisal Huq Ave

Fish
Market

To Kaukhali Village (40km);
Bagerhat (70km);
Khulna (90km);
Kuakata (100km)

Sadar Rd

Amusement Park

Ghat for
launches

BIWTC Ghat Rd

Kirtonkhol River

By-Pass Rd

To
Patuakhali
(30km)

INFORMATION
Dutch-Bangla Bank.....................1 D3
Genius Café.................................2 D3

SLEEPING
Hotel Ababil................................3 D3
Hotel Ali International..................4 D2
Hotel Athena International...........5 D2
Paradise Hotel.............................6 C2

EATING
Kirtonkhola Garden Restaurant.....7 D4
Rose Garden Restauant................8 D3
Yan Thai Restaurant..................(see 3)

TRANSPORT
BIWTC...9 D3
Buses for Kuakata.......................10 D3
Main Bus Station.........................11 A1
Rocket Reservation Office...........12 D3

8.30pm). Don't risk taking this boat during the monsoon as it often crosses very rough open-ocean.

This same boat also stops off at both Hatiya Island (1st/2nd/deck class Tk 375/255/60) and the even more off-the-beaten-track Sandwip Island (fares about 50% more). Memorable adventure is included in the price.

For information and reservations for the Rocket, visit the **BIWTC** (Bangladesh Inland Waterway Transport Corporation; Barisal harbour) or the **reservations office** (BIWTC Ghat Rd).

Numerous other vessels of all shapes and sizes drift slowly upriver to Dhaka at around 6pm nightly. Prices vary but a double cabin on a standard boat should cost around Tk 700, while deck class is an uncomfortable Tk

120 to Tk 150. A 'super luxurious' cabin will be more like Tk 1600 to Tk 1700. The journey takes around 10 hours. The departure point in Barisal is just south of the BIWTC terminal.

Recommended operators are **Suravi** (☎ 01711 332084), **Parabat** (☎ 01711 346080) and **Kirtonkhola** (☎ 01711 171605)

BUS

Buses from Dhaka to Barisal depart Dhaka from the Gabtali bus station (p67). Day coaches depart each way, mostly in the morning from around 6.30am, while night buses depart mostly between 6pm and 9pm. Buses for Dhaka (Tk 250, five to seven hours) depart from the northern entrance to Barisal, 4km from the town centre.

Buses also travel south to Kuakata (Tk 130, five hours, 110km, hourly between 6am and 4.30pm). Buses for Kuakata leave from the southern end of town.

AROUND BARISAL

The village of **Madhabpasa**, about 10km to the northwest of Barisal, has a **lake** that is known for attracting birds. There is also a **Hindu temple** close to the village. **Kaukhali** village, close to the city, has some interesting pottery factories where daily utensils and figurines for Hindu festivals are made in the oldest of manners.

KUAKATA

☎ 0441

This isolated beach at the southern tip of the delta, about 100km from Barisal, was named by the original Mogh (Rakhine) Buddhist settlers whose ancestors remain today. *Kua* means 'well', and *kata* means 'dug'.

The river mouths east and west of the beach ensure that the sea is rather murky, and sharks drying on racks along the beach similarly don't augur well for swimming. Though Kuakata isn't the archetypal turquoise, tropical ocean, the vibe is right. The town suffered heavily at the hands of Cyclone Sidr in November 2007.

There is a **Buddhist temple** close to the Parjatan Motel, about 100m from the beach on a slightly raised mound. The ugly tin-walled shrine holds a much prettier 100-year-old statue of Buddha, said to be the largest in the country. The nearby **forestry reserve** is pleasant but succumbing to illegal logging.

Some travellers report that hiring a fisherman to take you to nearby forested **islands** is a fun excursion.

Sleeping & Eating

Hotel Sunrise (☎ 63945; s Tk 100, d Tk 250-300) A rickety beach shack with more atmosphere than amenities. The engaging manager organises package tours to nearby areas and the not-so-nearby Sundarbans.

Parjatan Motel (☎ 64433; d Tk 500-750, with air-con Tk 1250; set Bangladeshi meal Tk 55) The rooms are decent but otherwise unremarkable. It is becoming outshone by the plethora of new establishments springing up along the main road. Be warned that 'eggs any style' means any style that is an omelette. French fries are Tk 10 and the tasty chicken-and-corn soup is Tk 20.

Hotel Neelanjna (☎ 01712 927904; r with/without air-con Tk 1890/690) The fancy pants hotel of Kuakata has sea views that alone justify the price. Everything is lovely and tidy without any signs of tropical rot setting in. All rooms are twin bed only so couples needn't worry about bringing any contraception! A discreet chat with the receptionist should see some reduction on the overpriced air-con rooms.

Shaphired Restaurant (mains Tk 60) Directly opposite the Parjatan Motel. It doesn't have a menu, but does have a nice attitude.

Getting There & Away

The road between Kuakata and Barisal isn't as good as that between Barisal and Dhaka, largely due to extensive renovations.

Buses to Barisal cost Tk 130.

Rajshahi Division

If Indiana Jones were a real man, then he'd be living in Rajshahi division. For tucked away in this unknown corner of the country are a plethora of ruins and reminders. In fact there's so much history stashed away up here that you sometimes feel that you can't move without tripping over some other forgotten temple or decaying palace. Though today largely removed from mainstream Bangladeshi life, the rich soils of Rajshahi division once held court for powerful Buddhist kingdoms, neutered Hindu empires and fell easily to the embrace of Islam; all of which have left their mark in the tumble-down walls that litter the region.

However, it's not just about relics: there are small villages where children will leap in the air in excitement at the sight of you; passionate market towns full of colour; and, if you're very lucky, views to the great Himalayan peak of Kanchenjunga.

But at the end of the day it's the sense of past glories that is the highlight of this region, and what is so remarkable about this historical fantasy is that you will almost certainly have these ancient sights all to yourself – even Indiana Jones hasn't got the secret map to Rajshahi's treasures.

HIGHLIGHTS

- Perusing the art of **Kantanagar Temple** (p111) and relishing the gorgeous countryside
- Standing in the footsteps of the Buddha at **Paharpur** (p104), the most impressive archaeological site in Bangladesh
- Counting back the years at **Mahasthangarh** (p103), the oldest known city in Bangladesh
- Chilling under the mango-tree mosques of **Gaud** (p120)
- Wondering where everyone else is in temple-riddled **Puthia** (p117) and philosophising with sadhus (itinerant holy men) in **Natore** (p118)

BOGRA
☎ 051

Bogra, a sprawling town with a small heart, serves primarily as a base from which to explore two of the country's most famous and impressive archaeological sites – Mahasthangarh (p103) and Paharpur (p104). The former is 10km north of town, and the breathtaking latter, 53km to the northwest. It would be an exaggeration to describe Bogra itself as attractive or exciting, but it does have a couple of little treats that make saving a morning for the town worthwhile. These include the Chandi (a boisterous central market area), an interesting rajbari (palace) and an eccentric dream zoo.

Information

There is a **Standard Chartered Bank** (Sherpur Rd) with an ATM, just visible from Sat Mata. You can hook up with the wider world at the **Skylink Cybercafe** (Kazi Nazrul Islam Rd; per hr Tk 20) just upstairs from the Quality Sweets & Restaurant. More computers are available at **Wait & Browse** (Nawab Bari Rd), just around the corner.

Sights

Two blocks east of Sat Mata, the **Nawab Syed Abdus Sobhan Chowdhury Memorial Museum** (admission to grounds Tk 10, to museum Tk 5; ☺ 10am-8pm) is one of only a handful of furnished rajbaris in Bangladesh. The mosaic ceiling of the audience hall is impressive, and the rooms have mannequins dressed to impress in both Bengali and British fashions. The last room you'll see is dedicated to modern art – it's a compelling display, but the lack of English explanation leaves it somewhat obscure. Look out also for the rare gharial (a type of crocodilian). We're sure you'll agree that they look far better nailed to the wall here than they would do in the wild…

The grounds of the museum have been turned into a rose- and lover-filled garden (all the lovers appear to help themselves to the roses) and a quirky **amusement park** with rickety fairground rides and charmingly naive statues of peasants, bullock carts and wild animals. In the far corner is a small row of cages containing depressed monkeys with heavy chains around their necks.

Just next to the museum's entrance is a statue '**zoo**' of painted cement animals, where you'll find monkeys seeing, hearing and speaking no evil (a first for a monkey), goril-

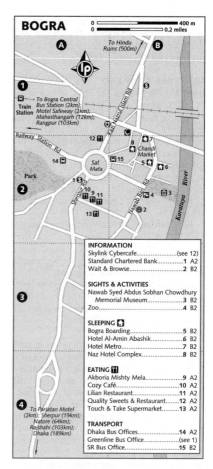

las shimmying a little sexy salsa and frogs that have outgrown the pandas. The cages these animals live in are often better than those their real-life cousins have to put up with. The real highlight though is the terrifying cave. Hand over your cash (Tk 15) and enter only if you dare!

Sleeping

BUDGET

Bogra Boarding (☎ 65609; Nawab Bari Rd; r without bathroom Tk 140, s/d with bathroom Tk 120/160) A three-storey building with an English sign and a charming old gentleman manager. The well-presented green and red rooms are tiny but relatively clean, and come with fans and mosquito nets.

Cheaper and less hygienic beds can also be found at the **Hotel Metro** (Nawab Bari Rd) and the **Naz Hotel Complex**, but neither contain the promise of a delightful night.

MIDRANGE & TOP END

Hotel Al-Amin Abashik (☎ 72937; s/d with air-con Tk 500/700, without air-con Tk 300/500) The more expensive room have sit-down toilets and more furniture and rooms of all prices come with that ever important mosquito net. If the cleanliness isn't all that you hoped for then ask them to clean it again and they'll quickly, and happily, get it scrubbed up for you. It's down a little mud side street and the sign is in Bengali only, but everyone seems to know where it is.

Motel Safeway (☎ 66087; safeway@bogra.desh.net; s/d Tk 990/1280) Gorgeous homely rooms that are some of the cleanest you'll come across in northern Bangladesh, though the bathrooms in the single rooms are cramped. The best thing about this hotel is the thick grassy lawn where you can relax beside the pond. It's a major hike from the town centre but is very handy for the bus station (though far enough away to avoid the noise).

Parjatan Motel (☎ 66753; r with/without air-con Tk 1200/750) The large Parjatan Motel comes with bird noise at the back and road noise at the front. Rooms are kept clean and have little balconies, but wear and tear is just beginning to make its presence felt. The price is absolutely right and the attached restaurant good news. The Parjatan is a long way south of the centre, but this gives plenty of room to breathe. To get into town just hop into any passing tempo (auto-rickshaw; Tk 5 to Sat Mata).

Eating

Quality Sweets & Restaurant (Kazi Nazrul Islam Rd; mains Tk 50) The Quality Sweets & Restaurant is overflowing with both character and drool inspiring food. It's tucked down a little alley off the main drag – there's no exterior English sign, but there is a small sign in English beside the interior door. The dhal here is especially good and much thicker than is normal in Bangladesh. Its sweet selection is deserving of the name.

Akboria Mishty Mela (⊙ 9am-9pm; mains Tk 50) A kickback café with a range of sickly-sweet Bengali cakes and almost equally sweet Western cakes. It also delves into coffee and light snacks, and Chinese meals are dished out upstairs.

Parjatan Motel (☎ 66753; mains Tk 160) It's nothing special but if you're staying here and can't face the long trek into town then you'll be pleased to know that the Bangladeshi and Chinese dishes at the Parjatan are satisfying.

Lilian Restaurant (☎ 61800; mains Tk 180) Small, intimate and a good place for a more drawn out Chinese or Thai meal. It's close to the Akboria Mishty Mela.

Cozy Café (☎ 00610; Sherpur Rd; mains Tk 180) The Cozy Café, where the young of the town come to see and be seen, is Bogra's trendiest eating experience and is very much a new concept for Bogra. The décor is dark and cool, the Chinese dishes really delicious, the staff will be genuinely pleased to see you and, if another reason were needed to stop by, they have a music collection that includes such old-school 'classics' as Bon Jovi, Europe and A-ha!

Finally, at the **Touch & Take Supermarket** you can stock up on hard-to-come-by food-stuffs and toiletries; unfortunately, despite the name, you do have to pay for items.

Getting There & Away

BUS

Buses usually arrive at Bogra's central bus station, 2km northwest of town at the junction of the Rangpur Bypass road and the road to Naogaon (close to the Motel Safeway). From here it's a Tk 10 rickshaw ride into town.

Ordinary buses travel to Dhaka (Tk 120, 4½ hours) via the Bangabandhu Bridge. Most coach offices for buses to Dhaka are west of Sat Mata, but the Green Line bus office is just to the south of Sat Mata. Deluxe air-con buses cost between Tk 350.

Buses leave the central station throughout the day for Natore (Tk 30, 2½ hours) and Rajshahi (Tk 70, three hours). There are several buses to Khulna (Tk 200, 8½ hours, depart around 9am) and Rangpur (Tk 60, 2½ hours, every 20 minutes from 5.30am to 6pm). Travellers to Paharpur can take regular buses throughout the day to Jaipurhat (Tk 50, 1½ hours) and a tempo or bus (Tk 10) on to Paharpur. Buses also run to Mahasthan (Tk 10, 30 minutes, 11km).

TRAIN

Bogra doesn't have great train connections and most people take the bus, but there is one train a day to Dhaka (1st/*sulob* class Tk

320/215, 1.07pm daily except Saturday) which arrives in Dhaka at 8.20pm, and a night train departing at 9.56pm nightly except Monday.

There are no direct trains from Bogra to Dinajpur or Rajshahi.

AROUND BOGRA
Sariakandi

For a bit of good adventure, consider heading 20km east via Gabtali (General Zia's home town) to Sariakandi and hiring a motorised boat to take you out onto the Jamuna River. It will cost around Tk 50 for half an hour. During the monsoonal season you can see broken embankments, and people living on the tiny islands created by the massive annual flooding.

The banks of the Jamuna are about the most erosion-prone places in the country, forcing farmers off their land during flood season. Many dispossessed farmers join the ranks of the rickshaw-wallahs.

Hat Bazar

Every Friday in a village just south of Bogra there's a hat bazar, a small open-air market that attracts so many people that they spill onto the highway. Roaming around the bazar can be great fun.

MAHASTHANGARH

The oldest known city in Bangladesh, dating back to at least the 3rd century BC, Mahasthangarh (an easy half-day trip from Bogra) is an archaeological site consisting largely of foundations and hillocks hinting at past riches.

The principal site, the Citadel, contains traces of the ancient city. Many other sites in the vicinity are lumped together under the name Mahasthangarh. The whole area is rich in Hindu, Buddhist and Muslim sites, but most have all but vanished. The Buddhists were here until at least the 11th century; their most glorious period was the 8th to the 11th centuries, when the Buddhist Pala emperors of North Bengal ruled. It is from this period that most of the visible remains belong.

Sights
MAHASTHANGARH SITE MUSEUM

This small but well-maintained **museum** (admission Tk 50; ☼ 2.30-6pm Mon, 10am-1pm & 1.30-6pm Tue-Thu & Sat, 10am-12.30pm & 2.30-6pm Fri Apr-Sep, 1.30-5pm Mon, 9am-1pm & 1.30-5pm Tue-Thu & Sat, 9am-1pm & 2-5pm

Fri Oct-Mar) has a lively set of objects discovered in the antique rich surroundings.

The highlights are the statues of Hindu gods, terracotta plaques depicting scenes from daily life and some well-preserved bronze images mostly found in monasteries from the Pala period. Other notable objects are the necklaces that look just like those sold in hippy markets all over the West and the fragments of toilet seats – they certainly don't make them like that anymore! The gardens are an attraction in their own right.

THE CITADEL

Adjacent to the museum, the **Citadel** forms a rough rectangle covering more than 2 sq km. It was once surrounded on three sides by the mighty Karatuya River. Hindus still make an annual pilgrimage to the Karatuya River in mid-April.

Probably first constructed under the Mauryan empire in the 3rd century BC, the site shows evidence of various Hindu empires, and Buddhist and Muslim occupations (though it's doubtful the helipad dates back that far). The Citadel fell into disuse around the time of the Mughal invasions. Most of the visible brickwork dates from the 8th century, apart from that added during restoration. Nowadays there isn't a lot left to see aside from the edge of the exterior walls and various unidentifiable grassy mounds. However, it's a perfect place for a walk and a picnic. The Citadel's interior is used as both agricultural land and a leisure area, with cricket matches taking place in the cool evening light. If cricket isn't your cup of tea then there will be plenty of other people around (some with flasks of tea) who will be keen to pass the time of day with you.

Outside the Citadel, opposite the museum, the remains of a 6th-century **Govinda Bhita Hindu Temple** (admission Tk 20) overlook a picturesque bend in the river. The temple, which looks like a broken-down step pyramid, is a quiet spot to get away from everyone. Opening hours are as for the Mahasthangarh Site Museum.

Back in the drab little town of Mahasthan (1.7km from Mahasthangarh) there is a small **Muslim shrine** that every other person will try to lead you to when you step off the bus – it's very missable! There are further **ancient sites** in the nearby countryside and any rickshaw-wallah will be keen as mustard to whip together a tour for you (around Tk 150).

Sleeping & Eating

If it's not full, you can stay at the **Archaeology Department Rest House** (d Tk 200), across the road from the museum, overlooking the Karatuya River. The three rooms have a fan, mosquito netting and bathroom. There's also a small dining room. The museum caretaker can hunt down the person in charge.

The town of Mahasthan has a few basic restaurants.

Getting There & Away

Buses run from Bogra to Mahasthan (Tk 10, 30 minutes, 11km). From here you can take a rickshaw (Tk 15 to Tk 20) or walk the 1.7km to the Citadel and museum. If there are no buses heading back to Bogra then you can hop in a shared baby taxi (mini auto-rickshaw, Tk 10).

PAHARPUR

The Somapuri Vihara at Paharpur was once the biggest Buddhist monastery south of the Himalaya. It dates from the 8th century AD. This is the most impressive archaeological site in Bangladesh; it was declared a protected archaeological site back in 1919, although the scholar-traveller Dr Buckman Hamilton had shown interest in it as far back as 1807. The name of the site has changed over the eons; it began life as Somapura (abode of the moon), then became Mahavihara (greatest monastery) before taking its current combination name. Getting to Paharpur is a bit of a pain on public transport, but it all adds to the element of discovery.

Sights

SOMAPURI VIHARA

The impressive stupa and temple complex at **Somapuri Vihara** is in the shape of a large quadrangle covering 11 hectares, with monks' cells making up the walls and enclosing a courtyard. The 20m-high remains of a stupa rise from the centre of the courtyard. Its cruciform floor plan is topped by a three-tier superstructure; the 3rd level has a large tower structure similar to that of Moenjodaro in Pakistan.

Look out for the clay tiles lining the base of the *mahavihara* (great monastery) which depict various people and creatures, including an animal that might be the rhinoceros that is now extinct in Bangladesh.

Lining the outer perimeter are over 170 small monastic cells. Seventy-two of these contain ornamental pedestals, the purpose of which still eludes archaeologists. It is possible they contained the remains of saintly monks who had resided here.

On the east side of the courtyard you can make out the outline of what was once a miniature model of the temple. On the western wing of the north side are remains of structures that baffle archaeologists. On the eastern wing of the south side is an elevated brick base with an eight-pointed star-shaped structure that must have been a shrine. To the west lie the remains of what appears to have been the monks' refectory and kitchen.

Except for the guardhouse to the north, most of the remains outside the courtyard lie to the south. They include an oblong building, linked to the monastery by a causeway, which may have been the wash house and latrines. In the same area is a bathing ghat, probably of Hindu origin. Only 12m southwest of the ghat is the rectangular Temple of Gondeswari, with an octagonal pillar base in the centre and a circular platform to the front.

The monastery is thought to have been successively occupied by Buddhists, Jains and Hindus, which explains the curious mixture of artwork. The Jains must have constructed a *chaturmukhar* (a structure with all four walls decorated with stone bas-reliefs of deities). The Hindus replaced Buddhist terracotta artwork with sculptural stonework of their own deities, and terracotta artwork representing themes from the *Mahabharata* and the *Ramayana*. Artefacts discovered at the site range from bronze statues and bas-reliefs of the elephant-headed Hindu god Ganesh, to statues of the Jain god Manzuri, bronze images of the Buddha and statues of the infant Krishna.

MUSEUM

The small **museum** (admission Tk 50; ⊙ 2.30-6pm Mon, 10am-1pm & 1.30-6pm Tue-Thu & Sat, 10am-12.30pm & 2.30-6pm Fri Apr-Sep, 1.30-5pm Mon, 9am-1pm & 1.30-5pm Tue-Thu & Sat, 9am-12.30pm & 2-5pm Fri Oct-Mar) gives a good idea of the range of cultures that have used this site. Stucco Buddha heads unearthed here are similar to the Gandhara style of Indo-Hellenic sculpture from what is now northwestern Pakistan. Sculptural work includes sandstone and basalt sculptures, but the stonework of Hevagara in passionate embrace with Shakti is the collection's finest item. The most important find, a large bronze Buddha, is usually away wooing fans on a seemingly endless world tour.

Sleeping & Eating

The small white building between the museum and the temple is the **Archaeological Rest House** (☎ 0571 89119; per person Tk 200). Staff at the museum should be able to point you to the appropriate person if you want to stay. The large and functional rooms are kept clean and offer superb value for money. As it's inside the grounds of the ruins you can even go for a lonely, and creepy, night stroll around the complex on your own. It all adds up to a very peaceful and romantic getaway for a day or so.

Basic meals can be obtained from the shacks near the museum entrance.

Getting There & Away

From Bogra, take a bus to Jaipurhat (Tk 50, 1½ hours, 44km). From there, buses leave regularly between 7am and 4pm for Paharpur (Tk 10, 25 minutes, 9km). To get to the sights from Paharpur village, take a rickshaw (around Tk 20).

You can always get a baby taxi back to Jaipurhat, but it will cost around Tk 250. Don't count on getting a bus from Jaipurhat to Bogra after 6pm.

RANGPUR
☎ 0521

Rangpur is the best of storybook-exotic Bangladesh, and a better introduction to the wonders of the entire subcontinent it would be hard to find. The central area is a rainbow-flavoured lollipop of markets and rickshaws. This playful atmosphere is like a heavyweight drug – once you've tasted it you'll forever be smitten.

A major transit point for the northern half of Rajshahi division (sometimes referred to as North Bengal), the town is, in addition to its bossy streets, home to several public buildings of the Raj era, including Carmichael College and Tajhat Palace. The town is also one place you may see members of the Kochi ethnic group, an Indo-Tibetan people related to the plains tribes of Assam, and recognisable by their rounder, more Southeast Asian faces.

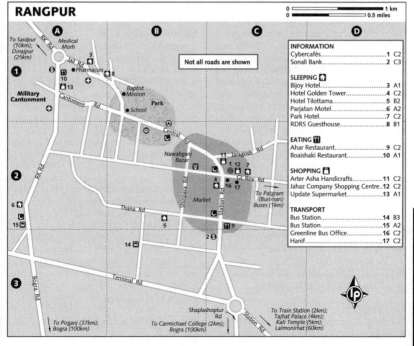

RANGPUR	
INFORMATION	
Cybercafés....................................1 C2	
Sonali Bank..................................2 C3	
SLEEPING	
Bijoy Hotel...................................3 A1	
Hotel Golden Tower......................4 C2	
Hotel Tilottama.............................5 B2	
Parjatan Motel..............................6 A2	
Park Hotel....................................7 C2	
RDRS Guesthouse.........................8 B1	
EATING	
Ahar Restaurant...........................9 C2	
Boaishaki Restaurant...................10 A1	
SHOPPING	
Arter Asha Handicrafts.................11 C2	
Jahaz Company Shopping Centre..12 C2	
Update Supermarket.....................13 A1	
TRANSPORT	
Bus Station..................................14 B3	
Bus Station..................................15 A2	
Greenline Bus Office....................16 C2	
Hanif...17 C2	

RAJSHAHI DIVISION

Orientation & Information

Rangpur is a sprawling place, but once you've got to grips with it you'll find it simple enough to navigate and there are only really two areas of interest to travellers. Rangpur 'centre' is based on Nawabganj Bazar (GL Roy Rd between Shinpara and Station Rds), a cacophony of clashing colours, and the more stately Medical Morh, where you'll find one of the better hotels. Separating them both is a pleasant stretch of parks, gardens and sports fields. The train station is about 3km south at the end of Station Rd. At the time of research there were no ATMs in town.

Cyber cafés (cnr Station & GL Roy Rds; per hr Tk 20)

Sonali Bank (Station Rd) About 500m south of Nawabganj Bazar, Sonali changes cash and travellers cheques. You need to show your passport for both.

Sights

TAJHAT PALACE

The domineering **Tajhat Palace** (admission Tk 100; ☉ 2.30-6pm Mon, 10am-1pm & 1.30-6pm Tue-Thu & Sat, 10am-12.30pm & 2.30-6pm Fri Apr-Sep, 1.30-5pm Mon, 9am-1pm & 1.30-5pm Tue-Thu & Sat, 9am-12.30pm & 2-5pm Fri Oct-Mar) is one of the finest rajbaris in Bangladesh. During the regime of General Ershad (1982–91), the palace was used by the High Court division of Bangladesh's Supreme Court, but today it houses a small museum stuffed with old manuscripts and bits and bobs from Paharpur and Mahasthangarh.

The palace, which is structurally intact but deteriorating fast, is similar to Ahsan Manzil in Dhaka. It has a frontage of about 80m and is crowned by a ribbed conical dome and features an imposing central staircase made of imported white marble. The balustrade originally featured marble sculptures of classical Roman figures, but these have long since disappeared.

The palace was constructed in the 19th century by Manna Lal Ray, a Hindu who was forced to emigrate from the Punjab and found his way to Rangpur. He became a successful jeweller, acquired a lot of land, eventually won the title of raja (landlord or ruler) and built this huge mansion. Local villagers believe there is treasure hidden in its walls.

The palace is 5km south of Nawabganj Bazar and 2km south of the train station, outside the de facto city boundaries.

KALI TEMPLE

The delightful architectural folly of **Kali Temple** is modelled on a Florentine dome (or at least a Bengali vision of an English adaptation of a Florentine dome) and is topped with blue-rinse Hindu gods. The courtyard also doubles as a village school and your arrival will send reams of children into a whiz.

The temple lies about 1km south of Tajhat Palace. Take a rickshaw from High Court Rd and ask around the neighbourhood for 'Kali mondir'.

CARMICHAEL COLLEGE

This famous old **college** is one of the largest in the country in terms of both area and student enrolment. Situated on the outskirts of town, the college dates from 1916. Similar in inspiration to Curzon Hall in Dhaka and with a grand frontage of over 100m, it is a splendid fusion of classical British and Mughal architecture. Its domes rest on slender columns and a series of arched openings all add to its mosque-like appearance. It is spacious and rural, with cows grazing on the main lawn and students keen to talk of the wider world while resting in the shade.

Sleeping

Bijoy Hotel (Jail Rd; s/d Tk 120/220) Basic cubes and lots of mosquitoes (net provided), but surprisingly comfortable beds and private bathrooms. Despite not being at all used to foreigners, the staff are super cool with the idea of you staying. There is no English sign, so ask around.

Hotel Tilottama (☎ 63482; Thana Rd; s Tk 150, d Tk 210-275) This happy budget option is on a quiet road and has staff who race around trying to make you comfortable. The airy green rooms are surprisingly tidy for the price and come with attached bathrooms. If you opt for the 'deluxe' room you get a tatty scrap of carpet and a proper sit-down toilet – albeit perched over a squat toilet… The business card boasts of a 'Lonely Atmosphere', which in Bangladesh can be a virtue indeed. It's quite hard to find, so ask, ask, ask!

The Park Hotel (☎ 66718; GL Roy Rd; s with/without air-con Tk 600/260, d with/without air-con Tk 425/750; ✷) For fancy budget travellers, this central hotel is a delight. The rooms might lack character but this means they are sterile clean. All have wooden bedheads and desks. In the pricier rooms you can relax on the toilet with a book, while in the cheaper ones it's a squat-and-run job. It has the best positioning of all the hotels.

Hotel Golden Tower (☎ 65920; Station Rd; s/d Tk 800/1000; ❄) A decent midway option in the heart of the downtown mess. The staff don't seem totally convinced by foreigners but if you get in you'll find that the low-ceilinged rooms are neat and air-con cool.

Parjatan Motel (☎ 63681; RK Rd; r with/without air-con Tk 1380/690; ❄) An excellent serving from the Parjatan group. This low-slung mellow yellow building is set in pleasant flower gardens on the edge of town. The rooms are universally clean and comfortable with balconies and large bathrooms. The air-con and non-air-con rooms are otherwise identical. There is also a restaurant (fixed Bangladeshi meal Tk 120) with the usual mix of Chinese, Bangladeshi and Western dishes. A rickshaw from the town centre costs in the region of Tk 10 to Tk 15.

ourpick RDRS Guesthouse (☎ 66490; www.rdrs bangla.net; s/d Tk 1086/1569; ❄ ▣ Ⓟ) Let's cut straight to the chase. Beautiful Swedish princesses have been known to stay here. Enough said! In addition to sleeping in the same bed as a Swedish princess, you will be helping out a highly deserving NGO which works on health, educational and agricultural projects throughout northwest Bangladesh. But even without all those incentives, this would be a sweet pick, because the ivy-clad red-brick building – with its polished and spacious rooms, piping hot showers, satellite TV, plenty of mosquitoes (bring your own net), internet access, pool table and superb restaurant (mains Tk 150) – is as good as northern Bangladesh gets. And, just in case you missed it the first time – Swedish princesses…

Eating

The best way to pick a place to eat is to head into Nawabganj Bazar and wander down some side streets. As well as the local holes-in-the-wall, there are some slightly pricier restaurants in this area that serve sensational food in surprisingly clean surrounds.

Boaishaki Restaurant (RK Rd; ☼ 6am-midnight; mains Tk 60-80) This place is so popular it's just silly, but as normal the locals know best. As well as delectable curries there are a few harder to come by dishes such as biryani. If the staff take a shine to you then you might find yourself leaving with a free red rose, and a cha or two better off.

Ahar Restaurant (cnr Thana & Station Rds; mains from Tk 100) At night it's damn near impossible to miss this flashing Christmas tree of a restaurant. During the day it's marginally more subtle, but even so the bright lights, bright pink interior and bright balloons are obviously of great appeal to the girls of Rangpur as this seems to be the only restaurant in the entire country where female diners outnumber male. The staff proudly announce that they can make 'anything', though they mean anything Bangladeshi. Still, the biryani is well worth the trip.

Shopping

Arter Asha Handicrafts (☎ 092 150; House 3, CP Sen Rd) This eye-catching boutique store specialises in handmade traditional clothes. Fashions and souvenirs at Arter Asha don't come cheap, but they do come classy.

Jahaz Company Shopping Centre (GL Roy Rd) The perfect place to splash out on the elaborate souvenir sari that you may wear once when you get home. As well as the overwhelming collection of clothes and jewellery, you'll also find electronic goods.

Update Supermarket (RK Rd) There's a healthy range of groceries and toiletries at the Update Supermarket. There's also an attentive employee who will try to promote every product within a 2m radius.

Getting There & Away

Commercial flights haven't operated to Rangpur for some time now, but it's worth checking with **GMG** (☎ 02-711 4155/7 in Dhaka) and **United Airways** (☎ 02-895 7640 in Dhaka; www.uabdl .com) to see if there has been any change.

The **Karma Para bus station** (RK Rd) sits snugly just south of the centre of town. There are regular buses for Bogra (Tk 65, two hours, every 20 minutes from 7am to 5.30pm). For towns such as Dinajpur and Thakurgaon you may have to change at Saidpur (Tk 30, one hour, regularly until 7pm). Many buses leaving this bus station get to their final destination via Bogra.

Only a few buses make the journey to Rajshahi (ordinary Tk 180, luxury Tk 220, 4½ hours); the last leaves at around 3pm. There are no chair coaches on any of these routes.

Greenline (☎ 63940; cnr Station & GL Roy Rds) and **Hanif** (☎ 62462) both operate coaches to Dhaka (Tk 450, five hours, 325km) at various times between 7am and 11pm.

There is a train to Dinajpur at 7.08pm (two hours) daily except Sunday.

SAIDPUR
☎ 0552

Saidpur is a quiet backwater town where the atmosphere of the Raj lingers. Near the old train station is one of Bangladesh's few surviving **English-style churches**. The southern part of town has some impressive **red-brick buildings** from the latter period of the Raj. The town used to be home to Rangpur airport and received a few visitors. But with no commercial flights currently operating, few people visit. If you want to slow the pace right down then this is a nice place to get into small-town life.

There are a couple of banks that might be persuaded to change cash at bad rates, but you'll have to continue on to Rangpur or Dinajpur to change travellers cheques. There

is an **internet café** (☻ 9am-11pm; per hr Tk 20) with s-l-o-w connections past the railway lines.

The dirty central **market** is a fun place to explore and is alive with the sights, sounds and smells of southern Asia. At the northern end of town, near the train station, is the rusty red 150-year-old **church**, built by the British. It's kept locked but the caretaker lives in the house next door and will open up for you. It's in surprisingly good condition and services are attended by the members of the 25 Christian families in the neighbourhood.

Sleeping & Eating

It's hard to think why you might choose to stay overnight in Saidpur, and even if you do there is only one hotel that accepts foreigners.

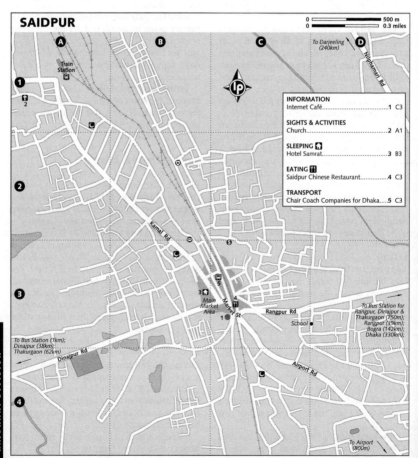

CHARS OF THE BRAHMAPUTRA *Bruno De Cordier*

An adventurous side trip, and a good way to see how rivers affect people's livelihoods, is to visit one of the chars in the Brahmaputra River. Chars are large sandbank islands that once belonged to the mainland. There are literally hundreds of chars, but their number and position change with the process of silting and erosion. There are estimated to be 230,000 char-dwellers in northern Bangladesh. They scratch out a living from agriculture, livestock and seasonal labour in towns on the mainland. When their makeshift villages flood and eventually disappear, they pack up and move to another sandbank.

To get to the chars, first go to the town of Kurigram and on to the village of Chilmari, about 40km south of Kurigram. There, take one of the long, engine-driven wooden 'service boats' that link the chars to the mainland.

Hotel Samrat (☎ 2105; Kamal Rd; s/d/VIP Tk 60/120/300) There's not much to recommend the standard rooms at the Samrat. However, the VIP room has chairs, a TV and a rooftop pretty much to itself. It's not pristine but it's private and has character.

There's a nice food culture on Market St; have a wander to see what's on offer. Opposite the Hotel Samrat is the **Saidpur Chinese Restaurant** (meals Tk 100), which is certainly the nicest place in town to eat.

Getting There & Away

The main bus station is about 1.5km east of the town centre. There are departures every few minutes until around 7pm for Rangpur (Tk 30, one hour) and Dinajpur (Tk 40 to Tk 50, one hour), and slightly less frequently for Thakurgaon (Tk 50, 1½ hours). If you're headed south for Jaipurhat (near the Paharpur ruins) you may have to wait so long for a direct bus that you're better off taking a series of buses.

There are chair-coach offices for Dhaka (Tk 200 to Tk 350) in the centre of town along Station Rd. Most coaches leave Saidpur after dark.

DINAJPUR

☎ 0531

On paper, Dinajpur is one of the largest centres in northwest Bangladesh, but in reality it acts like little more than an inflated village. The exotic central core is a cluttered labyrinth of mucky markets and soiled streets, and is the kind of place that can make home feel like a long way away.

The main reason for visiting is to ogle the nearby Kantanagar Temple and, in the town itself, interesting Dinajpur Rajbari with its adjoining Krishna Temple.

Orientation & Information

The train station is in the heart of town. The market, and most hotels and restaurants, are just north. South of the train station is the administrative area, including the circuit house, some imposing Raj-era buildings (the post office, mapping office etc) and a maidan (grassed area) that hosts cricket and badminton matches as well as political demonstrations.

You may be able to change money at **City Bank** (Hospital Rd), about 1km north of the train station, but there are no ATMs in the town. There are a few cyber cafés in town: **Dol's** (Hospital Rd), and **Aptouch** and **Galaxy Computer** off Station Rd.

Sights

Almost nothing now remains of the 100-year-old **Dinajpur Rajbari** save for a few mouldy walls and pillars, but the two Hindu temples standing within the grounds are both in good condition and well-worth hunting down. The rajbari is about 4km northeast of central Dinajpur. A rickshaw will cost at least Tk 20.

The **Krishna Temple**, to the left of the rajbari, is slapped in bright and bold paint, and full of columns and statues. Thanks to Dinajpur's Hindu population of around 38% (one of the highest in the country) the temple is still a living temple. Hindus coming out of the town to make *puja* fill the courtyard with laughter, and several Hindu families live permanently in the yellow-wash houses surrounding the temple.

If you are a colonial architecture buff, it's worth seeking out the formal-looking **town hall**, built with all the pomp the Brits could muster. The small garden fronting it contains a **statue** unusual for Bangladesh in that it's based on Classical Greek design.

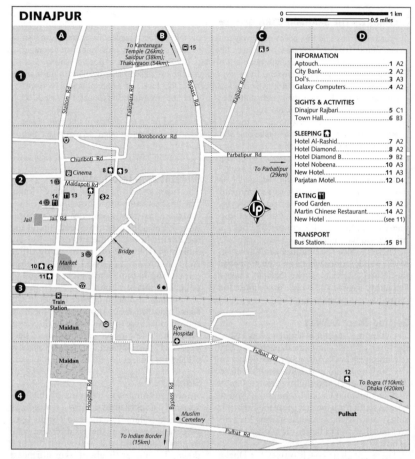

DINAJPUR

0 — 1 km
0 — 0.5 miles

To Kantanagar
Temple (26km);
Saidpur (38km);
Thakurgaon (54km)

Borobondor Rd

Churiboti Rd

Parbatipur Rd

To Parbatipur
(29km)

Cinema

Maldapoti Rd

Jail   Jail Rd

Bridge

Market

Train
Station

Maidan

Maidan

Eye
Hospital

Fulbari Rd

To Bogra (110km);
Dhaka (420km)

Pulhat

Hospital Rd

Bypass Rd

Muslim
Cemetery

To Indian Border
(15km)

Pulhat Rd

INFORMATION
Aptouch.................................1 A2
City Bank..............................2 A2
Dol's......................................3 A3
Galaxy Computers.................4 A2

SIGHTS & ACTIVITIES
Dinajpur Rajbari.....................5 C1
Town Hall.............................6 B3

SLEEPING
Hotel Al-Rashid.....................7 A2
Hotel Diamond......................8 A2
Hotel Diamond B...................9 B2
Hotel Nobeena....................10 A3
New Hotel...........................11 A3
Parjatan Motel.....................12 D4

EATING
Food Garden.......................13 A2
Martin Chinese Restaurant....14 A2
New Hotel ....(see 11)

TRANSPORT
Bus Station.........................15 B1

Sleeping

The accommodation scene in Dinajpur is dire indeed. We filtered out the real dives and were left with the following.

Hotel Al-Rashid (☎ 65658; s/d Tk 180/370) The small rooms on offer here are enough to keep jolly budget travellers happy. The rooms, though small, are well-maintained and come with mosquito nets, attached bathrooms and small alcoves with a desk. Staff will be utterly mystified by your presence, but happy to have you. To find it, look for the large pink building with the green Bengali sign.

Hotel Diamond (☎ 64629; s with/without air-con Tk 600/250, d with/without air-con Tk 850/350; ❄) Split between two separate buildings (opposite one and other) the Hotel Diamond is the best place in the city centre in which to stay. The large rooms are nice and inviting but the constant ring, ring of a thousand rickshaw bells on the street below will keep you up all night unless you have the air-con on full noise eruption. The budget rooms in the Hotel Diamond B are not all enjoyable, but they are pink, so that's nice.

Parjatan Motel (☎ 64718; Fulbari Rd; r from Tk 1380) Three kilometres out of town, this is one of the worst value Parjatan's in the country. The bland rooms, stained bed sheets and less than helpful management make the asking prices fairly ludicrous. Even so, it's the best place to sleep in Dinajpur.

There are a few cheaper places to stay though its highly unlikely that they will accept a foreign tourist. Still, if you're counting taka it might be worth hustling for a room at either the down-at-heel **New Hotel** or the marginally nicer **Hotel Nobeena**.

Eating

There is a range of small local restaurants, including some ultra-cheap choices (where hygiene is but a word) around the train station.

New Hotel (☎ 64155; Station Rd; meals Tk 40) The best Bangladeshi restaurant in the town centre by far, New Hotel's restaurant is very popular and open almost till midnight. There are vegetarian dishes here, too.

Food Garden (☎ 51899; Station Rd; mains Tk 130) A bright and cheerful new Chinese establishment that is popular at both lunch and dinnertime. It's a great respite from the searing intensity of the streets, and the clientele, who are generally better off Bangladeshis, won't overpower you with stares. It offers sensible half-portions and, should you feel like eating out on the dirty streets, take-away.

Martin Chinese Restaurant (☎ 64074; Station Rd; ☽ midday-9pm; mains Tk 130) The brightly coloured exterior of this restaurant sits in contrast to the gloomy interior, but even so the fussy waiters will bring forth a passable array of Chinese food. Expect to be dining alone.

Getting There & Away

BUS

The **bus station** (Rangpur Bypass Rd) is northeast of town. Buses go to Saidpur (Tk 40 to Tk 50, one hour), Thakurgaon (Tk 75, 1¾ hours) and Bogra ('luxury' bus Tk 200, 3½ hours). There are some direct luxury buses to Rajshahi (Tk 300, five hours), or a cheaper combination of local buses can be used with a change in Bogra.

Chair coaches to Dhaka (Tk 300, 7½ hours) depart between 5pm and 7pm. Some companies have offices in town.

For information on buses to Kantanagar Temple see p112.

TRAIN

A number of trains serve Dinajpur, though nobody ever really uses the train service as bus travel is so much quicker. There are two IC trains from Dinajpur to Parbatipur (30 minutes, depart 6.15am and 5.30pm). From here, going on to Dhaka (1st/*sulob* class Tk 510/230, 14 hours) is a long haul.

If you are headed for Khulna (1st/*sulob* class Tk 510/200) or Rajshahi (1st/*sulob* class Tk 175/60), you will need to go first to Parbatipur.

KANTANAGAR TEMPLE

Set in the graceful heart of gorgeous countryside, the rouge sandcastle of **Kantanagar Temple** (off Map p110; admission Tk 10; ☽ 7.30am-5.30pm) is a stunning block of religious artwork, and is surely one of the most impressive Hindu monuments in Bangladesh.

Built in 1752 by Pran Nath, a renowned maharaja from Dinajpur, it is the country's finest example of brick and terracotta style. Its most remarkable feature, typical of late-Mughal–era temples, is its superb surface decoration, with infinite panels of sculpted terracotta plaques depicting both figural and floral motifs.

The folk artists did not lack imagination or sense of humour. One demon is depicted swallowing monkeys, which promptly reappear from his ear. Other scenes are more domestic, such as a wife massaging her husband's legs and a lady combing lice from another's hair. Amorous scenes are often placed in obscure corners. These intricate, harmonious scenes are like a richly embroidered carpet.

This 15-sq-metre, three-storey edifice was originally crowned with nine ornamental two-storey towers, which collapsed during the great earthquake of 1897 and were never replaced. The building sits in a courtyard surrounded by offices and pilgrims' quarters (now occupied by several Hindu families), all protected by a stout wall. Visitors can no longer go inside the temple, which houses a Krishna shrine, but the intricate detail of its exterior will keep you engaged. A popular Hindu festival takes place here each November and would certainly be a colourful time to pop by.

Almost as much of an attraction is the utter peace and tranquillity of the site; after you've finished fawning over the temple take a stroll through the fields down to the nearby river. In the dry season the sandbanks exposed by the dropping water levels make a handy cricket pitch for local children.

It might be possible to stay at the **CDA training centre** at Proshikhan Kendra, 3km from the temple in the village of Mukundupur. It's a large complex and all rooms have an attached bathroom. Food is also available.

Getting There & Away

You can get a bus from Dinajpur to Kantanagar (Tk 14, 45 minutes, 26km). It's on the route to Thakurgaon but request Kantanagar, otherwise you may end up paying more and/or missing your stop.

From the main road where the bus drops you to the temple is 3km and a Tk 15 rickshaw ride for locals, but you would be lucky to get away with paying less than Tk 50. Ask the rickshaw to wait at the temple for you as there is no transport back again. The ride is along a pleasant, winding trail through a rural bliss of mustard, banana, rice and chilli fields, and little mud-and-wattle villages.

THAKURGAON

☎ 0561

Thakurgaon is one of the more pleasant towns in northern Bangladesh, with beautiful scenery and few motor vehicles. Very few foreign tourists visit as there are no attractions as such, but for some this very dearth of visitors will be the attraction.

If you're interested in seeing what local NGOs are doing, visit the office of the Humanitarian Agency for Development Services (HADS) and its farm on the southwestern edge of town. To arrange a visit drop by the HADS Guesthouse (which we don't recommend you stay in). There's also a **Rangpur Dinajpur Rural Services Project** (RDRS) office here.

Sleeping & Eating

RDRS Guesthouse (☎ 52032; s/d Tk 699/1099) Located a couple of kilometres south of town, this place is much less frequented by foreign tourists than the excellent branch in Rangpur. The staff here will take some time to recover from the shock of your arrival, but after this you will be presented with simple, but exceptionally clean and cool, rooms sheltered from all noise but that of twittering birds. There is a restaurant in which advance orders are essential (meals Tk 150), and plenty of English-speaking Bangladeshis keen for a chat work here. Altogether it represents superb value.

Hotel Salam International (☎ 53486; Howladar Market shopping centre, Bazar Rd; r Tk 700) As a foreigner, you are only likely to be allowed to stay in the vast, green 'deluxe' room. It's far from deluxe, but it does sleep three people

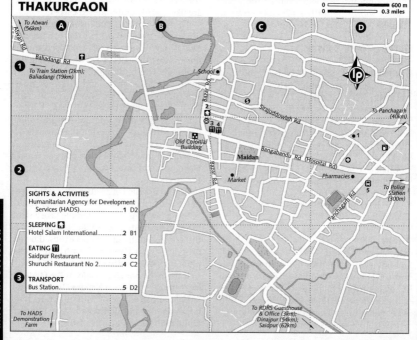

THAKURGAON

| 0 | 600 m |
| 0 | 0.3 miles |

SIGHTS & ACTIVITIES
Humanitarian Agency for Development
    Services (HADS).........................1 D2

SLEEPING
Hotel Salam International...............2 B1

EATING
Saidpur Restaurant........................3 C2
Shuruchi Restaurant No 2..............4 C2

TRANSPORT
Bus Station..................................5 D2

and the bathroom is even bigger than the sprawling room.

The **Saidpur Restaurant** (Hospital Rd) and the next door **Shuruchi Restaurant No 2** (Hospital Rd; mains Tk 50) are both equally decent places to stuff your gullet with all manner of meat and veg curries. Both attract the normal hordes of locals and starers.

Getting There & Away

All buses listed here depart from the bus station on the Dinajpur–Panchagarh Hwy, 500m south of Hospital Rd. Buses go south to Dinajpur (Tk 75, 1¾ hours, daily between 7am and 7.30pm), Saidpur (Tk 55, 1¾ hours, daily between 6.30am and 5.30pm) and Bogra (Tk 160, five hours, daily between 6.30am and 5.30pm).

BURIMARI

Burimari is a major crossing point into India, though it's hardly busy.

The customs office at the border is open from 8am to 6pm. It should take about 20 minutes to have your passport processed, but all the socialising and cha-drinking will slow you down.

There is nowhere to change money on the Bangladeshi side of the border, so make sure that before you leave India you grab enough taka to get you to your next destination.

If you arrive late at night at Burimari, you can stay at **Mahoroma Hotel** (s/d Tk 150/250), around the corner from the customs office. It has small but clean rooms with attached bathroom.

Getting There & Away

Getting to Burimari is a slow process. First take a bus from Rangpur to the dusty town of Lalmonirhat (Tk 45, every hour) on the other side of the Tista River and from there take another to Burimari (Tk 40). Once you arrive in Burimari, catch a three-wheeler to the customs office (Tk 10). Start early in the day if you are hoping to get to anywhere of significance in India before nightfall.

On the Indian side, at the town of Chengrabandha, there are no direct buses to Siliguri so you will have to go first to Jalpaiguri and then onto Siliguri (Rs 40). From Siliguri you can travel to Nepal, Darjeeling and Sikkim. There are also taxis and minibuses milling about in Chengrabandha.

If you're coming from India, you can arrange a coach to Dhaka (Tk 250 to Tk 400, 10 hours) directly from Burimari. The scenery is a typical introduction to the varying landscapes of Bangladesh.

RAJSHAHI
☎ 0721

Built on the northern bank of the Padma River, Rajshahi is a frantic and fun university town with enough colour and attractions to entertain for a few days. It also makes an excellent base from which to dig through the layers of history in Gaud, Puthia and Natore.

The river bank by the Padma River affords one of the best river views in the country and, in the late afternoon, a carnival-like atmosphere pervades with people strolling and chatting, children playing and vendors selling ice cream and other snack food.

Looking across the vast flood plain to the opposite bank you'll see India, where the river is called the Ganges. In the dry season it is sometimes possible to walk across the river bed, which aids the thriving smuggling trade along the border. The local trade in smuggled goods is most evident in Saheb Bazar.

Information

There are quite a few bookshops in New Market and to the north of Saheb Bazar. Rajshahi being a university town, the bookshops sell mainly academic texts, but the odd novel is available. There are several ATMs about the town centre which give cash advances on foreign cards.

Agrani Bank (Greater Rd) The best place to change money and travellers cheques.

Chartered Cyber Café (Saheb Bazar Rd; per hr Tk 20)

Syenthiya Computer (Saheb Bazar Rd; per hr Tk 20; ⏰ to 8pm) The best internet café, with broadband access.

Sights
VARENDRA RESEARCH MUSEUM

Founded in 1910 with the support of the maharaja of Dighapatia, the **Varendra Research Museum** (admission free; ⏰ 10am-5pm Sat-Wed, 2.30-5pm Fri) is managed by Rajshahi University (RU), and is the oldest museum in the country. The predominantly British-style building has some interesting Hindu-Buddhist features, including a trefoil arch over the doorways and windows. A small *rekha* temple forms the roof.

Inside, artefacts from all over the subcontinent are on display, including some rare examples from the ancient city of Mohenjodaro in Pakistan, and a superb collection of local Hindu sculpture.

RAJSHAHI DIVISION

RAJSHAHI

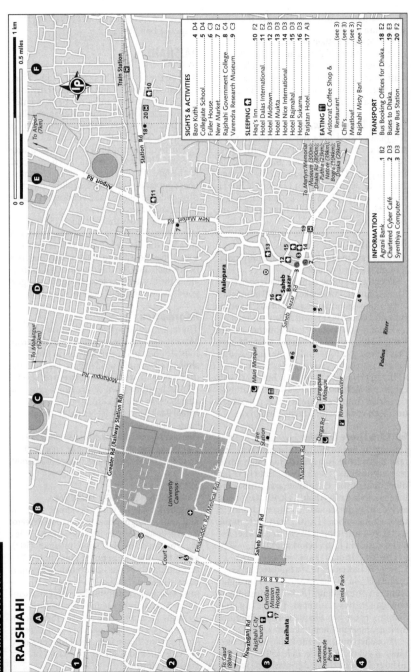

THE INFAMOUS INDIGO KUTHIS

In the 18th and early-19th centuries the trade in indigo – the plant that yields the indigo hue for dye – was highly profitable. By the mid-1800s the Rajshahi region alone had more than 150 indigo *kuthis*. The local zamindars (landowners) even loaned money to peasants so they could plant more indigo. Indeed, trade was so lucrative and the *kuthis* so numerous that factory labourers had to be imported.

The farmers, however, didn't profit at all and began changing crops. Using oppression and torture to keep the peasants growing indigo, angry zamindars sometimes went as far as committing murder and burning whole villages. An adage at the time held that 'no indigo box was despatched to England without being smeared in human blood'.

In 1859 the peasants revolted. The Indigo Revolt lasted two years and brought the cultivation of indigo to a halt. Eventually the government had no choice but to decree that the peasants could no longer be forced to plant indigo. As a result, by the end of the century the indigo trade had completely disappeared. Some of the *kuthis* were converted into silk factories but most simply fell into ruin.

MARTYRS' MEMORIAL MUSEUM

The collection of Liberation War mementos at the **Martyrs' Memorial Museum** (Shaheed Smriti Sangrahashala) at RU is a reminder of the dreadful days of the 1971 war. Unfortunately, the dilapidated state of the museum, with its dusty collection of war artefacts, is more likely to make one feel that the country has forgotten its heroes. Among the exhibits are blood-stained uniforms, a pen used by a fighter to write his last love letter, the deed papers of surrender by the Pakistani forces, and remains recovered from a mass grave of victims, among whom were intellectuals from RU.

BUILDINGS OF THE BRITISH RAJ

Near the centre of Rajshahi are some Raj-era buildings. **Rajshahi Government College**, which dates from 1873 when several maharajas donated money for its establishment, is an elegant two-storey edifice with beautiful semicircular arched windows. Others nearby include **Collegiate School** (1836), which consists of two single-storey structures east of the college, with verandas along the façades; and **Fuller House** (1909), a large two-storey red-brick building that is similar in appearance to the college.

BARO KUTHI

A block southeast of Rajshahi Government College, on a high bank of the Padma River, is a historic structure known as **Baro Kuthi**. It's one of the last remaining examples of the indigo *kuthis* (factories) that once flourished in the region. The simple buildings are of little architectural interest but their history is fascinating.

In the early-19th century Baro Kuthi was built by the Dutch for the silk trade, and served as a fort in times of emergency. Some rooms were probably used as a prison and for mounting cannons. After 1833, when Baro Kuthi was taken over by the British East India Company, it was used for the indigo trade (see above), which lasted about 25 years. It is reputed to have been the scene of countless crimes during that period.

NEW MARKET

If the town centre isn't bewildering enough then check out the cube of chaos that is the **New Market**, on the way to the train station. It is most active in the morning, and is a photographer's paradise.

Sleeping
BUDGET

Hotel Rajmahal (☎ 774 399; s/d from Tk 125/230) You can't grumble at the price and the rooms are reasonable, though ask to see a few first as some (the better rooms) have old sacks as carpets – novel, we'll grant you, but possibly not the most desirable of floor coverings. It's not certain that such temptations as a woman will be allowed to stay in this purely male environment. And to be honest you may not want to anyway.

Hotel Midtown (s/d Tk 200/400) When we passed by the receptionist was a 10-year old boy. Even so, he knew his stuff and treated us better than many an adult receptionist! This is a decent budget buy and as well as clean rooms they throw in an attached bathroom as well – can't really knock it can you?

RAJSHAHI DIVISION

MIDRANGE

Hotel Dalas International (☎ 773 839; Station Rd; s from Tk 300, d with/without air-con 800/500; ✿) Quite possibly the best central hotel and with a price that can't be faulted. Rooms are universally spacious and well-equipped with TV, chairs and big beds. It's handy for both the town centre and the bus and train stations. The English-speaking management loves a good old chin-wag.

Hotel Nice International (☎ 776 188; s with/without air-con Tk 500/200, d with/without air-con Tk 800/300; ✿) Rooms aren't as nice as the reception (and name) would suggest. Some smell like old carpet and old dahl, but then again so do many of the town's other cheap hotels and this place is no worse than them. If it's not too hot then opt for a non–air-con room as they are actually better value. It's located on a quiet side street.

Haq's Inn (☎ 810 420; Station Rd; s with/without air-con Tk 600/250, d with/without air-con Tk 950/500; ✿) A neat and tidy midrange option within easy stumbling distance of the train and bus station, which makes it ideal if you are just passing through. It's big enough to ensure that there are always shiny, clean rooms available.

Hotel Mukta (☎ 771 100; s with/without air-con Tk 650/120, d Tk 220; ✿) Locals will tell you that this is the top address in the city centre yet, for some bizarre reason, only the single rooms come with air-con. The rooms without air-con are miniscule and very hot, while those with air-con are much larger and airier and have better bathrooms. Even if it's not hot, you will want the air-con on full blast to drown out the sound of the road below. It's a friendly place, though becoming a little frayed around the edges.

Hotel Sukarna (☎ 770 670; s with/without air-con Tk 700/250, d with/without air-con Tk 700/400; ✿) The kindly English-speaking owner ensures that this hotel has a good vibe. There is a wide array of rooms from small depressing cheapies to comfortable and ample doubles with air-con. It's clean, well-maintained and good value.

Parjatan Hotel (☎ 770 247; just off Nawabganj Rd; s with/without air-con Tk 1000/450, d with/without air-con Tk 1200/700; ✿ Ⓟ) Try and ignore the grotesque '70s disaster architecture because this Parjatan establishment, situated in a quiet residential area out of town, is one of the better offerings in the chain. Even the cheaper rooms aren't half bad (though they do get steamy hot). If

you want a more luxurious room it's a good idea to book ahead as it's a very popular hotel. It contains all the standard Parjatan services including a quick-to-please restaurant. Add an extra 15% tax to room rates quoted. A rickshaw from the centre shouldn't cost more than Tk 15.

Eating

You can devour some of the best food in north Bangladesh in Rajshahi. For super cheap, super reliable restaurants open every hour, look no further than the flurry of places next to the Hotel Mukta. The best of this bunch is the Rahmania Hotel, which is Bangladesh through and through for around Tk 50 a meal.

Chili's (☎ 774 513; Saheb Bazar Rd; Chinese mains Tk 200) The Chili's emporium has a flurry of restaurants in the centre. The main tiger-stripe building gives you the chance to get flirty with a tasty Thai or Chinese meal upstairs, while downstairs you will discover a kebab joint and a 'fast food' restaurant (though exactly what the difference between kebabs and fast food is, isn't made clear).

ourpick Aristocrat Coffee Shop & Restaurant (Saheb Bazar Rd; ◷ 11.45am-10.30pm; mains Tk 150-200, cakes Tk 50) Locals dress sharp to come to this new restaurant and coffee shop situated above the Mercantile Bank. One half is a relaxed coffee shop with filter coffee, tempting cakes and a distinctly non-Bangladeshi vibe. The other half is the last word in Rajshahi sophistication and offers some of the best Indian and Chinese food you'll find in north Bangladesh – the chicken tikka masala is spot on as is the service.

Further fast food is available from the basement level **Meatloaf** (Saheb Bazar Rd; snacks Tk 70) – just pray that they don't play any while you're eating!

Rajshahi Misty Bari (Saheb Bazar Rd; ◷ 9am-8pm) is one of the better of the many Bengali sweet shops that clutter the centre.

You could also take a picnic to Simla Park, just beyond the circuit house on C&B Rd, overlooking the Padma River.

Getting There & Away
BUS

Most of the bus companies have their offices on Station Rd, next to the train and bus stations. Greenline has air-con buses to Dhaka (Tk 400, five hours, departing 8am, 3.15pm and 11.30pm).

You can also get ordinary buses to Bogra (Tk 60 to Tk 70, two hours, every 15 minutes between 6.15am and 5.45pm), Natore (Tk 30, one hour, every 20 minutes between 5am and 9.30pm), Jessore (ordinary/luxury Tk 140/180, 5½ hours, every 30 minutes between 6am and 6.30pm) and Rangpur (ordinary/luxury Tk 180/220, 4½ hours, every 45 minutes between 6am and 5pm).

CAR
Hire cars can be arranged through the Parjatan. The cost for a day drive to Gaud, Puthia and Natore (about 10 hours) should be around Tk 2400, including petrol.

TRAIN
IC trains depart from the **train station** (☎ 774 040) for Dhaka (1st/*sulob* class/air-con berth Tk 290/145/630, 6½ hours, 7am daily except Sunday).

There's a daily express to Jessore (1st/*sulob* class Tk 215/75, five hours) and Khulna (1st/*sulob* class Tk 260/90, seven hours), departing at 2pm.

PUTHIA
The delightful little village of Puthia (*pou*-tee-ah) is positively bursting at the seams with dilapidated palaces and bewitching temples, and is one of the shining highlights of Bangladesh. If Puthia were in almost any other country the ruins here would be seething in camera-snapping tourists, but lost as it is in the remote paddy fields of Bangladesh, you'll have it all to yourself.

The vegetation-chocked village centres on a cheerful bazaar and a number of lily covered ponds in which people fish, swim and wash both themselves and their buffalo.

Only 23km east of Rajshahi (16km west of Natore) and 1km south of the highway, the village is very accessible, which means that the scarcity of decent places to sleep poses no problem.

Information
Mr Bishwana, the caretaker of the temples and a gentleman in the truest sense of the word, works directly for the archaeology department and makes a charming guide. If he is not hanging around the Shiva Temple someone will quickly ferret him out for you. Even if you don't want a guide, he is the man with the keys to many of the sights so you will have to find him anyway. He can normally arrange for some lunch to be prepared at his house.

Sights
PALACES
The stately two-storey **Puthia Palace** was built in 1895 by Rani Hemanta Kumari Devi in honour of his illustrious mother-in-law, Maharani Sharat Sundari Devi. She was a major benefactor in the Rajshahi region, having built a boarding house for college students and a Sanskrit college, for which she was given the title 'maharani' in 1877. The building is in just good enough condition to serve as a college today. Though you probably won't be allowed inside, it's enough just to marvel at how grand the exterior is and how perfect the setting, with a large grassy maidan in front (which hosts regular afternoon cricket matches) and a frog-filled pond behind. In many ways the whole structure of this side of the village is similar to a medieval European village with its manor house, common ground and, further away, workers' houses.

Tahirpur Palace, 18km due north of Puthia, is up a back road along the Baralai River in Tahirpur. Rebuilt after the great earthquake of 1897, it's an imposing two-storey structure that, despite the collapse of its roof, remains largely intact.

TEMPLES
The most startling monument in Puthia village is the **Govinda Temple**, on the left-hand side of the rajbari's inner courtyard. Erected between 1823 and 1895 by one of the maharanis of the Puthia estate, it's a large, square structure with intricate terracotta designs embellishing the surface. In this sense, it's very similar in inspiration to the Kantanagar Temple (see p111), which is about a century older. Most of the terracotta panels depict scenes from the love affair between Radha and Krishna as told in the Hindu epics. The temple now contains a Krishna shrine and is visited by many of the local Hindu population.

There is a second, smaller **Govinda Temple** complex on the opposite side of the main pond. The couple of temples here have a beautiful domed, egg-shell roof and carvings that come close to rivalling that of the main Govinda Temple.

Built in 1823, the towering **Shiva Temple** sits at the entrance to Puthia, overlooking a pond.

It's an excellent example of the *pancha-ratna* (five-spire) Hindu style common in northern India. Unfortunately, many of the stone carvings and sculptures were disfigured during the 1971 Liberation War. The inside contains a huge black-stone phallic representation of Shiva. Many Hindus come to make *puja* here early in the morning or late evening and, with the mist rising off the pond and the light setting everything aflame, this is a beautiful time to come. An even more rewarding time to visit is during one of the two major pilgrimages that take place here – one in March/April and the other during the final week of August.

One of Bangladesh's finest examples of the hut-shaped temple is the **Jagannath Temple**, about 150m to the right (west) of the rajbari. This nicely restored 16th-century temple, measuring only about 5m on each side, features a single tapering tower that rises to about 10m. The temple's western facade is finely adorned with terracotta panels of mostly geometric design. Nearby are two much smaller rajbaris that are in a serious state of decay, despite now being government buildings. Even so, the atmosphere is out of this world.

Getting There & Away

There are numerous buses between Rajshahi and Natore (Tk 20, 30 minutes) throughout the day that pass through Puthia. On leaving Puthia, you can easily hail a bus travelling between the two towns on the main highway.

NATORE
☎ 0771

The small town of Natore is a place of split personality. On the one hand you've got the town centre itself; a dreary, noisy and depressing place. On the other hand you have elegant Natore Rajbari with its fanciful gardens and temple-hemmed ponds which, when combined with nearby Puthia, makes for an enchanting day trip from either Rajshahi or even Bogra.

Sights
NATORE RAJBARI
One of the oldest rajbaris in Bangladesh (dating from around the mid-1700s), the magnificent but dilapidated **Natore Rajbari** is actually a series of seven rajbaris, four of which remain largely intact. The main block, called Baro Taraf, is approached via a long avenue lined with impressively tall bottle palms, the white trunks of which resemble temple columns.

To the rear of Baro Taraf is a second block called Chhota-Taraf, consisting of two rajbaris. The principal one faces a pond and is one of the most beautifully proportioned buildings in Bangladesh.

The peaceful and idyllic gardens around the rajbari are as much an attraction as the building itself; bring a picnic to eat in the shade of a gnarled old tree. There are several large ponds here which form an interesting centre piece, around which are a couple of interesting Hindu temples, one dedicated to Kali and one to Shiva. Both are still used by the many Hindus in the area and attract the odd sadhu, making Natore about the only place in Bangladesh where you might bump into one of these wandering Hindu holy men. The beautiful complex attracts many locals in the evening who come to relax by the ponds and pass the time of day.

Natore Rajbari is at the northern edge of town, but to avoid getting lost it is easier to take the Natore–Bogra Rd and, 1km before the turn-off for Dighapatia Palace, take a left turn on an unmarked paved road that leads west towards the complex. It's 1.5km down that road, just beyond a school on your right.

UTTARA GANO-GHABAN
The building was once the palace of the Dighapatia Maharaja, the region's governor. It's now a government building called **Uttara Gano-Ghaban** (Dighapatia Palace) and serves as one of the president's official residences. Situated 3km north of town, off the road to Bogra, the beautifully maintained complex occupies about 15 hectares of land. It's enclosed within a moat and a high boundary wall, and is approached from the east through an imposing four-storey arched gateway. Unfortunately foreigners are not allowed to enter the complex.

Sleeping & Eating
Hotel Raj (☎ 66660; s/d Tk 60/120) Stay in a dark-green cell in this multistorey job opposite the bus stand (sign in Bengali only). It's very friendly, shockingly clean and as cheap as Bangladesh gets, which is very cheap indeed.

VIP Guest House (☎ 66097; s/d Tk 200/400) Nobody will argue with you when you say that this is the best place to stay in Natore and equally nobody will argue with you when you say that the sickeningly tacky bathroom doors aren't worth the price of admission. Away from the Snow White bathrooms, the large rooms are the cleanest and most comfortable for miles around and the attached restaurant the best place to eat (meals Tk 150). It's on the southern road into town.

The main drag is the best place for finding street food and a couple of restaurants.

Getting There & Away

Buses headed north and east leave from the intersection at the eastern end of town, while those headed for Rajshahi (Tk 30, one hour) leave from the west. There's a bus to Pabna (Tk 35, 1½ hours) and Bogra (Tk 40, 1½ hours).

PABNA
☎ 01731

Between Rajshahi and Dhaka, Pabna, which dates from medieval times, might be old but you'll be hard pressed to see its attractive side through the clouds of exhaust fumes and dust kicked up by throngs of passing trucks and buses. Despite this, the town has a couple of fine old buildings, a unique Hindu temple and two well-known rajbaris that make a quick stop well worthwhile.

Sights

JOR BANGLA TEMPLE

Built in the 18th century in the form of two traditional village huts intertwined and standing on a platform, the structure of this **temple**, 2km east of the town centre, is the best remaining example of the *jor bangla* (twin hut) style. However, the once clearly beautiful terracotta plaques carved with scenes of daily life are badly weathered and only of appeal to serious history buffs. Before construction was completed something sacrilegious occurred on the site, so the temple was never used.

A rickshaw from the centre will set you back around Tk 15.

RAJBARIS

The **Taras Rajbari**, viewed from the street through an unusually impressive archway, is a few hundred metres south of the town centre on the main road. Dating from the late 19th century, this grand red and white building

with a crazy coat of arms was evidently once an elegant palace, but it's now all too obviously the drab home of government offices.

Very close-by is a fairground-style **mosque** that is as bright and gaudy as you'll find in Bangladesh.

East of town, on the banks of the Padma River, **Sitlai Palace**, dating from 1900, is a grand rajbari that's fairly well preserved. Today it's occupied by a drug company, so you can't see the 30-room interior. The exterior is interesting however, with a broad staircase flagged with white marble, leading to a second-storey arched portico.

SHAHZADPUR MOSQUE

Just outside of Pabna is this splendid 15-dome pre-Mughal **mosque**, built in 1528 in traditional *bangla* (Pre-Mauryan and Mauryan) style with thick walls and various arched entrances.

Sleeping & Eating

Hotel Shilton (☎ 62006; s with/without air-con Tk 500/200, d with/without air-con Tk 600/250; 🅿) Easily the best place to stay in town, the spacious rooms are comfortable and offer what is, for Bangladesh, peace and quiet. It's clean, friendly and the staff speak English. Located at the southern end of town.

Hotel Park (☎ 64096; s with/without air-con Tk 600/220 d with/without air-con Tk 800/500; 🅿) On the main street, and the hotel everyone will point you towards. This is unfortunate because though the rooms themselves are okay, the bed sheets are far and away the most stained and grimy we've seen anywhere in Bangladesh. All rooms come with a bath, though of the sort that makes you feel dirtier *after* you've used it.

Sagotom Restaurant (Main Rd; mains Tk 80) This is the most popular restaurant in town on account of its delicious curries, biryanis and Chinese meals.

There are several other dirt-cheap hole-in-the-wall restaurants along the main road where a meal won't cost more than Tk 40.

Getting There & Away

Most buses leave from the main road just south of the town centre. There are buses to Dhaka via Aricha, although the expresses that originate in Rajshahi will probably be full. An ordinary bus to Dhaka costs Tk 200 to Tk 250, while the daily luxury bus (departing 9am) costs Tk 300.

Buses run to Rajshahi (Tk 150 to Tk 170, 2½ hours), Bogra (Tk 120 to Tk150, 1½ hours) and Kushtia (Tk 60 to Tk 70, one hour).

GAUD

A site of great historical importance, Gaud (or Gaur) has more historic mosques than any area in Bangladesh, except Bagerhat. It's over 100km west of Rajshahi, right on Bangladesh's western border – some of its sights are in India, some in Bangladesh.

The Hindu Senas established their capital here, after which the Khiljis from Turkistan took control for three centuries, to be followed in the late 15th century by the Afghans. Under the Afghans, Gaud became a prosperous city, surrounded by fortified ramparts and a moat, and spread over 32 sq km. Replete with temples, mosques and palaces, the city was visited by traders and merchants from all over Central Asia, Arabia, Persia and China. A number of mosques are still standing today, and some have been restored. None of the buildings from the earlier Hindu kingdoms remain.

Today there is something of a strange air lying over the town and it doesn't seem quite Bangladeshi. At first you can't work out what it is that's missing, but then you realise that nobody is responding to your greetings and, even more strangely, the streets are almost deathly quiet. No people, no cars, no trucks and, most weird of all, no rickshaws.

Sights
MOSQUES

Built between 1493 and 1526, the well-preserved **Chhota Sona Masjid** (Small Golden Mosque) is oddly named given that it's actually jet black with just patches of terracotta brickwork. Despite its misleading name, it's still a fine specimen of pre-Mughal architecture. The chief attraction here is the superb decoration carved on the black-stone walls. On both the inner and outer walls, ornate stonework in shallow relief covers the surface. It also features an ornate women's gallery, arched gateways and lavishly decorated mihrabs (niches). This living mosque draws in large crowds for Friday prayers, but outside prayer time its fine for foreigners to enter.

The gorgeous single-domed **Khania Dighi Mosque** (also known as Rajbibi Mosque), built in 1490, is in Chapara village and is in excellent condition. Though it also has some ornately decorated walls, embellished primarily with terracotta floral designs, it's the domed roof that is the attraction. Built of thousands of miniscule Lego-like bricks, it's one of the more arresting mosques in the country. Like the Chhota Sona Masjid it's a working mosque, in which Friday prayers are especially animated. It's fine for women to enter outside of prayer time but they must be respectfully dressed. The mosque's position, crouching under the mango trees beside a large lily- and duck-covered pond, only helps to enhance its beauty.

Built around 1470, the palace-like **Darasbari Mosque** is in poorer condition than the other two. Its domed roof long since gave up the ghost and collapsed and vanished into the rich soils. Talking of ghosts, what remains of this whimsical and secluded red-brick ruin seems like the perfect spot for spirits to float silently between the pillars.

MONUMENTS IN FIROZPUR

At nearby Firozpur you'll find several interesting structures that are all fairly well preserved and close to one another. One is the picturesque **Shah Niamatullah Mosque**, a three-domed mosque built in 1560 which overlooks a large pond. About 100m away is the **Mausoleum of Shah Niamatullah Wali**; it has three domes and four squat towers. The third structure, north of the mausoleum, is **Tahkhana Palace**, built by Shah Shuja in the early 17th century and the area's major Mughal-era building. A large two-storey brick edifice, it has a flat roof, which in those times was virtually unheard of in Bangladesh.

Sleeping & Eating

It's best to visit Gaud as a day trip from Rajshahi as there is little in the way of tourist facilities.

The **Archaeology Department Rest House** (Tk 250) has fairly basic but decent rooms. If you just show up, chances are excellent that you'll be allowed to stay because there is no other accommodation in Gaud, barring some extremely basic rooms above an equally basic **restaurant** where the bus stops near the Bangladeshi border post.

Getting There & Away

Getting to Gaud can take so damn long that you'll forget how close you are to Rajshahi. From the main bus terminal in Rajshahi, take a bus to Nawabganj (Tk 40, two hours) from where it should be possible to get a bus directly to Gaud (Tk 30) every hour or so. If you get blank looks when you ask for 'Gaud', (which you will!) try 'India' or 'border' instead.

The consolation of all of this messing about is that the scenery on the journey is quite unusual. There are fascinating expanses where village life takes place amid enormous expanses of trees with foot-worn pathways meandering between them. There are mud-brick huts interspersed throughout, mustard fields so bright you almost have to squint, and thousands of stumpy mango trees (May–June is the mango season).

On arrival in Gaud it is a good idea to call on the friendly soldiers at the border post. They can advise you where not to go; the strip of no-man's-land between the two countries is just as intensively farmed as surrounding areas, so it's easy to make a mistake.

Chittagong Division

Chittagong division contains some of the highlights of Bangladesh. And we mean literally HIGH lights. This fantastically diverse region stretches from the world's longest, unbroken beach at the brash resort of Cox's Bazar to Burmese-tasting hills 1000m high and a thousand stories thick. Much of the region feels like a different country altogether. If you've spent much time absorbing the ruler-straight horizons elsewhere in Bangladesh, it will be a pleasure to stare at ruffled peaks and troughs, and after visiting so many straight-edged mosques, the golden pinnacles of a Buddhist stupa are poetry indeed. Even the people themselves are different; gone are the clogging crowds of India, in are the gentle smiles of southeast Asia.

Chittagong division is truly a meeting point and, unfortunately, sometimes a battleground between two very different sets of ideas, religions, cultures, peoples and landscapes. All this means that it's not just one of the highlights of Bangladesh, but that it is one of the most fascinating areas of Asia.

HIGHLIGHTS

- Sailing around the countless unfathomably green islands littering the surface of Kaptai Lake at **Rangamati** (p130), home to the smiling Chakma tribe

- Giving into the enthusiasm of Bangladeshi holiday crowds at **Cox's Bazar** (p136) and cheering for floaters and tubes in the annual surfing contest. Yes, you read that right!

- Swinging the days away in a hammock on **St Martin's Island** (p141), Bangladesh's only coral island

- Chilling with the monks in **Chitmorong** (p133), a serene Buddhist village on the shores of a deep-blue lake

- Hiking a slippery mountain trail to the remote tribal villages surrounding **Bandarban** (p134), the most scenically beautiful chunk of Bangladesh

Rangamati ★

★Chitmorong
Bandarban ★

Cox's Bazar ★

St Martin's
Island ★

CHITTAGONG

☎ 31

The sticky city of Chittagong (the second-largest city in Bangladesh, with a population of around four million) is the country's busiest port. The constant stream of super ships that line its docks bring with them more than just material goods – they bring ideas, fashions and philosophies from around the world. It's this cosmopolitan exchange of minds that makes Chittagong such a fascinatingly different side of Bangladesh to explore for a few days.

History

Locals say the word Chittagong originated from *chattagram* (small village), though it more likely comes from the Rakhaing (Arakanese) phrase *tsi-tsi-gong* ('war should never be fought') inscribed on a tablet brought by an invading Buddhist army.

Despite its name, Chittagong has been consistently fought over. In 1299 Muslims occupied the city, until the Rakhaing retook it and retained it until 1660. The Mughals took possession next, only to be expelled by the Rakhaing in 1715. Finally, in 1766, the British raised their flag.

The evolution of the city followed a similar pattern to Dhaka, except that the oldest parts (where the city of Sadarghat now stands) were wiped out during the British and post-Independence periods. The Pakistani navy shelled the city during the Liberation War.

Orientation

Station Rd is basically the centre of town and is a good reference point. Towards its eastern end, on the corner of Jubilee Rd, is the large New Market building (Riponi Bitan).

The Central Bazar is a warren of lanes between the lower ends of Jubilee and Station Rds. It's almost impossible not to lose your way among the densely packed rows of clothing shops.

The more upmarket shopping area is along CDA Ave, at the intersection of Zakir Hossain and Nizam Rds, which is called GEC Circle. There are also a number of restaurants in this area.

Chittagong's business district is the Agrabad Commercial Area, the grid of streets between Sheikh Mujib Rahman Rd and the Hotel Agrabad, around which you'll find numerous international airline offices.

MAPS

Mappa publishes a good Chittagong city map. You may be able to buy one from a bookshop on CDA Ave, or from street vendors.

Information

GEC Circle has a couple of internet cafés, and there are banks in the Agrabad Commercial Area.

Dot.com (GEC Circle; per hr Tk 20) For internet access.

HSBC Near the Ethnological Museum; has an ATM.

Main post office (Suhrawardi Rd; ⏱ 8am-8.30pm Sat-Thu)

Standard Chartered Bank With branches on Station Rd and Central Bazar; and a 24hr ATM at Peninsula Chittagong Hotel lobby, CDA Ave.

Sights & Activities

OLD CITY

As in Dhaka, the city's oldest area is the waterfront area called Sadarghat. Also just like in Dhaka, this is a cacophony of sensual assaults. The early arrival of the Portuguese is evinced by the proximity of the Paterghatta district, just next to Sadarghat, which remains a Christian area. There isn't much to see in Paterghatta, but it's a quiet, clean place to walk around – until you get into the slums of the prawn-sellers around the waterfront near Feringhee Bazar, which will leave an enduring stench on your shoes and in your mind. A rowboat back to Sadarghat costs anything from Tk 5.

You can hire a boat from the boat terminal to go across the river (Tk 20, 10 minutes) to the **fish harbour and market**. The **Marine Fisheries Academy** is housed in a new building with a small museum.

Shahi Jama-e-Masjid, in Anderkilla (inner fort), was built in 1670 on a hillock and hence looks a bit like a fort. The mosque has a tall minaret, Saracenic or Turkish in design, which looms up out of the shops that have since surrounded it. In the early 1950s it was greatly enlarged and most of its original features altered, though a number of original inscriptions are still embedded in the walls.

The **Chilla of Badar Shah** derives its name from a Sufi (ascetic Muslim mystic) who came to Chittagong in 1336. It is a modest-sized place with a courtyard and worship area built around the grave of Badar Shah, and is within walking distance from the Shahi-Jama-e-Masjid. There are several *mazars* (graves) in the area, so make sure you're directed to the right one – ask for 'Badar Shah Chilla'.

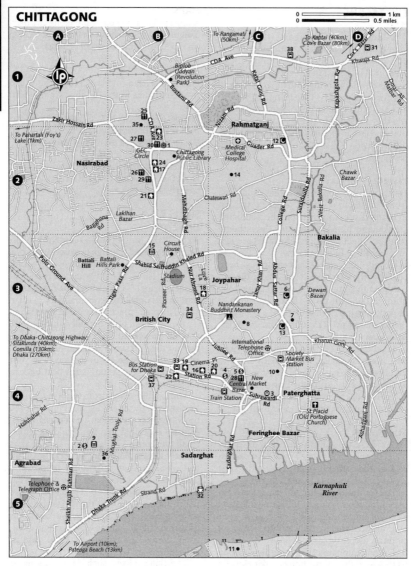

On the same road are some interesting shops that make traditional *tablas* (musical instruments).

BRITISH CITY

The British originally occupied the area just northwest of Sadarghat, a slightly hilly section where they built their usual collection of administrative and cultural edifices. Since the British departure, this area has become the central business district of Chittagong.

The **Zia Memorial Museum** (admission Tk 2; 10.30am-4.30pm Sat-Wed, 3.30-7.30pm Fri) is housed in an interesting mock-Tudor mansion. Among its much-revered collection is the microphone and transmitter with which

President Zia proclaimed the country's independence in 1971, and you can see the blood-stained and bullet-damaged wall at the foot of the stairs where Zia was shot.

The **Chandanpura Mosque** is north of the city centre on the road to Kaptai, near Dewan Bazar. It has no historical importance but is an attractive sight with its flamboyant design.

Fairy Hill is said to be named for the fairies and genies that were believed to occupy it when the Sufi saint Badar Shah first came to Chittagong. Legend says that he made a number of requests to the fairies before they would allow him to build a place of worship. It's behind the main post office and New Market – climb the path leading off Jubilee Rd just north of the pedestrian bridge near New Market. Ask directions for the **High Court**, the building on top of the hill – Fairy Hill was the common name during the Raj era and is rapidly being forgotten.

Atop **DC Hill** is the district commissioner's residence, but the surrounding area is open to the public. It is a pleasant place with many old trees.

The tear-inducing **WWII Memorial Cemetery** contains the graves of hundreds of soldiers from both Allied and Japanese forces who died on the Burma front. Most are inscribed with simple and powerful epitaphs of loss and love. The cemetery is maintained by the Commonwealth War Graves Commission.

MODERN CITY

There is little to see in Agrabad, the modern commercial section. The interesting **Ethnological Museum** (🕐 9am-1pm & 1.30-4pm Mon-Wed, 9am-noon Thu) has displays on Bangladesh's tribal people. Unfortunately, it isn't always open when it should be. Some of the exhibits are looking a bit tattered, but it covers all the major tribal groups of the nearby Chittagong Hill Tracts.

The museum's assumption that these cultures are doomed is depressing, though sadly, probably true.

QADAM MUBARAK MOSQUE

Built in 1719 in the Rahmatganj area, the late-Mughal **Qadam Mubarak Mosque** derives its name from a slab that bears an impression of the Prophet's foot *(mubarak)*.

PAHARTALI LAKE

Also known as **Foy's Lake**, this area has boating facilities and is a popular picnic spot; things get hectic on weekends. Early in the morning is a nice time to visit, and on a cool day, walking is pleasant in the denuded hills around the lake. There is a zoo here, but it's a wretched place. A high hill near the lake's edge affords grand views of Chittagong and the Bay of Bengal. You can get to the lake by rickshaw (Tk 15) or tempo (auto-rickshaw, Tk 5) from the junction of CDA Ave and Zakir Hossain Rd.

KARNAPHULI RIVER

An unusual adventure is to head out onto the Karnaphuli River, close to the airport, where you'll be blown away by the massive number of equally massive ships riding at anchor in this deep-water channel. To get here take a baby taxi (mini auto-rickshaw; with bargaining you might get it down to Tk

CHITTAGONG DIVISION

200 return) along the river in the direction of the airport. Just before you reach the junction turning away from the river and leading immediately to the airport, you will see a small jetty with little wooden boats moored up. Ask here about renting one for an hour or so to explore – Tk 200 should suffice for a small boat.

Be warned that this is a working port and there is also a naval base in close proximity, therefore cameras (and big boats) might prove problematic. If you manage to get out onto the river then you can count yourself a real explorer as we haven't heard of anyone managing to do this – so be sure to let us know what you find!

Sleeping
BUDGET

Very few of the true cheapies are willing to accept foreign guests, and budget travellers should be prepared to pay a little more in Chittagong than elsewhere.

Silver Inn Hotel (☎ 632 752; 335 Station Rd; s/d Tk 250/500, d with air-con Tk 800; 🔀) Next to the Golden Inn and, as the name suggests, suitably less classy. The rooms are large but that only means more space for all the grot to breed. Still you can certainly do worse in Chittagong and at least it will accept foreigners.

Hotel Miskha (☎ 610 923; 95 Station Rd; s/d Tk 280/400) You get a lot for your money at the Miskha, including a charming manager who thinks that everything is '100%' and can't do enough for you. The rooms have a slight old-world feel, though that might just be because none of the furniture has been changed for decades.

Hotel Park Residential (☎ 623 320; 5/6 Zakir Hossain Rd; s/d Tk 300/600, d with air-con Tk 800; 🔀) This is one of the few real cheapies in this upper-crust neighbourhood. The bad news is that we've seen rabbit hutches with more space and therefore the non–air-con rooms get stinking hot. On the plus side they're far cleaner and much brighter than any of the other cheapies in the city and the staff are insanely friendly.

MIDRANGE

Hotel Al-Faisal International (☎ 619 000; www.hotel alfaisal.com; 1050 Nur Ahmed Rd; s from Tk 400, d with/ without air-con Tk 1000-500; 🔀) One of the better midrange options, the large rooms have heat-repelling tiled floors and crispy clean

bed sheets. The manager is chatty and it's not far from the stadium so you can catch cricket-match-day enthusiasm. Add 5% extra tax on room rates.

Hotel Sylhet Super (☎ 841 451; 16 Station Rd; s with/without air-con Tk 700-300, d with/without air-con Tk 1000/450; 🔀) On the remote chance that the Hotel Golden Inn is full then let your little legs rush you without hesitation straight over the road to this place. The rooms are functional and contain no scary sights, and the staff are cool.

Hotel Golden Inn (☎ 611 004; 336 Station Rd; economy s with/without air-con Tk 750/400, d with/without air-con Tk 1100/725; 🔀 🖵) Save yourself some hassle by heading straight to this honey of a hotel. The spacious rooms are pleasantly thought out and starting to gather that nice old-fashioned air. It is a vast, echoing place with enough rooms to ensure that late comers never have to sleep in the stables. It also has rooms for three or four people which is handy for groups of friends travelling together. There is a restaurant, a rooftop courtyard with good views and a travel agency at the front of the building, convenient for buying domestic airline tickets.

Asian SR Hotel (☎ 285 0346; www.asiansrhotel .com; 291 Station Rd; s/d from Tk 600/1000, premium s/d from Tk 1000/1700; 🔀) Just two minutes walk from the train station, this new arrival on the midrange scene is great value. It doesn't have much flavour but if you want clean and functional lines for an unbeatable price then this is your man. It's so new that everything retains it's just-opened shiny appearance. A platoon of room staff will help you with everything – even with things you don't want help with! Add an extra 15% tax to room rates.

TOP END

our pick **Grand Park Hotel** (☎ 620 044; facl@myway .com; 787 CDA Ave; s/d Tk 2500/3000; 🔀 🖵) The Grand Park Hotel is easily the best value hotel in its class. The hotel is only small but the rooms gigantic – you literally need to pack supplies to walk from one end of the room to the other. All rooms have a nice old-world charm thanks to the copious use of wooden wardrobes, desks, bedheads and Hindu-inspired art. The bathrooms glitter in all their clean glory and the whole ensemble exudes a certain elegance that its competitors lack.

Meridian Hotel (☎ 654 000; meridian@techno-bd.net; 1367 CDA Ave; s/d from Tk 2618/2723) Firstly, this isn't a part of the chain you know only too well. However, despite the blatant copyright issue, this is a decent top-end option with low prices and large, character infused rooms of a certain old-world charm. The bathrooms are some of the best in Bangladesh and the curtains so kitsch that you cannot help but grow fond of them. The staff are very friendly, the furniture of a quality you rarely find today but the complimentary breakfast is very stingy.

Peninsula Chittagong (☎ 285 0860/9; www.peninsulactg.com; 486 CDA Ave; r from US$130; ✶ ▢) Touted as the 'best business-class hotel in Chittagong' it's a carbon copy of every other IKEA-class business hotel on the planet. This means high levels of peace, comfort and service but less character than a blank piece of paper. The highlight, literally, is the wonderful lofty views over the city from the massive bedroom windows. It has a plethora of Asian and continental restaurants, rooftop pool (non-guests Tk 300) and internet in all rooms.

Eating

Jubilee Rd is one of the best cheap restaurant areas, whilst CDA Ave is the place to go for more upmarket eating.

New Madina (Jubilee Rd; mains Tk 30-40) Full of character, this is the friendliest and tastiest of several similar hole-in-the-wall establishments.

Hotel & Restaurant Azad (Station Rd; mains Tk 40) There are many rock-bottom-price eating establishments on Station Rd, but this is one of the cleaner and brighter places. Biryani is the speciality.

Hotel Sonali (GEC Circle; meals from Tk 40) Hordes of local students and workers enjoy the chance to eat for next to nothing in a place that, with its funky paint job and terrace seating, inspires lingering meals and lasting conversations. A rare find indeed in the world of cheap restaurants.

Well Food Centre (GEC Circle; meals Tk 30-120) A modern complex of different restaurants in an airport-sterile environment. The 'Western meals' aren't really anything of the sort but the downstairs snacks are perfect for a light lunch.

Hotel Zaman (GEC Circle; mains Tk 100-150) Ignore the misleading name; this isn't a place to sleep but rather a place to indulge in sensational Bangladeshi food in a classy but comfortable atmosphere.

There are two **Sayeman** (CDA Ave; meals Tk 150-200) restaurants across the road from each other. One specialises in rich Mughali cuisine, the other in fiery Thai dishes.

The Crystal Lounge & Restaurant (☎ 886 688; 805 CDA Ave; mains Tk 170-200, snacks Tk 120) Sleek, modern and fashionable, you will feel like you're in the city when you eat here. Meals are mainly Western based with lots of pasta and steaks, but there are also filling sandwiches, delicious fruit smoothies and some Thai treats.

Bonanza Food Plus (☎ 652 079; 1692 CDA Ave; mains from TK 200; ✶) You certainly won't get sloppy dhal and stringy chicken at this sophisticated but well-priced restaurant. Many consider it to be the finest eating establishment in the city and it is, without doubt, the place to experience everything good about Bangladeshi food.

Getting There & Away

The Dhaka–Chittagong Hwy is probably the busiest, and scariest, highway to hell in the country and is prone to bumper-to-bumper traffic jams (though at least this slows everyone down). At all costs avoid travelling along it at night. Taking the train to Dhaka is far less nerve-racking.

AIR

GMG Airlines (☎ 655 659; gmgairlines.com; CDA Ave) has four or five flights a day to/from Dhaka (Tk 4220, 45 minutes) and to Cox's Bazar (Tk 3450, 30 minutes) on Tuesday, Thursday and Saturday.

United Airways (☎ 650 7671; www.uabdl.com; CDA Ave) has two to four flights daily to Dhaka (Tk 3945), as well as flights to Cox's Bazar (departs 9.45am Sunday and Thursday).

Best Air, with offices at the airport, also has daily flights between Chittagong and Dhaka for Tk 3390.

It has recently become possible to fly to select international destinations from Chittagong. GMG has flights to Bangkok for US$195.

BOAT

The **Bangladesh Inland Waterway Transport Corporation (BIWTC) terminal** is near the end of Sadarghat Rd, a few hundred metres to the west along the river bank. The administration office is clearly marked in English, but tickets are sold from a nondescript building just before the office. Book early if you want a 1st-class cabin.

Launches go to Barisal (1st/2nd/deck class Tk 850/560/120, 18 hours, departs 9am Monday). The same boat stops at Hatiya Island and Sandwip Island.

BUS

The largest bus station is **Bardarhat** (Cox's Bazar Rd), 4km north of the city centre. To get there, take a local bus (Tk 5) or rickshaw (Tk 10) from Nur Ahmed Rd. From here, buses leave for Cox's Bazar (Tk 120, four hours) and Bandarban (Tk 50, three hours) every 15 minutes between 6am and 6pm.

Buses leave from **Modapur bus station** (CDA Ave) for Rangamati (Tk 75 to Tk 80, luxury bus Tk 130, 2½ hours) and Kaptai (Tk 70, two hours, half-hourly 7am to 7pm).

Most Dhaka-bound private bus companies operate out of the old **BRTC bus station** (Station Rd). There are air-con chair coaches to Dhaka (Tk 450 to Tk 600, five to six hours).

Luxury buses to Cox's Bazar (Tk 250, four hours, every half hour between 5.30am and 7.30pm) and Sylhet (Tk 650, evening only departures) leave from the **Cinema Palace bus station** (Nur Ahmed Rd).

TRAIN

The four intercity (IC) trains a day to Dhaka (1st/*sulob* class Tk 290/125; six hours; depart 7am, 7.15am, 2.30pm and 11pm) go through Comilla (1st/*sulob* class Tk 140/60). There's a sleeper option (Tk 660) on night trains. Tickets should be booked two or three days in advance. There's an IC train to Sylhet (1st/*sulob* class Tk 490/190, 10 hours, departs 9pm).

Getting Around
TO/FROM THE AIRPORT

There isn't always a bus to meet incoming flights and the airport is a long way out from town – baby taxis cost at least Tk 150. You could try catching a bus to New Market (Tk 10) at the T-junction, 500m from the airport.

LOCAL TRANSPORT

Rickshaws and baby taxis are plentiful, and cost about the same as in Dhaka. Tempos and buses are cheaper, but are cramped and can be

frustrating if you don't speak Bengali – routes aren't easy to decipher.

AROUND CHITTAGONG

A few sites around Chittagong are challenging to get to but worth the effort.

Shakpura

This small village, 24km south of the city, has Buddhist and Hindu temples. The **Nindam Kanon Temple** is a meditation centre.

Buses to Shakpura (Tk 25, eight daily) leave from Bardarhat bus station in Chittagong.

Ship-Breaking Yards

Along the shore north of Chittagong, every kind of ocean-going vessel, from super tankers to tugboats, is dismantled – all with manual labour. At any one time there can be 30 ships beached on the shoreline between the towns of Bhatiara and Sitakunda. Armies of workers use blowtorches, sledgehammers and plain brute force to tear them apart. It's such a bizarre sight that the ship-breaking yards have become a popular setting in Bangladeshi movies, typically as bad-guy hang-outs.

Actually getting to visit the yards is virtually impossible nowadays, and with every negative exposé in the Western media it becomes harder still (see boxed text, below). Site supervisors are very reticent to let anyone wander around, particularly with a camera.

An easier and surprisingly impressive way of seeing the yards is from the air. Most Dhaka–Chittagong flights pass right over the top of the yards a few moments before landing.

Sitakunda

About 36km north of Chittagong, this sleepy town has one attraction – the historic Hindu **Chandranath Temple**. There are great views from the top, which can be a real treat in flat Bangladesh. Unless you have a particular interest in Hindu temples and don't mind an

---

SHIPSHAPE?

Ship-breaking is a controversial industry. Greenpeace, among other organisations, says it can threaten public health, the environment, and the rights and lives of workers. For more information on Greenpeace's stance on Chittagong's ship-breaking yards, visit www.greenpeaceweb.org/shipbreak/.

hour's uphill climb, it's only really worth visiting during the **Shiva Chaturdasi Festival**, held for 10 days in February and attracting thousands of Hindu pilgrims.

To get there, take a bus for Feni (Tk 25, 45 minutes) from the Kadamtale bus station in Chittagong (Map p124).

CHITTAGONG HILL TRACTS

Decidedly untypical of Bangladesh topography and culture, the 13,180 sq km of the Hill Tracts comprises a mass of hills, ravines and cliffs covered with dense jungle, bamboo, creepers and shrubs.

About half the tribal population are Chakma; the remainder are mostly Marma (who represent about a third of the tribal population) and Tripura. Among the many much smaller groups, the Mru (called Murung by Bangladeshis) stand out as the most ancient inhabitants of the area.

The culture and lifestyle of the Adivasis (tribal people) are very different from that of the Bangladeshi farmers of the plains. Some tribes are matriarchal, and all have similar housing – made entirely of bamboo and covered by thatched roofs of dried leaves. In most other respects, the tribes are quite different, each having its own distinctive rites, rituals, dialect and dress, eg Chakma women wear indigo-and-red striped sarongs.

The women are particularly skilled in making handicrafts, while some of the men still take pride in hunting with bows and arrows.

The area, full of the flavours of Burma, is utterly fascinating and very beautiful. It also offers a chance to stretch the legs with some exciting hiking between tribal communities.

History

Under the British, the Hill Tracts gained special status and only Adivasis could own land there, but the Pakistani government abolished the special status of the Hill Tracts as a 'tribal area' in 1964. The construction of the Kaptai Lake for hydroelectricity in 1960 was an earlier blow, submerging 40% of the land used by the Adivasis for cultivation, and displacing 100,000 people. The land provided for resettlement was not sufficient and many tribal people became refugees in neighbouring northeastern India.

During the Liberation War, the then Chakma king sided with the Pakistanis, so

WARNING

The safety situation in the Chittagong Hill Tracts has improved enormously over the past few years and trips to both Bandarban and Rangamati will almost certainly be problem free. However, this doesn't mean everything is roses and you should certainly only consider exploring remoter parts of the region with a reputable tour operator.

when independence came, the Adivasis' plea for special status fell on deaf ears. The Chakma king left for Pakistan and later became that country's ambassador to Argentina.

Meanwhile, more and more Bengalis were migrating into the area, usurping the land. In 1973 the Adivasis initiated an insurgency. To counter it, the government, in 1979, started issuing permits to landless Bengalis to settle there, with title to tribal land. This practice continued for six years and resulted in a mass migration of approximately 400,000 people into the area – almost as many as all the tribal groups combined. Countless human-rights abuses occurred as the army tried to put down the revolt.

From 1973 until 1997 the Hill Tracts area was the scene of a guerrilla war between the Bangladeshi army and the Shanti Bahini rebels. The troubles stemmed from the cultural clash between the tribal groups and the plains people.

Sheikh Hasina's government cemented an internationally acclaimed peace accord in December 1997 with tribal leader Jyotirindriyo Bodhipriya (Shantu) Larma. Rebel fighters were given land, Tk 50,000 and a range of other benefits in return for handing in their weapons. The peace deal handed much of the administration of Khagrachhari, Rangamati and Bandarban districts to a regional council. The struggle to have the accord fully honoured continues today.

Information

Whether a permit is required to visit the Hill Tracts can change from month to month. At the time of writing, permits were absolutely required.

To obtain a permit, fax your details to the district commissioner (DC) of the district you intend to visit three days before you enter the region (see p130 for fax numbers).

CHITTAGONG DIVISION

DISTRICT COMMISSIONER FAX NUMBERS

Bandarban
District commissioner 0361-62509

Khagrachhari
District commissioner 0371-61674
Superintendent of police 0371-61755

Rangamati
District commissioner 0351-63020
Superintendent of police 0351-63127

The DC should forward your details to the relevant 'foreigner checkpoints', but this doesn't always happen. You must provide your name, native country, passport number, district you intend to visit, purpose of visit, duration of stay, occupation, mode of transport, probable date of visit, expected date of return and signature.

It is a good idea to type your details and keep the original on your person – it will look far more official to checkpoint police than a handwritten application. Also try to procure some sort of receipt to show that you have faxed the information in good time. It's also sensible to fax the same details to the relevant superintendent of police. None of this guarantees that you'll be allowed to visit, but it will increase your chances.

Finally, always carry numerous photocopies of your permit with you to give out like sweets at the numerous checkpoints.

Most people book accommodation in advance through a tour operator who then sort out all the paper work for you, but even then it still takes at least three days to complete all the formalities.

Tours

The following companies operate reliable and interesting tours to the Chittagong Hill Tracts.

Bengal Tours (Map p62; ☎ 02-882 0716; www.bengal tours.com; House 66, Rd 10, Block D, Banani) In Dhaka.

Guide Tours (Map p62; ☎ 02-988 6983; www .guidetours.com; Darpan Complex, 1st fl, Gulshan Circle II, Gulshan) In Dhaka. In addition to tours, it has also recently opened the Hillside Resort (p135), 4km from Bandarban.

Unique Tours & Travels (☎ 02-988 5116; unique@ bangla.net; 51B Kemal Ataturk Ave, Banani, Dhaka)

Rangamati

☎ 0351

The elongated village of Rangamati, 77km east of Chittagong, is beautifully situated over a series of islands in Kaptai Lake and is, alongside Cox's Bazar, the place every Bangladeshi wants to take their summer holidays. The town was originally laid out as an administrative centre and modern-day hill station in the 1960s, after the damming of the Karnaphuli River and though it has grown to encompass a large area it hasn't lost its small town vibe. Even so the real charm of Rangamati lies not in the town itself but rather in the lush, undulating and verdant surrounding countryside.

The vast majority of Adivasis here are Chakma, and much of their ancestral land is flooded by the lake. The population of the town is, however, overwhelmingly Bangladeshi.

ORIENTATION & INFORMATION

Rangamati village extends for about 7km from the army checkpoint and Tribal Cultural Institute Museum to the Parjatan Motel. The main road passes banks, the fish market and Hotel Sufia before it crosses a long causeway, at the end of which is a traffic circle (roundabout). The road to the right leads to the Parjatan Motel (after crossing a steel bridge), while the road to the left leads to the main bazar and the main launch ghat (steps or landing).

Despite the presence of a couple of banks and many Bangladeshi tourists, it is impossible to change money in Rangamati – even cash will draw blank looks, and as for an ATM…

There is also no internet service in town, nor, somewhat incredibly, any reliable mobile phone reception.

SIGHTS & ACTIVITIES

The newly constructed **Tribal Cultural Institute Museum** (Manik Charri Rd; admission Tk 10; ⏰ 9am-5pm Sat-Thu) is one of the better museums in Bangladesh with well thought out displays on the tribes of the Hill Tracts, including costumes, bamboo flutes, coins, silver-and-ivory necklaces and a tiger trap – it's hard to imagine what they actually do with a large, angry tiger once they get one in such a flimsy wooden trap! There is also a map showing where the different tribes live.

The institute is opposite the army checkpoint as you enter town from the direction of Chittagong.

There are several modern Buddhist *viharas* (monasteries) in and around the town. The biggest and busiest is the **Bana Vihara**, on a headland at the northern end of town. In one open-walled hall there are elaborate thrones for the head abbot, in the form of a Naga serpent. The parkland in which the temple is set is a popular place for a walk and there are a number of stalls selling devotional items and candles to the numerous passing pilgrims. While walking around the parkland keep an eye peeled for the unusual statue of the starving Buddha, the multistorey temple and the numerous pesky monkeys!

The Chakma king has his rajbari (palace) on a neighbouring island. The rajbari is not open to visitors but the **Raja Vihara** on the same island has a large bronze statue of Shakyamuni (the historical Buddha) overseen by a small and friendly monastic community. The island is reached by small launches that leave from the mainland just opposite the island.

A **boat trip** on Kaptai Lake, the country's largest artificial lake, with stops at tribal villages along the way, is the undisputed highlight of a visit to Rangamati. The lake is ringed with banana plantations and thinning patches of tropical and semi-evergreen forests. The level of the lake varies considerably throughout the year. When it starts to fall in March, the emerging land is farmed before the lake rises again in the monsoon season.

While the lake itself is beautiful, the villages you'll see around it make the trip special. Bring binoculars for bird-watching (which is excellent) and better viewing of some of the thatched villages and fishing boats. Tourist boats usually stop at Chakma villages, allowing you to see traditional bamboo houses and small Buddhist shrines made of bamboo.

There are three main places from which to hire a boat: across the hanging bridge near Parjatan Motel; at the main ghat; and at Tobulchuri ghat. The latter is probably the best, while the first is the most expensive. An hour in one of the rainbow splashed boats should cost around Tk 200 split between a

RANGAMATI

0 — 1 km
0 — 0.5 miles

INFORMATION	
Agrani Bank	1 B1
Janata Bank	2 B2
Sonali Bank	3 B1

SIGHTS & ACTIVITIES	
Bana Vihara	4 B1
Boats for Hire	5 B3
Fish Market	6 B2
Raja Vihara	7 B1
Tobolchuri Ghat	8 B2
Tribal Cultural Institute Museum	9 A1

SLEEPING	
Hotel Golden Hill	10 C1
Hotel Green Castle	11 C2
Hotel Lake View	12 C2
Hotel Sufia	13 B2
Parjatan Motel	14 B3

EATING	
Café Link	15 B2
Girishova Restaurant	16 B2
Green Restaurant	17 C1
Mayer Doa Restaurant	(see 13)

TRANSPORT	
Bus Station	18 C1
Buses to Chittagong	19 C2

small group (bigger groups should expect to pay a little more).

The boat trips are generally very well organised and, if you don't really know where you want to go, the boatmen will have their own hour, two-hour, half day and full-day long tours. In fact just clambering on board and letting them make all the decisions isn't a bad idea as almost anywhere they take you will turn out to be both interesting and beautiful.

Foreigners are supposed to have armed police guards for any trip out onto the lake. In practise, if you only want to go for an hour sunset jaunt, most boatmen will take you without the requisite escort. Nobody really seems to know why you still need a man with a machine gun watching over you (those egrets can be mighty vicious sometimes) and their presence won't exactly endear you to the inhabitants of any village you stop at. One thing to keep in mind if you're thinking of trying to sneak out onto the lake without a guard is that though you are unlikely to get into trouble for doing so, your boatman may be reprimanded.

A good place to visit, not far from Rangamati, is the Buddhist monastery **Jawnasouk Mountain Vihara**, just across the lake. A trip out to Kaptai is a longer and very rewarding day trip, while another interesting journey is through the narrow, steep-sided waterway that leads into the lake's upper basin, where you can also swim.

SLEEPING

Considering that Rangamati is one of Bangladesh's tourist hot spots, it's something of a surprise to discover that the accommodation and eating scene is generally fairly dire and almost universally overpriced.

Hotel Golden Hill (☎ 62146; s/d Tk 150-200) Gorgeous lake views and the double rooms are pretty healthy. Single rooms have a toilet but you'll need to wash in the lake! Friendliest of the budget hotels by far. The staff can organise boat trips for you.

Hotel Lake View (☎ 62063; s/d Tk 200/400) The best aspect of this budget hotel are the legendry lake views. You could spend hours sitting on the balcony watching life unfold on the waters below. This is good news, because you certainly wouldn't want to spend hours sitting in the rooms, which are little more than airless and non-too clean cells. Single women won't feel comfortable here. It's also known as Hotel Al-Amin.

Hotel Sufia (☎ 62145; s/d Tk 400/600, ste Tk 1500/2000) A sensible option on the main road, just before the causeway. The non–air-con rooms are undoubtedly the ones to go for if the lack of hot water doesn't bother you. Some rooms have balconies overlooking a small portion of the lake. The suites place size above quality, but are good for families.

Hotel Green Castle (☎ 61200; s with/without air-con Tk 750/350, d Tk 1000/700) Despite the name this hotel is neither green nor a castle, but it does have good lake views. Once again room size takes precedent over room quality. Cheaper rooms have squat toilets and cramped bathrooms. In most towns this would be considered a non-descript hotel, but in Rangamati it holds its own.

Peda Ting Ting (☎ 62082; cottages Tk 1000) This place, hidden on a secluded island, is a 20-minute boat ride from town. Foreigners are supposed to have a police escort to visit this indigenous-run venture, which makes staying at its cottages a little problematic – a shame because this would be an idyllic place to wile a way a few days. Instead do what everyone else does and stop by for lunch or a drink at its excellent restaurant (mains Tk 180), serving traditional indigenous fare.

Parjatan Motel (☎ 63126; d with/without air-con Tk 1200/600, 4-/8-bed cottage Tk 1000/1500) Location, location, location – we all know that's what sells and the location of this Parjatan venture, overlooking a quiet hyacinth-clogged backwater of the lake, is simply priceless. But the management haven't allowed this to let them rest on their laurels and what they've got going on here is one of the better Parjatan establishments. Rooms are quaint and clean and some come with balconies overlooking the lake. The electricity supply is as erratic as the hot water. Book in advance.

EATING

Around the main ghat is a gaggle of cheap restaurants selling the usual stuff for the usual prices.

Mayer Doa Restaurant (meals Tk 30-50) Next to the Hotel Sufia, the menu of the Mayer Doa advertises simple Bangladeshi dishes, but the tastes the cooks produce are far from simple. The chefs recommend the fish (Tk 40). The red-and-green painted sign is in Bengali only.

Green Restaurant (mains Tk 60-80) A new and increasingly well-regarded Bangladeshi restaurant that sticks to hygiene laws, located next to the Hotel Golden Hill.

Café Link (☎ 63433; Masjid Market, Banarupa; mains Tk 130) A cosy and intimate Chinese restaurant on the first-floor of a shopping centre (look out for the flashing fairy lights). There are only about a dozen tables and the service is fast and friendly. It also has a few lighter snacks such as sandwiches, and will box meals up to take away for picnic lunches.

You can't beat the view at **Girishova Restaurant**, which is literally floating on the lake surface and is perfect for a sunset tea or a light meal. The sign is in Bengali only but it's impossible to miss.

Of the hotel restaurants, the one at **Parjatan** (☎ 63126; mains Tk 150) is easily the best and its excellent curries are worth dropping by for even if you aren't staying there.

GETTING THERE & AWAY

Buses from Chittagong leave for Rangamati (Tk 75 to Tk 80, 2½ hours) periodically from Modapur bus station (p128). You'll pass a couple of security checkpoints en route, where you are called off to fill out formalities and prove you have applied for a permit.

From Rangamati, buses for Chittagong leave from outside Hotel Green Castle throughout the day from around 7am. Buses also leave from the more manic bus station opposite the Golden Hill Hotel. There is no direct route to Kaptai; you'll have to go back to Chittagong to catch a bus from there.

There are also public launches leaving Rangamati for the town of Kaptai, but check the schedule carefully as the situation changes frequently. The trip takes 1½ hours (four hours return). There is also a speedboat that does the round-trip in two hours. These boats leave from the main launch ghat.

GETTING AROUND

Due to its hilly topography, Rangamati is a rare example of a Bangladeshi town without rickshaws. Baby taxis operate as share taxis (five or six passengers); the cost is usually Tk 30 divided by the number of passengers, regardless of where you're going. The other option is to jump on a passing bus.

Kaptai

It takes a special sort of person to find something positive to say about Kaptai, 64km east of Chittagong. You could wax lyrical about its gorgeous lakeside setting or proffer poetic praise about its mountainous backdrop, but let us not kid ourselves here. The scenery might be breathtaking, but Kaptai itself is the proverbial hellhole. In some dim and distant age, this former hunting reserve must have been idyllic but nowadays it's a smoky, dirty port town full of grim-lipped soldiers, noisy trucks spitting out ice-cap melting quantities of fumes and, almost certainly, lots of ladies of ill-repute out to please said soldiers and truckers. (OK, if there aren't lots of these kind of girls then there certainly should be.)

On a positive note Kaptai ghat looks quite picturesque at night. The town is known for its large dam and hydroelectricity plant but don't even think about trying to take pictures of them.

Kaptai is a flat town with one main street where you'll find all the (highly basic) eateries, hotels, boarding houses, teahouses and general stores. At the dam wall there's a crane that lifts stacks of bamboo, ferried in incredible-length rafts across the lake, over and into the Karnaphuli River, from where they float down to Chittagong.

So why, if it's so grim, should you go there? Simply, it makes a good goal for a longer boat trip from Rangamati, but try and leave Rangamati in the morning, allowing you ample time to amble down the waterways and return to Rangamati by nightfall.

SLEEPING

There is a government circuit house in Kaptai. As always you'll need permission from the district commissioner to stay; his office is nearby. Otherwise, there are some very basic boarding houses, most of which are dirty and cheap.

GETTING THERE & AWAY

Unless you have a private vehicle, you cannot travel here straight from Rangamati; instead you'll have to head back to Chittagong for the bus. Direct buses to Kaptai (Tk 30) leave from Chittagong's Modapur bus station throughout the day.

You might also be able to get a launch from Rangamati, but check it out carefully as the situation changes frequently.

Chitmorong

The Buddhist hamlet of **Chitmorong**, approximately 4km from Kaptai on the Chittagong Rd, is draped in peace and spirituality. Built around a large modern Buddhist monastery and a much older, wooden monastery, the village is a centre for the Marma tribe, most of whom have resisted the recent push of Islam and Christianity and stuck to their Buddhist beliefs. Very few foreigners visit so the reception is certain to be warm and a monk is likely to take you gently by the hand and lead you around the monastery grounds. When you're inside the main monastery look out for the montage of snaps from the monk's holidays in Sri Lanka and Malaysia. You should leave a small donation at the monastery. The **Buddhist water festival** is held here around mid-April.

There is nowhere to stay in the village but down by the boat ghat there are a couple of little wooden shacks selling clean and tasty meals (in fact Chitmorong makes a better lunch stop than Kaptai).

Chitmorong is on the opposite side of the lake from the Kaptai–Chittagong road and you'll need to hop into one of the double oar row boats (Tk 2) to access the village. Actually finding the boat ghat on the Kaptai–Chittagong road is a little hard – ask all passers-by and look out for the painted fence posts and a couple of tea stalls.

Bandarban

Put simply there is no better place in which to experience the magic of the Hill Tracts than in the bolshy small town of Bandarban, which lies on the Sangu River, 92km from Chittagong. The river is the centre of local life: bamboo rafts up to 500m long, steered by a single solitary boatman, drift leisurely downstream, while country boats make slow trips to neighbouring villages. Most inhabitants belong to the Buddhist Marma tribe. The town itself, which has a couple of interesting sights, isn't overly attractive, but the surrounding countryside is some of the finest in Bangladesh and offers one of the few opportunities to really escape the masses. Instead of the honking of horns and awe-struck stares of the masses you'll have nothing much to listen to but birdsong and the only things likely to be fluttering about you will be bright, floppy winged butterflies. All up this is not a town to rush through in a hurry.

At the checkpoint before coming into town, officials may request that you call upon the district commissioner. His office is just around the corner from the Hotel Purabi.

There is an **internet café** (per hr Tk 50) under Hotel Greenhill.

SIGHTS

The small **Tribal Cultural Institute** has a museum and library. Opening hours are vague but the curator is very knowledgeable. The museum specialises in tribal costumes and jewellery and is better than many big town museums. Most of the information labels are in English. The **Bohmong Rajbari** is the residence of the Bohmong king.

Perched on a hill top a few kilometres out of town is a large glowing, golden **Buddhist stupa** (ask for the 'Bala Gata'). It's a Burmese blast through and through and is one of the most impressive stupas in the country. When entering you should leave your shoes outside.

There is a **tribal bazar** (☯ Wed & Sun), where trading is conducted in Marma rather than Bengali.

ACTIVITIES

Bandarban is the centre of Bangladesh's fledgling **hiking** industry. With current permit restrictions it would probably be fairer to describe this activity as gentle walking rather than hiking, and for the casual visitor a half-day walk is about the longest hike you can presently engage in. Even so hiking around the breathtaking Bandarban countryside and visiting little known traditional tribal villages will be one of the highlights of a visit to this highlight-studded country.

One drawback with all these walks is that you will be required to take an armed police escort. The government says that this is for your own safety and Bengalis talk about terrible, but unspecified, dangers that await any foreigner wandering off alone.

Dangers aside, the police escorts are normally highly reluctant to actually put one foot in front of the other and walk anywhere and, on arrival in a village, having a couple of armed men with you doesn't exactly encourage much cultural interaction! On top of all this the police will then expect a tip for their services – we would suggest you refrain from paying and hopefully they'll eventually give up on accompanying foreigners. If you are polite but persistent, and take a known local guide from the Hillside Resort (see opposite) then you might be able to get away without taking an escort on the shorter walks. One highly recommended, knowledgeable and English-speaking guide is Lallim Bawm, who also works as a waiter at the Hillside Resort.

A couple of the easiest and most convenient hikes are listed here.

Shailapropat Waterfall & Bawm Village Hike

This very painless hike is entirely along a quiet, surfaced road and is the most popular 'hike' with Bangladeshis, though that's only because they can complete it while sat in a nice shiny car! The walk itself, which takes about an hour in either direction, is hilly and, at times, quite steep, but it's far nicer than the goal, which is a small waterfall carpeted in litter. Very close to the waterfall is the Bawm tribal village of Faruk Para, where you can buy some beautiful baskets, woven fish traps and rugs.

Sangu River Hike

A harder and more interesting hike, which can also be combined with a boat ride, is to the Sangu River which you can see snaking through the fertile valley below the Hillside Resort. Once at the river you can take a country boat down to Bandarban town from where it's a hard two-hour climb back to the resort. With a bit of luck you'll see some of the bamboo rafts hundreds of metres long drifting down river. It is also possible to swim in secluded corners of the river.

Haatibandha Village Hike

Maybe the most interesting short walk, which takes about an hour in either direction, is this one to the Tripura tribal village of Haatibandha. Much of the route involves following steep, muddy tracks which can be very slippery after rain. Entering the village for the first time is like entering a new country – all around you are rounded Burmese faces and with luck you will meet women decked out in hundreds of bead necklaces, bangles that coil serpent-like around their arms, and strange earrings that look more like bolts and stretch out the wearers ear lobes. Very few people make it to this village and it's essential that you obtain the permission of the village headman to be there and remember to tread carefully with your photos.

Longer Hikes & Excursions

With prior arrangement, and the security situation allowing, it's often possible to arrange highly adventurous hikes and excursions further afield, including one to Chimbuk Hill, one of the highest points in the country, and the surrounding Murong villages. An even more challenging expedition is the overnight trip to the stunning Bogra Lake. This trip involves a two-hour jeep ride, a boat journey and then a five-hour hike. You will stay the night in forgotten tribal villages. At the time of research the biggest draw of all, the hike to the summit of Mt Keokradang – which at 1230m is as high as you can go in Bangladesh – is sadly forbidden, but with the slowly improving security situation this may change. For any of these longer hikes it is essential to arrange everything through an established tour operator such as Guide Tours (p130) or Bengal Tours (p130).

SLEEPING & EATING

Hillside Resort (Milonchhori; ☎ 01199 275691; Chimbuk Rd; dm Tk 150, basic s/d/q cottages from Tk 500/800/1000, luxury s/d/tr cottages Tk 750/1200/1450) Thrown haphazardly across a steep jungle-smothered hillside, this brilliant Guide Tours–run resort, 4km and a Tk 120 baby taxi ride from Bandarban, has a wide array of cottages built of authentic bounce-as-you-walk-bamboo and is the best place to stay. None of the accommodation can be described as luxurious, though there are hot water showers, but it blends in with the vibe of the area perfectly. A lullaby of jungle noises will send you peacefully to sleep (though you're in for a rude awakening when a squirrel or monkey leaps onto your cottage roof in the middle of the night!). The service is polished and professional without being formal and the restaurant (mains Tk 150) whips up the finest cuisine in all the Hill Tracts. It's worth trying to avoid Friday, Saturday and holidays when half of Chittagong descends on the place. Book ahead through Guide Tours Dhaka office (p59), and it will arrange all your permits (including any for Rangamati and other parts of the Hill Tracts).

Otherwise there are some basic places in the town itself. **Hotel Greenhill** (s/d Tk 80/150) is on the main intersection, while **Hotel Purabi** (s Tk 80-100, d Tk 160) has a friendly manager. Aside from the restaurant at the Hillside Resort, eating options are limited; there are some basic restaurants and teahouses on the main street.

GETTING THERE & AWAY

Buses leave from Chittagong's Bardarhat bus station for Bandarban (Tk 50, three hours) throughout the day.

Purbani Coach Service at the Bandarban bus station has several buses to Cox's Bazar (Tk 120) per day.

The checkpoints on the way in to Bandarban can be frustrating, particularly if you have obtained your permit independently of a tour company. The bus may even continue without you so it doesn't have to wait the 45 minutes it takes you to convince officials that you have applied for a permit.

COX'S BAZAR
☎ 0341

Welcome to beach life, Bangladeshi style. The usual question, 'Why have you come here?' doesn't get asked because the answer is obvious – you've come to be at the seaside. Bangladeshis adore Cox's Bazar and all across the country people will ask whether you have been. For Bangladeshis the infatuation is because Cox's Bazar is so unlike the rest of the country, but a foreign visitor, used to the clean, liberal sands of Spain, Australia or California, is likely to be far less enamoured. The beach itself is a lovely, long (very long!), and surprisingly clean slip of sand, but by no stretch of even the most enthusiastic imagination can it be described as the 'number one natural wonder of the world', which is exactly how Bangladeshis, through an online web vote (which you will be asked constantly to partake in) are promoting it. The way to get the most out of Cox's Bazar is not to think of it as a beach holiday, but rather to treat it as a way to relax with middle-class Bangladeshi at play by just surrendering to their holiday enthusiasm.

Information
There is a Dutch-Bangla Bank ATM in the town centre.

Cyber Café (per hr Tk 25) For internet access.

Niloy Cyber Café (per hr Tk 30) Internet access; on the main road.

Post office (Motel Rd) On the edge of the Hotel Shaibal grounds. It's poorly marked – look for the letter box outside.

Dangers & Annoyances
Make no mistake about this – foreign women cannot swim or sunbathe in swimsuits and we dread to think about the levels of harassment you would endure if you were to try. Bangladeshi women who swim do so in their *salwar kameez* (long, dress-like tunic worn over baggy trousers) and you'd be very wise to do the same. Even foreign men are unlikely to enjoy the experience of swimming here and as for sunbathing, well that is a massive no, no for both sexes.

The northern end of the beach next to the airport may be invitingly quiet, but armed robberies have occurred here, even in daylight. The entire beach is not safe at night.

Sights & Activities
The main reason to come to Cox's Bazar is for the **beach**. The route to the beach, along Sea Beach Rd, can be crowded and dirty, but once on the beach you will find the sand surprisingly clean. There are plenty of places from where you can rent a sun lounge and umbrella (Tk 5 to Tk 10), and staff will offer security so you can leave your belongings unattended while you go for a dip. You could also plant yourself in front of a big hotel, where guards will watch over your gear if you go swimming, and shoo away kids selling shell necklaces. They will also deal with the crowds of gawkers, if they get too intrusive (which they will).

If you're intrigued by the wooden fishing boats chugging along the shore, you can check them out from the Bakhali River on the north side of town, where they're moored. Some of the boats look uncannily like pirate ships; and given that piracy is on the rise in the Bay of Bengal there's the possibility that they might be!

The colourful **Buddhist Water Festival** takes place here each year (13 to 18 April). And a gob-smackingly unlikely local **surfing competition** is held most years in late September/ early October. That there are any waves in Bangladesh is shock enough to most surfers, that there are any Bangladeshi surfers even more so and that they have a competition is enough to render most surfers silent with surprise. But that this conservative Muslim nation can actually conjure up enough female surfers to include an entire women's division in the contest is, quite frankly, about the most extraordinary thing we've ever heard!

Aggameda Khyang, a Buddhist monastery at the eastern end of town, is representative of Burmese-style architecture. Its distinctive appearance would stand out anywhere, but nestled among trees in the middle of Cox's Bazar it's all the more fascinating. The main sanctuary is built around massive timber columns. The teak flooring adds an air of timelessness to

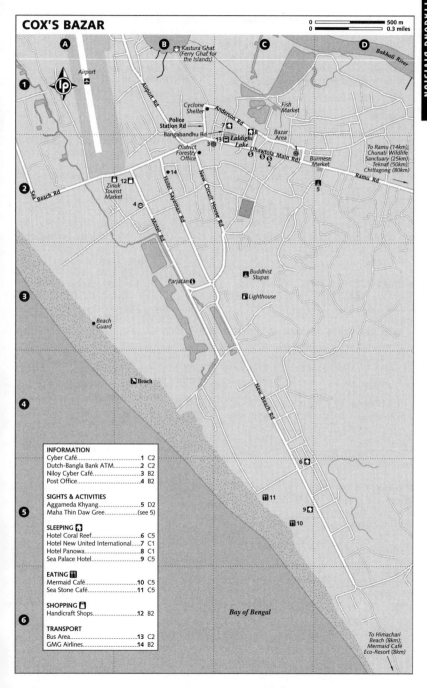

COX'S BAZAR

Kastura Ghat
(Ferry Ghat for
the Islands)

Bakhali River

Airport

Airport Rd

Cyclone
Shelter

Anderson Rd

Fish
Market

Police
Station Rd

Bangabandhu Rd

Bazar
Area

Laldighi
Lake

Uhawtola

District
Forestry
Office

Burmese
Market

Main Rd)

To Ramu (14km);
Chunati Wildlife
Sanctuary (25km);
Teknaf (50km);
Chittagong (80km)

Ramu Rd

Sea Beach Rd

Zinuk
Tourist
Market

Hotel Sayeman Rd

New Circuit House Rd

Motel Rd

Parjatan

Buddhist
Stupas

Lighthouse

Beach
Guard

Beach

New Beach Rd

Bay of Bengal

To Himachari
Beach (8km);
Mermaid Café
Eco-Resort (8km)

0   500 m
0   0.3 miles

the place. You may be asked for a donation – Tk 10 is reasonable.

Behind Aggameda Khyang is **Maha Thin Daw Gree**, a vast spread of Buddhist buildings amid the trees. Almost invisible from the road, this interesting display of Buddhas was built in 1790.

Sleeping

The whole Cox's Bazar area is now so over-developed that it more resembles a Costa del Sol disaster zone than a quaint tropical beach hide-out. In recent years the area of interest to tourists, including all the decent hotels and restaurants, has crept ever further south away from the town centre and there is now little reason to visit the town itself except maybe to change money or use the internet. You can often hook up some sweet accommodation deals by booking a package in advance from Dhaka.

BUDGET

There are some cheap dives in the town centre around Laldighi Lake, but none are very appetising.

Hotel New United International (☎ 63753; Bangabandhu Rd; s with shared/attached bathroom Tk 60/100, d Tk 100/200) A good-value budget choice if they'll let you in. It's cleaner and brighter than some of its contemporaries, and far enough away for you to get some shuteye.

Hotel Panowa (☎ 63282; s/d Tk 120/300) Down a lane to the east of Laldighi Lake, the Panowa is about the only cheapie that will accept foreigners, but it's hardly appealing. The cheaper rooms have shared bathrooms. The stunning bougainvillea out front is nice though!

MIDRANGE & TOP END

There are a ridiculous number of massive hotel complexes south of the town in the 'hotel-motel zone'. All seem somehow completely inappropriate for the beach and their uncontrolled spawning along the fore-shore seems to be creating serious beach erosion problems.

Mermaid Café Eco-resort (☎ 017131 60029; r around Tk 1500) By far the most exciting development is this new accommodation venture by the same people behind the superb Mermaid Café (right). Due to open for business as this book hits the shelves, the complex may even live up to the eco in its name as the resort will be powered entirely by solar energy and wind

turbines, and built using locally obtained, sustainable materials. As well as rooms, it will also have a spa in which all the oils are made using orange skins and other fruit extracts left over from the fruit juices made at their café.

Hotel Coral Reef (☎ 64469; hotelcoralreef@yahoo.com; Motel Rd; r with/without air-con Tk 1950/1200; ✖ 🖳) Of the many, many mega hotels, this is one of the more charming (and smaller). The immaculate rooms make you feel too dirty to be in them. The staff are helpful and the restaurant receives positive reviews. A 30% discount off the above rates is almost standard.

Sea Palace Hotel (☎ 63692; www.hotelseapalaceltd .com; Motel Rd; ✖ 🖳) This monster sized complex is divided into two hotels. The Western Plaza is the cheaper of the two blocks (room with/without air-con Tk 1850/1200, plus 25% tax) and has slightly tiered but otherwise clean and spacious rooms. You can expect an immediate 45% discount on the above rates. The Crown Plaza (room from Tk 3000, plus 25% tax) is the big boys choice and though the standard rooms are utterly devoid of personality they do have baths as well as showers (in case you're really dirty). They're also mercifully free of the tacky, fake chandeliers that blights the reception. After the almost guaranteed discount you will only be paying Tk 2000 a room with all taxes, making this a certified bargain.

Eating

our pick **Mermaid Café** (☎ 017131 60029; ✪ 11am-midnight; mains from Tk 200) This Goa-style beach shack serves what is quite possibly the best food in all of Bangladesh. In fact both the food, the setting and the vibe are so good that we have received more positive reports from travellers on this one restaurant than everything else in Bangladesh put together! The gorgeous owners have gone out of their way to ensure that as many of the ingredients as possible are organically produced (a harder task than you might imagine as most farmers are hooked on the delights of pesticides and chemical fertilisers) in the local area. The effort has really paid off – even the rice is of a quality you will rarely have tasted before. In addition to the excellent food there is also a great music collection and a small art gallery with frequently changing exhibitions. There are two branches, very close to one and other and right on the beach. One specialises in fresh seafood and the other in pasta and meat dishes. It even has an old surfboard or two that it will rent out.

Sea Stone Café (☎ 01818 067709; meals from Tk 200) Very similar to the next-door Mermaid in style and feel, this chilled-out beachside café knows exactly what Western tourists want from a beach café, and the fish dishes are sensational. Equally sensational are the ocean views and the warm owners.

Entertainment
The Mermaid Café organises full-moon parties (yes we fell over in surprise too) throughout the season. There may be a little less drink and drugs going round than at a Thai or Goan party, but you might be surprised at how much fun you can have without these!

Shopping
There are various handicraft and Burmese shops near Aggameda Khyang, selling handwoven fabrics, saris, cheroots and jewellery. Avoid buying any coral or seashell items – very bad karma. There is also the Burmese Market east of the town centre.

Getting There & Away
GMG Airlines (☎ 63900; Hotel Sayeman Rd) supposedly has flights to/from Dhaka (Tk 4670) everyday and Chittagong (Tk 3450) on Tuesday, Thursday and Saturday, but don't rely on this schedule.

Most buses leave from around the Laldighi Lake area. Buses to Dhaka (non–air-con Tk 400 to Tk 500, luxury Tk 700 to Tk 1000; eight to 10 hours) generally leave in the evening and arrive early the next morning.

Buses to Chittagong (local bus Tk 140, luxury bus Tk 300, four hours) leave regularly until 4.30pm. Buses to Teknaf (Tk 75, three hours) depart until 6pm.

Getting Around
Some rickshaw drivers are hotel touts; be clear where you want to go and how much you want to pay. On the other hand, not all their hotel recommendations are bad ones.

Bangla Tours, located in the Dream Castle Hotel in the hotel-motel zone, is a reliable car-hire firm for trips further afield.

AROUND COX'S BAZAR
The road from Cox's Bazar, south along the seashore to Teknaf, is hemmed in by gentle, jungle-covered mole hills, though unfortu-nately this forest is quickly succumbing to deforestation. It's also a not so temporary home to many Rohingya refugees from Myanmar (Burma).

This forest is home to a wealth of plant and animal life including a handful of elephants. Bird-watching in the newly formed and easily visited **Chunati Wildlife Sanctuary** (about halfway along the Chittagong–Cox's Bazar road) is especially rewarding. The park has a number of easy-to-follow short walking trails and some lofty look-out towers. If you're very lucky you might even come to face to face with one of the wild Asian elephants that hide in the depths of the park.

Beaches
Himachari Beach, just 12km south, is a secluded and pretty spot, but it's **Inani Beach**, that is the real claim to fame. Considered one of the world's longest and broadest beaches (180m at high tide and 300m at low tide), it's one of the few places where you might, and only might, be able to swim and sunbathe in peace.

The people behind the Mermaid Café have established an 'art village' down here with the idea of attracting local and foreign artists to spend time together working on projects. They are trying to model it on the Auroville commune in India. It's open to tourists and the Mermaid Café can arrange boat trips from Cox's Bazar, and lunch.

The government is keen to promote international beach tourism here and there is talk of an interesting, and no doubt controversial, government-sponsored project taking off at Inani Beach. The idea, and it remains just a fairly well-developed idea, is to open an exclusive tourist zone at the southern end of the beach. From what we understand, this will be open only to Western tourists and richer, more 'Westernised' Bangladeshis. The government is hoping to make it a little Goa, complete with alcohol and at least two of the three S's!

To get to Inani independently, take a bus to Teknaf and get off at Court Bazar (30km), a tiny village 2km before Ukhia. From there, you can rickshaw or tempo west to the beach, 10km away.

Ramu & Lamapara
Ramu and Lamapara are noted for their Buddhist khyangs (temples). Ramu is an un-distinguished town 14km east of Cox's Bazar,

just off the Chittagong road. Some hills in this area are topped with pagodas.

In addition to its khyangs, Ramu, a subsidiary capital of the Rakhaing (Arakan) kingdom for nearly three centuries, is noted for a beautiful **monastery** containing images of the Buddha in bronze, silver and gold, and inlaid with precious and semiprecious stones. Start at the far end of the street of Buddhist buildings, at the lovely **U Chitsan Rakhina Temple**, and work your way back towards the town centre.

The beautiful Burmese **Bara Khyang** at Lamapara has the country's largest bronze Buddha statue. The temple's three wooden buildings house a number of precious Buddhist images in silver and gold, set with gems. Lamapara is a palm-shaded village about 5km from Ramu, and accessible only by zigzagging paved village paths. It's impossible to find it on your own, so take a rickshaw or a baby taxi (from Tk 100 to Tk 150 return).

About 2km from Lamapara, at the village of Ramkot, there are Buddhist and Hindu **temples** perched on adjacent forested hills.

Sonadia Island

According to legend, a ship laden with gold sunk here centuries ago during an attack by Portuguese pirates and an island formed around the shipwreck. The tiny, 4.63-sq-km island, 7km from Cox's Bazar, was once renowned for pink pearls, but more profitable commercial fishing has seen this tradition slowly fade away. Fishermen set up camp in winter, and Bangladeshi tourists make the trip here to buy dried pomfret fish.

Sonadia acts as a temporary sanctuary for migrating birds such as petrels, geese, curlews, ducks and other waterfowl. There are no public launches, so you'll have to hire a boat (Tk 700 or more for a day trip divided between up to 10 people) at Kastura ghat, or around the port, ask if any fishermen are heading that way.

Maheskhali Island

About 6km northwest of Cox's Bazar, Maheskhali (mosh-*khal*-ee) Island makes a pleasant day trip. If there are any festivals underway among its mixed Buddhist, Hindu and Muslim population, you might be invited to stay and watch.

Walking along the jetty into the town of Ghoroghata, you'll see a hill to the north, about a 20-minute rickshaw ride away. This **holy spot** is the principal tourist attraction, with a famous stupa on top. The climb takes five minutes and affords a good view of the island from the top.

A few hundred metres away is a wooded area that hides **Adinath**, a mandir (temple) and ashram dedicated to Shiva. It's a delightfully serene place set in a beautiful garden.

If it's the dry season and you have the time, you might consider some hiking. There are paths along the top of the cliffs that line the eastern side of the island. Swimming is also an option, particularly at the sandy beaches on the island's western side.

When you return to town, ask to be pointed towards the small fishing settlement nearby, where you can watch **boat-building** activity. During the dry season you can also watch people fishing and drying their catch.

In the north of the island, the little town of Hohanak has a **betel bazar** on Monday and Thursday evening.

If you get stuck for the night there are a couple of super-basic guesthouses.

To reach the island, take a speedboat from Kastura ghat in Cox's Bazar, which will leave when there are about 10 people on board (Tk 60, 15 minutes). You will have to pay Tk 2 to get onto the impressively rickety pier at Kastura ghat. Also be prepared to clamber over wooden boats tied together as a makeshift pier extension when the tide is out. The last speedboat leaves from the island at around 6pm. Some travellers have recommended taking a guide as the rickshaw-wallahs on the island speak no English and can be aggressive in their demands.

TEKNAF

This bustling smugglers' town is on the southern tip of the narrow strip of land adjoining Myanmar, 92km south of Cox's Bazar. The Bangladesh–Myanmar border is formed by the Naaf River, a branch of which divides the town. Most of the town is a crowded area of narrow alleys.

It is illegal to cross into Myanmar from here, and since its army has planted minefields along the border to deter illegal immigrants and smugglers, it's not wise to try.

Sights & Activities

Just south of the market and police station, you'll find jeeps that provide transport to surrounding villages. The last village on the mainland, **Shahpuri**, is a bumpy 30-minute ride. Its main attraction is the beautiful view from the embankment through the mangrove swamps to the Myanmar coast. Another option is a ride south to Badarmokam at the tip of the peninsula, where the white sandy beach is quite deserted and particularly nice at sunset.

The main reason for visiting Teknaf is to reach St Martin's Island (below), 38km south.

Sleeping & Eating

Hotel Dwip Plaza (d Tk 400) This clean establishment is not always stoked to have foreigners. Rooms have squat toilets.

Hotel Ne-Taung (r with/without air-con Tk 1000/500;) Close to the ferry, this ramshackle Parjatan-run hotel is the normal lacklustre Parjatan offering. However it's the best in town, has hot water and some rather nice gardens. Its restaurant serves reasonably priced Bangladeshi food.

Finding cheap food is no problem, but don't expect culinary excellence. There are some basic restaurants near the market and on the main highway, just west of the bridge over the creek.

Getting There & Away

Buses run between Cox's Bazar and Teknaf (Tk 75, 70km, hourly until 6pm). Expect three arse-aching hours.

ST MARTIN'S ISLAND

Idyllic St Martin's Island is everything that brash Cox's Bazar is not. It's the country's only coral island, and home to a friendly, tomorrow-never-comes population of around 7000. The majority of the island's inhabitants are Muslim, and live primarily off fishing.

St Martin's Island is a special place with beaches that really do match the hype, but whether it will remain as such is a big question. Entrepreneurs are increasingly becoming aware of the island's economic potential, though unfortunately not its environmental and cultural vulnerability. For the moment though it remains a place more for the discerning Bangladeshi tourist and therefore most foreign visitors find it a far more relaxing beach hang-out than its big brother up the coast.

Activities

Locals assert that St Martin's is a better place to **dive** and **snorkel** than Australia's Great Barrier Reef. While this might be about as true as Cox's Bazar being one of the wonders of the world, it is certainly possible to ogle the world beneath the waves here between November and March. **Oceanic** (0171 867911; www.oceanicbd .com) charge experienced divers Tk 3000 per session with a guide and all equipment. To find it, take a left at the small road at the end of the restaurant strip on the beach; it's a couple of hundred metres along on the right.

Sleeping & Eating

Simana Perie (01819 018027; dm Tk 600, r Tk 900-1000;) This place certainly has positioning going for it as it's located right on the western beach. It's also aware of the fact that not everybody wants multi-storeyed blocks and instead comprises of a series of eight 'cottages', which represent decent value.

Hotel Prashad Paradise (01815 152740; r Tk 1200) The first hotel you'll see immediately as you step onto the island. Rooms are clean and have a balcony. This is a good example of the type of hotel under construction, and some would say demonstrative of the sad direction the island is taking.

Blue Marine Resort (01817 060065; s/d Tk 1200/1500;) Probably the best place to stay on the island, even though it has looked to Cox's Bazar for architectural inspiration. It has rooms that gleam, a generator guaranteeing 24-hour power and a couple of self-catering cottages (Tk 2000) that are more block houses than quaint cottages.

There is no dearth of shops and teahouses on St Martin's. As you step off the pier you'll walk through a strip of seemingly makeshift restaurants. Their fierce competitiveness makes for some great meals. The numero uno place to eat is the **Marine Drop Restaurant** (mains Tk 100-150), a wooden beach shack on the soft sands of the western beach. It offers delicious seafood and even hosts the odd barbeque night.

Getting There & Away

From Teknaf several ferries a day cruise to the island in around two hours. Prices vary slightly depending on which boat company you use but average prices are Tk 500 to Tk 600 depending on class. Cabins are also available on some boats for s/d Tk 1500/2500. Most boats leave Teknaf around 9am and return around 3pm. **Keari Sindbad** (815 7647) runs the most reliable boats and is the only company to operate through the monsoon (boats depart around three times a week at this time of year but schedules are highly weather dependent).

Many tour companies and hotels in Cox's Bazar run rushed day trips to the island for between Tk 12,000 and Tk 13,000.

COMILLA
☎ 081

Comilla is a boisterous and bustling market town 90km southeast of Dhaka and a few kilometres west of the Indian state of Tripura. It receives very few foreign visitors, and everywhere you go you will be an object of intense and friendly curiosity. It is a base for those visiting the fascinating and extensive Buddhist ruins of Mainimati (p144).

The heart of Comilla is the manic and colourful Kandirpar Circle, from which four major arteries extend. Fazlul Haque Rd heads eastward, eventually becoming Chowk Bazar Rd and the road to Chittagong. Heading east along this street you'll come to Rajshinda Market and Chowk Bazar, a major commercial area. For internet access, head to **EarthNet-Bd** (per hr Tk 30).

Sights

On the northwestern outskirts of town, along the road north to Sylhet and 1km off the Dhaka road, the beautifully maintained **Maynamati War Cemetery** is a sombre and moving testimony to wasted lives. British, African, Indian and Australian troops from WWII are all buried here. Japanese troops also penetrated the area and 40 Japanese soldiers are among the hundreds buried in the manicured grounds.

Just behind Kandirpar Circle is a park and huge lake with a traffic-free walking route that locals love to parade around in the cool of the evening. Unfortunately neither the lake nor the park has been treated with the respect they deserve.

Just past Chowk Bazar, on the outskirts of town, are some impressive **Hindu temples**.

Sleeping

Hotel Abedin (☎ 76014; Station Rd; s/d with shared bathroom Tk 60/120) From outside this bright-green hotel looks like a charmingly old-fashioned place, but on the inside the corridors leading to the rooms have some resemblance to a boat (or possibly a prison depending on your

mood). The rooms themselves are very tight and noisy, but fairly well-kept. It's hard to find as the sign is in Bengali only.

Ashik Residential Resthouse (☎ 68781; Nazrul Ave; s with/without air-con Tk 1000/575, d with/without air-con Tk 1400/700; 🖳) The air-con rooms are overpriced but those without air-con are decent. The comfortable rooms are unusually large, and have tables and sit-down toilets. Some have balconies. The staff are English-speaking.

Hotel Noorjahan (☎ 68737; Dhaka-Chittagong Rd; r Tk 1200) Quite possibly the most exclusive service station in the world! Every bus on the Dhaka–Chittagong run stops off here in order to let the passengers feast in the excellent restaurant (see below), but just upstairs are a handful of clean and calm rooms (get one facing away from the road for maximum peace). However, it's the service that really clinches the deal. The army of staff will go out of their way to ensure you have a relaxing stay and you'll even be given your own 'nanny' – a guy whose job it is to look after foreign 'guests' (which, with the scarcity of such people, must make this the easiest job in the world). A further bonus is the tacky decorations. The only real downside is the distance from town (a baby taxi will cost you around Tk 100).

Eating

For cheap Bangladeshi food, the area around the train station in the centre of town has several good restaurants.

Meet Point Restaurant (Kandirpar Circle; mains Tk 80) Smartly suited waiters bring forth spot-on Bengali dishes at this heaving restaurant. The sign is in Bengali only but it's very easy to find as it's right on the main circle.

Diana Hotel (Kandirpar Circle; mains Tk 80) Real Bangladeshi food in atypically clean surrounds. The curries are delectable and the naan is piping-hot perfection.

Hotel Noorjahan (☎ 68737; Dhaka-Chittagong Rd; mains Tk 80-150) If you're travelling between Dhaka and Chittagong and don't stop to eat at one of the three restaurants in the Noorjahan complex then people will assume you have taken leave of your senses, and quite frankly they'd be correct. Choose between the Bangladeshi, Chinese or kebab restaurants and afterwards be sure to dip into the sweets collection and wash it down with a strong coffee.

Silver Spoon (Station Rd; mains Tk 150) Enjoyable Chinese fare with a menu sensibly divided

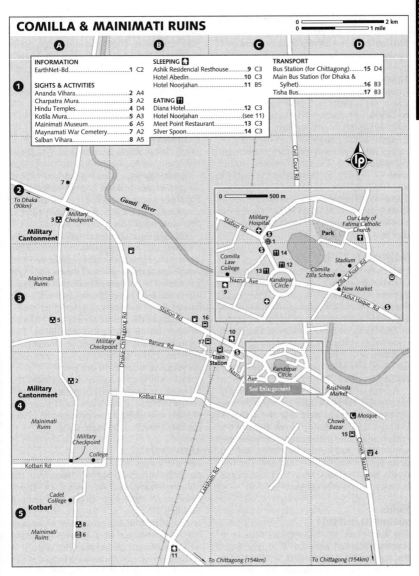

COMILLA & MAINIMATI RUINS

INFORMATION	
EarthNet-Bd...................................1	C2

SIGHTS & ACTIVITIES	
Ananda Vihara..............................2	A4
Charpatra Mura............................3	A2
Hindu Temples.............................4	D4
Kotila Mura...................................5	A3
Mainimati Museum......................6	A5
Maynamati War Cemetery...........7	A2
Salban Vihara...............................8	A5

SLEEPING	
Ashik Residencial Resthouse..........9	C3
Hotel Abedin..............................10	C3
Hotel Noorjahan.........................11	B5

EATING	
Diana Hotel................................12	C3
Hotel Noorjahan ....(see 11)	
Meet Point Restaurant................13	C3
Silver Spoon...............................14	C3

TRANSPORT	
Bus Station (for Chittagong)........15	D4
Main Bus Station (for Dhaka &	
Sylhet)....................................16	B3
Tisha Bus...................................17	B3

into single, half and full serves. It's a good place to hide from the world.

Getting There & Away

BUS

Buses for Dhaka (Tk 60, two hours), and other cities to the north, leave from Station Rd, just west of the railway line. **Tisha Bus** (☎ 65856; Wapda Rd), off Station Rd, operates coaches to Dhaka (Tk 100, every 20 minutes between 5.40am and 7pm).

Buses for Chittagong (Tk 100/150, four hours, every 20 minutes between 5.30am and 5.30pm) and other towns to the south leave from the Chowk Bazar Rd bus station, about 2km east of Kandirpar Circle.

If you're heading to Mymensingh and don't want to go via Dhaka, go north to Bhairab Bazar, in Dhaka division, and pick up connections there.

TRAIN

Comilla is on the Dhaka–Chittagong line. There are a couple of daily express trains to Dhaka (air-con berth/1st/*sulob* class Tk 360/170/90, six hours, departs 1.37am and 1.54pm) and a couple of non-daily departures (which often have more convenient departure times). Two go to Sylhet (1st/2nd class, Tk 195/135, 6½ hours, departs 12.47am and 10.57am – service doesn't run Monday). There are at least three daily express trains to Chittagong (1st/*sulob* class Tk 140/80, departs 11.44am, 2.20pm and 3.15pm) as well as further non-daily trains.

MAINIMATI RUINS

Hidden away for years in the low Mainimati–Lalmai ridge of hills are the remains of the bygone Buddhist splendour of Mainimati. Between the 6th and 13th centuries, Mainimati was famous as an important centre of Buddhist culture and today the scattered ruins count as some of the most breathtaking in Bangladesh. The three most important of the 50-odd Buddhist sites are Salban Vihara, Kotila Mura and Charpatra Mura.

A large section of Mainimati is a military cantonment. It was while the army was clearing the area with bulldozers that the archaeological site in the Kotbari area was discovered. Some of the major ruins are within the cantonment, and cannot be visited without permission from military officers. For this reason, most visitors see only the museum and the ruins outside the cantonment.

Sights

MAINIMATI MUSEUM

The best place to start explorations is at **Mainimati Museum** (admission Tk 50; ☯ 2.30-6pm Mon, 10am-1pm & 1.30-6pm Tue-Thu & Sat, 10am-12.30pm & 2.30-6pm Fri Apr-Sep, 1.30-5pm Mon, 9am-1pm & 1.30-5pm Tue-Thu & Sat, 9am-12.30pm & 2-5pm Fri Oct-Mar). The collection includes terracotta plaques, bronze statues, 4th-century silver and gold coins, jewellery, kitchen utensils and votive stupas embossed with Buddhist inscriptions. The marvellous terracotta plaques reveal a rural Buddhist art alive with animation and vivid natural realism.

Also on display is an unusually large bronze bell from one of the Buddhist temples and some 1000-year-old large, well-preserved black-stone carvings of Hindu gods and goddesses, including Vishnu, Ganesh and Parvati.

The museum's custodian, Mr Pramanik Abdul Latif, is happy to chat. His office is opposite the museum.

SALBAN VIHARA

While **Salban Vihara** (admission Tk 50; ☯ 2.30-6pm Mon, 10am-1pm & 1.30-6pm Tue-Thu & Sat, 10am-12.30pm & 2.30-6pm Fri Apr-Sep, 1.30-5pm Mon, 9am-1pm & 1.30-5pm Tue-Thu & Sat, 9am-12.30pm & 2-5pm Fri Oct-Mar) lacks Paharpur's imposing stupa, the remains give a better idea of the extent of the structure, as they were rebuilt more recently.

This 170-sq-metre monastery has 115 cells for monks, facing a temple in the centre of the courtyard. The royal copper plates of Deva kings and a terracotta seal bearing a royal inscription found here indicate that the monastery was built by Sri Bhava Deva in the first half of the 8th century. The original cruciform plan of the central temple was reduced in scale during subsequent rebuilding. The entire basement wall was heavily embellished with decorative elements such as terracotta plaques and ornamental bricks.

Just opposite the Salban Vihara (and the museum) is a rare patch of open woodland around which you can take a short pony ride (Tk 40) or a quiet, undisturbed walk. There are also a couple of pleasant tea shops.

KOTILA MURA

Like all the ruins in the cantonment, **Kotila Mura** cannot be visited without permission from the military. Situated 5km north of Salban Vihara, it comprises three large stupas representing Buddha, Dharma and Sangha, the 'Three Jewels of Buddhism', plus some secondary stupas, all enclosed by a massive boundary wall. The ground plan of the central stupa is in the shape of a *dharma chakra* (wheel of the law). The hub of the wheel is represented by a deep shaft in the centre, and the spokes by eight brick cells. The two stupas on either side each contain a sealed relic-chamber that has yielded hundreds of miniature clay stupas.

CHARPATRA MURA

Situated 2km north of Kotila Mura, **Charpatra Mura** is another oblong Buddhist shrine perched on a hilltop in the cantonment. The main prayer chamber of the shrine is to the west, and is approached from a spacious hall to the east through a covered passage. The roof was originally supported on four thick, brick columns, and a covered entrance led to the prayer chamber.

ANANDA VIHARA

Also in the cantonment, 1.5km south of Kotila Mura, this **mound** is the largest of the ancient sites on the ridge, occupying over 100 sq metres. Similar in plan to Salban Vihara, it was badly damaged and plundered during WWII, so there's not much to see. You could have a quick look on your way to Kotila Mura.

Getting There & Away

From Kandirpar Circle, you can get an occasional tempo to Kotbari for Tk 8. Otherwise rent your own baby taxi for Tk 100.

Sylhet Division

Damp and green Sylhet division, a place of myriad waterways and gentle bumplike hills crowned in lurid green tea plantations, is one of the more scenically attractive parts of the country. Aside from the regional capital, Sylhet, which is a town of worldly ambition and religious contentment, this is a state kitted out with the naturalist in mind. Such people will find endless opportunities for entertainment in the forests and lakes that weave a tapestry around the numerous rivers and fruit plantations.

It is tea, though, that is the real heart of life here. Sylhet division produces over 55 million kg of tea annually, with more than 150 tea estates spread over 40,000 hectares. It's the chance to visit a tea estate and learn something about the processes that culminate in your morning cuppa that has put the friendly town of Srimangal, in the south of the division, firmly on the fledgling Bangladesh tourist map.

The area along the northern border of this diverse region, at the foot of the Khasi-Jaintia hills, is tribal land and for the adventurous anthropologist the opportunity to make friends with the shy Khashia (or Khasi), Pangou and Tripura people is an exciting notion. Another major tribal group of the area are the Monipuri (Manipuri), much more integrated into mainstream Bangladeshi life. The best-known feature of their culture is the tribe's classical dance, which tells the story of Krishna's love affair with the female cowherd Radha. She symbolises human spirituality, while Krishna is the embodiment of divine love. Regardless of cultural background this love and spirituality is what shines through in all the people you meet here.

HIGHLIGHTS

- Learning the secrets of your morning cuppa in the montage of tea estates surrounding **Srimangal** (p152)

- Feeding black magicians with fish food at the **Shrine of Hazrat Shah Jalal** (opposite), a 14th-century Sufi mystic in Sylhet

- Swinging through the trees of the densely vegetated **Lowacherra National Park** (p154) in search of the elusive gibbons

- Ticking off ruddy crakes, pochards and bee-eaters on the *haors* (wetlands) near **Sunamganj** (p151)

SYLHET
☎ 0821

Sylhet is a strange kind of place. The majority of British Bangladeshis are from the city or its environs and are likely to wax lyrical over the place. Those with stronger ties to the homeland continue to pour money back into the local economy and this has helped to create one of the most surreal city centres in Bangladesh. A string of apparently flashy Western-style shopping malls built on their money have taken over the centre, but on entering one you discover that they're nothing but a façade of half-empty sari shops. It doesn't take long to realise that this façade extends to the city as a whole and that Sylhet is actually little more than a village with shoes too big for it. Despite this, it remains one of the most cosmopolitan towns in Bangladesh and you're almost certainly going to meet more people here speaking with a strong Brummie or East London accent (some more genuine than others) than anywhere else in the country. More depressingly for Bangladesh, you also won't fail to notice the dozens of adverts and billboards promising easy visas to a better life in the US, UK and other European countries. These startling contrasts help to make Sylhet an almost essential stop for anyone who wants to understand something of this country.

Orientation & Information

On the south side of the Surma River you'll find the train and bus stations, but not much more. The river is traversed by two bridges. Kean Bridge, the more central one, was repaired after being damaged by Pakistani bombers during the Liberation War. In making the crossing, rickshaw-pullers are aided by rickshaw-pushers; these 'assistants' are paid Tk 2 for their service. This bridge is almost a sight in its own right – only a subcontinental bridge could contain so much seething humanity.

Zinda Bazar Rd is littered with restaurants and shopping centres, as is the intersection of Telihaor and Taltala Rds.

There are only a couple of internet cafés in town and none offer fast connections. The most central one is **Ahana Net & Cyber Café** (Jaintiapur Rd; ⏰ 9am-8pm; per hr Tk 20).

There is a **Standard Chartered Bank** (Airport Rd) with an ATM opposite Darga Gate, and others below both the Hotel Asia and the Surma Valley Rest House.

Sights
SHRINE OF HAZRAT SHAH JALAL

In the north of the city, off Airport Rd, is the **Shrine of Hazrat Shah Jalal**, a 14th-century Sufi saint. The shrine is one of the biggest pilgrimage sites in the country and a fascinating place to visit. Being buried near the saint is considered a great honour. Shah Jalal's sword and robes are preserved within the large new mosque, but aren't on display. The tomb is covered with rich brocade, and at night the space around it is illuminated with candles. The atmosphere is quite magical. It's never entirely clear whether non-Muslims can visit the shrine, though it seems to be OK if you are suitably solemn and well dressed. Women, however, are definitely not allowed up to the tomb.

The pond in front of the shrine complex is filled with sacred catfish that are fed by pilgrims and are, according to legend, metamorphosed black magicians of the Hindu raja Gour Govinda, who was defeated by Shah Jalal in 1303. Nearby is a deep, dark well containing something mysterious. What exactly that is remains a little uncertain – if our translation was correct, it's a giant goldfish with 'Allah' written on its forehead, but then again it might just as likely be the Loch Ness monster!

The complex is thronging with people day and night, including many beggars and disabled people asking for alms, so if you wish to donate bring plenty of small change with you.

Nearby, on a hillock named **Rama Raja's Tilla**, you can get some partially blocked views of the city. Legend has it a Hindu temple that once stood here was destroyed by an earthquake, instigated by Shah Jalal.

OSMANI MUSEUM

In Nur Manzil, near the centre of town and east of Noya Sarok Rd, is the **Osmani Museum** (admission free; ⏰ 10.30am-5.30pm Sat-Wed, 3-8pm Fri Apr-Sep, 9.30am-4.30pm Sat-Wed, 3-8pm Fri Oct-Mar). This small, colonial-era house is dedicated to General Osmani, a key figure in the Liberation War. As it's one of the few tourist sights in town, you should visit, but be warned – it's slightly less interesting than an algebra lesson. It contains such thrilling articles as a 'chair' (and that is exactly what it is). Electricity is a hit-and-miss affair and if you're lucky you'll get a man following you around with an oil lamp to illuminate the displays for you.

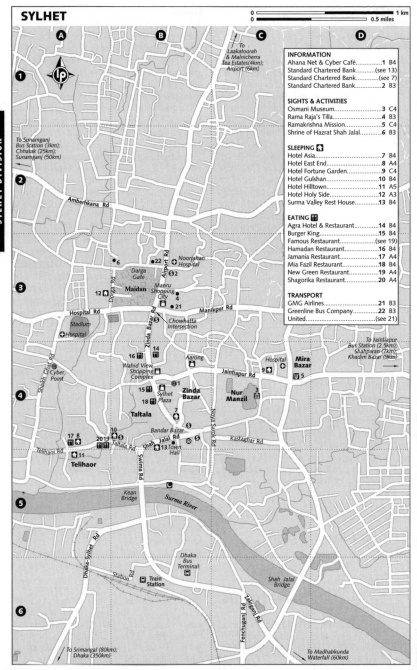

SYLHET

0   1 km
0   0.5 miles

INFORMATION
Ahana Net & Cyber Café.............**1** B4
Standard Chartered Bank.........(see 13)
Standard Chartered Bank.........(see 7)
Standard Chartered Bank.........**2** B3

SIGHTS & ACTIVITIES
Osmani Museum.........................**3** C4
Rama Raja's Tilla........................**4** B3
Ramakrishna Mission..................**5** C4
Shrine of Hazrat Shah Jalal........**6** B3

SLEEPING 🏠
Hotel Asia.................................**7** B4
Hotel East End...........................**8** A4
Hotel Fortune Garden.................**9** C4
Hotel Gulshan...........................**10** B4
Hotel Hilltown..........................**11** A5
Hotel Holy Side.........................**12** A3
Surma Valley Rest House............**13** B4

EATING 🍴
Agra Hotel & Restaurant............**14** B4
Burger King...............................**15** B4
Famous Restaurant..................(see 19)
Hamadan Restaurant.................**16** B4
Jamania Restaurant...................**17** A4
Mia Fazil Restaurant..................**18** B4
New Green Restaurant...............**19** A4
Shagorika Restaurant.................**20** A4

TRANSPORT
GMG Airlines.............................**21** B3
Greenline Bus Company.............**22** B3
United.....................................(see 21)

SYLHET DIVISION

A block to the northeast is the **Ramakrishna Mission**, where Hindu melas are often held.

Sleeping

BUDGET

A number of budget hotels are in the centre of town, in Taltala, along Taltala Rd, and in the adjoining Telihaor area.

Hotel Asia (☎ 711 278; Bandar Bazar; s/d Tk 100/300, d with air-con Tk 800; ✍) Do yourself a favour and grab a bargain at this hotel in the heart of a colourful neighbourhood. The rooms are plain and honest budget treats that come without stains and mess. Go for one without air-con as they are better value.

Hotel East End (☎ 719 210; Telihaor Rd; s/d Tk 150/300, d with air-con Tk 1000; ✍) This friendly hotel with easy English-speaking staff represents good bang for your buck. The rooms are immaculately clean, though strangely the non-air-con rooms are the better deal, thanks to tiled floors which just make everything much more hygienic.

Hotel Hilltown (☎ 716 077; Telihaor Rd; s with/without air-con Tk 255/850, d with/without air-con Tk 350/1000; ✍) The range of rooms on offer at this old stand-by fills an entire A4 sheet, which means almost everyone can find something suitable. Rooms are tiled and clean but lack character, and corridors can be a bit long and lonely. The standard air-con doubles are better than most. You can arrange car hire from the handful of travel agencies situated just outside and there's a good restaurant on site too.

Hotel Gulshan (☎ 717 263; Taltala Rd; s/d Tk 300/500, d with air-con Tk 800; ✍) A long-time favourite with visitors to Sylhet and easily the best in its class, this enormous hotel is almost as big as Bangladesh and much better managed. All rooms are clean and some have sit-down toilets and TV, but only the most expensive ones have hot water. The restaurant doesn't have an atmosphere worth partaking in.

MIDRANGE & TOP END

Hotel Holy Side (☎ 722 278; Dorga Rd; s/d from Tk 650/950; ✍) A very good value midrange/top-end establishment. This welcoming place has the bonus of proximity to the shrine of Hazrat Shah Jalal (though it's not so close that your eardrums take a battering), invitingly soft beds and clean bathtubs to get sloshy in. It's opposite the maidan, which ensures something interesting is always taking place right outside the door. Add an extra 15% tax to room rates.

Hotel Fortune Garden (☎ 715 590; www.hotelfortunegarden.com; 29A Bongobir Rd; s/d Tk 700/1000, d with air-con from Tk 1400; ✍ 🖵) Sylhet's top-dog hotel is sterile to the core and offers no hint of being in Bangladesh, but it does offer exceptional value for taka and you know a decent night's kip is guaranteed. The staff are entertainingly disorganised.

Surma Valley Rest House (☎ 712 671; Shah Jalal Rd; r from Tk 1450; ✍) This sparkling and central hotel is one to write home about and certainly one of the better-value hotels in Bangladesh. Rooms are comfortable enough to mean that leaving will be an effort, and though not huge, the space is nicely used and full of little homely touches. In fact the only minus point we could come up with is its proximity to a noisy mosque, but surely that 5am prayer call will grow on you!

Eating

If you're staying in the Telihaor area, you'll have lots of choices, including the friendly **New Green Restaurant** (meals Tk 40-50), **Shagorika Restaurant** (meals Tk 40-50) and the unmistakably turquoise **Jamania Restaurant** (meals Tk 50), which receives rave reviews from travellers. For something marginally posher, and we mean marginally, try the **Famous Restaurant** (meals Tk 60), which is on the same road.

Mia Fazil Restaurant (Zinda Bazar Rd; meals Tk 60) One of tonnes of identical Bengali restaurants. This one reserves a warm welcome for foreigners and always makes room for you, no matter how busy (and it normally is). Look for the yellow Bengali sign.

Agra Hotel & Restaurant (Zinda Bazar Rd; meals around Tk 60) As full of character as it is full of characters, this popular restaurant, tucked away in a corner, won't give you much privacy with its cramped quarters, but will give you great food.

Burger King (Zinda Bazar Rd; meals Tk 50-100) The name might ring a bell but nothing else about this 2nd-floor restaurant will. Its greasy burgers and kebabs will provide a welcome break from all that healthy rice (don't worry, it's good for the heart).

Hamadan Restaurant (☎ 812 872; 4th fl, Al-Hamra Shopping Centre, Zinda Bazar Rd; dishes from Tk 150-200) This is Sylhet's special-occasion restaurant and it's certainly a nice break from the heat and crush outside. Unfortunately the food, which is mainly Chinese and Thai, is hardly worthy of the fuss – we've had tomato salads that contained more meat than our chicken dish! To find it, take the escalators to the third floor and climb the stairwell at the back left-hand corner of the building.

Getting There & Away

AIR

Both United Airways (which also has an office at the airport) and **GMG Airlines** (☎ 721 225; Feroz Centre, Manikpur Rd) have frequent daily flights to Dhaka (Tk 3720).

BUS

A daytime bus trip between Dhaka and Sylhet is an interesting journey through varied countryside. All the luxury bus companies have offices on the road leading to the shrine of Hazrat Shah Jalal.

Greenline have a luxury bus for Dhaka (Tk 450, five hours) at 12.30am, but other companies offer more sensible departure times.

Buses to Chittagong (Tk 650, 10 hours) generally set sail in the evening only.

Buses to Sunamganj (Tk 50 to Tk 75, 2½ hours, every 20 minutes between 6am and 8.30pm) leave from the Sunamganj bus station a few kilometres northwest of town, along Amberhkana Rd.

Buses northeast to Jaintiapur (Tk 40, three hours, between 6.45am and 5.35pm) and Tamabil (Tk 75, 2½ hours) leave from the small **Jaintiapur bus station** (Jaintiapur Rd), several kilometres east of the town centre.

TRAIN

The **train station** (☎ 83968) is on the south side of town. There are three daily express trains for Dhaka (1st/*sulob* class Tk 270/150, between 7½ and nine hours, depart at 7.30am, 2.45pm and 10.15pm). The night train also has a sleeping car (air-con/fan Tk 610/425).

Trains to Chittagong (1st/*sulob* class Tk 320/190, 10 hours, depart 10am and 10.40pm) also stop at Comilla (1st/*sulob* class Tk 195/120, 6½ hours).

Most of these trains also stop at Srimangal (1st/*sulob* class Tk 90/50, two hours).

Getting Around

TO/FROM THE AIRPORT

The airport, 7km north of town, has numerous taxis and baby taxis (mini rickshaws) waiting. For a ride into town, expect to pay about Tk 300 for a taxi, Tk 100 for a baby taxi.

AROUND SYLHET
Tea Estates

Tea-estate managers haven't cottoned on to their tourist potential, so don't expect a tour on a dune buggy followed by a complimentary cuppa. At best, you'll get permission to be there, and maybe a quick tour with a staff member.

There are a couple of tea estates just beyond the city's northern outskirts on Airport Rd and these are probably the easiest to visit. It's not normally a problem just to stroll straight in – someone is certain to adopt you and show you around. At the **Laakatoorah Tea Estate**, you might be lucky enough to get an interesting lecture from the manager on the history of tea production.

The largest number of tea estates in the northern half of Sylhet division are further on, around **Jaflang**, near the Indian border. This is one of the most scenic parts of Sylhet division and a major tribal area, where many Khasi are found. The bus from Sylhet takes 2½ hours to Tamabil and another 30 minutes to Jaflang. Remind the bus-wallah that you want to get off at Jaflang – it's easy to miss.

Shrine of Shah Paran

Around 8km east of Sylhet, just off the highway to Jaintiapur, is the **Shrine of Shah Paran** in the tiny village of Shahparan. It's a single-domed mosque that attracts about 2000 pilgrims a day; you'll see charter buses from Dhaka all around the place.

Madhabkunda Waterfall

A three-hour drive southeast of Sylhet (and equally accessible from Srimangal by road and rail), and a 3km rickshaw ride from Dakshinbagh train station, is the famous **waterfall** of Madhabkunda. It is popular with busloads of Bangladeshi tourists. You may also be able to find some elephants, which are still being used to haul huge logs, in this general area. There's a Parjatan tourist spot nearby, with a restaurant, picnic area and toilet facilities.

TAMABIL

The Tamabil border crossing (open between 6am and 5pm), 55km north from Sylhet, is primarily used to import coal from India, though foreigners occasionally cross here. Getting to the border can be messy – some travellers have reported being confused as to where the official crossing actually is, but all declare the hassle well worth the scenery between Dawki and Shillong in India: it's spectacular. Coming from India, Sylhet division is a nice way to ease yourself into Bangladesh.

To cross from Tamabil to Dawki, you *must* deposit Tk 300 departure tax into any Sonali Bank branch. Once you have done this, you are required to show your deposit receipt to border officials. The closest Sonali Bank branch is in Jaintiapur, 13km from Tamabil.

Plan in advance to have some rupee/taka on you – there is nowhere to change money in Tamabil, and the bank at Dawki is none too cooperative.

Getting There & Away
FROM BANGLADESH
Buses run from Sylhet to Tamabil (Tk 75, 2½ hours). From here, it's a 15-minute hike to the border.

Once in India, it's a 1.5km walk (or Rs 30 taxi ride) to the town of Dawki, from where buses run to Shillong (Rs 70, 2½ hours). If you are stranded in Dawki, there is a small hotel on the hill, above the Sikh temple, though it's super basic and often loath to take foreigners – start your journey early in order to avoid getting caught out.

The last bus leaves Dawki for Shillong around 11am. If you miss it, there are a number of taxis eager to take you the two hours to Shillong, but you'll pay dearly for the honour!

FROM INDIA
The border post is at Dawki in Meghalaya, accessible by bus from Shillong, 70km away. From Dawki, it is a 1.5km walk to Tamabil, where formal but friendly border officials may be able to help you negotiate a taxi to Sylhet, which shouldn't cost more than about Tk 700.

There is nowhere to stay the night in Tamabil, but nearby Jaflang has a couple of budget hotels and restaurants. It is also easier to organise onward transport from here.

SUNAMGANJ
☎ 0871
Approximately 70km west of Sylhet, this small town offers little for tourists. However, the local *haors* (wetlands) are rife with bird life. From midwinter through to the end of March and sometimes April, migrants, winter birds and residents all get together for a big bird party. Varieties of rails, raptors, ducks, sandpipers and others congregate.

The three *haors* that seem to be the best for bird-watching are several hours upstream

---

TWITCHING IN THE SUNAMGANJ HAORS   *Dave Johnson*

For a worthwhile tour of the Sunamganj *haors*, you'll need at least four days to find some exciting bird species. Baer's pochard is probably the rarest bird, and not difficult to spot if you're there at the right time; other pochards include the white-eyed and red-crested varieties. The Baikal teal and the falcated teal are both impressive winterers, along with an assortment of crakes, including the ruddy crake and the little crake. You'll also see the spotted redshank and the blue-bearded bee-eater, and the assortment continues with various sandpipers and lapwings. A number of raptors are here as well, including several fishing eagles, such as the grey-headed and spotted Pallas' eagles. So little has been done to record species here that it's not unreasonable to expect to see new, previously unrecorded species during each trip.

The trip begins at Aila Haor, four hours upriver. A knowledgeable boatman will know exactly where to go. It's another two hours on foot into the *haor* area, but it's worth it for the rich bird life awaiting. It may be dark by the time you return to the boat, so carry a torch. You'll sleep on the boat and continue to Pasua early next morning.

Pasua Haor, four hours upriver, lies just over an embankment from the river. You can sit and watch the wildlife or walk for a couple of kilometres on the fringes of the marshy basin. After another four hours' travel the next morning, you'll arrive at Tangua Haor, bordering India and the furthest point of the trip. In this area, scrub and grassland are a bonus, and you'll see some interesting grassland species of birds.

On the return trip to Sunamganj, river travel is spartan yet peaceful, and it is an exceptional way to experience rural life in Bangladesh, where so much takes place on or near a river's edge.

from the Surma River. Visiting all of them is a four-day affair, which, except for true bird enthusiasts, is probably more than most travellers want. An overnight trip would get you into some of the most fascinating rural areas in Bangladesh. See boxed text, p151 for a fascinating account of a birder's trip up here.

Getting There & Away

From Sylhet, there are regular buses to Sunamganj (Tk 50 to Tk 75, 2½ hours), leaving from **Sunamganj bus station** (Amberhkana Rd). Buses from Sunamganj to Sylhet depart approximately every 20 minutes from the bus station.

SRIMANGAL
☎ 08626

Put the kettle on and let's have a nice cup of tea. But have you ever wondered what goes into producing that little bag? Well, in Srimangal (or Sreemongal), the tea capital of Bangladesh, you can find out all about it. This hilly area, with tea estates, lemon orchards and pineapple plantations, is one of the most pic-turesque and enjoyable parts of the country. For miles around, tea estates form a perennially green carpet on the sloping hills, and it's the one area (besides the Sundarbans) where it is possible to look around and not see another human being. In addition to learning all there is to know about tea, you can also go primate-potty in a range of forest national parks, get the low-down on tribal life and discover that pineapples don't actually grow on trees.

Information

Within a stone's throw of each other on the main drag, College Rd, is a Rupali Bank, Sonali Bank and IFIC Bank, but they'll probably think you crazy if you ask about changing money with them.

Cyber Corner (per hr Tk 25) At the end of the long corridor under the Hotel Mukta.

E-Zone Cyber Café (per hr Tk 30) Excellent connections on the outskirts of town.

Tours

Adventure Tourism (☎ 01712 317483; enjoylife_45@ yahoo.com; RK Mission Rd) Run by the ambitious Mr

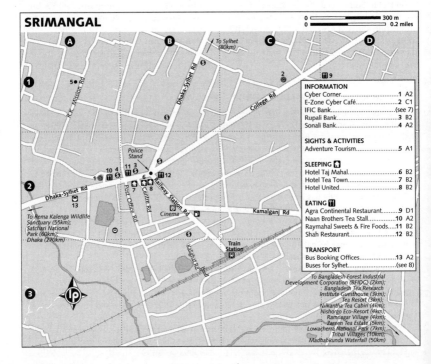

SRIMANGAL

| | 0 | 300 m |
| | 0 | 0.2 miles |

INFORMATION
Cyber Corner.........................1 A2
E-Zone Cyber Café...............2 C1
IFIC Bank.............................(see 7)
Rupali Bank..........................3 B2
Sonali Bank..........................4 A2

SIGHTS & ACTIVITIES
Adventure Tourism................5 A1

SLEEPING
Hotel Taj Mahal....................6 B2
Hotel Tea Town.....................7 B2
Hotel United.........................8 B2

EATING
Agra Continental Restaurant.........9 D1
Naan Brothers Tea Stall..............10 A2
Raymahal Sweets & Fire Foods....11 B2
Shah Restaurant.......................12 B2

TRANSPORT
Bus Booking Offices...................13 A2
Buses for Sylhet.....................(see 8)

To Bangladesh Forest Industrial
Development Corporation (BFIDC) (2km);
Bangladesh Tea Research
Institute Guesthouse (3km);
Tea Resort (3km);
Nikantha Tea Cabin (4km);
Nishorgo Eco-Resort (4km);
Ramnagar Village (4km);
Zareen Tea Estate (5km);
Lowacherra National Park (7km);
Tribal Villages (10km);
Madhabkunda Waterfall (50km)

To Rema Kalenga Wildlife
Sanctuary (55km);
Satchari National
Park (60km);
Dhaka (270km)

Rashed Husan. Adventure Tourism organises day tours (Tk 800 per person) taking in a tea estate, the Lowacherra National Park, some tribal villages and various other sights of interest in the region. It's an effective way to tick off all the sights quickly and painlessly, but his guides aren't very knowledgeable. If he doesn't find you, you can find him through the Hotel Tea Town. He also rents out bikes (Tk 150 to Tk 200 per day).

Sleeping

Hotel Taj Mahal (Dhaka-Sylhet Rd; s/d Tk 50/100) The world's most beautiful monument to love it isn't, but it is the sort of place that looks like it sees a lot of paid-for adulation… Even so, for the price it's hard to fault and the small rooms are kept fairly clean.

Hotel United (☎ 88297; Dhaka-Sylhet Rd; s/d Tk 100/200) Next door to the Taj Mahal, the Hotel United offers cramped rooms that are shockingly clean and good value and come with rare extras like mosquito nets and sit-down toilets. It's friendly and they are happy for women to stay, but couples get single beds only.

Hotel Tea Town (☎ 370; Dhaka-Sylhet Rd; s/d Tk 300/400, ste from Tk 800) The town centre's glitziest hotel has sparkling floors and, in the suites, sit-down toilets and hot-water showers. The cheaper rooms lack such mod cons but are just as well tended.

ourpick Bangladesh Tea Research Institute Guesthouse (BTRI; ☎ 71225; r Tk 400) Live, breathe, touch and taste it. There is simply no escaping it. Tea – it's everywhere in Srimangal, so what better place to stay than right here in the heart of the Bangladesh tea universe. Located a couple of kilometres out of town, this charming guesthouse is right opposite the Research Institute and has large, well-furnished rooms with thick carpets, regal green curtains, inviting bathtubs and, best of all, lovely verandas with tables and chairs, where you can sit back with – what else – a perfect cuppa and admire the beautifully maintained gardens. Meals are available for around Tk 200 per day. It's a good idea to book accommodation in advance.

Nishorgo Eco-Resort (www.nishorgo.org; r Tk 1000) Several positive reports have come in of a newly opened accommodation venture run by Nishorgo, the recently formed and very active government-run group in charge of all the protected areas in the country. It has several basic, thatched 'jungle' huts that come

with attached bathrooms. To stay at this resort, located halfway between Srimangal and Lowacherra National Park, contact Mr Kazi Shamsul Hogue (☎ 0171 5041207).

Tea Resort (☎ /fax 207/8; r Tk 1100-2300) The Tea Resort, tucked away amongst the tea gardens 3km from Srimangal is, unfortunately, not among the best places to stay in the country – though it could very easily become one. The cheap rooms had cockroaches when we visited and looked very tatty, and while the more expensive rooms are better, they are still overpriced. We have also received less than positive comments regarding the restaurant. So why are we mentioning it? Simple: because it seems to be the *de rigueur* when visiting Srimangal to stay here and most people book in advance.

Eating

Food is something of a struggle in Srimangal and especially hard is breakfast. The best bet at this early hour is to buy some of the delicious, home-made shortbread biscuits that many of the little grocery shops sell and find a tea stall hidden from penetrating gazes. One such place that comes highly recommended is the Naan Brothers Tea Stall, halfway down the main road (look out for the sacks of rice and pulses in the neighbouring grocery shop). There is no sign and it doesn't kick into gear until after 9am.

ourpick Nilkantha Tea Cabin (Ramnagar village) The Nilkantha Tea Cabin, around 5km south of town, produces the almost world-famous Willy Wonka-esque five-colour tea. Yes, it does have five distinct layers of colour and five equally differing tastes. In addition to the five-colour tea (Tk 50), there are dozens of other flavours (from Tk 5) and the tea cabin has turned into a social institution for the young of the area. A baby taxi from town shouldn't cost more than Tk 20.

Shah Restaurant (Railway Station Rd; meals around Tk 50) In the heart of town, a few doors south of the main intersection, the Shah turns out filling and tasty meals.

Raymahal Sweets and Fire Foods (Dhaka-Sylhet Rd; meals around Tk 50) An excellent range of sugary treats and Western fast-food imitations.

Agra Continental Restaurant (☎ 71141; Guho Rd; mains Tk 200; ☼ midday-11pm) Every town needs a Chinese restaurant and this new establishment on the edge of town is one of the genre's better examples. It's the only relaxing, sit-down place to eat in town and is frequented by locals on special occasions.

Getting There & Away
BUS
To take a local bus to Dhaka (Tk 100, five hours) or Sylhet (Tk 65, three hours), you will have to hail one on the road. You can try the same for Comilla (Tk 200, six hours), Kamalganj (Tk 15) and Lowacherra National Park (Tk 10).

There are three booking offices for coaches along the main road in close proximity to each other. These service Dhaka (non–air-con/air-con Tk 200/250, five hours, every 30 minutes) and Chittagong (Tk 350, 12 hours). Buses for Sylhet also have offices on the main drag near the main intersection.

TRAIN
There are three trains a day to Dhaka (1st/ sulob class Tk 200/110; 5½ hours; depart 9.56am, 5.05pm and 12.37am), except for Tuesday and Wednesday when there are only two. Afternoon trains also have air-con compartments (Tk 300) and evening trains have sleepers (Tk 500).

AROUND SRIMANGAL
Sights & Activities
CYCLING
The area around Srimangal is one of the best in Bangladesh for cycling. Despite the rolling terrain, the roads are reasonably level; if overly encumbered rickshaw-wallahs can do it, so can you, even on the ubiquitous one-speed Chinese bike.

There's an intricate network of roads connecting all the tea estates to the main highways. Only the major routes are tarred or bricked, but the dirt roads are in good condition. Even if you just head east out of town on Kamalganj Rd and stay on the main roads, you will find yourself weaving in and out of heaven in no time.

It can be difficult to determine where one estate stops and another starts. Bear in mind that you might inadvertently pedal into private property. Though you will find that most people are more likely to treat you like a guest than a trespasser, it is appropriate to seek management's permission to be there.

TEA ESTATES
There are so many tea estates that it's not easy to determine which are the best for visiting. Some are more receptive to visitors than others.

One of the most frequently visited and welcoming estates is **Zareen Tea Estate**, where the tea bushes bounce across the tops of the cartoonlike hills that so typify this area. The turnoff for the gardens is located roughly halfway between the Tea Resort and Lowacherra National Park.

The sprawling **Finlays** estate, just on the edge of Srimangal, is less visitor-certain, but it's not normally a problem to wander a short way into the bushes and talk to the tea-pluckers.

The **Bangladesh Tea Research Institute** (BTRI; ☎ 71225) isn't a commercial estate as such, but rather the scientific headquarters of Bangladeshi tea production. New strains of tea and new growing techniques are tried out here, and the staff are knowledgeable and very happy to spread that knowledge. There is also a production factory, which with a bit of luck you might be allowed to visit, and a tea-tasting room which you are almost certain to be ushered into. It is polite to give advance notice of your visit. See also p156.

LOWACHERRA NATIONAL PARK
Around 8km east of Srimangal, on the road to Kamalganj, **Lowacherra National Park** (known to locals as Shaymoli) is a wild and mysterious patch of tropical semi-evergreen forest absolutely crawling with life. Not only is this 1250-hectare park (which forms part of a 2740-hectare protected zone known as the West Bhanugach Reserve) one of the finest wildlife venues in the country, but it's also one of the easiest to visit. Though the forest may look like a primeval jungle, it has been greatly influenced by the activities of humans, and as recently as 1920 it was managed as a timber-production plantation. Since then the forest has been largely allowed to revert to a natural state, and after years of mismanagement the government has finally got its act together and given the park firm protection, established a number of visitor walking trails and is in the process of training up 'eco-guides'.

The undisputed highlight of the park is the critically endangered hoolock gibbon – the subcontinent's only ape species and one that you have a pretty good chance of seeing crashing through the trees. A further 19 mammal species have been identified including capped langur, the delightful slow loris, orange-bellied Himalayan squirrel and bark-

---

TEA GARDENS & TEA ESTATES

Tea production in Bangladesh dates from 1854, when Malnicherra Tea Estate, just north of Sylhet, was set up by the British. The tea grew well here and by the end of the century there were around 150 tea estates, almost all under British ownership. About the same number exist today but, since Independence, less than half are British-owned. The rest mainly belong to wealthy Bangladeshis and, to a lesser extent, the government's Tea Board.

When the British began growing tea in Sylhet, they didn't bother training the indigenous people. Rather, they brought experienced Indian labourers, mainly from tea estates in Bihar, Orissa and Bangla (West Bengal). Today, virtually all of the labourers, or 'coolies', are descendants of these original Hindus. Small Hindu shrines are a common feature of tea estates with worker colonies.

Each estate provides an elementary school and a doctor. Since many of the estates are in remote locations, few of the workers' children are able to go beyond the primary grades. However, the tea workers have the only trade union in Bangladesh that effectively bargains with management, so their contracts often include special privileges, such as a festival allowance. New Year's Eve is one of the most festive times, in part because the tea season is over. Hinduism does not ban alcohol and many workers get a bit tipsy at festival time. Several private 'clubs' outside Srimangal cater to the owners and managers year-round. Faced with these long-standing traditions, the government looks the other way.

When you are visiting a tea estate, as you must, don't make the mistake of touring on a Friday, the day of rest, or visiting between mid-December and the start of March, as everything will be at a standstill. The picking season is during the wetter months, from early March to early December, when the factories are in full operation.

---

ing deer. The bird-watching here is equally superb and so far some 246 species have been recorded, with the blue-bearded bee-eater and the red-breasted trogon being big stars. Another highlight are the orchids, of which there are more than 20 varieties (the wet season is the best time to see them).

Remember though that this isn't the open African savanna but a dense forest, and despite the impressive number of animals you would have to put in a good deal of effort to get anything other than a fleeting glimpse. One thing you won't miss though are the insects, and rather than concentrating on the bigger mammals you will find your visit more rewarding if you focus instead on the bugs and birds. Of these bugs, the most visible are the ropelike columns of aggressive ants, the flamboyant butterflies and, maybe less welcome, the enormous orb spiders (also called banana spiders). You won't be able to miss these black, red and yellow monsters hanging from spiderman-sized webs between trees, but don't worry, they might look like the devil incarnate but they are in fact harmless – or so we're told!

There are three marked walking trails taking anything from half an hour to three hours, and the visitors centre has printed booklets with walking maps and some pointers on things to look out for. You can also hire 'eco-guides' from here, but try and chat to them first as many don't speak much English and have very little real knowledge of the plants and animals contained within the forest.

To access the reserve from Srimangal, take the paved road east towards Kamalganj. The poorly marked turn-off to your left (north), which is easy to miss, is about 4.75km past the Tea Resort compound and another 2.75km beyond the well-marked turn-off for the Nurjahan and Madabpore tea estates. The dirt road into the forests, which crosses the railroad tracks, is less than 1km long and an easy walk. A bus from Srimangal costs Tk 10.

TRIBAL VILLAGES

There are 11 Khashia villages (called *punji*) and several Monipuri villages (called *para*) scattered among the tea plantations in the Srimangal area. Khashia villages are usually on hilltops surrounded by betel-nut trees, which is their cash crop. When visiting a Khashia village you should first call in on the local chief, as the community will not extend full hospitality without his permission. The easiest way of visiting one of the Khashia communities is to ask one of the guides at Lowacherra National Park to lead you to one of the villages situated on the nearby park fringes.

DR MAINULHUQ

Dr Mainulhuq is a scientist working for the Bangladesh Tea Research Institute. He spoke to us about the production and history of tea in Bangladesh.

Where did tea originate from and when did it arrive in Bangladesh? Tea originated in China around 2500 BC, when an emperor was meditating beside some boiling water. Whilst he was doing this, a tea leaf fell into the water. After he had finished meditating, he drank the water and tea was born. Robert Bruce, who worked for the British Army, saw Assamese people drinking tea and came up with the idea of growing it in Bangladesh. Production first began in 1854.

How much tea is produced per year in Bangladesh? We make around 55 to 60 million kg of tea a year, of which about 10 to 15 million kg is exported to Pakistan, the Middle East and Europe. Almost all the tea we produce here is black tea. I think only one estate makes green tea.

Tell us something of the life cycle of a tea bush? Firstly, all tea bushes are the same species, each one in the world. It is the altitude they are grown at and the processing that gives them their distinct flavours. Srimangal is very low, just 75m above sea level, which makes it one of the lowest tea-growing areas in the world. The many trees you will see planted among the tea bushes are to give them shade, because this low altitude means it gets very hot. The tea leaves can be first plucked after only a year. For the first five years of the bush's life it is considered young tea, but mature tea, after the bush is over about eight years old, is best. The life of the plant is around 100 years but its economic life lasts until the bush is around 60 years old. After a tea bush dies we replace it with another crop, such as citronella, which quickly allows the soil to recuperate before we replant with tea again after two years. We have to trim the tea plants frequently, otherwise they would grow into trees. We keep them at elbow height for ease of picking.

Why is it only women who pick the tea? Women are much better at it because they have smaller and more delicate hands, which helps with the picking, and they are better at concentrating than men.

Can you tell us how to make the perfect cup of tea? Well, firstly you must never use tea bags, because the tea dust pollutes it. You should use 2.5g of tea leaves with 190mL of water and leave it to brew for five minutes. If you like milk tea, put the milk in last so that you can gauge the strength of the tea properly.

One of the easiest Monipuri villages to visit is called **Ramnagar**, close to the Bangladesh Tea Research Institute; if you call in on the institute you will be able to get directions.

SATCHARI NATIONAL PARK

About 60km southwest of Srimangal on the Dhaka–Sylhet Hwy is the small **Satchari National Park** (formerly known as the Telepara Forest Reserve). This 243-hectare park is part of a much larger protected region. Although less popular than Lowacherra, it is a superb slab of tropical forest with a higher diversity of plants and animals than Lowacherra, and with far less human disturbance.

There are a number of marked walking trails of between 30 minutes and three hours, seven streams, a population of hoolock gibbons, fishing cats, Phayre's langur, jungle fowl, pygmy woodpeckers and oriental pied hornbills.

The Satchari National Park is on the south side of the main road, about 1km east of the Satchari bus stop and Telepara Tea Estate, where the highway takes a sharp left bend. You could get the driver of the Dhaka–Sylhet bus to drop you off here, if you don't mind missing the early hours when bird-watching is best. Alternatively, get a bus from Srimangal and walk to the trail head 1km away. To return to Srimangal, flag down one of the Dhaka–Sylhet buses, or walk back to Telepara Tea Estate and catch one there.

REMA KALENGA WILDLIFE SANCTUARY

The **Rema Kalenga Wildlife Sanctuary**, near Satchari National Park, is a very rarely visited region of upland forest that provides a home to numerous bird species, capped langur, slow loris and fishing cats. It has a similar system of walking trails to Satchari.

Directory

CONTENTS

ACCOMMODATION

There are international-standard hotels in Dhaka, Chittagong and Sylhet, but most accommodation is well down the price scale.

Couples, married or not, shouldn't plan a dirty weekend in Bangladesh. Most midrange and top-end hotels will have no problems with you sharing a room, but most of the time you'll find it contains only two single beds. Some budget hotels refuse to allow unmarried couples to stay and many of them are not very welcoming to single women travellers. If you are in a couple (married or not) and one of you is of Bangladeshi or Indian descent, you may well have trouble getting a room of any description in any hotel – including in some of Dhaka's most expensive establishments!

> ### PRACTICALITIES
>
> - The *Daily Star*'s supplementary magazine on Fridays is a good source of information on what's going on in Dhaka.
> - Almost every hotel TV is satellite TV.
> - Electricity (when there is electricity) is 220V, 50 Hz AC and is either a two-pronged connection with round rather than flat holes or a three-pin UK-style plug but rounder and with thicker pins.
> - Officially Bangladesh is metric, but some local measures are still used. For instance, a *seer* equals 850g and a *maund* is 37kg. Yards are interchanged with metres, and miles are often confused with kilometres.

Prices are often characterised as 'with air-con' or 'without air-con'; the latter is often significantly cheaper and usually less appealing. Outside of this major distinction, prices vary according to whether there is a TV and/or an attached bathroom. It's rarely necessary to book rooms in advance. Note that in the bigger cities it's often easy to negotiate room discounts of up to 50% on the better-class hotels. In this guide, rates are generally broken down into budget (under Tk 500 for a double), midrange (Tk 500 to Tk 1000) and top end (over Tk 1000).

Government Rest Houses & Circuit Houses

There are government rest houses and circuit houses in every district. They aren't officially accessible to travellers, but the district commissioner may let you stay if there are few alternative options around.

The Archaeology Department has rest houses at Paharpur, Mainimati and Mahasthan. Rooms are basic but cheap at typically Tk 200 for a double.

Hotels

The word 'hotel' denotes a hotel or restaurant; the correct term for a hotel is 'residential hotel'. Lower-end establishments often make this distinction on their signs, and you'll avoid confusion if you use this term when asking for directions.

Many hotels don't have English signs and some buildings look like hotels but aren't. You'll save yourself time and trouble if you learn to recognise the word 'hotel' in Bengali script (see p191).

Absolute bottom-end accommodation usually consists of a tiny room with fan, shared bathroom and maybe mosquito nets. This typically costs around Tk 80/120 for a single/double. Apart from space and hygiene deficiencies, these places often refuse to accept foreigners.

Midrange hotels are better value and there is an increasing number of them. Expect to pay from Tk 400/600 (or more in Dhaka) for a single/double with attached bathroom. For this you will usually get a small room with a reasonably soft bed, and a clean bathroom with a cold shower. Double this price and you're into the upper midrange or lower top-end class of hotel and can expect a large room, soft beds without too many nasty stains, hot water and sit-down toilets.

ACTIVITIES
Cycling
Bangladesh's lazy terrain makes it an ideal place for cycling. Even the slightly more hilly areas aren't arduous, they're just scenic. Good places for cycling include Srimangal (p154) in Sylhet division and Thakurgaon in Rajshahi division.

For information about cycling in general, see p173.

Hiking
The best places to do some hiking are forest reserves and national parks. Some, like Satchari National Park (p156) and Lowacherra National Park (p154) in Sylhet division, have hiking trails marked out and offer magical jungle experiences.

Unquestionably the best place for fully fledged hikes is the Chittagong Hill Tracts (p129), particularly around Bandarban. For the moment at least, the security situation prevents anything much more taxing than gentle day hikes, but a little determination and preplanning might open up multiday sensory-overload treks. The Adivasis (tribal people) in this area are considerably more hospitable than the central government likes

to give them credit for, and the landscape in which they live is unforgettable.

River Trips
To come to Bangladesh and not travel by boat down a swampy river is like going to Paris and not suffering from a look of utter disdain from a snooty waiter. It's not just inconceivable – it's plain old wrong! Although river trips in Bangladesh are unavoidable if you're doing any sort of extensive travel, it's also worth putting in the effort to do a good one. There are some river trips you can do around Dhaka either independently or through an organised tour company. See p59 for details.

The ultimate boat ride in Bangladesh is a journey on the Rocket. This crazy ferry ride between Dhaka and Khulna via Barisal isn't for the light-hearted but it's the stuff that legendary travel stories are made of. See p175 for more details.

Surfing
It's not Hawaii but for the most adventurous of wave riders surprisingly consistent beach breaks can be found between Cox's Bazar and St Martin's Island. The most consistent time of year is during the monsoon, but you'll need to rise early to beat the daily onshore winds. The best overall time is late September/early October when swells will be consistent, wind patterns more favourable and temperatures pleasant. Almost no foreigners have surfed in Bangladesh but you might be surprised to learn that there is a small Bangladeshi surf community around Cox's Bazar who even hold a fun contest in late October, which includes a Bangladeshi women's division – this country never fails to surprise! For more on Bangladeshi surfing, keep an eye on www.oceansurfpublications.co.uk.

BUSINESS HOURS
Unlike in most South Asian countries, business hours are strictly adhered to in Bangladesh and you shouldn't expect to get anything done on Friday, which is the official day off. Banking hours from Saturday to Wednesday are 9am to 3pm, and on Thursday 9am until 2pm. Select ATMs, like those attached to Standard Chartered Bank, Dutch-Bangla Bank or the less common HSBC, are open 24 hours or at least until very late.

Government offices are open Saturday to Thursday from 9am until 2pm. Private businesses generally operate between 9am and 5pm (closed Friday), while shops, including bazars, tend to be open from 9am or 10am to 8pm or 10pm. Some shops and bazars are open for half a day on Friday.

CHILDREN

Travelling with young children in Bangladesh would be very tough and child-care facilities are almost zero. However, Bangladeshis are fascinated by foreign children and everyone will go out of their way to help. You will have a constant queue of would-be nannies wanting to take your child under their wing.

From a health standpoint, dishes of boiled rice and unspiced *dahl* (yellow lentils), scrambled or boiled eggs, oatmeal and a variety of fruits and vegetables should be enough to keep kids happy.

You'll be hard pressed coming across highchairs and nappy-changing facilities, but formula and disposable nappies can be found at some supermarkets in towns and cities.

Lonely Planet's *Travel with Children* is a collection of experiences from travelling families, and includes practical advice on how to avoid hassles and have a fun travel experience with kids.

CLIMATE CHARTS

The climate in Bangladesh is dramatic, to say the least. It is subtropical and tropical with temperatures ranging from as low as 3˚C overnight in the cold season to a daytime top of above 40˚C in the hot season. Annual rainfall varies from 1000mm in the west to 2500mm in the southeast, and up to 5000mm in the north, near the hills of Assam.

Three-quarters of the annual rainfall occurs between June and September. The 90% to 95% humidity in this season is almost unbearable.

In the cold season the weather is drier and fresh, with average daytime temperatures of 24ºC. Rainfall is negligible, although even in winter a brief shower may come along.

While early March can still be pleasant, by April, as the monsoon approaches, humidity increases and lethal hailstorms aren't uncommon. The monsoon season usually starts between late May and mid-June. It doesn't rain solidly all day – there tends to be an initial downpour, followed by clear skies. You should avoid visiting at this time of year!

See also When to Go (p12).

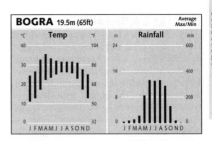

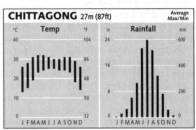

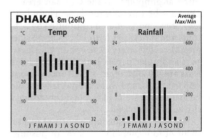

COURSES

The best places for learning Bengali are the **Effective Bangla Learning Centre** (EBLC; Map p62; ☎ 1710 926392; www.eblcbd.com; House 16A, Rd 25A, Banani, Dhaka) and **HEED** (Health, Education, Economic Development; Map p62; ☎ 881 2390, 989 6028; hlc@agni .com; House 104, Rd 12, Block E, Banani, Dhaka).

CUSTOMS

The usual '200 cigarettes, 1L of alcohol' rule applies, though a relatively casual approach is employed at border crossings. Foreigners are permitted to bring in US$5000 without declaring it and Bangladeshis can bring in US$2500.

On departure, tourists are allowed to reconvert 25% of the total foreign currency encashed in the country. This is only possible at the airport in Dhaka, and you will need to have your encashment slips with you as proof.

DANGERS & ANNOYANCES

Bangladesh generally receives a rough ride in the Western press and many people regard it as a dangerously unstable country. The truth couldn't be further away from this and by and large Bangladesh is overwhelmingly friendly and hospitable. The biggest annoyance you will probably have to face is unabating friendliness – interested crowds are everywhere and questions about your nationality, religion and marital status never cease.

Having said that, there are some very rare but very real dangers in Bangladesh; foreigners have been robbed, raped and kidnapped.

Pickpocketing on crowded buses is not as endemic as in some other Asian countries, but armed robbery on buses, particularly at night and using crude weapons such as knives, acid bulbs and home-made shotguns, does take place. Try to travel in daylight hours only. A number of foreigners have been mugged, often at gunpoint, in the Gulshan area of Dhaka – be careful after dark. There have also been reports of theft committed by both touts and officials at both Dhaka and Sylhet airports. Keep a very close eye on your passport and other papers here. Rickshaws and taxis present all manner of theft and mugging opportunities, and women especially should be extremely careful of any taxi containing a driver and his 'friend'.

We have had some rare reports of harassment of foreigners in the form of pushing, stone throwing and spitting, but such incidents are very uncommon.

There are also ripples of terrorist activity, targeted assassinations, politically motivated attacks and, sometimes, violent religious rivalry. The latest attack at the time of writing was in May 2007, when bombs exploded at train stations in Dhaka, Sylhet and Chittagong though there were no fatalities. There have been a number of similar attacks in recent years that have seen four people killed. However, between late November and early December 2005 a number of bomb attacks took place across the country that left 23 people dead and 144 injured. Foreigners have never been targeted in these incidents, but many travel advisories warn foreign nationals to stay away from large gatherings to cut down on the 'wrong place, wrong time' possibility.

Foreigners are more likely to get tangled up in a hartal (strike). These frequently turn violent and many people have been killed or seriously injured as a result. The National Day of Mourning (21 February) is a potentially chaotic day (see opposite). Major riots, affecting many towns, took place in August 2007 resulting in deaths and many injuries. A curfew was enforced in many problem areas including Dhaka. This has since been lifted but at the time of writing a state of emergency, originally imposed in January 2007, was still being enforced (see p24 for more information). However, it has to be said that this will have no effect on your travel plans and most foreigners aren't even aware of it.

The Chittagong Hill Tracts (p129) is the only part of the country where you need really worry for your safety, and even here the problem areas are out of bounds to foreign tourists.

To sum up, the military-backed caretaker government has done much to ease tensions in Bangladesh and improve both the security and corruption situation, and in all honesty the biggest danger you face is from being involved in a road accident. Even so, it pays to keep yourself informed as to what's going on by regularly consulting travel advisories and newspapers.

Also see Dangers & Annoyances in the Dhaka chapter (p50).

Scams

Tourism has not really established itself in Bangladesh, and neither have tourist-related scams. You might actually be surprised at the sheer honesty of most people. However, as with anywhere in the world, not everyone is a good guy.

The most common scam you will encounter is short-changing for small transactions. The best guard against this is vigilance when you're receiving change, or a polite query about unlikely restaurant bills. A similar scam is bus boys conveniently 'forgetting' to give you your change, even though they have a fistful of taka. Nine times out of 10 you're more likely to be chased because *you've* forgotten, but keep this at the back of your mind.

Some travellers have reported being approached by dubious charities, initially appearing legitimate. Some professional beggars wave fraudulent or at least out-of-date pharmaceutical prescriptions asking for assistance in purchasing medicine for children.

Finally, there are the usual hassles with rickshaw, baby taxi (mini three-wheeled autorickshaws) and taxi drivers, though even here the level of harassment is minimal compared to some nearby countries, and in many towns it's possible to just hop on a rickshaw without pre-negotiating a price and not suffer the consequences!

EMBASSIES & CONSULATES
Embassies & Consulates in Bangladesh
If you are going to spend a considerable length of time in a remote area, it is a good idea to register with your embassy.

Australia (Map p62; ☎ 881 3101-5; fax 811 125; 184 Gulshan Ave, Gulshan II, Dhaka)

Bhutan (Map p62; ☎ 882 6863; fax 882 3939; House 12, Rd 107, Gulshan II, Dhaka)

Canada (Map p62; ☎ 988 7091-7; fax 882 3043; House 16/A, Rd 48, Gulshan II, Dhaka)

China (Map p62; ☎ 882 4862; fax 882 3004; House 2 & 4, Rd 3, Block 1, Baridhara, Dhaka)

Denmark (Map p62; ☎ 882 1799; fax 882 3638; House 1, Rd 51, Gulshan, Dhaka)

France (Map p62; ☎ 881 3811-4; fax 882 3612; House 18, Rd 108, Gulshan, Dhaka)

Germany (Map p62; ☎ 882 3521-5; fax 885 3528; 178 Gulshan Ave, Gulshan II, Dhaka)

India (Map p62; ☎ 988 8789; fax 984 3050; House 2, Rd 142, Gulshan I, Dhaka)

Italy (Map p62; ☎ 882 2781-3; fax 882 2578; Plot 2/3, cnr Rds 74 & 79, Gulshan II, Dhaka)

Japan (Map p62; ☎ 881 0087; fax 882 4469; Plot 5 & 7, Dutabash Rd, Baridhara, Dhaka)

Malaysia (Map p62; ☎ 882 7759-60; fax 882 7761; Plot 1, cnr of United Nations Rd & Rd 6, Baridhara, Dhaka)

Myanmar (Burma; Map p62; ☎ 989 6331; fax 882 3740; House 3, Rd 84, Gulshan II, Dhaka)

Nepal (Map p62; ☎ 989 2490; fax 882 6401; cnr United Nations Rd & Rd 2, Baridhara, Dhaka)

Netherlands (Map p62; ☎ 882 2715-8; fax 882 3362; House 49, Rd 90, Gulshan II, Dhaka)

Norway (Map p62; ☎ 882 3880; fax 882 3661; House 9, Rd 111, Gulshan, Dhaka)

Pakistan (Map p62; ☎ 882 5388-9; fax 885 0637; House 2, Rd 71, Gulshan, Dhaka)

Russia (Map p62; ☎ 882 8142; fax 882 3735; House 9, Rd 79, Gulshan, Dhaka)

Sweden (Map p62; ☎ 883 3144-7; fax 882 3948; House 1, Rd 51, Gulshan II, Dhaka)

Switzerland (Map p62; ☎ 881 2874-6; fax 882 3872; House 31/B, Rd 18, Banani, Dhaka)

Thailand (Map p62; ☎ 881 2795-6; fax 885 4280; 18-20 Madani Ave, Baridhara, Dhaka)

UK (Map p62; ☎ 882 2705-9; fax 882 3666; 13 United Nations Rd at Dutabash Rd, Baridhara, Dhaka)

US (Map p62; ☎ 885 5500; fax 882 3159; Madani Ave, Baridhara, Dhaka)

FESTIVALS & EVENTS
A festival in Bangladesh is usually called a mela. Although it's normally specific to just one religion, Bangladeshi curiosity is such that it's a given that everyone else in a town or village will rock up as well. Festivals may also be related to harvests as well as Hindu and Buddhist ceremonies. Minor melas are mainly related to weddings, exhibition fairs or even election victories.

The main nonreligious Bangladeshi holidays are:

February
National Mourning Day (21 February) A solemn occasion in remembrance of those killed on this day in 1952 in protests to establish Bengali as an official language of East Pakistan. Unesco have declared this day International Mother Language Day.

April
Honey-Hunting Festival (1 April) The honey-collecting season officially begins with much pomp at Burigoalini on the edge of the Sundarbans (p94).

Pohela Baishak (14 & 15 April) The Bangladeshi New Year celebration is the biggest festival in Bangladesh with large parades and many cultural events exploding in marvellous technicolour across the nation. Dhaka and Rangamati host the biggest events.

May
Rabindra & Nazrul Jayanti (11 & 25 May) The anniversaries of the birth of national poet Kazi Nazrul Islam on May 11 and Nobel laureate Rabindranath Tagore on May 25 are celebrated with public readings and songs.

Islamic Festivals
Muslim holidays, known as Eids, follow a lunar calendar. The dates depend on the phases of the moon, and fall about 11 days earlier each successive year. The following festival calendar is based on festival dates between the years 2008 and 2011. Along with public holidays, these events are observed nationally, with government offices, banks and most businesses closing. They tend to lack the street flair of Hindu holidays.

February–March
Eid-e-Miladunnabi Birth of the Prophet Mohammed.

July–August
Shab-e-Barat This holiday marks the sighting of the full moon 14 days before the start of Ramadan. The night of *barat* (record), according to Mohammed, is the time that

BISWA IJTEMA

Every January up to three million Muslims from across the world descend on the Dhaka suburb of Tongi for the world's second-largest Muslim gathering (after the haj to Mecca in Saudi Arabia). The three-day event, which has been running since the 1940s, concentrates on prayers and meditation and is not a forum for political debate. Non-Muslim foreigners are normally well received.

God registers all the actions men are to perform in the ensuing year. It is a sacred night when alms and sweets are distributed to the poor.

Jamat-ul-Wida Start of the month of Ramadan and the fasting period.

Ramadan Referred to as Ramzan in Bangladesh. Fasting, the third pillar of Islam, incurs merit whenever observed, but is an absolute duty during Ramzan. For the entire month, between sunrise and sunset, abstinence from food, liquids, smoking, impure thoughts and physical pleasures is obligatory. Fasting begins at dawn and is broken when the evening call to prayer is heard. The *iftar* (meal) taken when the fast is broken includes samosa (a pastry triangle stuffed with spiced vegetables or minced meat), *piaju* (deep-fried lentil-and-onion balls), various kebabs, and *moori* (aniseed) and *cheera* (flattened rice) preparations. Travellers, the elderly, the sick and the very young are pardoned from fasting during Ramzan (though they are supposed to make up for it at a later date). The fast is not observed as rigorously in Bangladesh as in some Middle Eastern countries, and some snack shops in the larger cities will stay open during the day but put up curtains so diners have a little anonymity. In smaller villages it may be more difficult to find a meal during the day. Travelling at this time can be very hard, if not impossible.

September–October

Eid-ul-Fitr One of the two major Muslim holidays, it celebrates the end of Ramzan with the sighting of the new moon. It's a holiday as important to Muslims as Christmas is to many Westerners. The festival is characterised by alms-giving and prayer, feasting, merriment and gifts. Eid Mubarrak or Happy Eid are the common greetings.

November–January

Eid-ul-Adha Known as the Eid of Sacrifice or, informally, Bloody Eid, this two-day festival falls 69 days after Eid-ul-Fitr. It remembers Abraham's sacrifice of his son Ishmael, celebrated with the slaughter of a cow, sheep or goat. After the morning prayers the head of the family takes the animal out to the entrance of the house, faces it toward

Mecca and kills it with a quick slash of the throat. The meat is divided among the poor, friends and family. During the week preceding the festival, open-air fairs do a brisk trade in cattle and goats. The animals are brightly adorned with ribbons, garlands and tassels. This festival also marks the beginning of the hajj (pilgrimage) to Mecca.

Ashura The Ashura festival (also called Muharram) takes place in the Muslim month of Muharram. It commemorates the martyrdom of Hussain, grandson of the prophet Mohammed, on the battlefield of Kerbala in modern-day Iraq in the Christian year 680.

Hindu Festivals

Hindu holidays generally fall at much the same date each year. They usually mark the changing of the seasons.

January–February

Saraswati Puja Towards the end of January clay statues of Brahma's consort Saraswati are made in preparation for this ceremony, held around the beginning of February. The goddess of knowledge is always depicted playing a *veena* (an Indian stringed instrument) and accompanied by a swan, but outside these limitations there's a lot of variety.

February–March

Holi The Festival of Colours is celebrated in late February/early March. Commonly known as the spring festival, it is celebrated, less so here than in other countries, with the throwing of coloured water and powders and the construction of bonfires.

June–July

Rath Jatra This festival celebrates Jagannath, the lord of the world and a form of Krishna, along with his brother and sister. These three images are set upon a Jagannath (chariot) and pulled through the streets by devotees. The 7m chariot in Dhamrai, 32km northwest of Dhaka, is typical.

October

Durga Puja The most important Hindu festival celebrated in Bangladesh. Statues of the goddess Durga astride a lion, with her 10 hands holding 10 different weapons, are placed in every Hindu temple. Celebrations culminate on the day of the full moon when the statue is carried into the water after sunset. A huge festival takes place along the Buriganga River in Dhaka (see also p59).

For a list of other holidays see opposite.

GAY & LESBIAN TRAVELLERS

There is a high degree of sexual repression (and frustration) in Bangladesh. Authorities generally deny the existence of homosexuality and the criminal code left by the British Raj punishes male homosexual acts with deportation, fines and/or prison, but these laws are hardly ever used. Lesbianism is studiously denied by the legal system.

Unofficially, many believe homosexuality is quite prevalent. Bangladeshi society can be privately tolerant towards homosexuality among young men, but only if it is a 'phase' that doesn't interfere with marriage prospects. Lesbians have to stay even deeper in the closet.

The great irony is that in a country where it is largely inappropriate for men and women to shake hands, it is socially acceptable for two men to hold hands. Such public displays of affection between men are common but don't signify a nonplatonic relationship.

Gay travellers are wise to be discreet in Bangladesh. The upside is that you will be spared the hassles that many unmarried heterosexual couples have in checking into hotels, given the assumption that you are just friends.

HOLIDAYS
Public Holidays
The following holidays are observed nationally, and government offices, banks and most businesses are closed.

Birthday of the Father of the Nation (Sheikh Mujibur Rahman's birthday) 17 March
Independence Day 26 March
May Day 1 May
Bank Holiday 30 June
National Mourning Day (Anniversary of the death of Sheikh Mujibur Rahman) 15 August
National Revolution Day 7 November
Biganj Dibash (Victory Day) 16 December
Christmas Day 25 December. Known as Bara Din (Big Day). Churches are adorned with lights and some hold cultural evenings with dances and prayers.
Bank Holiday 31 December

INSURANCE
Any policy you get should cover medical expenses and an emergency flight home. Always check the fine print. Some policies exclude coverage of 'dangerous activities', which can include motorcycling and trekking.

For theft and loss you will require documentation from the Bangladeshi police; getting it can be a hassle and often requires a 'fee'.

Worldwide travel insurance is available at www.lonelyplanet.com/travel_services. You

can buy, extend and claim online any time – even if you're already on the road.

See also p182 for health insurance details.

INTERNET ACCESS
Many top-end hotels provide universal power adaptors in rooms, but outside of those rare cases you'll need to bring your own. If you are travelling with a laptop or some other electronic device, remember to bring a 220V, 50 Hz AC adaptor. If you forget to bring one, you may be able to track one down in Dhaka. The Stadium Market would be a good bet.

Connections in top-range hotels are normally good but certainly won't be cheap. Thankfully, internet cafés are everywhere in Bangladesh – even small towns are getting tech-savvy. They are usually cheap and open till quite late. The lowest price is around Tk 20 per hour and the average is Tk 30 to Tk 45; connections are normally reasonable.

LEGAL MATTERS
Drug offences are taken seriously in Bangladesh and can result in the death penalty if considerable quantities are seized. Anyone, including foreigners, caught smuggling virtually any amount of drugs or gold often ends up with a prison sentence for life. As a matter of practice, courts permit those charged to have access to a lawyer.

Under the Vienna Convention on Consular Relations, to which Bangladesh is a signatory, any foreign national under detention has a right to request that their embassy be notified of their situation.

MAPS
The best map publisher, **Mappa** (Map pp56-7; ☎ 881 6710; www.themappa.com; 112 Green Rd, Farmgate) produces English-language maps, which are updated regularly. All are available at bookshops and New Market in Dhaka (Map pp56–7), and on occasion from street vendors.

The Parjatan Corporation also produces a Dhaka city map and a Bangladesh map. Though not as detailed as the professionally produced maps, they can be useful references. These are available at the **Parjatan Tourist Office** (Map pp56-7; ☎ 914 0790, 811 7855-9; 233 Airport Rd, Tejgaon) and occasionally at Parjatan Hotels.

MONEY
The local currency of Bangladesh is the taka (Tk; rhymes with Dhaka), which is further

divided into 100 paisas. There are 10, 20 and 50 paisa, and Tk 1, Tk 2 and Tk 5 coins. There are notes in denominations of Tk 1, Tk 2, Tk 5, Tk 10, Tk 20, Tk 50, Tk 100 and Tk 500.

Torn notes may be refused by merchants. Most banks will exchange them for you.

Bangladesh is a long way behind much of the world when it comes to banking and exchanging money. Most banks outside the big cities won't exchange money in whatever form you present it – even dollar or euro cash receives wide-eyed stares of bewilderment. It's best to change as much money as you are likely to need in Dhaka, Chittagong and Sylhet. You might get lucky elsewhere, but many travellers find themselves getting caught short when no bank for miles around will exchange money or travellers cheques for them and every ATM spits out their card in disgust!

For information on costs, see p12, and for exchange rates see Quick Reference on the inside front cover.

ATMs

Major towns and cities have ATMs, and there appear to be more on the way. However, the vast majority don't accept foreign bank or credit cards. The most reliable are those belonging to Standard Chartered Bank, Dutch-Bangla Bank and HSBC, and with any of these three you shouldn't have any problems with a Visa card, but Cirrus or MasterCard might present problems. Unfortunately, these machines are only found in the biggest towns and cities (indicated in regional chapters). ATMs are usually open-all-hours guarded booths.

Cash

It is a good idea to bring US dollars with you to change into local currency when you can't change travellers cheques or use a credit card. US dollars are the preferred currency, with euros running a very distant second. Again, only banks like Standard Chartered and HSBC in the biggest centres are likely to change cash for you.

At some banks you may have to show your passport even when changing cash.

Credit Cards

Visa, MasterCard and American Express are usually accepted by major hotels and restaurants in Dhaka and Chittagong.

Cash advances on credit cards can be made at Standard Chartered and HSBC banks. HSBC ATMs do not accept Cirrus cards.

Moneychangers

There are a few authorised moneychangers that legally convert cash on the spot at good rates. They're open all hours and can convert taka into US dollars as well. If it looks like a well-run establishment, chances are it is.

With the liberalisation of the economy, there is essentially no black market.

Tipping

Baksheesh (*bohk*-sheesh), in the sense of a tip or gift rather than a bribe (an admittedly fine line), is part of life in Bangladesh. Don't see it as begging; it's part of Islamic morality that rich people give some of their income to those less fortunate. There are some peculiarities to this system though; if you're going to be repeatedly using a service, an initial tip ensures that decent standards will be kept up.

Don't feel persecuted – well-to-do locals also have to pay baksheesh. Always be conscious of the expectations that will be placed on the next foreigner in light of the amount you give and don't feel embarrassed about not giving baksheesh to someone who rendered absolutely no service at all.

In expensive restaurants in Dhaka that are mostly frequented by foreigners, waiters often expect a small tip, typically about 5%. In any other type of restaurant it is not necessary to tip.

Travellers Cheques

Put simply, don't bother! Only the biggest international banks are likely to accept them and even then it will be with great reluctance.

POST

Bangladesh's postal system works well. You may be sceptical when you're watching an old man weigh your letter on a set of scales that should be in an antique shop, but rest assured it will get sent and arrive in around 10 to 15 days.

If you've overdone the shopping, consider mailing stuff home to yourself – it's amazingly cheap.

Receiving mail can be more frustrating. The poste restante service in Dhaka is at the main post office (Map pp56–7). It's probably safer to try and get mail sent to a personal address or tour company office.

SHOPPING

You don't get hassled to buy things here, mainly because there isn't very much produced with the tourist market in mind. Even quality postcards are hard to come by.

Things not to buy are products made from wild animals, reptiles, seashells and coral, all of which are under pressure to survive in this crowded country. There is also a trade in the country's artistic treasures, which are often plundered from Hindu temples.

Handicrafts

Souvenirs include jewellery, garments, brasswork, leatherwork, ceramics, jute products, artwork, woodcarvings and clay or metal sculptural work. Unique items include *jamdani* (loom-embroidered muslin or silk) saris, jute doormats, wall pieces, glass bangles and reed mats. Quality is generally high and the prices generally low.

Jute carpets, if you have the room, are a real deal. The better ones are similar to Oriental wool carpets. They don't last as long as the real thing, but a 2m-by-3m (6ft-by-9ft) jute carpet costing US$50 (and a fortune in excess baggage) will last five or more years.

The chain of Aarong shops has a range of high-quality goods, although the fixed prices are higher than in the markets, where it's normal to bargain prices down.

Clothing

You may decide to replace everything in your backpack. The Bangladeshi garment industry is one of the biggest producers of Western clothing, and you can either purchase it from some of the high-street fashion-label stores around Gulshan or buy much cheaper seconds and overruns at the enormous Banga Bazar (Map p51), sometimes referred to as Gulistan Hawker's Market. There's also a good range at New Market (Map pp56–7). See p65 for more information.

Rickshaw Art

One distinctly Bangladeshi souvenir is a piece of authentic rickshaw art. These colourful back flaps of rickshaws are lightweight and easy to pack in the flat of your bag or backpack. Rickshaw art is not a tourist industry, so you'll have to shop where the rickshaw-

wallahs shop. The few centrally located shops are on Bicycle St in Dhaka, a local name for the area where most bicycle parts and a few whole bicycles are sold. See p54 and the box text on p34 for more information.

SOLO TRAVELLERS

Those who are travelling alone on the assumption that they will meet other travellers on the road should think again. You may, but you'll probably be able to count them on one hand. To increase your chances, the best thing to do is join a short tour (to the Sundarbans would be perfect) to suss out candidates.

Travelling alone through Bangladesh can be a rewarding experience, and won't cost you much more money than travelling with company – basic single rooms are often less than half the cost of a double. Then again, it may be worthwhile splashing out on a cabin or sleeper on a boat or train for peace of mind. On your own you will have to stay particularly alert, and exercise a greater degree of caution with regards to where you go and when.

TELEPHONE

Though there are a surprising number of mobile phones floating around Bangladesh, some towns still don't have land lines. Don't expect that every hotel and restaurant will have a phone number.

International calls are easy to make. Many phones have direct-dial service via satellite. Rates are 25% lower all day on Friday and on other days from 11pm to 8am. Local calls present no problems, but between cities it is often difficult to hear the other end. The only way to make a 'public' phone call is to use the telephone and fax services available at numerous small business centres. Charges are roughly Tk 100/110/120 per minute to Australia/Europe/USA, ie roughly double the actual rate. Major hotels charge two or three times as much. The numbers for long-distance information are ☎ 103 (domestic) and ☎ 162 (international). International operators speak English; others usually don't.

Mobile Phones

If bringing your own phone, make sure your service provider has turned on the global-roaming facility on your phone and be prepared to remortgage your house to pay the bill when you get back home! Note that you may have to manually find a Bangladeshi network on your own phone. Reception is normally decent.

Phone Codes

To call a number in Bangladesh from outside the country, dial country code ☎ 880, followed by the city or mobile code without the leading 0, and then the number.

To call a different city from within Bangladesh, dial the city code including the leading zero, followed by the number.

To call another country from Bangladesh, dial ☎ 00 followed by the country code and city code.

City codes can be found in phone books and, for major cities, in this guide under the city headings in each regional chapter.

Phonecards

There is an increasing number of phonecards appearing on the market, which can be bought at some small business centres and phone shops in large cities. Shop around for the best deal for the country you'll be calling most.

TIME

Bangladesh has one time zone: an hour behind Thailand, half an hour ahead of India, six hours ahead of GMT, 10 hours ahead of New York (11 during daylight savings time), four hours behind EST in Australia and five hours ahead of France.

TOILETS

In midrange and top-end establishments you'll find sit-down toilets that flush, but most toilets are mildly malodorous squat types. Sit-down toilets are sometimes described as 'high commode' and squat toilets as 'Indian style'.

The ritual in squat toilets is to use your left hand and water. A strategically placed tap and jug are usually at hand. If you can't master the local method or don't even want to try, toilet paper is widely available. Sometimes a basket is provided where paper and tampons can be discarded.

Some women report that when trying to use toilets in cheap restaurants, they've been told the facilities are unsuitable. Polite protestations that they're more suitable than the floor may help.

There are very few facilities at bus stations and other public places, and what facilities exist, are pretty horrific. It pays to do your thing back at your hotel. By and large you will find that Bangladeshi hospitality extends to letting you use a toilet, if you ask nicely enough, or you could simply buy a drink at a nice hotel for an excuse to sit down (pun absolutely intended).

In rural areas it can be difficult to find both toilets and privacy. For women in a desperate situation, a long skirt will make this awkward position a little less so.

TOURIST INFORMATION

The national tourist office is the Bangladesh Parjatan Corporation. It has more of a presence in terms of nationwide hotels than nationwide information. It also theoretically runs tours, but private-sector operators have eclipsed its tour service. Outside of the **Parjatan main office** (Map pp56-7; ☎ 914 0790, 811 7855-9; www .bangladeshtourism.gov.bd; 233 Airport Rd, Tejgaon), information counters at Parjatan hotels have little to offer but brochures, though they are often the nicest place to stay in town.

Parjatan hotels can be found in Benapole, Bogra, Chittagong, Cox's Bazar, Dhaka, Dinajpur, Kuakata, Madhabkunda, Mongla, Rangamati, Rangpur, Rajshahi, Sylhet, Teknaf and Tungipara.

The Parjatan website is useful. For other useful tourist-oriented internet resources see p14.

In general, it's better to consult a private tour company for anything other than the most basic tourist-related questions. Special mention must also be made here to **Mahmud Hasan Khan** (☎ 0171 4044498; mahmud.bangladesh@ gmail.com; www.mahmud.bigbig.com) and his brother **Mahfuz Hossain Khan** (☎ 0171 1048456; mahfuz1972@ gmail.com). Mahmud is essentially the guardian angel of travellers in Bangladesh and can be found dispensing invaluable advice on the Thorn Tree forum of lonelyplanet.com. Neither brother officially works in the tourist industry, though if they can wrangle time off their day jobs, they will be happy to accompany you as a guide for a fee. Instead in the classic manner of all Bangladeshis, they do it only as a hobby to ensure that tourists leave Bangladesh with good impressions.

TRAVELLERS WITH DISABILITIES

Putting it bluntly, disabled travellers will struggle in Bangladesh. Some footpaths are difficult for even the able-bodied to traverse. In fact, with its squat toilets, over-crowded buses and absence of elevators in all but the finest buildings in Dhaka, it would seem that the country has contrived to keep out everyone except the most fit and able.

On the other hand, hiring help to check out accessible hotels and restaurants, toilets and other facilities and to help you get around is going to be quite cheap. Also, Bangladeshis are good at coming to the aid of foreigners before they are even asked.

VISAS

With some obscure exceptions, visas are required for citizens of all countries. Israeli passport holders are forbidden from entering Bangladesh.

Visas on arrival (either by air or land) have not been available for some years, but in March 2008, 15-day landing permits started to be issued again in exceptional circumstances. The immigration department doesn't encourage tourists to arrive without a visa and there is no guarantee you will be granted entry (especially if you have just arrived from a country with a Bangladeshi embassy), but the word is that some people had managed to obtain them. For the moment, we recommend that you do all you can to obtain a visa in advance, but this is an encouraging sign that visa rules might be further relaxed.

Visa validity and the granted length of stay seems to vary from embassy to embassy, but normally you will be issued with a visa valid for two or three months from the date of issue, and good for stays of one to two months. Visa fees vary according to nationality, whether you are seeking single or multiple entry and which embassy you are applying through, but they normally cost around US$50/€30/£25.

Requests for visas for stays longer than three months are usually denied. If you decide to extend your stay, extensions can be obtained, though this requires tangling with Bangladeshi bureaucracy and isn't a good idea (see below).

Visa Extensions & Change of Route Permits

To apply for visa extensions and change of route permits you will need to visit the **Immigration and Passport Office** (Map pp56-7; ☎ 889 750; Agargaon Rd, Dhaka; ☉ Sat-Thu). This is also the office where long-term visitors are required to register.

Travellers have reported poor service and misinformation at this office. You will need to be both persistent and patient.

If you overstay your visa, you will be fined for each extra day. In some cases travellers have been charged even more, given no receipt and the extra charge has not been explained.

Extensions up to a total stay of three months are generally easy to obtain. If you've been in Bangladesh for three months and wish to extend beyond that, the process can take up to a week or more, and there is no assurance that you'll receive an extension. The more convincing your reasons for wanting an extension, the better your chances of getting one.

Processing of requests to stay longer than three months is notoriously inefficient, so start the process early – at least a fortnight before the expiration date, if you've already been there three months.

If you exit Bangladesh by means other than that by which you entered (ie you flew in but are leaving by land), you will need a change of route permit, also sometimes referred to as a road permit. Change of route permits shouldn't take more than 24 hours, but sometimes take up to 72 so start the process early. The permit is free. You will need a couple of passport photos.

WOMEN TRAVELLERS

Bangladeshi opinions about Western women are still being formed. By and large the default response to the bewildering sight of you is respect, so don't do anything that would make you less than worthy of it. Bangladesh is safer than a lot of Muslim countries, but it's wise to be careful. How you carry yourself subtly determines how you are treated. A woman who is politely assertive can ask for space and usually gets it. The other side of the harassment coin, and almost as much of a nuisance, is that people are constantly making elaborate arrangements to protect you from harassment.

Dressing like a local is not obligatory but it will certainly impact on the way you are treated. You will still get attention, but the attention you get will be more respectful and appreciative of the fact that you have made the effort. Invest in a *salwar kameez* (a long dress-like tunic worn over baggy trousers). A dupatta (long scarf) to cover your head increases the appearance of modesty and is a handy accessory. You can get away with wearing baggy trousers and a long loose-fitting shirt in most parts of the country. Long, loose skirts are also acceptable and provide the added advantage of a modicum of privacy in the absence of a public toilet. Make sure you wear a headscarf at places of worship. Most mosques don't allow women inside, although some have a special women's gallery. If in doubt, ask.

Keep in mind that in this society women are not touched by men, but because you're a foreigner, it might happen. A clear yet tactful objection should end the matter.

Tampons are available from some upmarket supermarkets (like Agora) for around Tk 60 a packet. Sanitary napkins and panty liners are widely available, but be sure to carry adequate supplies if you're travelling away from major cities.

A good place to take a breather from the patriarchal streets is Adda, an informal space for women to eat and chat, at Narigrantha Prabartana, the feminist bookshop run by Unnayan Bikalper Nitinirdharoni Gobeshona (UBINIG; Policy Research for Development Alternatives) in Dhaka. Men are welcome, so long as they are accompanied by a woman. See p49 for further details.

Eating

In a Bangladeshi middle-class home you would most likely be expected to eat first with the men while the women of the house-hold tuck themselves away in another part of the house or dutifully serve the meal. In rural areas you might not eat with either, but be served first and separately, as a gesture of respect. Accept either graciously. Protest would cause great embarrassment on the part of your host.

In restaurants you may be shown to the curtained women's rooms. This is a courteous offer that you can decline, though you may find that the curtain provides something of a respite from the eyes that will be on you if you sit elsewhere.

Getting Around

On buses, unaccompanied women are expected to sit at the front. If you are travelling with 'your husband' you are expected to sit on the window side, away from the aisle. Avoid travelling alone at night; Bangladeshi women avoid going out alone at night as much as possible.

Sleeping

Women, with or without men, are sometimes unwelcome in budget hotels, usually because the manager thinks the hotel is not suitable. This knee-jerk reaction can sometimes be overcome if you hang around long enough. On the other hand, staying in one of these cheaper establishments, especially if you are going solo, can be more trouble than it is worth. Midrange hotels that are accustomed to foreigners are the best bet. Unmarried couples are better off simply saying they're married.

Transport

CONTENTS

THINGS CHANGE...

The information in this chapter is particularly vulnerable to change. Check directly with the airline or a travel agent to make sure you understand how a fare (and ticket you may buy) works and be aware of the security requirements for international travel. Shop carefully. The details given in this chapter should be regarded as pointers and are not a substitute for your own careful, up-to-date research.

GETTING THERE & AWAY

ENTERING THE COUNTRY

To enter Bangladesh you will need a passport that's valid for at least six months beyond the duration of your stay, an onward/return ticket and a visa.

Rules and procedures for entering and exiting Bangladesh seem to be in a constant state of flux. For many years it hasn't been possible to obtain a visa on arrival at the airport, though there are rumours that some people had recently managed to wrangle visas on arrival. Despite this promising move, it's still best to play it safe and make sure you arrive with a visa and your passport in order. See p167 for more information.

If you are exiting by land but you entered by air, a 'change of route' permit is required (see p167). Note that Bangladesh currently refuses entry to Israeli passport holders.

AIR
Airports & Airlines

There are three international airports in Bangladesh. Osmani International (ZYL) in Sylhet, Patenga (CGP) in Chittagong and Zia International Airport (DAC) in Dhaka. **Zia International Airport** (☎ 02-819 4350) is the busiest of the three. Located 12km north of the city centre, on the road to Uttara, it doesn't have 'gateway to the world' written on it, but it

does have a bank, some duty-free shops and a couple of restaurants.

For a long time Bangladesh had only one major airline, Biman. The US Federal Aviation Administration has classified Biman as category two, which means that it is not in absolute compliance with international aviation safety standards. They run domestic flights between Dhaka, Chittagong and Sylhet, and internationally throughout South and Southeast Asia and occasionally even to Europe. Privately run GMG Airlines is a newer, brighter and better option. It links Dhaka, Chittagong, Sylhet, Cox's Bazaar, Barisal and Jessore, but internationally it only serves South and Southeast Asia. GMG has just been joined by United Airways, which runs an almost identical service, in equally good planes, as GMG. In 2007 two new airlines, funded by British and Bangladeshi businessmen, took to the skies. These are Best Air and Royal Bengal. At the time of writing it seemed that both were offering very limited internal services, and the much-hyped London–Bangladesh route seems to have quietly vanished from the advertising hype.

Airlines flying to and from Bangladesh:
Biman (BG; ☎ 02-956 0151; www. Bimanair.com; hub Zia International Airport, Dhaka)
British Airways (BA; ☎ 02-881 5111; www.british airways.com; hub Heathrow Airport, London)
Dragon Air (KA; ☎ 02-881 8782; www.dragonair.com; hub Hong Kong International Airport)
Druk Air (Bhutan Airlines; KB; ☎ 02-891 1066; www .drukair.com.bt; hub Paro Airport)

CLIMATE CHANGE & TRAVEL

Climate change is a serious threat to the ecosystems that humans rely upon, and air travel is the fastest-growing contributor to the problem. Lonely Planet regards travel, overall, as a global benefit, but believes we all have a responsibility to limit our personal impact on global warming.

Flying & Climate Change

Pretty much every form of motor travel generates CO_2 (the main cause of human-induced climate change) but planes are far and away the worst offenders, not just because of the sheer distances they allow us to travel, but because they release greenhouse gases high into the atmosphere. The statistics are frightening: two people taking a return flight between Europe and the US will contribute as much to climate change as an average household's gas and electricity consumption over a whole year.

Carbon Offset Schemes

Climatecare.org and other websites use 'carbon calculators' that allow jetsetters to offset the greenhouse gases they are responsible for with contributions to energy-saving projects and other climate-friendly initiatives in the developing world – including projects in India, Honduras, Kazakhstan and Uganda.

Lonely Planet, together with Rough Guides and other concerned partners in the travel industry, supports the carbon offset scheme run by climatecare.org. Lonely Planet offsets all of its staff and author travel.

For more information check out our website: lonelyplanet.com.

Emirates (EK; ☎ 02-989 2801; www.emirates.com; hub Dubai International Airport)

Etihad Airways (ETD; ☎ 02-883 1258; www.etihad airways.com; hub Abu Dhabi Airport)

GMG Airlines (Z5; ☎ 02-882 5845; www.gmgairlines .com; hub Zia International Airport, Dhaka)

Gulf Air (GF; ☎ 02-811 3237; www.gulfairco.com; hub Bahrain Airport)

Indian Airlines (IC; ☎ 02-955 5915; www.indian-air lines.nic.in; hub Indira Gandhi International Airport, Delhi)

Malaysia Airlines (MH; ☎ 02-988 8211; www.malaysia airlines.com; hub Kuala Lumpur International Airport)

Pakistan International Airways (PK; ☎ 02-934 9293; www.piac.com.pk; hub Quaid-e-Azam International Airport, Karachi)

Qatar Airlines (QR; ☎ 02-955 6491; www.qatar airways.com; hub Doha Airport)

Singapore Airlines (SQ; ☎ 02-881 1504; www .singaporeair.com; hub Changi Airport)

Thai International (TG; ☎ 02-813 4711-18; www .thaiair.com; hub Bangkok International Airport)

United Airways (☎ 02-893 2338; www.uabdl.com; hub Zia International Airport)

Tickets

Compared with India, fares to Bangladesh aren't very cheap and, if you don't mind the hassle of obtaining an Indian visa, a cheaper way of entering the country is often by coming overland from Kolkata (you'll need to leave via this route as well). Buying a one-way ticket out of Bangladesh is very expensive – go to India first!

There are many good travel agents in Dhaka. Those listed in the Dhaka chapter accept payment by credit card or travellers cheques (see p50).

Asia

There are flights to/from all nearby Asian countries except Myanmar. Most connections are direct to Dhaka's Zia International Airport, except for Biman flights between Chittagong and India or Thailand. During hajj (the pilgrimage to Mecca), airlines usually increase their services so that it is even possible to fly directly out of Sylhet.

BHUTAN

Druk Air offers the only service between Dhaka and Paro, and the fare is high (US$190/380 one way/return). There are only two flights a week. If the schedule isn't convenient, you could fly to Paro via Kolkata, using Druk Air and Biman; connections are good and the cost is only marginally more.

INDIA

GMG has frequent daily flights between Dhaka and Kolkata and slightly less frequent flights to Delhi. There are also connections between Chittagong and Kolkata several times a week.

From India expect to pay around US$65/115 for a one-way/return flight from Kolkata or US$235/470 from Delhi to Dhaka.

MYANMAR
To fly to Myanmar you will need to go via Thailand or India.

NEPAL
There are daily flights between Dhaka and Kathmandu with GMG. The flight takes 65 minutes and the one-way fare is around US$110.

THAILAND
Thai Airlines, GMG and Druk Air fly from Bangkok to Dhaka. Thai Airlines has flights every day, as does GMG. Thai Airlines charges around US$600 for a round-trip.

If you purchase your ticket from one of the many discount agencies in Bangkok, you'll get a much better deal.

Australia
The easiest way to get to Bangladesh from Australia is to fly to Bangkok, Singapore or Kuala Lumpur, then fly from there to Dhaka, or to fly to Kolkata in India, and fly or travel by land into Bangladesh. Flights from Sydney to Dhaka can be found for as little as A$1000 whereas advance-purchase airfares from the east coast to Bangkok are from A$900 return.

Quite a few travel offices specialise in discount air tickets. Some travel agents, particularly smaller ones, advertise cheap fares in the travel sections of weekend newspapers such as the *Age* in Melbourne and the *Sydney Morning Herald*.

Reputable agents with branches throughout Australia:

Flight Centre Australia (☎ 133 133; www.flight centre.com.au)

STA Travel Australia (☎ 134 782; www.statravel .com.au)

Continental Europe
Though London is the travel-discount capital of Europe, there are several other cities where you can find a range of good deals. Generally there is not much variation in airfares for departures from the main European cities.

All the major airlines usually offer some sort of deal, and travel agents generally have a number of deals on offer, so shop around.

Good places to start:

Barceló Viajes (☎ 902 11 62 26; www.barceloviajes .com) In Spain.

CTS Viaggi (☎ 199 50 11 50; www.cts.it) In Italy.

NBBS Reizen (☎ 0180 39 33 77; www.nbbs.nl) In the Netherlands.

Nouvelles Frontières (☎ 0 825 000 747; www .nouvelles-frontieres.fr) In France.

STA Travel (☎ 069 743 032 92; www.statravel.de) In Germany.

STA Travel (☎ 0900 450 402; www.statravel.ch) In Switzerland.

The best airlines serving Dhaka from Europe are British Airways and the Middle Eastern airlines (with a stopoff in their home country).

UK & Ireland
Airline-ticket discounters are known as 'bucket shops' in the UK. Despite the somewhat disreputable name, there is nothing under-the-counter about them. Discount air travel is big business in London. Advertisements for many travel agents appear in the travel pages of the weekend broadsheets, such as the *Independent* on Saturday, and the *Sunday Times*. Look out for the free magazines, such as *TNT*, that are widely available in London – start by looking outside the main railway and underground stations.

Good starting points:

STA Travel (☎ 0871 2 300 040; www.statravel.co.uk)

Trailfinders (☎ 0845 058 5858; www.trailfinders.co.uk)

USA
Discount travel agents in the USA are commonly known as 'consolidators' (although you won't see a sign on the door saying 'consolidator'). San Francisco is the consolidator capital of America, although some good deals can be found in Los Angeles, New York and other big cities. Consolidators can be found through the *Yellow Pages* or the major daily newspapers. The *New York Times*, the *Los Angeles Times*, the *Chicago Tribune* and the *San Francisco Examiner* all produce weekly travel sections in which you'll find travel-agency ads.

There are basically two ways to get to Bangladesh from the USA. From the west coast virtually everyone flies to Dhaka via Bangkok or Singapore. You can also fly direct to India and connect from there, but it will cost more.

From the east coast most people fly via Europe. Biman no longer operates direct flights to/from the USA, so you will have to transit somewhere en route.

One recommended travel agent is **STA Travel** (☎ 800-781 4040; www.statravel.com).

LAND
Border Crossings

There are numerous points to cross into India, but only a few of these are set up with immigration facilities to service foreigners.

Theoretically the same system is supposed to be in place for all of these crossings, but in practice this isn't the case. There is a Tk 300 departure tax, officially at least, at all land border crossings, but some travellers have reported not having to pay this. This tax must be paid in advance at a Sonali Bank branch (either in Dhaka, another big city or at the closest branch to the border). There have also been reports of people managing to leave without a change of route permit, and others being turned back for not having one. A change of route permit is officially required if you have entered Bangladesh by air and leave via a land crossing. These can be obtained at the Immigration and Passport Office (p167). Customs are fairly lax with foreigners. The same rules regarding what you can bring into the country (in the way of cigarettes and alcohol) apply at border crossings as at airports, though in practice a blind eye is usually turned to your luggage at land crossings.

AKHAURA

This border is close to Dhaka, along Akhaura Rd, 4km west of Agartala in India. The border is open from 8am to 6pm daily.

Officials on both sides operate an unofficial money-changing service, which may be necessary for a small amount to get you to Akhaura, if you're coming into Bangladesh. The distance between Dhaka and Agartala (in India's Tripura state) is 155km.

In India it is cheap to fly from Kolkata to Agartala, from where a Bangladeshi visa can be issued.

Coming into Bangladesh you will find plenty of rickshaws heading to the town of Akhaura, 5km away.

BENAPOLE

Officials at this border seem to be particularly prone to request change of route permits. Without one, you run a big risk of being turned back.

For more information on crossing this border, see p82.

In India **BRTC** (Bangladesh Road Transport Corporation; 21/A Mirza Ghalib St, Salt Lake City, Kolkata) runs direct services from Kolkata to Dhaka on Tuesdays, Thursdays and Saturdays. The privately run **Shyamoli Paribahan** (☎ 033-2252 0802; 6/1 Marquis St; ⏰ 10am-5pm) operates a daily service to Dhaka with a change in Benapole (Rs 550 one way).

BURIMARI

Burimari is 13km northwest of the village of Patgram. It can be reached by direct bus from Dhaka or Rangpur.

For more information, see p113.

GODAGARI

To get to the Godagari border from Rajshahi, take a Nawabganj-bound bus. In the town of Godagari, the border is quite well marked.

The towns of Godagari and Lalgola are separated by the Padma River. In the dry season it is possible to walk across it, otherwise there will be boats waiting to take you across. In the town of Lalgola, on the Indian side, there is a train station. This crossing is surprisingly little used by foreign tourists.

HILI

Much trade between Bangladesh and India goes on via this border. The Indian town of Balurghat is 25km from Hili, on the state highway. The border can be seen from the side of the road – it's usually lined with hundreds of trucks. This crossing is little used by foreign tourists.

TAMABIL

The catch with crossing at this border is the need to present a receipt that shows you have deposited a travel tax of Tk 300 into a Sonali Bank. Travellers have been turned back because they have failed to do so.

For more information on crossing this border see p150.

Car

To drive in Bangladesh, you will need an International Driver's Licence. The import of a vehicle requires a *carnet de passage en douane* (a document from the motoring organisation in the country in which the

---

FROM MYANMAR (BURMA)

Overland routes between the subcontinent and Myanmar have been closed since the early 1950s. Even if the border were to be opened to foreigners in the future (it is periodically opened for Bangladeshis), roads across the frontier are in bad condition. When the 133km Bangladesh–Myanmar Friendship Bridge is completed (the foundation stone was laid in April 2004) things may change.

In the meantime it is not possible to cross from or into Myanmar. Given the forbidden-fruit fascination that off-limits border areas have for many travellers, some people have been tempted to make a discreet trek across the Bangladeshi border into Rakhaing (Arakan) state. While this may have been fun in the past, and the punishment not too severe, things are different now: Myanmar's army has planted minefields along the border.

---

vehicle is registered, which says you will not sell the vehicle abroad without paying import duties) and an entry permit from a Bangladeshi embassy.

Train

At the time of writing, an announcement was made that after around 50 years without a service, rail travel between Bangladesh and Kolkata was finally set to kick into life.

GETTING AROUND

There are three words that can be used to sum up Bangladeshi public transport. Cheap, uncomfortable and scary. If you so wished, you could travel straight across the country for little more than a few hundred taka using rickety old buses or squashed into a 2nd-class train carriage. However, the journey won't be pleasant, particularly in the cheaper seats on any form of Bangladeshi public transport. Travelling here can also be a scary experience. Buses are the worst offenders – the drivers show no regard whatsoever for the safety of their passengers or other road users, though the one saving grace is that most roads are fairly quiet, and if the bus does topple over it's only likely to drop into a paddy field rather than off the edge of a cliff. The Dhaka–Chittagong road and Dhaka–Bogra road are real death traps: take the train instead. Do all you can to avoid travelling anywhere by road at night.

The distinguishing feature of internal travel in Bangladesh is the presence of a well-developed and well-used system of water transport. Rivers and streams outstretch roads in total distance, making water transport an essential of daily life. For the traveller, a long Bangladeshi ferry ride, especially on the smaller rivers where you can watch life along the banks, is one of the undisputed highlights of a trip to Bangladesh.

Nevertheless, travelling by boat is slow compared to travelling by bus and it's usually avoidable, so many travellers never go out of their way to take a long trip, settling instead for a short ferry ride across a river or two, but this really is a mistake.

AIR
Airlines in Bangladesh

Bangladesh currently has five domestic airlines: Biman, GMG Airlines, United Airways, Royal Bengal and Best Air.

Biman's planes have done an awful lot of air miles and the interiors are a bit tattered, but the pilots are enormously experienced.

The other three are privately owned and are classier, safer and also win points for punctuality and service. United, Royal Bengal and Best Air are recent start ups and remain relatively untested so far.

GMG is probably the best airline to use but don't expect much reliability on routes. United is starting to receive positive reports.

Airlines mostly fly between Dhaka and regional cities; there are only a couple of direct flights between regional cities, including Cox's Bazar–Chittagong.

Prices are low (Dhaka–Sylhet is around Tk 3700), but do change frequently.

BICYCLE

Bangladesh is great for cycling and this is an interesting way to see the country. With the exception of the tea-estate regions in the Sylhet division, the Chittagong Hill Tracts and the road between Chittagong and Teknaf,

Bangladesh is perfectly flat – you can pedal around very easily with a single-gear bike.

Cities, particularly Dhaka and Chittagong, are not easy or safe places to ride, given manic traffic and pollution. If you leave early, say 5.30am, you should be able to get out of the city without incident. Alternatively, you can put your bike on the roof of a baby taxi (three-wheeled auto-rickshaw) or bus. Some travellers have reported not being allowed to take their bikes on board trains.

The trick to cycling in Bangladesh is to avoid major highways as much as possible; look for back streets that will get you to the same destination. Unfortunately, maps of Bangladesh aren't detailed enough to be of much use, so be prepared for some interesting though unintentional detours.

Most paths are bricked and in good condition, and even if it's just a dirt path, bikes will be able to pass during the dry season. A river won't hinder your travel, since there's invariably a boat of some sort to take you across. At major bridges a sympathetic truck driver is likely to pile both you and your bike in the back for the crossing.

The ideal time to go cycling is in the dry season from mid-October to late March; during the monsoon many tracks become impassable.

Though cycling can by and large be a relaxing way to explore Bangladesh, don't get complacent about your belongings; snatches from saddlebags are not unheard of.

It's best to bring your bicycle and all other gear with you, though bike repair shops, catering to all those cycle-rickshaws, are two-a-penny almost everywhere.

BOAT
Ferry
The river is the traditional means of transport in a country that has 8000km of navigable rivers, though schedules, even for the ferries crossing the innumerable rivers, are prone to disruption. During the monsoon, rivers become very turbulent and flooding might mean relocation of ghats (landings); during the dry season, riverbeds choked with silt can make routes impassable. Winter fogs can cause long delays, and mechanical problems on the often poorly maintained boats are not unknown.

The main routes are covered by the Bangladesh Inland Waterway Transport Corporation (BIWTC), but there are many private companies operating on shorter routes and some competing with the BIWTC on the main ones. Private boats tend to be slower and less comfortable but cheaper than BIWTC boats.

Bangladesh averages about five major ferry sinkings a year, frequently at night and with an average of 100 people drowning each time. Despite this very unenvious safety record, you should try to experience at least one ferry ride whilst in Bangladesh. The one that most people take is the Rocket between Dhaka and Khulna (opposite).

CLASSES
There are four classes of ticket on Bangladeshi boats: 1st, 2nd, inter and deck class. Deck class simply means a space on deck, for which you'll need to bring your own bedding, mattress, food and water. Inter stands for intermediate, and gives you a berth in a cabin with 10 to 16 wooden-slat bunks. In deck class you may find your ability to sleep in cramped, noisy spaces stretched to the limit. Bedding is provided only in 1st class. It's quite unusual for a foreigner to use either the intermediate or deck class.

On all craft with 1st-class tickets you must book in advance to be assured of a cabin. On popular routes, especially the Rocket route between Dhaka and Khulna, you may have to book a couple of weeks ahead during the dry season. If you're catching a boat at one of the smaller stops, your reservation for a 1st-class cabin will have to be telegraphed to another office, and may take some time. Inter- and deck-class tickets can be bought on board, so there's always a scramble for room.

If you haven't managed to book a 1st-class cabin, it's worth boarding anyway and buying a deck-class ticket, as you may be offered a crew member's cabin. Renting a crew cabin is common and accepted practice, but it's technically against the rules, so there's scope for rip-offs. Don't necessarily believe the crew member when they tell you that the fee you pay them is all that you will have to pay – you need to buy at least a deck-class ticket to get out of the ghat at the other end of the trip, and other hastily thought of hidden charges may crop up. Some travellers have even had these sorts of problems when renting the captain's cabin.

It's a hassle finding the ship assistant, but if you want to avoid the possibility of minor rip-offs, involve him in negotiations for a crew cabin. He is responsible for matters relating to passengers and accommodation.

If you travel deck or inter class (and having a crew berth counts as deck class), you can't use the pleasant 1st-class deck, from where the best views are to be had. You might of course be able to sneak in, but don't complain too loudly if you're thrown out.

Prices in this book are generally for 1st/2nd/deck class.

TIPS

In winter, thick fog can turn a 12-hour trip into a 24-hour one, although the captain sometimes doesn't decide that it's unsafe to proceed until he has a very close encounter with a riverbank. If you're travelling deck class, make sure that you're sleeping in a spot where you won't roll off the boat if it comes to a sudden stop!

Porters waiting to leap on docking ferries jostle and fidget like swimmers on the starting blocks – if you don't fancy a swim, don't stand in front of them.

Watching the countryside drift by is amazing and relaxing. If you're lucky, you may spot a sluggish river dolphin. Sometimes you find yourself gliding over thick growths of water hyacinth close to the jungle-covered bank; at other times you're churning along a river so wide that neither of the banks are visible.

The Rocket

Rocket is the generic name that is given to special (paddle-wheel) BIWTC boats that run daily between Dhaka and Khulna, stopping at Chandpur, Barisal, Mongla and many other lesser ports en route.

The BIWTC is in the throes of trying to procure more Rockets, given the chequered history of the four in its possession. As the result of some major incidents that have left hundreds dead, the boating community is becoming more and more conscious of safety on the waterways.

If you're heading to the Sundarbans, Kolkata or the ruins at Bagerhat, travelling by Rocket is a great way to go for a major part of the journey. The north–south journey all the way to Khulna takes less than 30 hours, departing from Dhaka at 6pm every day but Friday and arriving at 8pm the following night. Going in the other direction,

the Rocket leaves Khulna at 3am and arrives in Dhaka at 5.40am.

CLASSES

Inter and deck classes are similar to those in ferries, and again, foreigners are highly unlikely to be sold tickets in either of these classes.

Rockets are not particularly glamorous by Mississippi paddle-wheel standards, but they do have paddle wheels. All have two levels. The front half of the upper deck of the old paddle-wheel steamer is reserved for 1st-class passengers, most of them, typically, Bangladeshis – this is not a tourist boat. There are eight cabins in this section – four doubles and four singles. Inside, floors are carpeted and each cabin has a washbasin and a narrow bunk bed or two with reasonably comfortable mattresses, freshly painted white walls, wood panelling and good lighting. Bathrooms with toilets and showers are shared. Bathrooms get progressively less clean as the trip goes on.

The central room has overhead fans, a long sofa and dining tables where meals are eaten. Meals are not included in ticket prices. There are both Bangladeshi and Western options, or you can go for a walk into the lower-class areas, where you can buy cheaper snacks.

The real highlight of 1st class, though, is the outside deck at the front of the boat, where you can sit while stewards serve tea and biscuits, and the Padma flows by.

Second class is at the back of the boat. Rooms are smaller than those in 1st class, and have no washbasin and no bed linen. There are small fans, though, and some chairs outside your door for scenery-gazing. If you are staying back here, it might be possible for you to dine in 1st class, for a fee, naturally.

In Dhaka tickets are available from the well-marked BIWTC office (Map pp56–7) in the modern commercial district of Motijheel. Book your tickets in advance. The boat leaves from Sadarghat terminal on the Buriganga River and, on rare occasions, from Badam Tole, a boat terminal 1km north. When leaving from Khulna, you should be allowed to sleep the night before in your cabin as departure is at 3am. They move the boat to a different anchorage for the night, so get aboard early. Sometime after midnight the boat steams back to the loading dock.

Prices in this book are generally for 1st/2nd/deck class.

Traditional River Boats

There are about 60 types of boats plying the rivers of Bangladesh. Steamers are only one type – the rest are traditional wooden boats of all shapes and sizes, some with sails but most without. These smaller boats plying the smaller rivers are the only way to see life along the riverbanks. On a bigger boat out on the wide Padma, you'll see lots of big launches, traditional boats and maybe some river dolphins, but you might not see people fishing with their nets, children waving from the shore, farmers working in unimaginably green paddy fields and women brightening up the river banks with their colourful saris.

The problem with taking boats on the minor rivers, and the reason why travellers almost never do this, is the difficulty in finding out where to board them and where they're heading. There is no 'system'; you simply have to ask around. If you see two towns on a map with a river connecting them, you can be sure that boats travel between them, and if there's no obvious road connecting them, there will be lots of passenger boats plying the route.

Barisal (p96) is a great place in which to embark on such memorable adventures.

BUS

Bus travel is cheap and, though it might not seem so, relatively efficient. A six-hour trip on a coach costs around Tk 200, and about half as much for a local bus.

The country has an extensive system of passable roads. When your bus encounters a river crossing, it generally comes on the ferry with you, and the smoky queues of buses waiting to be loaded is one of the more frustrating aspects of travel here. If you don't mind paying another fare, you can always leave your bus and get on one at the head of the queue.

For the lengthy ferry crossings of the mighty Padma, you may have to leave your bus and pick up another one from the same company waiting on the other side. These major inland ghats are a mass of boats, people and vehicles, so expect to be confused – pick out someone on your bus and follow them off the ferry. In any case, the bus assistant continues with the passengers, so you're unlikely to get left behind if you take a while finding your bus after the crossing.

It's illegal to ride on top of a bus, like the locals do, but the police won't stop you. If you do ride on top, though, remember that low trees kill quite a few people each year.

RUSHING ROULETTE

Bus travel in Bangladesh is something of a 'rushing roulette'. The astounding number of accidents that occur every day attests to the fact that Bangladeshi bus drivers are among the most reckless in the world. Currently around 12,000 people a year die on Bangladeshi roads (yes, that's 32 people a day)! Some people claim that this is because of the sheer volume of traffic – an opinion you might find hard to believe when you see how empty the highways are! You may even be advised that buses are simply too dangerous to catch, and that the only safe way to travel between cities is to fly.

If you're not involved in an accident, you will most likely witness one, or at least its aftermath. The main problem is that roads aren't really wide enough for two buses to pass without pulling onto the verge, which is inevitably crowded with rickshaws and pedestrians. All this swerving, yelling and honking can amount to the most exhausting and stressful experience you're likely to have sitting down.

Exercise some judgment. The law of probabilities suggests that a local bus covered with dints will continue to be. Coaches, on the other hand, tend to be more looked after. If you find yourself on a bus with a driver who is more reckless than the average reckless driver, don't be bashful about just getting off. Far better to be stranded on the side of the road than lying on it. However, the most important rule of all might be: DON'T travel at night. Nobody appears to have discovered the on/off switch for their vehicle's lights and the sheer number of unlit people, animals, cars, bikes, UFOs etc on the road after dark would be bad enough on its own, but even worse, on certain routes (such as the Dhaka–Chittagong road) trucks are forbidden from driving in daylight hours and all make the mad dash at night. All this makes night driving more risky than a suicide attempt.

Most bus stations are located on the outskirts of towns, often with different stations for different destinations. This helps reduce traffic jams in town (if you've come from India you'll appreciate the difference), but it often means quite a trek to find your bus. Chair-coach companies, however, usually have their own individual offices, often in the centre of town, and it's at these offices, not at the major terminals, that you must reserve your seat.

Chair Coaches

The safest and most comfortable options are chair coaches, which are distinguished by their adjustable seats and extra leg room. Where possible, take one of these large modern buses on journeys of more than three or four hours. They are not faster on the road – nothing could possibly go faster than the usually out-of-control ordinary buses! However, departure hours are fixed and seats must be reserved in advance, so unlike with regular buses, there's no time wasted filling up the seats and aisles. In addition, they are less crowded, often with no people in the aisles and, most importantly for taller people, there's plenty of leg room.

Most chair-coach services travelling between Dhaka and cities on the western side of the country operate at night, typically departing sometime between 5pm and 9pm and arriving in Dhaka at or before dawn. Whilst you'll save on a night's accommodation, you'll arrive at your destination very tired, having had little sleep. Worse still, the already dangerous daytime roads are treacherous at night. You would do well to try and avoid night buses.

There are two classes of chair coach – those with air-con and those without. Those with air-con cost about twice those without. All chair coaches are express buses, but not vice versa. Some serve snacks and drinks on board, and occasionally screen videos – but trust us, a video coach isn't as good as it sounds!

Some of the best chair-coach companies are **Eagle Paribahan** (☎ 02-710 1504), **Green Line** (☎ 02-710 0301), **Hanif Enterprise** (☎ 02-831 3869) and **Soudia** (☎ 02-801 8445).

Ordinary Buses

Among the ordinary buses there are express buses and local ones, which stop en route. The latter charge about 25% less but are slow. In more remote areas local buses may be your only option. Most buses are large, but there are a few minivans (coasters).

The buses run by private companies tend to be in much better condition than those of the state-run BRTC buses.

Ordinary buses are seemingly made for the vertically challenged – the leg room does not allow anyone to sit with their knees forward. On long trips this can be exceedingly uncomfortable, so try and get an aisle seat. Another option, and one that will really make you feel like the rich foreigner, is to purchase two seats so that you can spread out a little more. Having said that, though, when an elderly lady is left standing in the aisle for eight hours because of a lack of seats, you'd have to have a heart of steel not to give in and give up your additional seat!

Women travelling alone sit together up the front, separate from the men. If there is an accident, this is the most dangerous part of the bus to be on. Women travelling with their husbands normally sit in the main section, preferably on the window side. On long-distance bus trips cha (tea) stops can be agonisingly infrequent and a real hassle for women travellers – toilet facilities are rare indeed and sometimes hard to find when they do exist.

One of the most underappreciated professions would have to be that of bus-wallah. These are the men who half hang out the door helping people on and off, load goats onto the roof, bang on the side of the bus telling the driver to stop and go, and uncannily keep track of who needs how much change. They are usually extremely helpful – they often rearrange things so you are comfortably seated and rarely fail to let you know when the bus has arrived at your destination.

CAR

Travelling by private car has some obvious advantages and disadvantages. On the plus side, it gives you the freedom to quickly and easily go where you please, when you please, and allows for all manner of unexpected pit stops and adventures. On the minus side, it does insulate you somewhat from Bangladesh and it is far more expensive than public transport.

Travelling by car has two possibilities: either you'll be driving your own vehicle or you'll be the passenger in a rental car, which comes complete with its own driver.

TRANSPORT

Hire

Self-drive rental cars are not available in Bangladesh, and that's probably a good thing. However, renting cars with drivers is easy, at least in the big towns.

In Dhaka there are innumerable companies in the rental business; the best ones are recommended on p68. Expect to pay about Tk 3000/2400 a day for a car with/without air-con, plus fuel and driver expenses. Almost all taxis now run on LPG as well as diesel – filling a tank with gas will cost around Tk 100, but as yet this can only be done in the biggest cities, which means that on any extended road trip you will need to refill with diesel, which currently costs an ever rising Tk 68 a litre. There's only one other extra: when you stay out of town overnight, you must pay for the driver's food and lodging, which should come to around Tk 350. They don't try to hide this, but make sure you determine beforehand what those rates will be, to avoid any misunderstandings. Insurance isn't required because you aren't the driver.

Outside Dhaka, the cost of renting vehicles is often marginally less, but actually finding an available car and driver is much harder and virtually impossible if you want an air-con vehicle. Asking at the nearest Parjatan office or the town's top hotel can normally produce results (though they will add a percentage fee).

Owner-Drivers

Driving in Bangladesh, especially on the Dhaka-Chittagong Hwy or within 100km of Dhaka, takes a bit of guts (stupidity?). On the major highways, you'll be pushed onto the curb every few minutes by large buses hurtling down the road. Dhaka presents its own unique driving perils because of the vast number of rickshaws and baby taxis. It's a far better – and safer – option to hire a car and driver (see above).

It's sad to say, but if you're in a serious or fatal traffic accident (and, God forbid, you're responsible), the local custom is to flee, if you can. No-one has much faith in the justice system, so there is an element of self-law in the form of an angry crowd. Newspaper reports of road accidents typically end with words like 'the driver absconded on foot' or 'miscreants beat the driver to a bloody pulp'.

HITCHING

Hitching is never entirely safe in any country in the world, and we don't recommend it.

Travellers who decide to hitch should understand that they are taking a small but potentially serious risk. People who do choose to hitch will be safer if they travel in pairs, and let someone know where they are planning to go. Solo women are particularly unwise to hitchhike. Unless you get picked up by an expat or fellow tourists, you will be expected, as the locals do, to pay for any ride.

LOCAL TRANSPORT

Bangladesh has an amazing range of vehicles – on any highway you can see buses, cars, trucks, rickshaws, baby taxis, tempos (oversized auto-rickshaws), tractors with trays laden with people, motorbikes, scooters, bicycles carrying four people, bullock and water-buffalo carts, and bizarre homemade vehicles all competing for space. One local favourite in Rajshahi division is a sort of minitractor powered by incredibly noisy irrigation pump motors.

In Dhaka and Chittagong motorised transportation has increased tremendously over the last 10 years, and traffic jams in Central Dhaka are a nightmare. The problem continues to be due more to rickshaws than cars, and Dhaka has to be the only place on the planet where you can get caught up in a snarling hour-long traffic jam consisting entirely of rainbow-coloured bicycles and cycle-rickshaws.

What freaks out new arrivals the most is the total chaos that seems to pervade the streets, with drivers doing anything they please and pedestrians being the least of anybody's worries. Accidents do happen and sometimes people are killed, but the odds of your being involved are still fairly slim.

Where possible it can be wise to negotiate fares beforehand to avoid hassles at the other end, though you will be surprised at how often people don't overcharge you on principle. If you are hassled, a good strategy is to keep the discussion going long enough for a crowd to form, which won't be long. This crowd of strangers is something of a people's court, and more often than not is an impressively fair adjudicator. Once deliberations are over and the court has handed down its verdict, the honourable thing for both parties to do is graciously acquiesce.

Baby Taxi

In Bangladesh three-wheeled auto-rickshaws are called baby taxis. As with the rickshaw-wallahs, baby-taxi drivers almost never own their vehicles. They're owned by powerful fleet-owners called *mohajons,* who rent them out on an eight-hour basis. Also like rickshaws, they're designed to take two or three people, but entire families can and do fit.

In Dhaka and Chittagong baby taxis are everywhere – most people use these instead of regular taxis. Faster and more comfortable than rickshaws on most trips, baby taxis cost about twice as much. You'll also find them at Dhaka and Chittagong airports and they charge less than half the taxi fare, but the ride into town from either airport is long and not ideal after a tiring long-haul flight. Outside of these two metropolises, baby taxis are much rarer. In towns such as Rangpur, Dinajpur and Barisal they virtually don't exist.

In Dhaka you can go from Gulshan II to Central Dhaka for around Tk 100. For distances that won't clock over Tk 25, you are better off taking a rickshaw.

In addition to baby taxis, every so often you'll see a *mishuk* (mee-*shuk*), which is a similar vehicle that is slightly narrower and, if you look closely, is driven by a motorised chain like that on a bicycle.

Boat

Given that there are some 8433km of navigable inland waterways, boats are a common means of getting around. You may have to pay a few taka here and there to be ferried from one side of a river to the other, or hire a wooden boat to get from town to town.

Bus

The only real difference between local buses and long-distance buses is how you catch them – in the case of local buses, literally. It can be something of a death-defying process. Firstly, assess whether the bus will get you to your desired destination by screaming the name of the destination to the man hanging out the door. If he responds in the affirmative, run towards him, grab firmly onto a handle, if there is one, or him if there isn't, and jump aboard, remembering to check for oncoming traffic.

Rickshaw

In Bangladesh all rickshaws are bicycle driven; there are none of the human-puller variety. Rickshaw-wallahs usually do not speak English and often don't know much

of the layout of their town beyond their own area, so if you'll be going a good distance and you're not sure where you're going, don't expect them to be able to help much in locating your destination – you probably won't be able to explain yourself anyway. You may find some English-speaking wallahs hanging around outside top-end hotels.

To hail a rickshaw, stick your arm straight out and wave your hand downwards – the usual way of waving your arm upwards used in the West appears to a Bangladeshi as 'Go away! To hell with you!'

Fares vary a lot, and you must bargain if you care about paying twice as much as locals, although it still isn't very expensive. In any case, it is unrealistic to expect to pay exactly what Bangladeshis do. If you can get away with paying a 25% premium, you'll be doing exceptionally well. At the other end of the paying spectrum, there is sometimes a temptation to be overly generous. Try not to succumb to the warm feeling you know you'll get from doing so, and just be reasonable. Around Tk 50 per hour or Tk 6 per km, with a minimum fare of Tk 10 (and up to double that much in Dhaka), is normal.

Unlike in some other places, you can relax your guard in Bangladesh as most people are not out to rip you off. In fact, you're more likely to be surprised at how proud and honest these hard-working men can be.

Taxi

Taxis are abundant in Dhaka. You might be able to hail one down on the side of the road if they are on their way to their usual hang-out, but if they're all occupied you are better off heading straight to an intersection or top-end hotel, where you will find a fleet of them waiting. Taxis are all metered, though there is no way any driver will use the meter with a foreigner, so you should negotiate the fare before boarding.

Outside Dhaka there are precious few taxis. In Chittagong you'll find a few at the airport or at large hotels and around GEC Circle. In Sylhet, Khulna, Saidpur and possibly Rajshahi you'll see no taxis except for a few at the airport. They are not marked, so you'll have to ask someone to point them out to you.

Tempo

This is a larger version of a baby taxi, with a cabin in the back. Tempos run set routes, like buses, and while they cost far less than baby taxis, they're more uncomfortable because of the small space into which the dozen or so passengers are squeezed. On the other hand, they're a lot faster than rickshaws and as cheap or cheaper. Outside Dhaka and Chittagong they're a lot more plentiful than baby taxis – you will find them even in relatively small towns.

TRAIN

Trains are a lot easier on the nerves, knees and backside than buses, and those plying the major routes aren't too bad, while in 1st class they are positively luxurious. However, travel is slowed down by unbridged rivers requiring ferry crossings, circuitous routing and different gauges. This means that a train ride can sometimes take up to twice as long as a bus ride.

The recent introduction of computerised ticketing has made the purchase of train tickets from major stations far less of a headache than it used to be.

Classes

Intercity (IC) trains are frequent, relatively fast, clean and reasonably punctual, especially in the eastern zone. Fares in 1st class are fairly high (about a third more than an air-con chair coach), but in *sulob* (2nd class with reserved seating and better carriages than ordinary 2nd class) the fare is comparable to that in a non–air-con chair coach, and the trip is a lot more pleasant.

The carriages in 1st class, which have three seats across, facing each other and separated by a small table, initially seem little different from those in *sulob*, which have four seats across without tables. However, the difference is that there's always room for just one more passenger in *sulob*, whereas in 1st class what you see is what you get. Some IC trains also have an air-con 1st class, which is well worth the extra money. Seats here are of the soft and comfortable variety and are similar to those found on trains in the West. This class is always very popular but seats are limited – it's a good idea to reserve at least several days in advance to get a seat or berth in air-con 1st class, though a quiet word to the station master can often work wonders.

There are generally no buffet cars, but sandwiches, Indian snacks and drinks are available from attendants. If you're lucky, these attendants will be sharply dressed waiters handing out dainty china cups of tea.

Second-class cars with unreserved seating are always an overcrowded mess and on mail trains (which do allow for some passenger cargo) your trip will be even slower than on an IC train. However, you may come out of the experience with a few good stories.

The only sleepers are on night trains, and the fare is about 40% more than 1st class.

On the poorly maintained local trains, 2nd class is crowded and uncomfortable, though remarkably cheap – less than a third the price of 1st class. Unreserved 2nd class has so many class categories and combinations above it (1st class, *sulob*, seating, sleeping, air-con, non–air-con) that it's technically lower than 3rd class and it feels like it. On some trains there are only 2nd-class compartments.

Costs

As a rough indication, the 259km journey from Rajshahi to Dhaka costs Tk 630 for a 1st-class air-con berth, Tk 425 for a 1st-class air-con seat, Tk 290 for a 1st-class non–air-con seat and Tk 165 for *sulob*.

Prices in this book are generally for 1st/*sulob* class, and 1st-class prices are usually for air-con seats.

Reservations

For IC and mail trains, ticket clerks will naturally assume that you, as a seemingly rich foreigner, want the most expensive seats, unless you make it clear otherwise. Buying tickets on local trains is a drag because they don't go on sale until the train is about to arrive, which means that while you're battling the ticket queue all the seats are being filled by hordes of locals. It's almost always better to take a bus than a local train.

Printed timetables are not available, so understanding the convoluted rules of train travel is not easy, even for railway staff. It usually isn't too difficult to find a stationmaster who speaks English. Dhaka's modern Kamlapur station is the exception – schedules are clearly marked on large signs in Bengali and English, but you'll have to double-check to make sure they are correct. Some schedules, particularly on the Dhaka–Sylhet route, change by half an hour or so between the summer and winter seasons, and the signs may not be updated. You can phone the station, but inquiries in person are more likely to yield a reliable result. When making

TRAIN STATION PHONE NUMBERS

City	Reservations	General Inquiries/Station Manager
Dhaka	☎ 935 8634	☎ 01711 691612
Chittagong	☎ 635 162	☎ 01711 691550
Sylhet	☎ 717 036	☎ 01711 691656
Rajshahi	☎ 776 040	
Khulna	☎ 723 222	

inquiries, it's best to keep things as simple as possible: specify when and where you want to go, and which type of train you want to catch.

If your queries are too much for counter staff, try the District Information Officer (DIO) at Kamlapur station (in the administration annexe just south of the main station building).

If the crowds that silently follow you around the platform get you down (and they will), ask for the waiting room to be unlocked, or establish yourself in the office of an official who speaks English.

Rural railway stations are prone to power failures – hang onto your luggage if the lights go out.

TRANSPORT

Health

CONTENTS

Travellers tend to worry about contracting infectious diseases in this part of the world, but infections are a rare cause of *serious* illness or death in travellers. Pre-existing medical conditions such as heart disease, and accidental injury (especially traffic accidents), account for most life-threatening problems. Becoming ill in some way, however, is very common.

Environmental issues such as heat and pollution can cause health problems. Hygiene is generally poor throughout the region so food- and waterborne illnesses are common. Many insect-borne diseases are present, particularly in tropical areas. Fortunately most travellers' illnesses can either be prevented with some common-sense behaviour or be treated easily with a well-stocked traveller's medical kit. Medical care remains basic so it is essential to be well prepared before travelling to Bangladesh.

The following advice is a general guide only and does not replace the advice of a doctor trained in travel medicine.

BEFORE YOU GO

Pack medications in their original, clearly labelled, containers. A signed and dated letter from your physician describing your medical conditions and medications, including generic names, is very useful. If carrying syringes or needles, be sure to have a physician's letter documenting their medical necessity. If you have a heart condition, bring a copy of your ECG taken just prior to travelling.

If you take any regular medication, bring double your needs in case of loss or theft. In most South Asian countries, including Bangladesh, you can buy many medications over the counter without a doctor's prescription, but it can be difficult to find some of the newer drugs, particularly the latest anti-depressant drugs, blood-pressure medications and contraceptive pills, in particular outside Dhaka.

INSURANCE

Even if you are fit and healthy, don't travel without health insurance – accidents do happen. Declare any existing medical conditions you have – the insurance company *will* check if your problem is pre-existing and will not cover you if it is undeclared. You may require extra cover for adventure activities such as scuba diving. If your health insurance doesn't cover you for medical expenses abroad, consider getting extra insurance. If you're uninsured, emergency evacuation is expensive.

Find out in advance if your insurance plan will make payments directly to providers, or whether the company will reimburse you later for your overseas health expenditures. (In many countries, including Bangladesh, doctors expect payment in cash.) Some insurance policies offer lower and higher medical-expense options; the higher ones are primarily for countries that have extremely high medical costs, such as the USA. You may prefer a policy that pays doctors or hospitals directly rather than you having to pay on the spot and make a claim later. If you have to claim later, make sure you keep all documentation. Some policies ask you to call back (reverse charges) to a centre in your home country, where an immediate assessment of your problem is made.

VACCINATIONS

Specialised travel-medicine clinics are your best source of information; they stock all available vaccines and will be able to give specific recommendations for you and your trip. The doctors will take into account factors such as your vaccination history, the length of your trip, activities you may be undertaking and underlying medical conditions, such as pregnancy.

Most vaccines don't produce immunity until at least two weeks after they're given, so visit a doctor four to eight weeks before your planned departure. Ask your doctor for an International Certificate of Vaccination (otherwise known as 'the yellow booklet'), which will list all the vaccinations you've received.

Recommended Vaccinations

The World Health Organisation (WHO) recommends the following vaccinations for travellers to South Asia:

Adult diphtheria & tetanus Single booster recommended if none in the previous 10 years. Side effects include sore arm and fever.

Hepatitis A Provides almost 100% protection for up to a year; a booster after 12 months provides at least another 20 years' protection. Mild side effects such as headache and sore arm occur in 5% to 10% of people.

Hepatitis B Now considered routine for most travellers. Given as three shots over six months. A rapid schedule is also available, as is a combined vaccination with Hepatitis A. Side effects are mild and uncommon, usually headache and sore arm. In 95% of people, lifetime protection results.

Measles, mumps & rubella Two doses of MMR are required unless you have had the diseases. Occasionally a rash and flulike illness can develop a week after receiving the vaccine. Many young adults require a booster.

Polio In 2003 polio was still present in Nepal, India and Pakistan, but it has been eradicated in Bangladesh. Only one booster is required for an adult for lifetime protection. Inactivated polio vaccine is safe during pregnancy.

Typhoid Recommended for all travellers to Bangladesh, even if you only visit urban areas. The vaccine offers around 70% protection, lasts for two to three years and comes as a single shot. Tablets are also available, however the injection is usually recommended as it has fewer side effects. Sore arm and fever may occur.

Varicella If you haven't had chickenpox, discuss this vaccination with your doctor.

These immunisations are recommended for long-term travellers (more than one month) or those at special risk:

Japanese B Encephalitis Three injections in all. Booster recommended after two years. Sore arm and headache are the most common side effects. Rarely, an allergic reaction comprising hives and swelling can occur up to 10 days after any of the three doses.

Meningitis Single injection. There are two types of vaccination: the quadravalent vaccine gives two to three years' protection; meningitis group C vaccine gives around 10 years' protection. Recommended for long-term backpackers aged under 25.

Rabies Three injections in all. A booster after one year will then provide 10 years' protection. Side effects are rare – occasionally headache and sore arm.

Tuberculosis A complex issue. Long-term adult travellers are usually recommended to have a TB skin test before and after travel, rather than vaccination. Only one vaccine given in a lifetime.

Required Vaccinations

The only vaccine required by international regulations is yellow fever. Proof of vaccination will only be required if you have visited a country in the yellow-fever zone within the six days prior to entering Bangladesh. If you are travelling to Bangladesh from Africa or South America, you should check to see if you will require proof of vaccination.

MEDICAL CHECKLIST

Recommended items for a personal medical kit:

- antibacterial cream, eg Muciprocin
- antibiotic for skin infections, eg Amoxicillin/Clavulanate or Cephalexin
- antibiotics for diarrhoea, eg Norfloxacin or Ciprofloxacin; for bacterial diarrhoea, Azithromycin; for giardia or amoebic dysentery, Tinidazole
- antifungal cream, eg Clotrimazole
- antihistamine – there are many options, eg Cetrizine for daytime and Promethazine for night
- antiseptic, eg Betadine
- antispasmodic for stomach cramps, eg Buscopa
- contraceptive method
- decongestant, eg Pseudoephedrine
- DEET-based insect repellent
- diarrhoea treatment – consider an oral rehydration solution (eg Gastrolyte), diarrhoea 'stopper' (eg Loperamide) and antinausea medication (eg Prochlorperazine)
- first-aid items such as scissors, elastoplasts, bandages, gauze, thermometer (but not mercury), sterile needles and syringes, safety pins and tweezers
- Ibuprofen or another anti-inflammatory

HEALTH

- indigestion tablets, such as Quick Eze or Mylanta
- iodine tablets to purify water (unless you are pregnant or have a thyroid problem)
- laxative, eg Coloxyl
- migraine medicine – take your personal medicine
- paracetamol
- permethrin to impregnate clothing and mosquito nets
- steroid cream for allergic/itchy rashes, eg 1% to 2% hydrocortisone
- sunscreen and hat
- throat lozenges
- thrush (vaginal yeast infection) treatment, eg Clotrimazole pessaries or Diflucan tablet
- Ural or equivalent, if you're prone to urine infections.

INTERNET RESOURCES

There is a wealth of travel health advice on the internet. For further information, **Lonely Planet** (www.lonelyplanet.com) is a good place to start. The **World Health Organization** (WHO; www.who.int/ith) publishes a superb book called *International Travel and Health*, which is revised annually and available online at no cost. Another website of general interest is **MD Travel Health** (www.mdtravelhealth.com), which provides complete travel-health recommendations for every country and is updated daily. The **Centers for Disease Control and Prevention** (CDC; www.cdc.gov) website also has good general information.

FURTHER READING

Lonely Planet's *Healthy Travel – Asia & India* is a handy pocket size and packed with useful information including pretrip planning, emergency first aid, immunisa-

tion and disease information, and what to do if you get sick on the road. Other recommended references include *Traveller's Health* by Dr Richard Dawood and *Travelling Well* by Dr Deborah Mills – check out the website (www.travellingwell.com.au).

IN TRANSIT

DEEP-VEIN THROMBOSIS

Deep-vein thrombosis (DVT) occurs when blood clots form in the legs during plane flights, chiefly because of prolonged immobility. The longer the flight, the greater the risk. Though most blood clots are reabsorbed uneventfully, some may break off and travel through the blood vessels to the lungs, where they may cause life-threatening complications.

The chief symptom of DVT is swelling or pain of the foot, ankle or calf, usually but not always on just one side. When a blood clot travels to the lungs, it may cause chest pain and difficulty in breathing. Travellers with any of these symptoms should immediately seek medical attention.

To prevent the development of DVT on long flights you should walk about the cabin, perform isometric compressions of the leg muscles (ie contract the leg muscles while sitting), drink plenty of fluids, and avoid alcohol and tobacco.

JET LAG & MOTION SICKNESS

Jet lag is common when crossing more than five time zones; it results in insomnia, fatigue, malaise or nausea. To avoid jet lag try drinking plenty of fluids (nonalcoholic) and eating light meals. Upon arrival, seek exposure to natural sunlight and readjust your schedule (for meals, sleep etc) as soon as possible.

Antihistamines such as dimenhydrinate (Dramamine), promethazine (Phenergan) and meclizine (Antivert, Bonine) are usually the first choice for treating motion sickness. Their main side effect is drowsiness. A herbal alternative is ginger, which works like a charm for some people.

IN BANGLADESH

AVAILABILITY OF HEALTH CARE

In general, medical facilities are not up to international standards and serious cases are likely to be evacuated. Facilities are severely limited outside the major cities and, as a result, it can be difficult to find reliable medical care in rural areas. Your embassy and insurance company can be good contacts. Recommended clinics are listed on p50 in the Dhaka chapter.

Self-treatment may be appropriate if your problem is minor (eg traveller's diarrhoea), you are carrying the relevant medication and you cannot attend a recommended clinic. If you think you may have a serious disease, especially malaria (see p186), do not waste time – travel to the nearest quality facility to receive attention.

Buying medication over the counter is not recommended, as fake medications and drugs that have been poorly stored or are out-of-date are common.

INFECTIOUS DISEASES
Coughs, Colds & Chest Infections
Respiratory infections are common in Bangladesh. This usually starts as a virus and is exacerbated by environmental conditions such as pollution in the cities, or cold and altitude in the mountains. Commonly a secondary bacterial infection will intervene – marked by fever, chest pain and coughing up discoloured or blood-tinged sputum. If you have the symptoms of an infection, seek medical advice or commence a general antibiotic.

Dengue Fever
This mosquito-borne disease is becoming increasingly problematic in the tropical world, especially in the cities. As there is no vaccine available it can only be prevented by avoiding mosquito bites. The mosquito that carries dengue bites day and night, so use insect avoidance measures at all times. Symptoms include high fever, severe headache and body ache (dengue was previously known as 'breakbone fever'). Some people develop a rash and experience diarrhoea. There is no specific treatment, just rest and paracetamol – do not take aspirin as it increases the likelihood of haemorrhaging. See a doctor to be diagnosed and monitored.

Hepatitis A
A problem throughout the region, this food- and waterborne virus infects the liver, causing jaundice (yellow skin and eyes), nausea and lethargy. There is no specific treatment for hepatitis A, you just need to allow time

for the liver to heal. All travellers heading to South Asia should be vaccinated against hepatitis A.

Hepatitis B
The only sexually transmitted disease that can be prevented by vaccination, hepatitis B is spread by body fluids, including sexual contact. In some parts of South Asia up to 20% of the population are carriers of hepatitis B, and usually are unaware of this. In Bangladesh the number of carriers is just below 10%. The long-term consequences can include liver cancer and cirrhosis.

Hepatitis E
Transmitted through contaminated food and water, hepatitis E has similar symptoms to hepatitis A, but is far less common. It is a severe problem in pregnant women and can result in the death of both mother and baby. There is currently no vaccine, and prevention is by following safe eating and drinking guidelines.

HIV
HIV is spread via contaminated body fluids. Avoid unsafe sex, unsterile needles (including those in medical facilities) and procedures such as tattoos. The rate of HIV infection in South Asia is growing more rapidly than anywhere else in the world.

Influenza
Present year-round in the tropics, influenza (flu) symptoms include high fever, muscle aches, runny nose, cough and sore throat. It can be very severe in people over the age of 65 or in those with underlying medical conditions such as heart disease or diabetes – vaccination is recommended for these individuals. There is no specific treatment, just rest and paracetamol.

Japanese B Encephalitis
This viral disease is transmitted by mosquitoes and is rare in travellers. Like most mosquito-borne diseases it is becoming a more common problem in affected countries. Most cases occur in rural areas and vaccination is recommended for travellers spending more than one month outside of cities. There is no treatment, and a third of infected people will die, while another third will suffer permanent brain damage.

Malaria

For such a serious and potentially deadly disease, there is an enormous amount of misinformation concerning malaria. You must get expert advice as to whether your trip puts you at risk. Outside Dhaka, the risk of contracting malaria far outweighs the risk of any tablet side effects. Remember that malaria can be fatal. Before you travel, seek medical advice on the right medication and dosage for you. Malaria in South Asia, including Bangladesh, is chloroquine resistant.

Malaria is caused by a parasite, transmitted through the bite of an infected mosquito. The most important symptom of malaria is fever, but general symptoms such as headache, diarrhoea, cough or chills may also occur. A diagnosis can only be made by taking a blood sample.

Two strategies should be combined to prevent malaria – mosquito avoidance, and antimalarial medications. Most people who catch malaria are taking inadequate or no antimalarial medication.

Travellers are advised to prevent mosquito bites by taking these steps:

- Use a DEET-containing insect repellent on exposed skin. Wash this off at night, as long as you are sleeping under a mosquito net. Natural repellents such as citronella can be effective, but must be applied more frequently than products containing DEET.
- Sleep under a mosquito net impregnated with permethrin.
- Choose accommodation with screens and fans (if not air-conditioned).
- Impregnate clothing with permethrin in high-risk areas.
- Wear long sleeves and trousers in light colours.
- Use mosquito coils.
- Spray your room with insect repellent before going out for your evening meal.

There are a variety of medications available:
Doxycycline This daily tablet is a broad-spectrum antibiotic that has the added benefit of helping to prevent a variety of tropical diseases including leptospirosis, tick-borne diseases and typhus. The potential side effects include photosensitivity (a tendency to sunburn), thrush in women, indigestion, heartburn, nausea and interference with the contraceptive pill. More serious side effects include ulceration of the oesophagus – you can help prevent this by taking your tablet with a meal and a large glass of water, and never

lying down within half an hour of taking it. It must be taken for four weeks after leaving the risk area.
Lariam (Mefloquine) Lariam has received much bad press, some of it justified, some not. This weekly tablet suits many people. Serious side effects are rare but include depression, anxiety, psychosis and having fits. Anyone with a history of depression, anxiety, other psychological disorders or epilepsy should not take Lariam. It is considered safe in the second and third trimesters of pregnancy. Tablets must be taken for four weeks after leaving the risk area.
Malarone This drug is a combination of Atovaquone and Proguanil. Side effects are uncommon and mild, most commonly nausea and headache. It is the best tablet for scuba divers and for those on short trips to high-risk areas. It must be taken for one week after leaving the risk area.

A final option is to take no preventive medication but to have a supply of emergency medication should you develop the symptoms of malaria. This is less than ideal, and you'll need to get to a good medical facility within 24 hours of developing a fever. If you choose this option, the most effective and safest treatment is Malarone (four tablets once daily for three days). Other options include Mefloquine and Quinine but the side effects of these drugs at treatment doses make them less desirable. Fansidar is no longer recommended.

Measles

Measles remains a significant problem in Bangladesh. This highly contagious bacterial infection is spread via coughing and sneezing. Most people born before 1966 are immune as they had the disease in childhood. Measles starts with a high fever and rash, and can be complicated by pneumonia and brain disease. There is no specific treatment.

Rabies

This is a common problem in South Asia. Around 30,000 people die from rabies in India alone each year, and there are more than 2000 deaths annually in Bangladesh. This uniformly fatal disease is spread by the bite or lick of an infected animal – most commonly a dog or monkey. You should seek medical advice immediately after any animal bite and commence postexposure treatment. Having pretravel vaccination means the postbite treatment is greatly simplified. If an animal bites you, gently wash the wound with soap and water, and apply iodine-based antiseptic. If you are not prevaccinated, you will need to receive rabies immunoglobulin as soon as possible. This is very difficult to obtain outside Dhaka.

STDs

Sexually transmitted diseases most common in Bangladesh include herpes, warts, syphilis, gonorrhoea and chlamydia. People carrying these diseases often have no signs of infection. Condoms will prevent gonorrhoea and chlamydia but not warts or herpes. If, after a sexual encounter, you develop any rash, lumps, discharge or pain when passing urine, seek immediate medical attention. If you have been sexually active during your travels, have an STD check on your return home.

Tuberculosis

While TB is rare in travellers, those who have significant contact with the local population, such as medical and aid workers, and long-term travellers, should take precautions. Vaccination is usually only given to children under the age of five, but adults at risk are recommended to have pre- and post-travel TB testing. The main symptoms are fever, cough, weight loss, night sweats and tiredness.

Typhoid

This serious bacterial infection is also spread via food and water. It gives a high and slowly progressive fever and headache, and may be accompanied by a dry cough and stomach pain. It is diagnosed by blood tests and treated with antibiotics. Vaccination is recommended for all travellers spending more than a week in South Asia. India and Nepal pose a particularly high risk and have the added problem of significant antibiotic resistance. In Bangladesh the risk is medium level but the infection is also antibiotic resistant. Be aware that vaccination is not 100% effective, so you must still be careful with what you eat and drink.

TRAVELLER'S DIARRHOEA

Traveller's diarrhoea is by far the most common problem affecting travellers – between 30% and 70% of people will suffer from it within two weeks of starting their trip. In over 80% of cases, traveller's diarrhoea is caused by a bacteria, and therefore responds promptly to treatment with antibiotics. Treatment with antibiotics will depend on your situation – how sick you are, how quickly you need to get better, where you are etc.

Traveller's diarrhoea is defined as the passage of more than three watery bowel actions within 24 hours, plus at least one other symptom such as fever, cramps, nausea, vomiting or generally feeling unwell.

Treatment consists of staying well hydrated; rehydration solutions such as Gastrolyte are the best for this. Antibiotics such as Norfloxacin, Ciprofloxacin or Azithromycin will kill the bacteria quickly.

Loperamide is just a 'stopper' and doesn't get to the cause of the problem. It can be helpful, for example if you have to go on a long bus ride. Don't take Loperamide if you have a fever, or blood in your stools. Seek medical attention quickly if you do not respond to an appropriate antibiotic.

Amoebic Dysentery

Amoebic dysentery is rare in travellers but is often misdiagnosed by poor-quality labs in South Asia. Symptoms are similar to bacterial diarrhoea, ie fever, bloody diarrhoea and generally feeling unwell. You should always seek reliable medical care if you have blood in your diarrhoea. Treatment involves two drugs: Tinidazole or Metronidazole to kill the parasite in your gut, and then a second drug to kill the cysts. If left untreated, complications such as liver or gut abscesses can occur. Bacterial dysentery is more common.

Giardiasis

Giardia is a parasite that is relatively common in travellers. Symptoms include nausea, bloating, excess gas, fatigue and intermittent diarrhoea. 'Eggy' burps are often attributed solely to giardia, but work in Nepal has shown that they are not specific to giardia. The parasite will eventually go away if left untreated but this can take months. The treatment of choice is Tinidazole, with Metronidazole being a second-line option.

ENVIRONMENTAL HAZARDS
Air Pollution

If you have severe respiratory problems, speak with your doctor before travelling to any heavily polluted urban centres. Dhaka is one of the most polluted cities in the world. This pollution also causes minor respiratory problems such as sinusitis, dry throat and irritated eyes. If troubled by the pollution, leave the city for a few days and get some fresh air.

HEALTH

DRINKING WATER

■ Never drink tap water, and avoid ice

■ Bottled water is generally safe – check the seal is intact at purchase and that it is labelled 'arsenic free' (see p38)

■ Avoid fresh juices – they may have been watered down

■ Boiling water is the most efficient method of purifying it

■ The best chemical purifier is iodine. It should not be used by pregnant women or those with thyroid problems.

■ Water filters should also filter out viruses. Ensure your filter has a chemical barrier such as iodine and a small pore size, eg less than four microns.

Food

Eating in restaurants is the biggest risk factor for contracting traveller's diarrhoea. Ways to avoid it include eating only freshly cooked food, and avoiding shellfish and food that has been sitting around in buffets. Peel all fruit, cook vegetables, and soak salads in iodine water for at least 20 minutes. Eat in busy restaurants with a high turnover of customers.

Heat

Parts of Bangladesh are hot and humid throughout the year. For most people it takes at least two weeks to adapt to the hot climate. Swelling of the feet and ankles is common, as are muscle cramps caused by excessive sweating. Prevent these by avoiding dehydration and excessive activity in the heat. Take it easy when you first arrive. Don't eat salt tablets (they aggravate the gut), but drinking rehydration solution or eating salty food helps. Treat cramps by stopping activity, resting, rehydrating with double-strength rehydration solution, and gently stretching.

Dehydration is the main contributor to heat exhaustion. Symptoms include feeling weak, headache, irritability, nausea or vomiting, sweaty skin, a fast weak pulse and a normal or slightly elevated body temperature. Treatment involves getting out of the heat and/or sun, fanning the victim and applying cool wet cloths to the skin, laying the victim flat with their legs raised, and rehydrating with water containing ¼ teaspoon of salt per

litre. Recovery is usually rapid but it is common to feel weak for some days afterwards.

Heatstroke is a serious medical emergency. Symptoms come on suddenly and include weakness, nausea, a hot, dry body with a temperature of over 41°C, dizziness, confusion, loss of coordination, fits and eventually collapse and loss of consciousness. Seek medical help and commence cooling by getting the person out of the heat, removing their clothes, fanning them, and applying cool wet cloths or ice to their body, especially to the groin and armpits.

Prickly heat is a common skin rash in the tropics, caused by sweat being trapped under the skin. The result is an itchy rash of tiny lumps. Treat by moving out of the heat and into an air-conditioned area for a few hours and by having cool showers. Creams and ointments clog the skin, so they should be avoided. Locally bought prickly-heat powder can be helpful.

Tropical fatigue is common in long-term expatriates based in the tropics. It's rarely due to disease and is caused by the climate, inadequate mental rest, excessive alcohol intake and the demands of daily work in a different culture.

Insect Bites & Stings

Bedbugs don't carry disease but their bites are very itchy. They live in the cracks of furniture and walls, and then migrate to the bed at night to feed on you. You can treat the itch with an antihistamine.

Lice inhabit various parts of your body but most commonly your head and pubic area. Transmission is via close contact with an infected person. They can be difficult to treat and you may need numerous applications of an antilice shampoo such as permethrin. Pubic lice are usually contracted from sexual contact.

Ticks are contracted after walking in rural areas. They are commonly found behind the ears, on the belly and in the armpits. If you have had a tick bite and experience symptoms such as a rash at the site of the bite or elsewhere, fever or muscle aches, you should see a doctor. Doxycycline prevents tick-borne diseases.

Leeches are found in humid rainforest areas. They do not transmit any disease but their bites are often intensely itchy for weeks afterwards and can easily become infected.

Apply an iodine-based antiseptic to any leech bite to help prevent infection.

Skin Problems

Fungal rashes are common in humid climates. There are two common fungal rashes that affect travellers. The first occurs in moist areas that get less air, such as the groin, armpits and between the toes. It starts as a red patch that slowly spreads and is usually itchy. Treatment involves keeping the skin dry, avoiding chafing and using an antifungal cream such as Clotrimazole or Lamisil. *Tinea versicolor* is also common – this fungus causes small, light-coloured patches, most commonly on the back, chest and shoulders. Consult a doctor.

Cuts and scratches become easily infected in humid climates. Take meticulous care of any cuts and scratches to prevent complications such as abscesses. Immediately wash all wounds in clean water and apply antiseptic. If you develop signs of infection (increasing pain and redness), see a doctor. Divers and surfers should be particularly careful with coral cuts as they become easily infected.

Sunburn

Even on a cloudy day sunburn can occur rapidly. Always use a strong sunscreen (at least factor 30), making sure to reapply after a swim, and always wear a wide-brimmed hat and sunglasses outdoors. Avoid lying in the sun during the hottest part of the day (10am to 2pm). If you become sunburnt, stay out of the sun until you have recovered, apply cool compresses and take painkillers for the discomfort. One percent hydrocortisone cream applied twice daily is also helpful.

WOMEN'S HEALTH

Pregnant women should receive specialised advice before travelling. The ideal time to travel is in the second trimester (be-

tween 16 and 28 weeks), when the risk of pregnancy-related problems is at its lowest and pregnant women generally feel at their best. During the first trimester there is a risk of miscarriage, and in the third trimester complications such as premature labour and high blood pressure are possible. It's wise to travel with a companion. Always carry a list of quality medical facilities available at your destination and ensure you continue your standard antenatal care at these facilities. Avoid rural travel in areas with poor transportation and medical facilities. Most of all, ensure your travel insurance covers all pregnancy-related possibilities, including premature labour.

Malaria is a high-risk disease in pregnancy. WHO recommends that pregnant women do not travel to areas with Chloroquine-resistant malaria. None of the more effective antimalarial drugs are completely safe in pregnancy.

Hepatitis E is a particular problem for pregnant women – if it is contracted in the third trimester, 30% of women and their babies will die.

Traveller's diarrhoea can quickly lead to dehydration and result in inadequate blood flow to the placenta. Many of the drugs used to treat various diarrhoea bugs are not recommended in pregnancy. Azithromycin is considered safe.

In the urban areas of Bangladesh, supplies of sanitary products are readily available. Birth-control options may be limited so bring adequate supplies of your own form of contraception. Heat, humidity and antibiotics can all contribute to thrush. Treatment is with antifungal creams and pessaries such as Clotrimazole. A practical alternative is a single tablet of Fluconazole (Diflucan). Urinary tract infections can be precipitated by dehydration or long bus journeys without toilet stops; bring suitable antibiotics.

HEALTH

Language

Bengali (also widely known as Bangla) is the national language of Bangladesh and the official language of the state of West Bengal in India. Bengali is the easternmost of the Indo-European languages with its roots in Prakrit, the vernacular (ie commonly spoken) form of Pali, which was the original language of the Buddhist scriptures. In addition to Arabic, Urdu and Persian words, the Sanskrit of Brahmin Hindus was assimilated into the local speech, giving Bengali a strong resemblance to Hindi, with some variation in pronunciation. The vocabulary was further expanded through contact with European traders and merchants. Today, Bengali has a number of regional variations, but remains essentially the same throughout Bangladesh.

HISTORY

The modern development of Bengali as a symbol of the cultural individuality of Bangladesh began under the British. In keeping with the Raj's policy of working within local cultures, Bengali was taught to officers, who used it in their dealings with locals. This resulted in the fusion of the vernacular of the peasants with high-caste literary Bengali, which had fallen into disuse under Muslim rulers, who favoured Urdu. The Hindus took to Bengali with enthusiasm, seeing it as a means toward reasserting their cultural heritage, and the 19th century saw a renaissance in Bengali literature. Author Rabindranath Tagore gave Bengali literature kudos when he won the Nobel Prize for literature (see p32).

It wasn't until Partition, and the departure of most of the Hindu ruling class, that Bangladeshi intellectuals felt the need for Bengali as a means of defining their culture and nationalism.

There is a much lower proportion of English-speakers in Bangladesh than in India. It's surprising how many conversations you can have in which you think that you're being understood. English has lapsed for three main reasons: there aren't distinct regional languages which make a lingua franca (common language) necessary; the symbolic importance of Bengali in the independence movement; and the many weaknesses in the public education system. In recent years, however, the value of English has risen considerably, especially if the number of colleges and schools advertising tuition is anything to go by.

Making the effort to learn some Bengali will not only be greatly appreciated; at times it's your only hope. You'll find that most billboards and street signs are written in Bengali script only.

Lonely Planet's *Hindi, Urdu & Bengali Phrasebook* provides a far more in-depth guide to the language, with a selection of useful words and phrases to cover most travel situations. There are a few Bengali phrasebooks available in Dhaka in the New Market bookshops, although the standard of English in some isn't very good. The Heed language centre in Dhaka produces a useful Bengali-English/English-Bengali dictionary and a basic course instruction booklet. See Courses (p159) in the Directory chapter for information on learning Bengali while you're in the country.

PRONUNCIATION

Pronunciation of Bengali is made difficult by the fact that the language includes a variety of subtle sounds with no equivalents in English.

Vowels

Most Bengali vowel sounds are very similar to English ones. The most important thing is to focus on the length of vowels (like the difference between the sounds **a** and **aa**).

a	as the 'u' in 'run'
ą	as in 'tap'
aa	as in 'rather'
ai	as in 'aisle'
ay	as in 'may'
e	as in 'red'
ee	as in 'bee'
i	as in 'bit'
o	as in 'shot'
oh	as in 'both'
oy	as in 'boy'
u	as in 'put'
ui	as in 'quick'

Consonant Sounds

In Bengali there's an important distinction between 'aspirated' and 'unaspirated' consonants, which are produced with or without a puff of air respectively; you'll get the idea if you hold your hand in front of your mouth to feel your breath and say 'pit' (where the 'p' is aspirated) and 'spit' (where it's unaspirated). In this language guide we've used the apostrophe (eg **b′**) to show aspirated consonants – pronounce these as if there's a strong 'h' sound after them.

The other feature that will be unfamiliar to English-speakers is the 'retroflex' consonant. To produce the sound you bend your tongue up and back so the tip touches the ridge on the roof of the mouth behind the teeth. In this language guide the retroflex variants of **d**, **r** and **t** are represented by **đ**, **ŗ** and **ţ** respectively.

The sounds **v**, **w** and **z** are only found in words taken from English, and are pronounced the same as in English.

Word Stress

The pronunciation guides included in this book show words divided into syllables with dots (eg *bo*·ch'ohr 'year') to help you pronounce them. Word stress in Bengali is very subtle, and varies in different regions of the Indian subcontinent. Stress normally falls on the first syllable (eg *b′a*·loh 'good'). Just follow our pronunciation guides – the stressed syllable is always in italics.

ACHA

Acha, the subcontinent's ambiguous 'OK/ Yes/I see' is used widely, but the local slang equivalent is *tik assay* or just *tik*. The words *ji* or *ha* are more positive – if the rickshaw-wallah answers *acha* to your offered price, expect problems at the other end; if it's *tik* or *ji* he's unlikely to demand more money.

ACCOMMODATION

Where's a ...?
... কোথায়?
... *koh·ţ′a·e*

guesthouse
গেস্ট হাউস   gest *ha*·us

hotel
হোটেল   *hoh*·tel

resthouse (government-run guesthouse)
রেষ্ট হাউস   rest *ha*·us

tourist bungalow
টুরিষ্ট বাংলো   *tu*·rist *baang*·loh

youth hostel
ইউথ হস্টেল   ee·uţ′ *hos*·tel

What's the address?
ঠিকানাটা কি?
ţ′i·ka·na·ta ki

I'd like to book a room, please.
আমি একটা রুম বুক করতে চাই, প্লিজ।
aa·mi *ąk*·ta rum buk *kohr*·ţe chai pleez

Do you have a ... room?
আপনার কি ... রুম আছে?
aap·nar ki ... rum *aa*·ch'e

double	ডবল	*do*·bohl
single	সিঙ্গেল	*sin*·gel

How much is it per ...?
প্রতি ... কত?
proh·ţi ... *ko*·ţoh

person	জনে	*jo*·ne
night	রাতে	*raa*·ţe
week	সপ্তাহে	*shop*·ţa·he

May I see it?
আমি কি এটা দেখতে পারি?
aa·mi ki e·ta *dek′*·ţe *paa*·ri

I'll take it.
আমি এটা নিব।
aa·mi e·ta *ni*·boh

heating	হিটার	*hi*·tar
hot water	গরম পানি	*go*·rohm *pa*·ni
running water	কলের পানি	*ko*·ler *pa*·ni

The ... doesn't work.
... কাজ করে না।
... kaaj *koh*·re na

air conditioner	এয়ারকন্ডিশনার	e·aar·
		kon·đi·shoh·nar
fan	ফ্যান	fặn
toilet	টয়লেট	*toy*·let

Can I leave my bags here?
আমার ব্যাগ কি এখানে রেখে যেতে পারি?
aa·mar bặg ki e·k'a·ne *re*·k'e *je*·te *paa*·ri

I'm leaving now.
আমি এখন যাচ্ছি।
aa·mi q·k'ohn *jach*·ch'i

I had a great stay, thank you.
আমার খুব ভাল লেগেছে, ধন্যবাদ।
aa·mar k'ub *b'a*·loh *le*·ge·ch'e *d'ohn*·noh·bad

CONVERSATION & ESSENTIALS

Muslim men usually shake hands when greeting, but women generally just accompany their greeting with a smile. Hindu men and women greet others by joining the palms of their hands together and holding them close to the chest as they slightly bow the head and say their greeting.

Men might hear people greet them with *ba·ha·dur*, an honorific implying that you're wise and wealthy and should pay top price. Married or otherwise 'respectable' women might be addressed as *be·gohm*, roughly the equivalent of 'Madam'. However, in most situations you'll be referred to as *bohn·d'u*, meaning 'friend'.

'Please' and 'Thank you' are rarely used in Bengali. Instead, these sentiments are expressed indirectly in polite conversation. The absence of these shouldn't be misread as rudeness.

If you want to thank someone, you may use the Bengali equivalent for 'Thank you (very much)', *(o·nek) d'oh·noh·baad*, or, alternatively, pay them a compliment.

Hello. (Muslim greeting)
আস্সালাম ওয়ালাইকুম। as·*sa*·lam wa·*lai*·kum

Hello. (Muslim response)
ওয়ালাইকুম আস্সালাম। wa·*lai*·kum as·*sa*·lam

Hello. (Hindu greeting and response)
নমস্কার। *no*·mohsh·kar

See you later.
পরে দেখা হবে। *po*·re dặ·k'a *ho*·be

Goodbye/Good night. (Muslim)
আল্লাহ হাফেজ। *al*·laa *ha*·fez

Goodbye/Good night. (Hindu)
নমস্কার। *no*·mosh·kar

Yes.
হ্যাঁ। hặng

No.
না। naa

Please.
প্লিজ। pleez

Thank you (very much).
(অনেক) ধন্যবাদ। (o·nek) *d'oh*·noh·baad

Excuse me. (eg before a request)
শুনুন। *shu*·nun

Excuse me. (to get past)
একটু দেখি। ek·tu *de*·k'i

Sorry.
সরি। *so*·ri

Forgive me.
মাফ করবেন। maf *kohr*·ben

How are you?
কেমন আছেন? kặ·mohn *aa*·ch'en

Fine, and you?
ভাল, আপনি? *b'a*·loh *aap*·ni

What's your name?
আপনার নাম কি? *aap*·nar naam ki

My name is ...
আমার নাম ... *aa*·mar naam ...

I'm pleased to meet you.
আপনার সাথে পরিচিত *aap*·nar *sha*·ţ'e *poh*·ri·chi·toh
হয়ে খুশি হয়েছি। *hoh*·e *k'u*·shi *hoh*·e·ch'i

A pleasure to meet you, too.
আমিও। *aa*·mi·o

Two verbs that will undoubtedly come in very handy are *a·ch'e* (there is, has), and *lag·be* (need). You can ask *k'a·na a·ch'e?* (Is there food?) or *b'ang·ţi a·ch'e?* (Do you have change?). The negative form of *a·ch'e* is simply *nai*. Saying *bak·sheesh nai* means you don't have any baksheesh to give. You can say *pa·ni lag·be* (lit: water is needed), or say *lag·be na* (lit: don't need) to turn down any unwanted offer.

DIRECTIONS

Where's a/the (station)?
(স্টেশন) কোথায়? (*ste*·shohn) koh·ţ'ai

What's the address?
ঠিকানা কি? *ţ'i*·kaa·na ki

How far is it?
এটা কত দূর? e·ta *ko*·ţoh dur

How do I get there?
ওখানে কি ভাবে যাব? oh·*k'a*·ne ki *b'a*·be *ja*·boh

Can you show me (on the map)?
আমাকে (ম্যাপে) *aa*·ma·ke (*mặ*·pe)
দেখাতে পারেন? *dặ*·k'a·ţe *paa*·ren

SIGNS

ভিতর	Enter
বাহির	Exit
ধুমপান নিষেদ	No Smoking
হোটেল	Hotel
বাস	Bus
শৌচাগার	Toilets
মহিলা	Ladies (also bus seats reserved for women)
পুরুষ	Men
পুলিশ স্টেশন	Police Station
হাসপাতাল	Hospital

Cities

ঢাকা	Dhaka
খুলনা	Khulna
রাজশাহি	Rajshahi
সিলেট	Sylhet
চট্গ্রাম	Chittagong
বরিশাল	Barisal

by ...	... করে	... koh·re
bus	বাসে	ba·se
rickshaw	রিকশা	rik·sha
taxi	ট্যাক্সি	tak·si
train	ট্রেনে	tre·ne
on foot	পায়ে হেটে	paa·e he·te

Turn ...	... টার্ন করবেন	... taarn kohr·ben
at the corner	কর্নারে	kor·na·re
at the traffic lights	ট্রাফিক লাইটে	trq·fik lai·te
left	বামে	baa·me
right	ডানে	daa·ne

near ...	...এর কাছে	...·er ka·ch'e
on the corner	কর্নারে	kor·na·re
straight ahead	সোজা	shoh·ja
there	ঐ যে	oy je
north	উত্তর	ut·tohr
east	পূর্ব	pur·boh
south	দক্ষিন	dohk'·k'in
west	পশ্চিম	pohsh·chim

HEALTH

Where's the nearest ...?
কাছাকাছি ... কোথায়?
ka·ch'a·ka·ch'i ... koh·t'a·e

doctor		
ডাক্তার		dak·tar
hospital		
হাসপাতাল		hash·pa·tal
(night) pharmacist		
(রাতে খোলা) ঔষধের দোকান		(raa·te k'oh·la) oh·shud'·er doh·kan

I need a doctor (who speaks English).
আমার একজন ডাক্তার লাগবে (যিনি ইংরেজিতে কথা বলতে পারেন)।
aa·mar qk·john dak·tar laag·be (ji·ni ing·re·ji·te ko·t'a bohl·te paa·re)

I'm sick.
আমি অসুস্থ।   aa·mi o·shush·t'oh
It hurts here.
এখানে ব্যাথা করছে।   e·k'a·ne bq·t'a kohr·ch'e
I've been vomiting.
আমার বমি হচ্ছিল।   aa·mar boh·mi hoh·ch'i·loh
I have (a/an) ...
আমার (একটা) ...   aa·mar (qk·ta) ...
আছে।   aa·che

asthma	এ্যাজমা	qz·ma
(a) cough	কাশি	ka·shi
diabetes	ডাইবেটিস	dai·be·tis
diarrhoea	ডাইরিয়া	dai·ri·a
fever	জ্বর	jor
headache	মাথা ব্যাথা	ma·t'a bq·t'a
nausea	বমি ভাব	boh·mi b'ab
sore throat	গলা ব্যাথা	go·la bq·t'a

EMERGENCIES

Help!
বাচান!   ba·cha·o
I'm lost.
আমি হারিয়ে গেছি।   aa·mi ha·ri·ye gq·ch'i
Go away!
চলে যান!   choh·le jan
Where are the toilets?
টয়লেটে কোথায়?   toy·let koh·t'a·e

It's an emergency.
এটা একটা এমারজেন্সিস।
e·ta qk·ta e·mar·jen·si
Could you please help?
একটু সাহায্য করতে পারেন?
ek·tu sha·haj·joh kohr·te paa·ren
Can I use your phone?
আপনার ফোন ব্যাবহার করতে পারি কি?
aap·nar fohn bq·boh·har kohr·te pa·ri ki

Call ...!
... ডাকেন!   ... da·ken
an ambulance
এ্যাম্বুলেন্স   qm·bu·lens
a doctor
ডাক্তার   dak·tar
the police
পুলিশ   pu·lish

LANGUAGE

I'm allergic to ...
আমার ... –এ এল্যার্জি আছে।
aa·mar ... ·e *q*·lar·ji *aa*·ch'e

antibiotics	এ্যান্টিবায়োটিক	*qn*·ti·bai·o·tik
aspirin	এ্যাসপিরিন	*qs*·pi·rin
penicillin	পেনিসিলিন	*pe*·ni·si·lin
antiseptic	এ্যান্টিসেপটিক	*qn*·ti·sep·tik
condoms	কন্ডম	*kon*·dohm
contraceptives	কন্ট্রাসেপটিভ	*kon*·tra·sep·tiv
insect repellent	ইনসেক্ট রিপেলেন্ট	*in*·sekt *ri*·pe·lent
painkillers	ব্যাথার ঔষুধ	*bq*·t'ar o·shud'

LANGUAGE DIFFICULTIES

Do you speak (English)?
আপনি কি (ইংরেজি) বলতে পারেন?
aap·ni ki (ing·*re*·ji) bohl·te *paa*·ren
Yes, I understand.
হ্যা, আমি বুঝতে পারছি।
hɑng *aa*·mi *buj'*·te paar·ch'i
No, I don't understand.
না, আমি বুঝতে পারছি না।
na *aa*·mi *buj'*·te paar·ch'i na
I don't speak (Bengali).
আমি (বাংলা) বলতে পারি না।
aa·mi (*bang*·la) bohl·te *paa*·ri na
I can't read Bengali characters.
আমি বাংলা অক্ষর পড়তে পারি না।
aa·mi *bang*·la ok·k'ohr pohr·te *paa*·ri na
What does *'ach'·*ch'a' **mean?**
'আচ্ছা' মান কি?
ach'·ch'a *maa*·ne ki

Could you please ...?
... প্লিজ? ... pleez
repeat that
আবার বলন *aa*·bar *boh*·len
speak more slowly
আরা ধির বলন *aa*·roh *d'i*·re *boh*·len
write it down
লিখ দন *li*·k'e den

NUMBERS

Counting up to 20 is easy, but after that it becomes complicated, as the terms do not follow sequentially. In Bengali 21 isn't *bish·ek* or *ek·bish* as you might expect, but *ek·ush*; 45 is actually *poy·ṭal·lish*, but the simpler *pach·chohl·lish* is understood.

0	০	shun·noh
1	১	ɑk
2	২	dui
3	৩	ṭeen
4	৪	chaar
5	৫	paach
6	৬	ch'oy
7	৭	shaaṭ
8	৮	aat
9	৯	noy
10	১০	dosh
11	১১	q·gaa·roh
12	১২	baa·roh
13	১৩	ṭq·roh
14	১৪	chohd·doh
15	১৫	poh·ne·roh
16	১৬	shoh·loh
17	১৭	sho·te·roh
18	১৮	aat'·aa·roh
19	১৯	u·nish
20	২০	beesh
30	৩০	ṭi·rish
40	৪০	chohl·lish
50	৫০	pon·chaash
60	৬০	shaat
70	৭০	shohṭ·ṭur
80	৮০	aa·shi
90	৯০	nohb·boh·i
100	১০০	ɑk shoh
200	২০০	dui shoh
1000	১০০০	ɑk haa·jaar
100,000	১০০০০০	ɑk laak'
1 million	১০০০০০০	dosh laak'
10 million	১০০০০০০০	ɑk koh·ti

SHOPPING & SERVICES

For many words, such as 'hotel' and 'post office', the English word will be understood.

Where's a/the ...?
... কোথায়? ... koh·t'a·e
bank
ব্যাংক bɑnk
department store
ডিপার্টমেন্ট স্টোর đi·*part*·ment stohr
khadi shop
খাদির দোকান k'a·dir *doh*·kan
market
বাজার *baa*·jar
tourist office
পর্যটন কেন্দ্র *pohr*·joh·tohn *ken*·droh

Where can I buy (a padlock)?
(একটা তালা) কোথায় কিনতে পাওয়া যাবে?
(*qk*·ta *ṭa*·la) koh·t'a·e *kin*·te pa·wa ja·be
I'm just looking.
আমি দেখছি।
aa·mi *dek*·ch'i

I'd like to buy (an adaptor plug).
একটা (এ্যাডপ্টার প্লাগ) কিনতে চাই।
qk·ta (*ą·đąp*·tar plag) *kin*·țe chai
How much is it?
এটার দাম কত?
e·tar dam *ko*·țoh
Can you write down the price?
দামটা কি লিখে দিতে পারেন?
dam·ta ki *li·k'e di*·țe paa·ren
Can I look at it?
এটা দেখতে পারি?
e·ta *dek'*·țe *paa*·ri
That's too expensive.
বেশী দাম।
be·shi dam
Can you lower the price?
দাম কমান।
dam *ko*·man
I'll give you (30 taka).
আমি (তিরিশ টাকা) দিব।
aa·mi (*ți*·rish *ta*·ka) *di*·boh

Do you accept ...?
আপনি কি ... নেন?   *aap*·ni ki ... nen
  credit cards
  ক্রেডিট কার্ড   *kre*·đit kađ
  debit cards
  ডেবিট কার্ড   *đe*·bit kađ
  travellers cheques
  ট্রাভেলার্স চেক   *trą*·ve·lars chek

TIME & DATE

Bengalis use the 12-hour clock. There's no such concept as 'am' or 'pm' – the time of day is indicated by adding *shok·aal* (morning), *du·pur* (afternoon) or *raaț* (night) before the time. To tell the time, add the suffix *-ta* to the ordinal number which indicates the hour.

What time is it?	কয়টা বাজে?	*koy*·ta baa·je
It's (10) o'clock.	(দশটা) বাজে।	(*dosh*·ta) baa·je
Five past ...	... বেজে পাঁচ।	... *be*·je pach
Quarter past ...	সোয়া ...	*shoh*·aa ...
Half past ...	সাড়ে ...	*shaa*·țe ...
Quarter to ...	পৌনে ...	*poh*·ne ...
At what time ...?	কটার সময় ...?	*ko*·tar *sho*·moy ...
At (10)am.	সকাল (দশটা)।	*sho*·kaal (*dosh*·ta)

today	আজকে	*aaj*·ke
yesterday ...	গতকাল ...	*go·țoh*·kaal ...
tomorrow ...	আগামিকাল ...	*aa·ga·mi*·kaal ...
morning	সকাল	*sho*·kaal
afternoon	দুপুর	*du*·pur
evening	বিকাল	*bee*·kaal

Monday	সোমবার	*shohm*·baar
Tuesday	মঙ্গলবার	*mohng·gohl*·baar
Wednesday	বুধবার	*bud'*·baar
Thursday	বৃহস্পতিবার	*bri·hosh·poh·ți*·baar
Friday	শুক্রবার	*shuk·roh*·baar
Saturday	শনিবার	*shoh·ni*·baar
Sunday	রবিবার	*roh·bi*·baar

January	জানুয়ারি	*jaa·nu·aa*·ri
February	ফেব্রুয়ারি	*feb·ru·aa*·ri
March	মচ	maarch
April	এপ্রিল	*ep*·reel
May	মে	me
June	জুন	jun
July	জুলাই	*ju*·lai
August	আগস্ট	*aa*·gohst
September	সেপ্টেম্বার	*sep·tem*·baar
October	অক্টোবার	*ok·toh*·baar
November	নভেম্বার	*no·b'em*·baar
December	ডিসেম্বার	*di·sem*·baar

TRANSPORT
Public Transport

Which ... goes to (Comilla)?
কোন ... (কুমিল্লা) যায়?
kohn ... (ku·*mil*·laa) ja·e

bus	বাস	bas
train	ট্রেন	tren
tram	ট্রাম	trąm

When's the ... (bus)?
... (বাস) কখন?
... (bas) *ko·k'ohn*

first	প্রথম	*proh·t'ohm*
next	পরের	*po·rer*
last	শেষ	shesh

What time does it leave?
কখন ছাড়বে?   *ko·k'ohn ch'aaț·be*
How long will it be delayed?
কত দেরি হবে?   *ko·toh de·ri ho·be*
Is this seat available?
এই সিট কি খালি?   ay seet ki *k'aa·lee*
Where do I buy a ticket?
কোথায় টিকেট কিনবো?   *koh·ț'a·e ți·ket kin·boh*
Where's the booking office for foreigners?
বিদেশিদের জন্য   bi·de·*shi·der john·noh*
বুকিং অফিস কোথায়?   *bu·king o·feesh koh·ț'a·e*
Do I need to change train?
আমাকে কি চেঞ্জ   *aa·maa·ke ki chenj*
করতে হবে ট্রেন?   *kohr·țe ho·be tren*
How long does the trip take?
যেতে কতক্ষন   *je·țe ko·tohk·k'ohn*
লাগবে?   *laa·ge*

LANGUAGE

A ... ticket (to Dhaka).
(ঢাকার) জন্য একটা ... টিকেট।
(d'aa·kaar) john·noh qk·ta ... ti·ket

1st-class	ফার্স্ট ক্লাস	farst klaas
2nd-class	সেকেন্ড ক্লাস	se·kend klaas
one-way	ওয়ানওয়ে	wan·way
return	রিটার্ন	ri·tarn
student	ছাত্র	ch'at·roh

I'd like a/an ... seat.
আমাকে একটা ...   aa·ma·ke qk·ta ...
nonsmoking
ধূমপান নিষেধ এলাকায়   d'um·paan ni·shed' e·la·ka·e
smoking
ধূমপান এলাকায়   d'um·paan e·la·ka·e

What's the next stop?
পরের স্টপ কি?
po·rer stop ki
Please tell me when we get to (Sylhet).
(সিলেট) আসলে আমাকে বলবেন, প্লিজ।
(si·let) aash·le aa·maa·ke bohl·ben pleez
I'd like to get off at (Mongla).
আমি (মঙ্গলাতে) নামতে চাই।
aa·mi (mong·laa·te) naam·te chai
Where's the queue for female passengers?
মহিলা প্যাসেঞ্জারদের লাইন কোথায়?
moh·hi·la pq·sen·jar·der la·in koh·t'a·e
Where are the seats for female passengers?
মহিলা প্যাসেঞ্জারদের সিট কোথায়?
moh·hi·la pq·sen·jar·der seet koh·t'a·e

... bus	... বাস	... bas
city	শহর	sho·hohr
express	এক্সপ্রেস	eks·pres
intercity	ইন্টারসিটি	in·tar·see·ti
local	লোকাল	loh·kaal
ordinary	অর্ডিনারি	o·di·naa·ri

Is this taxi available?
এই ট্যাক্সি খালি?   ay tqk·si k'aa·li
Please put the meter on.
প্লিজ মিটার লাগান।   pleez mee·tar laa·gan
How much is it to ...?
... যেতে কত লাগবে?   ... je·te ko·toh laag·be
Please take me to this address.
আমাকে এই ঠিকানায়   aa·ma·ke ay t'i·kaa·nai
নিয়ে যান।   ni·ye jaan

Private Transport
I'd like to hire a/an ...
আমি একটা ... ভাড়া করতে চাই।
aa·mi qk·ta ... b'a·ra kohr·te chai
4WD
ফোর হুইল ড্রাইভ   fohr weel draiv
bicycle
সাইকেল   sai·kel
car
গাড়ি   gaa·ri
motorbike
মটরসাইকেল   mo·tohr·sai·kel

Is this the road to (Rangamati)?
এটা কি (রাঙ্গামাটির) রাস্তা?
e·ta ki (raang·a·maa·tir) raas·ta
Where's a petrol station?
পেট্রোল স্টেশন কোথায়?
pet·rohl ste·shohn koh·t'a·e
Please fill it up.
ভর্তি করে দেন, প্লিজ।
b'ohr·ti kohr·re dqn pleez
I'd like (20) litres.
আমার (বিশ) লিটার লাগবে।
aa·mar (beesh) li·tar laag·be

diesel	ডিজেল	di·zel
regular	পেট্রোল	pet·rohl
unleaded	অকটেন	ok·ten (octane)

I need a mechanic.
আমার একজন মেকানিক লাগবে।
aa·mar qk·john me·kaa·nik laag·be
The car/motorbike has broken down at (Sylhet).
গাড়ি/মটরসাইকেল (সিলেট) নষ্ট হয়ে গেছে।
gaa·ri/mo·tohr·sai·kel (si·let) nosh·toh hoh·e gq·ch'e
I have a flat tyre.
আমার গাড়ির একটা চাকা পাংচার হয়ে গেছে।
aa·mar gaa·rir qk·ta chaa·ka pank·char hoh·e gq·ch'e
I've run out of petrol.
আমার পেট্রোল শেষ হয়ে গেছে।
aa·mar pet·rohl shesh hoh·e gq·ch'e

lonely planet phrasebooks

Hindi,
Urdu & Bengali

with 2000-word two-way dictionary

Also available from Lonely Planet:
Hindi, Urdu & Bengali Phrasebook

LANGUAGE

Glossary

Adivasis – tribal people

baby taxi – mini auto-rickshaw
baksheesh – donation, tip or bribe, depending on the context
Bangla – the national language of Bangladesh (see *Bengali*); also the new name for the Indian state of West Bengal
bangla – architectural style associated with the Pre-Mauryan and Mauryan period (312–232 BC); exemplified by a bamboo-thatched hut with a distinctively curved roof
baras – ancient houseboats
bawalis – timber workers in the Sundarbans
Bengali – the national language of Bangladesh, where it is also known as Bangla, and the official language of the state of Bangla (formerly West Bengal) in India
BIWTC – Bangladesh Inland Waterway Transport Corporation
BNP – Bangladesh Nationalist Party
BRAC – Bangladesh Rural Advancement Committee
BRTC – Bangladesh Road Transport Corporation

cha – tea, usually served with milk and sugar
chair coach – modern bus with adjustable seats and lots of leg room
char – a river or delta island made of silt; highly fertile but highly susceptible to flooding and erosion

DC – District Commissioner

Eid – Muslim holiday

ghat – steps or landing on a river

hammam – bath house
haors – wetlands
hartals – strikes, ranging from local to national

jamdani – ornamental loom-embroidered muslin or silk
jor bangla – twin hut architectural style

kantha – traditional indigo-dyed muslin
khyang – Buddhist temple
kuthi – factories

madhu – honey; also *mau*
mahavihara – large monastery

maidan – open grassed area in a town or city, used as a parade ground during the Raj
mandir – temple
mau – honey; also *madhu*
maualis – honey-gatherers in the Sundarbans
mazars – graves
mela – festival
mihrab – niche in a mosque positioned to face Mecca; Muslims face in this direction when they pray
mishuk – smaller, less-colourful version of a baby taxi
mistris – rickshaw makers
mohajons – rickshaw- or taxi-fleet owners (also known as *maliks*)
Mughal – the Muslim dynasty of Indian emperors from Babur to Aurangzeb (16th-18th century)
mustan – Mafia-style bosses who demand, and receive, payment from baby-taxi drivers, roadside vendors and people living on public land

nakshi kanthas – embroided quilts
nava-ratna – nine towered; used to describe certain mosques
nawab – Muslim prince

paisa – unit of currency; there are 100 paisa in a taka
Parjatan – the official Bangladesh-government tourist organisation

Raj – also called the British Raj; the period of British government in the Indian Subcontinent, roughly from the mid-18th century to the mid-20th century
raj – rule or sovereignty
raja – ruler, landlord or king
rajbari – Raj-era palace built by a zamindar
Ramzan – Bengali name for Ramadan
rekha – buildings with a square sanctum on a raised platform
rest house – government-owned guesthouse
rickshaw – small, three-wheeled bicycle-driven passenger vehicle
rickshaw-wallah – rickshaw driver
Rocket – paddle steamer

sadhus – holy men
salwar kameez – a long, dress-like tunic *(kameez)* worn by women over a pair of baggy trousers *(salwar)*

shankhari – Hindu artisan
Shi'ia – Islamic sect that sees the authority of Mohammed as continuing through Ali, his son-in-law
Shiva – Hindu god; the destroyer, the creator
stupa – Buddhist religious monument
Sufi – ascetic Muslim mystic
sulob – upper-2nd class on a train (with reserved seating)
Sunni – school of Islamic thought that sees the authority of Mohammed as continuing through Abu Bakr, the former governor of Syria

taka – currency of Bangladesh
tea estate – terraced hillside where tea is grown; also tea garden
tempo – shared auto-rickshaw

vihara – monastery

zamindar – landlord; also the name of the feudal-landowner system itself
zila – district

Behind the Scenes

THIS BOOK

This sixth edition of *Bangladesh* was researched and written by Stuart Butler, with contributions from Heather Butler (p81), Bruno De Cordier (p109) and David Johnson (p151). The Health chapter was based on text written by Dr Trish Bachelor. Jose Santiago was author of the first edition, way back in 1985. Jon Murray researched the second edition, Betsy Wagenhauser and Alex Newton researched the third, Richard Plunkett researched the fourth edition and Marika McAdam researched the fifth.

This book was commissioned in Lonely Planet's Melbourne office and produced by the following:

Commissioning Editors Stefanie Di Trocchio, Sam Trafford, assisted by Maryanne Netto, Kalya Ryan
Coordinating Editors Dianne Schallmeiner, Branislava Vladisavljevic
Coordinating Cartographer Diana Duggan
Coordinating Layout Designer Jacqueline McLeod
Managing Editors Bruce Evans, Geoff Howard
Managing Cartographer Shahara Ahmed
Managing Layout Designer Adam McCrow
Assisting Editor Jeanette Wall
Assisting Cartographer Tadhgh Knaggs
Cover Designer Pepi Bluck
Project Manager Eoin Dunlevy
Language Content Coordinator Quentin Frayne

Thanks to Lisa Knights, Jelena Milosevic, Marg Toohey, Celia Wood

THANKS
STUART BUTLER

A huge thanks to everyone who knowingly or unknowingly helped out, especially Mahmud Hasan Khan and his brother Mahfuz. Also, thank you to Elisabeth Fahrni Mansur of Guide Tours, Mr Rashed Hasen, Lallim Bawm, Mr Shaheen for his expert driving, Adam Barlow, Nick Manning, Mr Ratan, Jafar Alam, Michael Bullo, Dr Mainulhuq, Philip Decosse, Bristy and Alam Shohag, and Yvonne Macieczyk.

Sorry to anyone I've missed – your help was priceless, but quite frankly I've been sat in front of this computer for so long now that I'm surprised I've remembered anyone.

Finally, and as always, I would like to thank Heather for everything she does and for being the best travel companion I could ever want.

OUR READERS

Many thanks to the travellers who used the last edition and wrote to us with helpful hints, useful advice and interesting anecdotes:

Ria-Maria Adams, Maria Ahmed, Marc Bergen, Sujan Bhattacharjee, Pieter Bossuyt, Claudio Cambon, Henry Coulter, Petr Drbohlav,

---

THE LONELY PLANET STORY

Fresh from an epic journey across Europe, Asia and Australia in 1972, Tony and Maureen Wheeler sat at their kitchen table stapling together notes. The first Lonely Planet guidebook, *Across Asia on the Cheap,* was born.

Travellers snapped up the guides. Inspired by their success, the Wheelers began publishing books to Southeast Asia, India and beyond. Demand was prodigious, and the Wheelers expanded the business rapidly to keep up. Over the years, Lonely Planet extended its coverage to every country and into the virtual world via lonelyplanet.com and the Thorn Tree message board.

As Lonely Planet became a globally loved brand, Tony and Maureen received several offers for the company. But it wasn't until 2007 that they found a partner whom they trusted to remain true to the company's principles of travelling widely, treading lightly and giving sustainably. In October of that year, BBC Worldwide acquired a 75% share in the company, pledging to uphold Lonely Planet's commitment to independent travel, trustworthy advice and editorial independence.

Today, Lonely Planet has offices in Melbourne, London and Oakland, with over 500 staff members and 300 authors. Tony and Maureen are still actively involved with Lonely Planet. They're travelling more often than ever, and they're devoting their spare time to charitable projects. And the company is still driven by the philosophy of *Across Asia on the Cheap*: 'All you've got to do is decide to go and the hardest part is over. So go!'

Ben Ernst, Rachel Fitzsimons, Peter Fox, Luke Gillian, Mary Gobey, Philip Gough, Martin Grznar, Renee Hoskins, Erik Jelinek, Abidur Khan, Lucie Kinkorova, Arun Kumar, Hayley Kuter, Gunilla Leander, Hong Liang Lee, Simon Liubinas, Daniel Lundborg, Matt McDonald, Katharine Nowitz, Grey Pang, Tony Pascual, Vitoon Puripunyavanich, Shafiur Rahman, Riddhi Sankar Ray Chaudhuri, Susanne Rettig, Simon Scholl, Cheryl Schroeder, Oona Solberg, Louise Storey, Tracy Tyson, Jyri Vahvanen, Joop Van Dijk, Twin Van Leeuwen, Donald & Sophie Vandenbosch-Dejaegher, Katleen Verloo, Marc Wennehes, Tony Woods.

ACKNOWLEDGMENTS
Many thanks to the following for the use of their content:

Globe on title page ©Mountain High Maps 1993 Digital Wisdom, Inc.

Index

INDEX

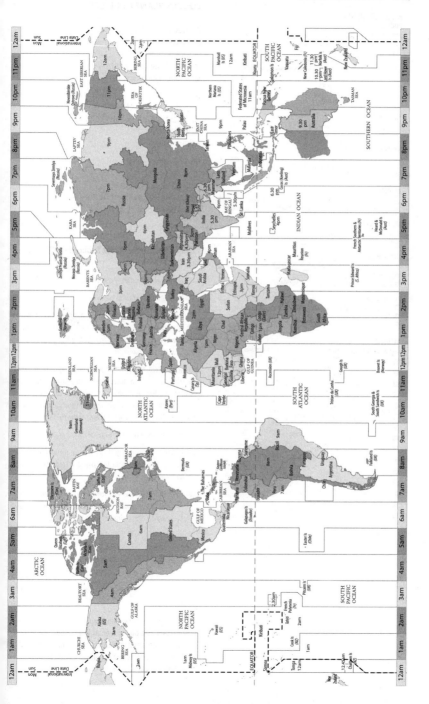

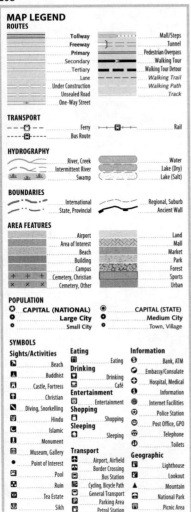

MAP LEGEND

ROUTES

Tollway
Freeway
Primary
Secondary
Tertiary
Lane
Under Construction
Unsealed Road
One-Way Street
Mall/Steps
Tunnel
Pedestrian Overpass
Walking Tour
Walking Tour Detour
Walking Trail
Walking Path
Track

TRANSPORT

Ferry
Bus Route
Rail

HYDROGRAPHY

River, Creek
Intermittent River
Swamp
Water
Lake (Dry)
Lake (Salt)

BOUNDARIES

International
State, Provincial
Regional, Suburb
Ancient Wall

AREA FEATURES

Airport
Area of Interest
Beach
Building
Campus
Cemetery, Christian
Cemetery, Other
Land
Mall
Market
Park
Forest
Sports
Urban

POPULATION

○ **CAPITAL (NATIONAL)**
● **Large City**
● Small City
◉ **CAPITAL (STATE)**
● **Medium City**
○ Town, Village

SYMBOLS

Sights/Activities
Beach
Buddhist
Castle, Fortress
Christian
Diving, Snorkelling
Hindu
Islamic
Monument
Museum, Gallery
Point of Interest
Pool
Ruin
Tea Estate
Sikh
Zoo, Bird Sanctuary

Eating
Eating

Drinking
Drinking
Café

Entertainment
Entertainment

Shopping
Shopping

Sleeping
Sleeping

Transport
Airport, Airfield
Border Crossing
Bus Station
Cycling, Bicycle Path
General Transport
Parking Area
Petrol Station
Taxi Rank

Information
Bank, ATM
Embassy/Consulate
Hospital, Medical
Information
Internet Facilities
Police Station
Post Office, GPO
Telephone
Toilets

Geographic
Lighthouse
Lookout
Mountain
National Park
Picnic Area
Waterfall

LONELY PLANET OFFICES

Australia
Head Office
Locked Bag 1, Footscray, Victoria 3011
☎ 03 8379 8000, fax 03 8379 8111
talk2us@lonelyplanet.com.au

USA
150 Linden St, Oakland, CA 94607
☎ 510 250 6400, toll free 800 275 8555
fax 510 893 8572
info@lonelyplanet.com

UK
2nd fl, 186 City Rd,
London EC1V 2NT
☎ 020 7106 2100, fax 020 7106 2101
go@lonelyplanet.co.uk

Published by Lonely Planet Publications Pty Ltd
ABN 36 005 607 983

© Lonely Planet Publications Pty Ltd 2008

© photographers as indicated 2008

Cover photograph: Children playing in jute crops, Tangail, Bangladesh. Karen Robinson/Panos Pictures. Many of the images in this guide are available for licensing from Lonely Planet Images: www .lonelyplanetimages.com.